MW00809741

Jews in Popular
Science Fiction

Jewish Science Fiction and Fantasy

Series Editor

Valerie Estelle Frankel

Jewish science fiction is a monumental literary genre worldwide, with hundreds of novels and short stories along with an enormous canon of films, plays, television shows, and graphic novels. It's also strikingly popular. Not only have works of this category just won the Hugo and World Fantasy Award while dominating bestseller lists, but talks on the subject are standing room only. The Own Voices movement has led to a renaissance of Jewish fantasy, even as its authors create imaginary worlds reflecting their unique cultures. This series seeks subtopics of exploration within the massive canon, defining aspects of Jewish genre fiction and its unique qualities. It features both monographs and anthologies focused on trends, tropes, individual authors, beloved franchises, and so on. Scholars of all disciplines are welcome, especially those in Jewish studies, literature, and media studies, while interdisciplinary and international perspectives are particularly encouraged.

Titles in the series

Jews in Popular Science Fiction

Marginalized in the Mainstream

Edited by Valerie Estelle Frankel

LEXINGTON BOOKS
Lanham • Boulder • New York • London

Published by Lexington Books
An imprint of The Rowman & Littlefield Publishing Group, Inc.
4501 Forbes Boulevard, Suite 200, Lanham, Maryland 20706
www.rowman.com

86-90 Paul Street, London EC2A 4NE

British Library Cataloguing in Publication Information Available

Library of Congress Cataloging-in-Publication Data
Names: Frankel, Valerie Estelle, 1980- editor.
Title: Jews in popular science fiction : marginalized in the mainstream / edited by Valerie
  Estelle Frankel.
Description: Lanham : Lexington Books, [2022] | Series: Jewish science fiction and
  fantasy | Includes bibliographical references and index. | Summary: "This book
  analyzes Jewish tropes in popular science fiction including Star Trek, Marvel, and
  other top franchises. The chapters examine representations of Jewish characters and
  culture in the genre that range from poignant metaphor to banal tokenism"— Provided
  by publisher.
Identifiers: LCCN 2022030648 (print) | LCCN 2022030649 (ebook) | ISBN
  9781666901450 (cloth) | ISBN 9781666901467 (epub)
Subjects: LCSH: Jews in mass media. | Science fiction, American—History and
  criticism. | Mass media—United States—History. | American literature—Jewish
  authors—History and criticism.
Classification: LCC P94.5.J482 U644 2022 (print) | LCC P94.5.J482 (ebook) | DDC
  791.45/6520924—dc23/eng/20220714
LC record available at https://lccn.loc.gov/2022030648
LC ebook record available at https://lccn.loc.gov/2022030649

∞™ The paper used in this publication meets the minimum requirements of American
National Standard for Information Sciences—Permanence of Paper for Printed Library
Materials, ANSI/NISO Z39.48-1992.

To my pandemic virtual game night pals—Rachel Bloom, Gabrielle DePesa, Jeremy Erman, Jonathan Erman, and Ben Pastcan. Every author needs friends to argue books and scifi with, and you've been amazing.

Contents

Introduction

Jews created American science fiction. It seems like a very broad and over-generous statement, but it's true. In 1926, Belgian immigrant Hugo Gernsback launched *Amazing Stories*, the first science fiction magazine. Unlike his predecessors like Jules Verne and H. G. Wells, he based his fiction in near-future technology: his electronics-based short story "Ralph 124C 41+" was impressive for predicting radar, microfilm, synthetic fabric, vending machines, tape recorders, the jukebox, the television, satellites, and spaceflight. This community soon produced science fiction clubs like his Science Fiction League, the science fiction publishers and agents who started in his magazines, as well as fanzines, cosplay, and the first scifi conventions.

Likewise, this was the golden age of comics, which was another industry where Jews could be hired, because it was so new. Two Jews invented Superman, who functions as a Jewish metaphor, a refugee sent to America like Moses, who hides his alien heritage and abilities behind a geeky, assimilationist façade, changing his Hebrew-sounding birth name to the Americanized Clark Kent. Matthew Diamond writes about this metaphor along with the Superman war comics and anti-fascist stance of the era. Batman, night to Superman's day, comes from the same era. If Superman is covertly yet recognizably Jewish, millionaire Bruce Wayne gives off a very goyish impression. At the same time, like Clark Kent, he seems a Jew's dream of assimilation, and such an insider that he seems to be overcompensating. Over the years, Jewish creators added more overtly Jewish characters to Gotham with Batwoman, Ragman, Harley Quinn, *Bombshells* characters, and recently, Whistle. Jonathan Sexton considers all these along with how well different creators handle the Jewish depiction . . . with even hints of Judaism for the Caped Crusader himself. While Marvel has a similar history with the Jewish team of Stan Lee and Jack Kirby creating the Avengers and X-Men to address minority life, my own essay covers more recent adaptations, considering how much Jewishness has been removed onscreen from X-Men's Kitty Pryde as well as Ragman, Felicity Smoak, Martin Stein, and Batwoman in the

1

Arrowverse. Even in this era of multicultural celebration, only Magneto and the cartoon version of Harley Quinn have kept much of their heritage—and both present it as a problematic source of their villainy.

After World War II, fantasy novels boomed, arguably kicked off by J. R. R. Tolkien's *Lord of the Rings*. In Arthur S. Harrow's "The Quest for the Kosher Dragon," he considers to what extent Tolkien included Jews in his fantasy world and comes up with surprising answers. Meanwhile, it took a Jewish creator, Rod Serling, to not only invent a dramatic new type of storytelling with *The Twilight Zone,* but also film Holocaust episodes in a decade in which people weren't prepared to discuss the subject. Professor Judy Klass examines these stories, through her university classes that push students to examine the metaphors as well as the origin of so many science fiction tropes.

In this era, Jewish science fiction writers (like mainstream Jewish American writers) began telling overt stories of their culture, instead of the previous generation's metaphors about alienation and ostracism in an increasingly fascist world. The first Jewish science fiction anthology, *Wandering Stars,* dates to this time, as do memorable Jewish science fiction works by Peter S. Beagle, Harlan Ellison, Avram Davidson, Harry Harrison, Alfred Bester, Cynthia Ozick, and others. Many of these novels incorporate the Jewish supernatural like ghosts, dybbuks, and particularly the famous golem. Mara W. Cohen Ioannides and Fraser Sherman each tackle this top Jewish monster and divide up its appearance in a long list of novels and comics along with the "golem" TV episodes—usually synonymous with token Jewish episodes. They both discover quite a spectrum of depictions as they consider how the legend and the Jewish characters are presented traditionally or subverted.

Erin Giannini does a similar exploration, but of "space Nazis" and whether the Third Reich's appearance across top shows, from *Supernatural* to the Buffyverse to *Marvel's Agents of S.H.I.E.L.D.* to *Doctor Who*, is done with sensitivity or with sloppy storytelling that removes the Holocaust victims entirely.

Babylon 5 and *Buffy*'s non-Jewish showrunners featured Jewish main characters . . . though the latter's Willow Rosenberg was not shown practicing, beyond an occasional mention of Hannukah. In the nineties, other television writers, both Jewish and not, could be seen tackling multiculturalism and Jewish tropes with varying levels of sensitivity. Miriam Eve Mora considers the most infamous "space Jews" of this era—the Ferengi—and how suggestively Jewish their different creators made them. Sarah Katz considers them and *Star Wars*' problematic Watto while she looks deeper at the metaphor of colonization, especially in how much it fuels the Bajoran–Cardassian conflict.

Star Trek didn't have a Jewish showrunner or much overt religion, but many contributors deepened the outsider symbolism surrounding Spock. The show also tackled Nazism, the Eichmann trial, and the harms of prejudice. A generation later, the next *Star Trek* show made Worf the alien on the bridge—and further, an alien raised by Theodore Bikel. Worf in many ways is a *Baal Teshuvah*, who did not grow up in his culture but becomes devoted to Klingon ways as an adult. He teaches young Klingons about belief and has a memorable crisis of faith in "Rightful Heir," in which he encounters a Messiah more in the Jewish tradition than the Christian. Ari Elias-Bachrach explores these themes through a Jewish lens.

Other scholars, rabbis, and enthusiasts examine top franchises through knowledge of Judaism and its laws. Caleb Horowitz considers the Mandalorians' creed and how it fits into a Jewish worldview of obedience and consequences with tension between sects. Ellen Levitt finds "Several Curious Connections" between Judaism and the beloved cartoon *Avatar: The Last Airbender*, as she sees Jewish values in the Air Nomads' Holocaust and the struggle to maintain faith and religious practice through great adversity . . . not to mention all the biblical motifs. With a fun twist, Rabbi Matthew Nover and Heather Nover write a Talmudic responsum for their students, exploring the religious and ethical nuances of the question, Is it permitted to kill a zombie?

Today, in the Own Voices era, Jewish science fiction and fantasy are booming, everywhere, from anthologies to graphic novels to picture books. Onscreen, there's a variety of Jewish representation, in *Shadowhunters, The Ghost and Molly McGee, Marvel's Runaways, Batwoman, Arrow, Moon Knight, Harley Quinn, Penny Dreadful: City of Angels, Hunters, The Plot Against America,* and *The Man in the High Castle,* along with Israeli speculative shows *Autonomies, Split,* and *Juda.* Comedies and nongenre shows offer far more, of course, as did previous decades. However, canonically Jewish characters like the Thing, Kitty Pryde, and Harley Quinn have had their Jewishness erased on the biggest screen. Even with the shows that keep their Jewish characters, questions must be asked concerning tokenism, impact, and authenticity.

Chapter One

"Discovery Requires Experimentation"

Centering Nazi-Fighting Ideology without Judaism in Genre Television

Erin Giannini

Despite its title, in the 2011 *Doctor Who* (1963–1989, 2005–present) episode "Let's Kill Hitler" (6.08), Hitler never actually gets around to being killed. Or, in fact, having much of an effect on the episode's narrative at all. Instead, he is shoved into a closet and ignored in the more immediate threat of a homicidal River Song (Alex Kingston) attempting to kill the Doctor (Matt Smith). As episode author and showrunner Steven Moffat said in an interview, his goal was "take the mickey" out of Hitler (Laws 2011), something UK television has tried (and failed) to do before with 1990s Galaxy network sitcom *Heil Honey, I'm Home* (canceled after a single episode aired). Further, River's quip to some Nazi goons, "Well, I was on my way to this gay Gypsy bar mitzvah for the disabled when I suddenly thought 'Gosh, the Third Reich's a bit rubbish. I think I'll kill the Fuehrer,'" hardly considers the indescribable suffering Hitler caused.[1] While critical review of the episode was primarily positive,[2] the use of a genocidal dictator as somewhere between a plot device and a throwaway gag suggests some troubling implications, including River's initial appropriation of a Nazi uniform after she regenerates from the Afro-British Mels to the ginger-haired white River and the Doctor and his companions' arrival accidentally saving Hitler from an assassination attempt. While both the Doctor and companions Amy (Karen Gillan) and Rory (Arthur Darvill) express dismay at saving Hitler's life, the implications of that are not delved into, likely due to both time and tone constraints of the episode.

This cavalier tone and narrative were troubling to some critics (and viewers) in 2011; however, with the steep rise in hate crimes in the past five years (in the United States) reaching its highest level in 2020,[3] the episode's tone seems more discordant, particularly when perpetrators adopt Nazi ideology and symbolism. This has not stopped other series, particularly in the sci-fi/fantasy genre, from incorporating either literal or figurative Nazis into their stories, from alt-history dramas such as *The Man in the High Castle* (2015–2019), *Hunters* (2020), and *The Plot against America* (2020) and vampire series *The Originals* (2013–2018) Nazi vampire antagonists, to *Doctor Who*'s Daleks, who in origin, ideology, and narrative have served as a Nazi metaphor since their 1963 debut.[4] Aside from the alternate history series, however, these Nazi or Nazi-esque antagonists' focus differs. That is, the targeting of the Jewish population of Europe was the cornerstone of Nazi ideology before and during the Second World War, advancing quickly from widespread segregation and demonization to extermination. While other groups were also selected for imprisonment and extermination, including the Romani people, gay people, and those with disabilities, over half of the twelve million victims of the Holocaust were Jewish. Yet many of these genre series that employ Nazis as the (ultimate) villain erase Judaism through metaphor; that is, those in danger from these Nazis—or Nazi-like—groups are targeted by what the villains perceive sets them apart or who are visually marked as other (e.g., demons, individuals with superpowers) without tying it to religious or ethnic identity, erasing a vital aspect of that toxic ideology. Yet, because Nazism and the Holocaust are inextricably linked, by employing Nazis as villains and erasing the identities, ethnicities, and religions of its victims runs the risk of creating narratives that are "triggering and often unproductive because the antisemitism, homophobia, anti-Romanyism, ableism . . . is just there as a prop for drama, and the human reality of what it meant to be in that environment is ignored."[5] Given the recent steep rise in hate crimes over the past half decade, some of which were perpetrated by individuals spouting Nazi ideology and embracing its Nazi iconography, a series such as *The Originals* choosing to have its vampire Nazis focus their rage on one of the program's white characters is a highly problematic appropriation that borders on erasure. The contemporary Hydra Nazis of *AoS* vent their hatred on Inhumans, who exist worldwide but whose abilities (e.g., regeneration, super strength, etc.) mark them as "Other." While the traditional targets of the Nazi regime are not mentioned, the fact that Hydra members' most personal and egregious actions are against women of color (Jiaying and Daisy) does, in a limited way, tie into more traditional portrayals, as does the later revelation of the existence of a selective breeding program amongst Hydra elites.[6] Thus, this article examines this erasure and its implications, with particular focus on the Initiative in *Buffy the Vampire Slayer* (1997–2003) and *Angel*

(1999–2004), the Daleks in *Doctor Who*, Hydra in *Agents of S.H.I.E.L.D. (AoS)* (2013–2020), and the Thule on *Supernatural* (2005–2020), which stands apart in the way it centers Judaism and Jewish identity as necessary to confront—and defeat—an ideology that should be long dead.

CRUCIBLES AND REALITY BOMBS: NAZIS AS METONYM AND METAPHOR

More than seventy years after the start of World War II, one can still see the physical effects of the conflict on the landscape of Europe, whether through the sustained destruction of bombing or the concentration camps left standing as both a testament to its worst outcomes and a memorial for those who suffered and died in them. With the exception of Pearl Harbor, however, the physical landscape of the United States was not attacked during the Second World War. That did not stop the Roosevelt administration from setting up several concentration camps within the United States for the internment of more than 100,000 Japanese Americans,[7] a few of which still remain standing and have been designated historical sites for education and edification. The comparative lack of destruction within the United States may be the reason why the war does not hold the same cultural resonance as it does for Europe. Even limiting it to an examination of a single country, such as the United Kingdom, and a single medium, like television, provides dozens of series across multiple genres in which the Second World War is the primary subject, stretching from the 1950s to the present day.

While the series *Doctor Who*, by its very remit, explores a variety of historical times and places in addition to other planets, galaxies, and star systems, one of their longest running and most well-known antagonists is the Daleks, who appeared in the second-ever serial of the series. Not surprisingly, their origin story has undergone some changes through the program's long history. One of the most resonant is the 1975 serial "Genesis of the Daleks" (12.04), in which the Doctor (Tom Baker) is sent back in time to their creation on the planet Skaro.[8] The planet, engaged in a seemingly endless conflict between the two main inhabitants—the Kaleds and the Thals—has become a radioactive wasteland and sickened the population. In order to gain an advantage both in the war and against the poisonous atmosphere, Kaled scientist Davros (Michael Wisher) creates what he terms the Daleks (an anagram of Kaled), mutated individuals encased in a protective, weaponized shell. To give them a further advantage, he removes emotions such as empathy, compassion, or nuance for any individual or species that is not "Dalek"; this has been an essential part of their characterization since their first appearance.

The costuming, words, and iconography throughout this episode, as well as earlier Dalek-centric episodes such as "The Dalek Invasion of Earth" (1964) blatantly tie the Daleks to the Nazis and to key moments in World War II.[9] In "Genesis," the Doctor has the chance to kill the incubating Daleks, but elects not to do so, despite his knowledge of their actions in the future, as he considers that he would essentially be committing genocide. "Genesis" thus is a more serious exploration of what River attempts to do in "Let's Kill Hitler"; that is, the question of the morality of killing one to save others.

While the Daleks are not the only homicidal alien race in the series, creator Terry Nation explicitly cited the Nazis as inspiration.[10] He also gave them a repeated phrase that indicates their merciless ruthlessness, as well as recalling the worst excesses of the Nazi regime: "Exterminate!" While this impulse was originally directed toward the Thals, it soon extended to anyone or anything considered "not Dalek": humans, Time Lords, Cybermen. Consequently, when the Emperor of the Daleks harvests human DNA to create a new version following their near-extermination in the Time War, these Daleks consider themselves "impure" and develop not only self-hatred but religious zealotry before being destroyed;[11] a later attempt to evolve beyond their homicidal xenophobia by again combining human and Dalek also leads to Daleks destroying their own as unacceptable.[12,13]

Once they are reunited with their creator, Davros (Julian Bleach), they attempt and nearly succeed in wiping out every other form of life beyond themselves across all of creation, stopped only by a "three-fold" Doctor (David Tennant): the Doctor himself, a cloned regeneration, and a companion, Donna Noble (Catherine Tate) dosed with Time Lord energy.[14] The combined focus on destruction and "purity" across the characters' history makes its connection to Nazism as explicit as possible without actually mentioning Nazis at all. (There is a further visual and auditory connection in "Journey's End," in which Daleks are patrolling outside Nuremberg and repeating "Exterminate" in German.) This includes rounding up British citizens and subjecting them to a device that literally disintegrates them.

While the Daleks may be one of the more obvious stand-ins in genre television, other series have used similar plots, motivations, and iconography to tie their antagonists to Nazism. The rhetoric of the battle between a faction of humans and a faction of the series' sentient zombies during the fifth season of *iZombie* was rife with both the human side (known as Dead Enders) and the self-proclaimed "zombie supremacists" embracing fascist language and worldviews focused on "purity." *Farscape*'s (1999–2004) Peacekeepers also focus on purity while wearing uniforms reminiscent of the Third Reich. The *Star Trek* franchise has delved into single-episode portrayals (*Star Trek*'s [1966–1969] Kodos the Executioner in "The Conscience of the King" [1.13] and the villains of "Patterns of Force" [2.21]) or as recurring antagonists (the

Cardassians in *Star Trek: Deep Space Nine* [1993–1999]; the Terran Empire in *Star Trek: Discovery* [2017–present]). It is a common enough characterization to merit its own page on *TV Tropes* ("A Nazi by Any Other Name").

The series *Buffy the Vampire Slayer* and its spinoff *Angel* delved into this imagery as well, albeit in different ways. The fourth season of the former introduced the Initiative, a government-funded and military-staffed research facility for studying demons ("hostile sub-terrestrial," in their words) and neutralizing them as a threat to humankind. While this is the public-facing purpose, it is merely a cover for a secret project to build human–demon hybrid soldiers.[15] They acknowledge no nuance in the demons or creatures they target, either locking them up or performing experiments on them whether they are considered benign or dangerous. This is most driven home when they capture and cage Oz, a human main character who's careful not to harm anyone when he becomes a werewolf.[16] Once the project leader Maggie Walsh (Lindsey Crouse) is killed by the first hybrid prototype (appropriately named Adam [George Hertzberg]), it is revealed that the experiments extend to the students/soldiers under her command; they are dosed with strengthening drugs and fitted with behavioral modification microchips without their consent. While Buffy continually expresses doubt about the Initiative's plans and motives for their actions, Riley Finn (Marc Blucas) is not only a member of the Initiative; it is the source of his friendships, housing, and (possibly) educational funding. When their more nefarious and fascistic goals are revealed, Riley completely breaks down, suffering a lack of identity that persists until he exits the series in the next season. His desire to do the right thing and embrace patriotic values is warped and weaponized by the organization. The penultimate episode of the season further reveals that all of this was done with governmental approval and funding in an attempt to "harness" the "underworld threat" to their own ends.[17]

Aside from the obvious metaphors of this particular arc, including the building of an ubermensch in the form of Adam and the scientists' nonconsensual experimentation, the fifth season of spin-off *Angel* reveals that the majority of the behavioral modification research that the Initiative employs was developed by actual Nazi scientists.[18] This has its real-world analogue in Operation Paperclip, in which Nazi scientists such as Wernher von Braun were hired by entities such as NASA;[19] their expertise meant that the United States declined to investigate their level of participation in Nazi atrocities.[20]

While this connection is more subtextual in *Buffy*, *Angel*'s episode "Hero" (1.09) is far more explicit. Angel (David Boreanaz), a vampire with a soul trying to atone for centuries of evildoing, is guided to those in need of help by visions sent by the "powers that be," seemingly benevolent entities. In the first season, these visions are filtered through Doyle (Glenn Quinn), a half-human, half-demon. In Doyle's final episode, he sees a group of half-demons being menaced by a group known as The Scourge. The Scourge are so-called "pure blood" demons whose sole purpose is to eliminate, in their words, "half-breeds . . . diluting our precious demon blood with their weak, simpering humanity."[21] Their uniforms are nearly identical to those of the Nazis, and they refer to half-demons as "vermin" that need to be "cleansed."[22]

"Hero" engages in further parallels, with the targeted population of half-demons constantly on the run, reliant on secret hiding places created in their living quarters to avoid capture, and the pyrrhic choice of either emigration or death. Both the Brakken demons and the Lister demons (the two targeted groups seen in the episode) are not only portrayed sympathetically (unlike most demons on both series), but the episode also weaves a reference to whether they can "pass" as human. (*Angel* will address this idea again in season two's "Are You Now or Have You Ever Been" with Judy, who loses her job and fiancé when they discover she is mixed race.)

If the parallel isn't clear enough, the people Angel, Doyle, and Cordelia (Charisma Carpenter) attempt to rescue are at least nominally religious, informing Angel of a prophesy regarding the "promised one," a messianic figure who will rescue them from the Scourge. This prophesy does come to pass; however, while the people they rescued assume it's Angel, it's actually Doyle who sacrifices himself to save them, as atonement for previously failing to help other victims of the Scourge. Angel does kill many members of the organization, but unlike the shutting down of the Initiative, the narrative doesn't suggest that the Scourge is entirely defeated at the end of the episode (although they are not mentioned again in the series). In that respect, it accurately suggests that such beliefs and actions are difficult to completely eliminate.

"YOU ALWAYS HAD THAT HITLER YOUTH LOOK TO YOU": THE SHIFTING TARGETS OF MODERN FASCISTS

Near the end of the first season of *Marvel's Agents of S.H.I.E.L.D.* (*AoS*), the series introduces a nemesis that will plague the team until its final episode: Hydra. Further, the Nazi-founded organization had infiltrated S.H.I.E.L.D. since S.H.I.E.L.D.'s founding and twisted their goals to Hydra's ends.[23] Both in flashbacks and in their present-day incarnation—befitting the genre of the series—Hydra attempts to gain power through alien artifacts and targeting "Inhumans": individuals whose biology grants them certain extraordinary powers. Unlike the previous examples, the Hydra of *AoS* is founded and run by actual Nazis, including Werner Reinhardt (Reed Diamond), a high-ranking

Nazi officer arrested and imprisoned in 1945.[24] Using his Hydra connections within S.H.I.E.L.D., Reinhardt performs extensive and savage experiments on an Inhuman woman to steal her regenerative abilities, de-aging himself and resuming control of a rebranded Hydra as a similarly rebranded self: Daniel Whitehall.[25]

Yet despite his and Hydra's attempts to obscure their Nazi origins, neither their policies nor their behaviors have changed, and S.H.I.E.L.D. will not allow them to forget it. When Hydra double agent Grant Ward (Brett Dalton) kidnaps S.H.I.E.L.D. agent Skye (Chloe Bennet) and tries to justify his alliance to her, she shuts him down. "I'm not a Nazi," he claims, to which she replies, "That is exactly what you are."[26] This particular storyline, in which Ward is targeted by fellow Hydra mole John Garrett (Bill Paxton) as a teenager, offers a commentary that is both prescient and familiar: Garrett weaponizes Ward's anger and feelings of exclusion and ill-usage—making him easy pickings[27]—by reinforcing and redirecting it toward his own enemies.[28]

While Ward gives Garrett a lot to work with, the series presents another option for him in its fourth season. When the team is trapped in an alternate reality known as the Framework, the Grant Ward here is not a double agent for Hydra within S.H.I.E.L.D. but for S.H.I.E.L.D. within Hydra. He's more thoughtful and less angry than his real-world counterpart, as at the crucial moment, he is mentored not by the equally angry Garrett but by Victoria Hand (Saffron Burrows). Hand is a no-nonsense, high-level S.H.I.E.L.D. agent, who focuses not on what Ward's done or what has been done to him, but what he is capable of; she accentuates skills and capabilities over negative emotion.[29] That within the "real world" of the series, Ward does not get a redemption arc before he is killed suggests the inescapable toxicity of the ideology to which he has aligned himself.

Hydra and its Nazi-focused ideology is the overarching antagonist of all seven seasons of *AoS*. Reinhardt/Whitehall is killed at the midpoint of the second season, and a different faction—one that worships an ancient, alien god named Hive—is introduced in the third, but they still pay tribute to the then-incarcerated Reinhardt, suggesting the connection to Hydra's Nazi origins among them is tenuous but not abandoned. In season seven, Hydra member Nathanial Malick (Thomas E. Sullivan) again visits Reinhardt in order to learn about his fatal experiments on Inhumans; as Reinhardt later enacts these experiments on an Inhuman named Jiaying (Dichen Lachmann), so too does Malick on her daughter, Daisy.[30] Both mother and daughter, however, have different reactions to the abuse suffered, with Jiaying becoming militantly anti-human and fighting for Inhuman dominance to avoid these abuses being enacted on others. In contrast, Daisy focuses on stopping Nathanial and saving her half-sister Kora (Dianne Doan) rather than engaging in a more large-scale social realignment.[31] Hydra's pervasive harm against many groups is stressed over and over.

Nazis also appear in *The Originals*. These vampire Nazis are targeting vampire–werewolf hybrids for their "impurity" in both the 1930s and 1940s and the present day.[32] They kidnap one of the main characters because of her "mixed" status, borrowing heavily from the *Underworld* film series, whose powerful vampires not only viewed werewolves as "less than" but feared the concept of a vampire–werewolf hybrid. The 1980s semi-anthology series *Friday the 13th: The Series* (1987–1990), which focused on finding and destroying Satanically cursed objects, offers a prescient episode featuring a reanimated Nazi named Rausch (Nigel Bennett), who rebrands himself as radio personality Carl Steiner. Steiner gains immense popularity by tapping into his listeners' rage against women, people of color, immigrants, and homosexuals that not-so-subtly suggests the late Rush Limbaugh (recently risen to prominence at the time this aired). Rausch is resurrected by an incarcerated fellow Nazi, Horst Mueller (Colin Fox), wielding a "Thule" amulet that allows him to communicate with (and control) his reanimated compatriot.[33] While the amulet is fiction, the Thule Society was a real organization interested in both occultism and Aryan dominance. Several prominent future Nazis (e.g., Rudolf Hess) were members before Hitler's rise to power. Yet despite both Rausch/Steiner's and Mueller's Nazi backgrounds, neither his radio rants nor his listeners target Jewish individuals as part of American society's "problems." The hate thus becomes universalized.

One of the few series that both employs Nazi villains and does not decenter the experience of Jewish individuals is *Supernatural*. Introduced in its eighth season, the Thule Society appears three times in the final seven seasons. In "Everybody Hates Hitler" (8.13), writer Ben Edlund builds on the historical Thule Society's mixture of occult interest and white supremacy to recast them as necromancers. During World War II, they are opposed by the Judah Initiative, a group of rabbis dedicated to fighting them by any means necessary (and thus undermining the myth of Jewish nonresistance); their greatest and most effective tool in the battle is the creation of a golem. In brief, golems, from Jewish folklore, are clay figures magically brought to life in times of peril for the Jewish community. Edlund ties this explicitly to known history when the Golem (John DeSantis) indicates he was created in the Vitsyebsk Ghetto, located in what is now Belarus, in which Nazis slaughtered nearly all its inhabitants in 1941.[34] Indeed, the episode starts there, with the activated Golem destroying all the Nazis in the camp except one—Commander Eckhardt (Bernhard Forcher)—who escapes to the present day using magic, and searches for a ledger listing both his fallen society members and the horrifying experiments he undertook on Jews and Romany to figure out how to resurrect the dead. When one of the resurrected Thule kills the last member of the original Judah Initiative, Rabbi Isaac Bass (Hal Linden), the responsibility for managing the Golem and fighting the Thule falls to his grandson, Aaron (Adam Rose), who is nonobservant and dismissed his grandfather's stories as crazy. With the assistance of Sam and Dean, the Thule are defeated, and Aaron takes control of the Golem in order to continue the fight.[35]

There are two elements here that are worth noting. One, the disconnect between generations, in which history is forgotten and knowledge lost. In the previous episode, Sam and Dean find out they are legacies in a society known as The Men of Letters, who compile knowledge and tools to fight evil. This knowledge is lost because of the disappearance of their grandfather, who never had the chance to pass it on to his son, John.[36] Aaron's story lightly mirrors this, in that he dismissed his true legacy and historical knowledge. In fact, while his grandfather attempted to school Aaron on his responsibilities as a member of the Judah Initiative, his talk of necromancers and dark magic made Aaron's parents regard such tales as a traumatic response to his experience in the war. This is not uncommon; many of the children whose parents survived the Holocaust are aware of the multiple manifestations of their parents' trauma,[37] including silence about their experiences; this can have physical repercussions across generations.[38] (As explicated above, the idea of shared generational trauma is literalized in *AoS*, with both Jiaying and her daughter Daisy undergoing the same torture by the same Nazi-led organization.) This may be why Aaron's parents sought to shield him from his grandfather, and yet it leaves him without the resources to fight against the same enemy. It puts Aaron in the position where the enemy knows more about Aaron's Jewish history than Aaron himself, making him particularly vulnerable.

It is also significant that the evil that Isaac Bass faced during World War II is active in the present day. While the Thule Nazis are dressed in contemporary clothing and thus able to pass undetected, their ideology remains unchanged. Eckhardt and the others continue to seek power and dominion over those they consider "lesser." Anti-Semitism and Nazi ideology are thus not "solved" by their defeat. Airing in 2013, "Everybody Hates Hitler," from the revenant quality of hate to Aaron's realization that the battle against it is ongoing, reads as somewhat prescient. When Aaron appears again in 2016's "The One You've Been Waiting For" (12.5), he is fully committed to his mission, traveling around the world with his Golem to stomp out the Thule and warning the Winchesters that the Thule are up to something significant. "The One You've Been Waiting For" examines inheritance and history from the other side, as a group of Thule attempt—and briefly succeed—at resurrecting Hitler. They use the blood of a young woman named Ellie Grant (Allison Paige), who, in the course of the episode, not only finds out she's adopted, but that she is Hitler's great-great-grandniece.[39] The focus on history, knowledge, and inheritance bookends it with "Everybody Hates Hitler," although, unlike Isaac and Aaron, the offspring of the Nazis and the Thule exist only to either reflect the older generation's views or to be used and discarded. After Ellie is kidnapped by the Thule and forcibly bled to resurrect her ancestor, he offers her a brief thanks and then orders her killed.[40] Ellie, Sam, and Dean eventually defeat the Thule (with Dean delivering the death shot to Hitler), and they do not appear again in the series.[41]

Each of the aforementioned series feature Nazis focused on domination, "purity," and power. However, unlike Hydra or the vampire Nazis of *The Originals*, *Supernatural*'s Nazis target—and are opposed by—characters who are and folklore that is explicitly Jewish. For Aaron and the Winchesters, defeating these resurrected Nazis not only requires knowledge, but knowledge of history. Moreover, that the Thule themselves are both of the past and in the present is itself a metaphor of the difficulties in destroying the damaging and lethal ideology they represent.

CONCLUSION

In his analysis of the proliferation of fascist villains in film, Noah Berlatsky, a critic who commonly discusses Jewish depiction in popular culture, suggests that relying on Nazis and other fascists as a "shorthand for iniquity and totalitarianism"—both metaphorical and actual Nazis—essentially trains the viewer not to notice the real ones within our social and political systems. That is, unlike supervillains such as Darth Vader in the *Star Wars* franchise or Thanos in the Marvel Cinematic Universe, real-world fascists don't announce their plans for world domination but instead speak to "belonging and duty and ferreting out traitors." They look more like our neighbors than Red Skull or Loki and express an "all-encompassing" hatred rather than one that "picks its vulnerable targets with care."[42] (As seen in series such as *Buffy* and *AoS*— with real-world resonances—these "vulnerable targets" can also include those recruited to fascism through appeals to duty, anger, or patriotism.)

Each of the series discussed do illuminate the dangers of fascism, including—but not limited to—control of information, targeting and eliminating dissent and difference, and ultranationalism disguised as patriotism. Given much more space than film, series such as *AoS*, *Angel*, or *Supernatural* can provide a lengthier examination of these dangers and their effects on those targeted. Yet the tendency of some of these programs to erase the ethnic and religious elements of Nazism for more "visible" signs of Otherness not only suggests a problematic reliance of visual signs of difference but makes its potential real-world victims more vulnerable and potentially erases a history that is vital to remember to prevent it from happening again.

NOTES

1. *Doctor Who,* season 6, episode 8, "Let's Kill Hitler," directed by Richard Senior, written by Steven Moffat, featuring Matt Smith, Karen Gillian, and Arthur Darvill, aired August 27, 2011, on the BBC, BBC Home Entertainment, 2011, DVD.

2. Dan Martin, "Doctor Who: Let's Kill Hitler—series 32, episode 8," *The Guardian*, August 27, 2011, www.theguardian.com/tv-and-radio/tvandradioblog/2011/aug/27/doctor-who-television; Patrick Mulkern, "Doctor Who: Let's Kill Hitler," Radio Times, August 27, 2011, beta.radiotimes.com/blog/2011-08–27/doctor-who-let's-kill-hitler; Ken Tucker, "Doctor Who Mid-season Premiere Review: 'Let's Kill Hitler' Was a Great Lark through Time and Space," *Entertainment Weekly*, August 28, 2011, ew.com/article/2011/08/28/doctor-who-lets-kill-hitler; Matt Risley, "Doctor Who: 'Let's Kill Hitler' Review," IGN, August 28, 2011, www.ign.com/articles/2011/08/28/doctor-who-lets-kill-hitler-review.

3. "FBI Releases 2020 Hate Crime Statistics," FBI National Press Office, August 30, 2021, www.fbi.gov/news/pressrel/press-releases/fbi-releases-2020-hate-crime-statistics.

4. *Doctor Who,* season 1, episode 2, "The Daleks," directed by Christopher Barry and Richard Martin, written by Terry Nation, featuring William Hartnell and Carole Ann Ford, aired December 21, 1963–February 1, 1964, on the BBC, BBC Home Entertainment, 2016, DVD.

5. Princess Weekes, "*The Originals* Has Introduced Nazi Vampires for . . . Reasons?" *The Mary Sue*, May 17, 2018, www.themarysue.com/the-originals-nazi-vampires/?fbclid=IwAR3a766XL7G6TSnYxBFE6kaHKycojUYzZHHfUy-jzkriec3agg_pdmC5VT0.

6. *Agents of S.H.I.E.L.D.,* season 5, episode 15, "Rise and Shine," directed by Jesse Bochco, written by Iden Baghdadchi, featuring Chloe Bennet and Dove Cameron. Aired March 30, 2018, ABC. Walt Disney Studios, 2018, DVD.

7. Italian and German U.S. residents—some of whom had citizenship and others who did not—were also placed in camps, but to a much smaller extent: approximately 1,100 Italians and 11,000 Germans living in the United States were interred during the war.

8. *Doctor Who,* season 12, episode 4, "Genesis of the Daleks," directed by David Maloney, written by Terry Nation, featuring Tom Baker, Elisabeth Sladen, and Ian Marter, aired March 8–April 12, 1975, on the BBC, BBC Home Entertainment, 2018, DVD.

9. Andrew Crome, "'There Never Was a Golden Age.' Doctor Who and the Apocalypse." In *Religion and Doctor Who: Time and Relative Dimensions in Faith,* edited by Andrew Crome (Eugene, OR: Cascade Books, 2013), 197.

10. John Ainsworth, ed., *Doctor Who: The Complete History,* no.1, 2016, 117–118.

11. *Doctor Who,* season 1, episode 13, "The Parting of the Ways," directed by Joe Ahearne, written by Russell T. Davis, featuring Christopher Eccleston and Billie Piper, aired June 18, 2005, on the BBC, BBC Home Entertainment, 2006, DVD.

12. *Doctor Who,* season 3, episode 5, "Evolution of the Daleks," directed by James Strong, written by Helen Raynor, featuring David Tennant and Freema Agyeman, aired April 28, 2007, on the BBC, BBC Home Entertainment, 2007, DVD.

13. The sole exception to this seems to "Asylum of the Daleks" (7.1 [33.1]), which features a planet that imprisons injured or otherwise broken Daleks rather than destroying them.

14. *Doctor Who,* season 4, episode 13, "Journey's End," directed by Graeme Harper, written by Russell T. Davis, featuring David Tennant and Catherine Tate, aired July 5, 2008, on the BBC, BBC Home Entertainment, 2008, DVD.

15. *Buffy the Vampire Slayer,* season 4, episode 13, "The I in Team," directed by James A. Contner, written by David Fury, featuring Sarah Michelle Gellar and Marc Blucas, aired February 8, 2000, on the WB, Twentieth Century Fox Home Entertainment, 2003, DVD.

16. *Buffy the Vampire Slayer,* season 4, episode 19, "New Moon Rising," directed by James A. Contner, written by Marti Noxon, featuring Sarah Michelle Gellar, Marc Blucas, and Seth Green, aired May 2, 2000, on the WB, Twentieth Century Fox Home Entertainment, 2003, DVD.

17. *Buffy the Vampire Slayer,* season 4, episode 21, "Primeval," directed by James A. Contner, written by David Fury, featuring Sarah Michelle Gellar, Alyson Hannigan, and Anthony Steward Head, aired May 16, 2000, on the WB, Twentieth Century Fox Home Entertainment, 2003, DVD.

18. *Angel,* season 5, episode 13, "Why We Fight," directed by Terrence O'Hara, written by Drew Goddard and Steven S. DeKnight, featuring David Boreanaz, J. August Richard, and Alexis Denisof, aired February 11, 2004, on the WB, Twentieth Century Fox Home Entertainment, 2005, DVD.

19. *Timeless* (2016–2018), a series whose premise revolves around time travel, features von Braun in an episode, telling the character of Rufus Carlin (Malcolm Barrett) that the politics mean less than the science ("Party at the Castle Varlar" 1.04). Historically, von Braun's allegiances to and actions in the Nazi regime are considered, at the very least, morally and ethically complex.

20. Ralph Vartabedian, "Who Got America to the Moon? An Unlikely Collaboration of Jewish and Former Nazi Scientists and Engineers," *Los Angeles Times*, March 1, 2020, www.latimes.com/california/story/2020-03-01/who-got-america-to-the-moon-a-unlikely-collaboration-of-jews-and-former-nazi-engineers; Annie Jacobson, *Operation Paperclip: The Secret Intelligence Program That Brought Nazi Scientists to America* (Boston: Back Bay Books, 2015).

21. *Angel,* season 1, episode 9, "Hero," directed by Tucker Gates, written by Howard Gordon and Tim Minear, featuring David Boreanaz, Glenn Quinn, and Charisma Carpenter, aired November 30, 1999, on the WB, Twentieth Century Fox Home Entertainment, 2003, DVD.

22. *Angel,* "Hero."

23. *Agents of S.H.I.E.L.D.,* season 1, episode 17, "Turn, Turn, Turn," directed by Vincent Misiano, written by Jed Whedon and Maurissa Tancharoen, featuring Clark Gregg, Brett Dalton, and Bill Paxton, aired April 8, 2014, ABC, Marvel Studios, 2014, DVD.

24. *Agents of S.H.I.E.L.D.,* season 2, episode 1, "Shadows," directed by Vincent Misiano, written by Jed Whedon and Maurissa Tancharoen, featuring Clark Gregg, Hayley Atwell, and Reed Diamond, aired September 23, 2014, ABC, Walt Disney Studios, 2015, DVD.

25. *Agents of S.H.I.E.L.D.,* season 2, episode 8, "The Things We Bury," directed by Milan Cheylov, written by D. J. Doyle, featuring Clark Gregg, Kyle McLachlan, Reed Diamond, and Brett Dalton, aired November 18, 2014, ABC, Walt Disney Studios, 2015, DVD.

26. *Agents of S.H.I.E.L.D.,* season 1, episode 20, "Nothing Personal," directed by Billy Gierhart, written by Paul Zbyszewski and D. J. Doyle, featuring Chloe Bennett, Brett Dalton, and J. August Richards, aired April 8, 2014, ABC, Marvel Studios, 2014, DVD.

27. Lulu Garcia-Navarro, "Masculinity and U.S. Extremism: What Makes Young Men Vulnerable to Toxic Ideologies?" *NPR,* January 27, 2019, www.npr.org/2019/01 /27/689121187/masculinity-and-u-s-extremism-what-makes-young-men-vulnerable -to-toxic-ideologie.

28. *Agents of S.H.I.E.L.D.,* season 1, episode 21, "Ragtag," directed by Roxann Dawson, written by Jeffrey Bell, featuring Clark Gregg, Brett Dalton, and Bill Paxton, aired May 6, 2014, ABC. Marvel Studios, 2014, DVD.

29. *Agents of S.H.I.E.L.D.,* season 4, episode 19, "All the Madame's Men," directed by Billy Gierhart, written by James C Oliver and Sharia Oliver, featuring Chloe Bennett, Henry Simmons, and Brett Dalton, aired April 25, 2017, ABC, Walt Disney Studios, 2018, DVD.

30. *Agents of S.H.I.E.L.D.,* season 7, episode 6, "Adapt or Die," directed by April Winney, written by D.J. Doyle, featuring Chloe Bennett and Clark Gregg, aired July 1, 2020, ABC, www.netflix.com/watch/81354117.

31. *Agents of S.H.I.E.L.D.,* season 7, episode 13, "What We're Fighting For," directed by Kevin Tancharoen, written by Jed Whedon, featuring Clark Gregg, Chloe Bennett, and Ming-Na Wen, aired August 12, 2020, ABC. Walt Disney Studios, 2020.

32. *The Originals,* season 5, episode 4, "Between the Devil and the Deep Blue Sea," directed by Michael Grossman, written by Beau DeMayo and Kyle Arrington, featuring Joseph Morgan and Phoebe Tonkin, aired May 9, 2018, The CW, Warner Brothers, 2018, DVD.

33. *Friday the 13th: The Series,* season 2, episode 19, "The Butcher," directed by Francis Delia, written by Francis Delia and Ron Magrid, featuring Chris Wiggins, John LeMay, and Nigel Bennett, aired April 29, 1989, in broadcast syndication. Paramount, 2016, DVD.

34. Peter Longerich, *Holocaust: The Nazi Persecution and Murder of the Jews* (London: Oxford University Press, 2010).

35. *Supernatural,* season 8, episode 13, "Everybody Hates Hitler," directed by Phil Sgriccia, written by Ben Edlund, featuring Jensen Ackles and Jared Padalecki, aired February 6, 2013, on the CW, Warner Brothers, 2013, DVD.

36. *Supernatural,* season 8, episode 12, "As Time Goes By," directed by Serge Ladouceur, written by Adam Glass, featuring Jensen Ackles and Jared Padalecki, aired January 30, 2013, on the CW, Warner Brothers, 2013, DVD.

37. Alix Kirsta, "The Trauma of Second-generation Holocaust Survivors," *The Guardian*, March 15, 2014, www.theguardian.com/lifeandstyle/2014/mar/15/trauma -second-generation-holocaust-survivors..

38. Tori Rodriguez, "Descendants of Holocaust Survivors Have Altered Stress Hormones: Parents' Traumatic Experience May Hamper Their Offspring's Ability to Bounce Back from Trauma," *Scientific American*, March 1, 2015, www .scientificamerican.com/article/descendants-of-holocaust-survivors-have-altered -stress-hormones; Patricia Dashorst, et al, "Intergenerational Consequences of the Holocaust on Offspring Mental Health: A Systematic Review of Associated Factors and Mechanisms," *European Journal of Psychotraumatology* 10 (2019), www .tandfonline.com/doi/pdf/10.1080/20008198.2019.1654065.

39. *Supernatural,* season 12, episode 5, "The One You've Been Waiting For," directed by Nina Lopez-Corrado, written by Meredith Glynn, featuring Jensen Ackles and Jared Padalecki, aired November 10, 2016, on the CW, Warner Brothers, 2017, DVD.

40. While the episode was filmed earlier, it aired two days after the 2016 election, making Hitler's comment: "Imagine what I could do with Twitter" more than a little chilling.

41. The Thule do appear in the eleventh season of the series; however, "The Vessel" (11.14) is primarily set in World War II rather than the present day.

42. Noah Berlatsky, "How Hollywood Lets Real Fascists off the Hook: Far from Helping Us Fight Fascism, Nazis on Film May Do the Opposite," *Pacific Standard*, February 12, 2019, psmag.com/ideas/nazi-movies-dont-prepare-you-to-fight-fascists.

WORKS CITED

Ainsworth, John, ed. *Doctor Who: The Complete History*, no. 1. Panini UK, 2016.

Baghdadchi, Iden, writer. *Agents of S.H.I.E.L.D.* Season 5, episode 15, "Rise and Shine." Directed by Jesse Bochco, featuring Chloe Bennet and Dove Cameron. Aired March 30, 2018, ABC. Walt Disney Studios, 2018, DVD.

Barnes, Jim, writer. *Timeless.* Season 1, episode 4, "Party at the Castle Varlar." Directed by Billy Gierhart, featuring Abigail Spencer, Malcolm Barrett, and Matt Lanter. Aired October 24, 2016, on NBC. Sony Pictures Television, 2017, DVD.

Bell, Jeffrey, writer. *Agents of S.H.I.E.L.D.* Season 1, episode 21, "Ragtag." Directed by Roxann Dawson, featuring Clark Gregg, Brett Dalton, and Bill Paxton. Aired May 6, 2014, ABC. Marvel Studios, 2014, DVD.

Berens, Robert, writer. *Supernatural.* Season 11, episode 14, "The Vessel." Directed by John Badham, featuring Jensen Ackles and Jared Padalecki. Aired February 17, 2016, on the CW. Warner Brothers, 2016, DVD.

Berlatsky, Noah. "How Hollywood Lets Real Fascists Off the Hook: Far from Helping Us Fight Fascism, Nazis on Film May Do the Opposite." *Pacific Standard*, 12 February 2019, psmag.com/ideas/nazi-movies-dont-prepare-you-to-fight-fascists. Accessed 1 January 2022.

Crome, Andrew. "'There Never Was a Golden Age.' Doctor Who and the Apocalypse." In *Religion and Doctor Who: Time and Relative Dimensions in Faith,* edited by Andrew Crome, 189–204. Eugene, OR: Cascade Books, 2013.

Dashorst, Patricia, Mooren, Trudy M., Kleber, Rolf J., de Jong, Peter J., and Rafaele J. C. Huntgens. "Intergenerational Consequences of the Holocaust on Offspring Mental Health: A Systematic Review of Associated Factors and Mechanisms." *European Journal of Psychotraumatology* 10 (2019). Accessed January 4, 2022, www.tandfonline.com/doi/pdf/10.1080/20008198.2019.1654065.

Davis, Russell T., writer. *Doctor Who.* Season 4, episode 13, "Journey's End." Directed by Graeme Harper, featuring David Tennant and Catherine Tate. Aired July 5, 2008, on the BBC. BBC Home Entertainment, 2008, DVD.

Davis, Russell T., writer. *Doctor Who.* Season 1, episode 13, "The Parting of the Ways." Directed by Joe Ahearne, featuring Christopher Eccleston and Billie Piper. Aired June 18, 2005, on the BBC. BBC Home Entertainment, 2006, DVD.

Delia, Francis, and Ron Magrid, writers. *Friday the 13th: The Series.* Season 2, episode 19, "The Butcher." Directed by Francis Delia, featuring Chris Wiggins, John LeMay, and Nigel Bennett. Aired April 29, 1989, in broadcast syndication. Paramount, 2016, DVD.

DeMayo, Beau, and Kyle Arrington, writers. *The Originals.* Season 5, episode 4, "Between the Devil and the Deep Blue Sea." Directed by Michael Grossman, featuring Joseph Morgan and Phoebe Tonkin. Aired May 9, 2018, The CW. Warner Brothers, 2018, DVD.

Doyle, D. J., writer. *Agents of S.H.I.E.L.D.* Season 7, episode 6, "Adapt or Die." Directed by April Winney, featuring Chloe Bennett and Clark Gregg. Aired July 1, 2020, ABC. www.netflix.com/watch/81354117

Doyle, D. J., writer. *Agents of S.H.I.E.L.D.* Season 2, episode 8, "The Things We Bury." Directed by Milan Cheylov, featuring Clark Gregg, Kyle McLachlan, Reed Diamond, and Brett Dalton. Aired November 18, 2014, ABC. Walt Disney Studios, 2015, DVD.

Edlund, Ben, writer. *Supernatural.* Season 8, episode 13, "Everybody Hates Hitler." Directed by Phil Sgriccia, featuring Jensen Ackles and Jared Padalecki. Aired February 6, 2013, on the CW. Warner Brothers, 2013, DVD.

"FBI Releases 2020 Hate Crime Statistics." FBI National Press Office, 30 August 2021, www.fbi.gov/news/pressrel/press-releases/fbi-releases-2020-hate-crime-statistics. Accessed January 4, 2022.

Fury, David, writer. *Buffy the Vampire Slayer.* Season 4, episode 13, "The I in Team." Directed by James A. Contner, featuring Sarah Michelle Gellar and Marc Blucas. Aired February 8, 2000, on the WB. Twentieth Century Fox Home Entertainment, 2003, DVD.

Fury, David, writer. *Buffy the Vampire Slayer.* Season 4, episode 21, "Primeval." Directed by James A. Contner, featuring Sarah Michelle Gellar, Alyson Hannigan, and Anthony Steward Head. Aired May 16, 2000, on the WB. Twentieth Century Fox Home Entertainment, 2003, DVD.

Garcia-Navarro, Lulu. "Masculinity and U.S. Extremism: What Makes Young Men Vulnerable to Toxic Ideologies?" *NPR,* January 27, 2019, www.npr.org/2019/01

/27/689121187/masculinity-and-u-s-extremism-what-makes-young-men-vulner-able-to-toxic-ideologie..

Glass, Adam, writer. *Supernatural.* Season 8, episode 12, "As Time Goes By." Directed by Serge Ladouceur, featuring Jensen Ackles and Jared Padalecki. Aired January 30, 2013, on the CW. Warner Brothers, 2013, DVD.

Glynn, Meredith, writer. *Supernatural.* Season 12, episode 5, "The One You've Been Waiting For." Directed by Nina Lopez-Corrado, featuring Jensen Ackles and Jared Padalecki. Aired November 10, 2016, on the CW. Warner Brothers, 2017, DVD.

Goddard, Drew, and Steven S. DeKnight, writers. *Angel.* Season 5, episode 13, "Why We Fight." Directed by Terrence O'Hara, featuring David Boreanaz, J. August Richard, and Alexis Denisof. Aired February 11, 2004, on the WB. Twentieth Century Fox Home Entertainment, 2005, DVD.

Gordon, Howard, and Tim Minear, writers. *Angel.* Season 1, episode 9, "Hero." Directed by Tucker Gates, featuring David Boreanaz, Glenn Quinn, and Charisma Carpenter. Aired November 30, 1999, on the WB. Twentieth Century Fox Home Entertainment, 2003, DVD.

Jacobson, Annie. *Operation Paperclip: The Secret Intelligence Program That Brought Nazi Scientists to America.* Boston: Back Bay Books, 2015.

Kirsta, Alix. "The Trauma of Second-generation Holocaust Survivors." *The Guardian*, March 15, 2014, www.theguardian.com/lifeandstyle/2014/mar/15/trauma-second-generation-holocaust-survivors.

Law, Roz. "Hitler, Crop Circles, School Uniforms and Moles—It's Just What the Doctor Ordered." *Sunday Mercury*, August 19, 2011, www.sundaymercury.net/entertainment-news/tv-news/2011/08/19/hitler-crop-circles-school-uniforms-and-moles-it-s-just-what-the-doctor-ordered-66331-29269160.

Longerich, Peter. *Holocaust: The Nazi Persecution and Murder of the Jews.* London: Oxford University Press, 2010.

Martin, Dan. "Doctor Who: Let's Kill Hitler—series 32, episode 8." *The Guardian.* August 27, 2011, www.theguardian.com/tv-and-radio/tvandradioblog/2011/aug/27/doctor-who-television.

Moffat, Steven, writer. *Doctor Who.* Season 7, episode 1, "Asylum of the Daleks." Directed by Nick Hurran, featuring Matt Smith, Karen Gillian, and Arthur Darvill. Aired September 1, 2012, on the BBC. BBC Home Entertainment, 2013, DVD.

Moffat, Steven, writer. *Doctor Who.* Season 6, episode 8, "Let's Kill Hitler." Directed by Richard Senior, featuring Matt Smith, Karen Gillian, and Arthur Darvill. Aired August 27, 2011, on the BBC. BBC Home Entertainment, 2011, DVD.

Mulkern, Patrick. "Doctor Who: Let's Kill Hitler." Radio Times. August 27, 2011, beta.radiotimes.com/blog/2011-08-27/doctor-who-let's-kill-hitler

Nation, Terry, writer. *Doctor Who.* Season 1, episode 2, "The Daleks." Directed by Christopher Barry and Richard Martin, featuring William Hartnell and Carole Ann Ford. Aired December 21, 1963–February 1, 1964, on the BBC. BBC Home Entertainment, 2016, DVD.

Nation, Terry, writer. *Doctor Who.* Season 12, episode 4, "Genesis of the Daleks." Directed by David Maloney, featuring Tom Baker, Elisabeth Sladen, and Ian

Marter. Aired March 8–April 12, 1975, on the BBC. BBC Home Entertainment, 2018, DVD.

Noxon, Marti, writer. *Buffy the Vampire Slayer.* Season 4, episode 19, "New Moon Rising." Directed by James A. Contner, featuring Sarah Michelle Gellar, Marc Blucas, and Seth Green. Aired May 2, 2000, on the WB. Twentieth Century Fox Home Entertainment, 2003, DVD.

Oliver, James C., and Sharia Oliver, writers. *Agents of S.H.I.E.L.D.* Season 4, episode 19, "All the Madame's Men." Directed by Billy Gierhart, featuring Chloe Bennett, Henry Simmons, and Brett Dalton. Aired April 25, 2017, ABC. Walt Disney Studios, 2018, DVD.

Raynor, Helen, writer. *Doctor Who.* Season 3, episode 5, "Evolution of the Daleks." Directed by James Strong, featuring David Tennant and Freema Agyeman. Aired April 28, 2007, on the BBC. BBC Home Entertainment, 2007, DVD.

Risley, Matt. "Doctor Who: 'Let's Kill Hitler' Review." IGN, August 27, 2011, www.ign.com/articles/2011/08/28/doctor-who-lets-kill-hitler-review.

Rodriguez, Tori. "Descendants of Holocaust Survivors Have Altered Stress Hormones: Parents' Traumatic Experience May Hamper Their Offspring's Ability to Bounce Back from Trauma." *Scientific American*, March 1, 2015, www.scientificamerican.com/article/descendants-of-holocaust-survivors-have-altered-stress-hormones/.

Tucker, Ken. "'Doctor Who' Mid-season Premiere Review: 'Let's Kill Hitler' Was a Great Lark through Time and Space." *Entertainment Weekly*, August 28, 2011, ew.com/article/2011/08/28/doctor-who-lets-kill-hitler/.

Vartabedian, Ralph. "Who Got America to the Moon? An Unlikely Collaboration of Jewish and Former Nazi Scientists and Engineers." *Los Angeles Times*, March 1, 2020, www.latimes.com/california/story/2020-03-01/who-got-america-to-the-moon-a-unlikely-collaboration-of-jews-and-former-nazi-engineers.

Weekes, Princess. "*The Originals* Has Introduced Nazi Vampires for . . . Reasons?" *The Mary Sue*, May 17, 2018, www.themarysue.com/the-originals-nazi-vampires/?fbclid=IwAR3a766XL7G6TSnYxBFE6kaHKycojUYzZHHfUy-jzkriec3agg_pdmC5VT0.

Whedon, Jed, and Maurissa Tancharoen, writers. *Agents of S.H.I.E.L.D.* Season 1, episode 17, "Turn, Turn, Turn." Directed by Vincent Misiano, featuring Clark Gregg, Brett Dalton, and Bill Paxton. Aired April 8, 2014, ABC. Marvel Studios, 2014, DVD.

Whedon, Jed, and Maurissa Tancharoen, writers. *Agents of S.H.I.E.L.D.* Season 2, episode 1, "Shadows." Directed by Vincent Misiano, featuring Clark Gregg, Hayley Atwell, and Reed Diamond. Aired September 23, 2014, ABC. Walt Disney Studios, 2015, DVD.

Whedon, Jed, writer. *Agents of S.H.I.E.L.D.* Season 7, episode 13, "What We're Fighting For." Directed by Kevin Tancharoen, featuring Clark Gregg, Chloe Bennett, and Ming-Na Wen. Aired August 12, 2020, ABC. Walt Disney Studios, 2020.

Zbyszewski, Paul, and D. J. Doyle, writers. *Agents of S.H.I.E.L.D.* Season 1, episode 20, "Nothing Personal." Directed by Billy Gierhart, featuring Chloe Bennett, Brett Dalton, and J. August Richards. Aired April 8, 2014, ABC. Marvel Studios, 2014, DVD.

Chapter Two

Destroyer, Defender, AI, Lover

The Golem in Speculative Fiction Prose and Comics

Fraser Sherman

Tales of bringing an artificial humanoid to life by science or sorcery go back long before Marvel's Vision or even Mary Shelley. The Greek god Hephaestus made metal servants for his workshop. Pygmalion brought the statue of Galatea to life. Egyptian legends spoke of animated figurines. And in Jewish Kabbalistic tradition, there's the golem.

The golem has been far more successful in reaching and appealing to a wider audience than most ancient legends of artificial life. Golems have appeared in films, comic books, novels, and short stories. It's a mark of their wide appeal that instead of a brand name, they're now generic. Rather than a humanoid formed by Kabbalistic means, "golem" is often used to refer to any magically created human figure, such as the flesh golems and iron golems of *Dungeons & Dragons*. Scientifically created humans receive the name too. Marge Piercy's *He, She and It* equates a cyborg character to a golem.[1]

The adaptability of the golem concept may be one reason why it's spread so far in fiction. Authors can present a golem as a protector of the Jews, or of the downtrodden and oppressed in general. A golem can be a brutal destroyer, barely controlled by its master, or an oppressed slave forced to obey its creator. A modern golem story can be a tale of horror, heroism, or human interest. When Marvel Comics canceled its *Golem* series after three issues, the editors admitted there were too many ways they could write a golem—supernatural horror, superheroic action, character study—and they couldn't figure out which path to take.[2]

This chapter looks at a selection of twentieth- and twenty-first-century novels, short stories, and comic books involving golems. Its scope is limited to golems, not robots, AIs, or other scientific or magical creations analogous to the figures of Jewish folklore.

KABBALISM AND FOLKLORE

The seeds that grew into the golem are found far back in Jewish tradition. A passage in the Talmud, for instance, makes a brief reference to the fourth-century Babylonian sage Rava creating a man who could not or would not speak. The Kabbalistic *Sefer Yezirah*, *The Book of Splendor*, discusses how combining the letters of the Jewish alphabet/name of God can unleash powers of magical creation.[3]

According to philosopher and historian Moshe Idel, the first written accounts that deal with creating a golem appear in the medieval period, though Idel thinks the tradition predated that era. Kabbalists wrote that just as God created Adam out of clay, a mystic of exceptional spiritual development could do the same. Even the most enlightened Kabbalist is not God's equal, however, so the golem is not fully human. It doesn't have a soul or at least not the higher, most divine elements of the soul, and therefore cannot speak.[4]

Kabbalistic writings list multiple methods for creating a golem, all centering on the use of words and letters. For example, the Kabbalist might recite the letters in the name of God or in the Hebrew alphabet, rearranged into multiple combinations; etch the word *emet* (truth) in the golem's forehead; or place a parchment holding the name of God in the golem's mouth. Unmaking the golem requires reversing the ritual: recite the same letters in reverse, change *emet* to *met* (death), or remove the parchment from its mouth.[5]

Over the following centuries, the Kabbalists discussed the ritual and its significance, but showed little interest in what might be done with a golem, or what the golem's internal life might be like.[6] Then, in the nineteenth century, Jakob Grimm made a reference in his writing to Polish Jews creating golems. As Grimm described the tale, the Jews created golems to labor for them, but the clay creatures, left alive, kept growing larger. Invariably they had to be uncreated.[7]

Although Grimm offered no source for the tale, and none has been found, it was widely accepted as an authentic piece of folklore. It inspired writers in the Romantic movement to use the golem in their fiction as they'd used other supernatural creatures. This in turn prompted Jewish writers and scholars to tell their own stories. By the end of the century, the golem was as much a literary figure as a mystical one.[8] Writers developed stories of the golem, not only as a protector or a brutal fighter, but a comical figure. Tell him to fill a kitchen water barrel and he might keep pouring water in until the room was flooded.

It was the nineteenth century that attached the golem legend to sixteenth-century scholar Judah ben Loew, known as the Maharal. There's no historical record showing ben Loew had any interest in the Kabbala, but the Golem of Prague nevertheless became a well-known figure in folklore and fiction. In this narrative, ben Loew created a golem to protect the Jews of the Prague Ghetto from persecution. The golem ended up running wild and out of control, so the Maharal eventually uncreated it. The remains, in some stories, were hidden in the synagogue attic, in a building still visitable today.[9]

The golem reached a much wider audience in 1914, courtesy of Austrian author Gustav Meyrink's novel, *The Golem*. Appearing on the eve of World War I, this strange, dreamlike novel sold 200,000 copies. Accidentally exchanging hats with Penrath, an elderly resident of Prague, the narrator finds himself experiencing Penrath's life in the old Jewish ghetto several decades earlier. That would be confusing enough, but Penrath has forgotten much of his past, a defense against memories of a past traumatic event.[10]

Without even trying, Penrath finds himself embroiled in his neighbors' feuds, plots, and affairs. At one point he's picked up on suspicion of murder and languishes for months in prison. When he's finally released, the judge reveals he was cleared of the crime some time earlier, but they couldn't release him before prisoners whose names begin with A through O. The influence of Kafka's *The Trial* seems obvious.

Despite the title, the Golem doesn't appear but constantly lurks around the fringes of the story. Penrath learns the legend of its creation by an unnamed Prague rabbi to perform menial labor on the Sabbath. When the Golem eventually ran wild, the rabbi uncreated it.

The Golem allegedly returns every thirty-three years and possibly dwells in-between in a room with no exits. At one point, Penrath apparently finds the room, but not the Golem. Other characters describe the Golem as the spiritual concept the rabbi developed before creating it physically. Or could it be a manifestation of a "spiritual epidemic"? Perhaps it's a metaphor: at one point Pernath compares his fellow ghetto residents to golems, becoming lumps of clay as soon as some element—"the glimmer of an idea, a trivial ambition"—dies away.

Meyrink's mysterious, mystical take fits in a novel that places great emphasis on dream experiences and Tarot cards. Soldiers in the Great War saw a parallel between the golem and the war technology that slaughtered them without compassion or feeling—though Meyrink, writing before the war began, could hardly have foreseen the carnage.

Like Meyrink, and like most speculative fiction dealing with religious and folk traditions, later golem stories pick and choose the elements they want to include. Most authors hand-wave the idea that the creator must be an enlightened mystic or even Jewish. A stoned computer scientist, a sleepwalking woman, an Irish Catholic boy, all can create a golem if the plot requires it.

Writers, particularly in comics, ignore that the golem, despite his lack of a soul or a voice, looks like a man, though possibly an abnormally large man. Fictional golems often appear as sculpted figures with crude faces, clearly more clay than man. The more destructive and dangerous a golem is, the more likely it is to appear monstrous.

DEFENDERS

Jewish Americans such as Jerry Siegel, Joe Shuster, Jack Kirby, and Stan Lee shaped the comic book industry, but Jewish superheroes were rare. The Thing, for example, was conceived as a Jewish character with the personality of his cocreator, Kirby, but his religion wasn't overtly stated until the twenty-first century.[11] The first openly Jewish hero appeared in 1974, and it was a golem.

Strange Tales #174 introduced the "the thing that walks like a man," in a story by Len Wein and John Buscema. Rather than discover it upstairs in a synagogue, Jewish archeologist Abraham Adamson unearths it from the sands of the Sinai. As Adamson explains to his niece Rebecca, nephew Jason, and righthand man Wayne Logan, the Golem eventually left Prague to protect the downtrodden throughout the world, without regard for religion. Eventually, for no reason beyond the needs of the plot, it fell asleep in the desert, where Adamson somehow located it.[12]

When Egyptian deserters loot the camp, Adamson gets shot trying to protect his priceless Kabbalistic scrolls. The deserters realize killing a world-famous scholar will draw too much attention, so they kidnap Wayne, Rebecca, and Jason as hostages (the contrast between the evil, murderous Arabs and the innocent, suffering Jews is not subtle). Left behind, the dying Adamson begs the Golem to protect his family as it protected the Jews of old. Adamson desperately recites the rituals from his scrolls without effect. As he dies, however, his tear splashes on the Golem's foot, bringing it to life. It rescues the hostages, kills the Egyptians, then sinks back into slumber.[13]

Over the next couple of issues (by Mike Friedrich and Tony DeZuniga), Rebecca, Jason, and Wayne ship the Golem back to the United States. This draws the attention of Kaballa the Unclean, a sorcerer who despite his name practices elemental magic. Kaballa wishes to enslave the Golem so that he can use its Earth-based power alongside his air, water, and fire spirits. His attacks fail, even when the Golem is in mid-ocean and can't draw strength from the Earth.[14] By the end of the third and final story, Kaballa realizes the

Golem's strength stems from his love for Wayne and the Adamsons; destroy them and the Golem will fall.[15] A later issue of *Marvel Two-in-One* teamed the Golem up with the Thing to resolve the storyline.[16]

The short-lived series acknowledges the legend that golems are dangerous, likely to destroy even those the golem serves. The third issue references Jakob Grimm's account of a master who turned *emet* into *met* while standing under his golem,[17] so that it collapsed and crushed him. Nevertheless, the series consistently shows the Golem as a trustworthy, heroic defender, except when Kabbala seizes control of it. The series itself was one of many off-the-wall ideas Marvel and DC tried out in the 1970s. Some became hits while others, like the Golem, sank into deserved obscurity.

In 1977, Marvel introduced another golem in *Invaders* #13. In World War II Warsaw, Jewish scholar Jacob Goldstein attempts to create a Golem to protect his people. When a lightning bolt strikes his house, it fuses Goldstein with his clay figure. This may be a literal act of God or relate simply to Goldstein using radioactive heavy water to make the clay. When the Invaders, an American superhero team, arrive in Warsaw to bring Goldstein to the United States—a condition for his scientist brother to keep working for the Allies—they become captives of the Nazis. Goldstein, as the Golem, frees them, kills the Nazi leader, then erases the *e* of *emet* and returns to normal. He chooses to remain in Warsaw to protect his people.[18]

In 1991, DC released *Ragman*, an eight-issue limited series that added a Kabbalistic origin to a forgotten 1970s superhero. Rory Regan is a Vietnam veteran living with his father, a junk dealer in one of Gotham City's worst slums. A local gang wants to use the Regans' junk shop as a base for the local drug trade, so they murder Rory's father and put Rory in the hospital. After recovering, Rory snoops around the store and stumbles across a strange, patchwork costume in his father's closet.[19] The costume makes Rory faster, stronger, almost unkillable—bullets can't do much damage to cloth—and able to siphon souls from evildoers.[20]

After Rory reclaims the shop, a rabbi shows up and explains Rory's dad was actually a Polish Jew named Reganiewicz. The Ragman suit dates to the sixteenth century, when the Maharal's fellow rabbis became worried about employing a soulless golem to protect their people. Using the same Kabbalistic methods, they created the Ragman, a golem of cloth controlled by its human wearer. It's not a perfect solution, as the evil of the stolen souls can corrupt the Ragman, making him an executioner rather than a protector. Rory's father succumbed to the urge to kill; that failure, coupled with being unable to stop the liquidation of the Warsaw Ghetto, drove him to put the suit away.[21]

Rory uses the suit to protect the desperate folk in his neighborhood while resisting its darker impulses. Then a complication develops. A golem the rabbi created to replace the inactive Ragman has slowly become more human over the decades, almost acquiring a voice and a soul. Rory's becoming the Ragman has drained magic from the golem, undoing its transformation. The golem arrives in Gotham seeking to kill the Ragman and regain its humanity. Instead, it sacrifices its lifeforce to feed Rory the strength to master the suit.[22]

Ragman does a better job with its Golem lore than Marvel's Golem series. It's also more entertaining as a superhero story. Both the Ragman and the Golem have appeared in DC Comics irregularly since.

Mike Mignola and Christopher Golden's *Joe Golem and the Drowning City* is set in the 1975 of an alternate timeline, where New York is half underwater. Street kid Molly McHugh enlists the help of occult detective Simon Church and his assistant Joe when her mentor is kidnapped. She doesn't know that Joe is a golem, created five hundred years earlier to hunt and execute witches; Joe, his memory blocked by Simon's drugs, doesn't know this himself. In the course of stopping an occult threat, Joe loses his humanity, turning him into a mindless force of destruction. After he defeats the menace, a dying Church begs Molly to restore Joe to humanity. She promises to do so and sets out in search of Joe.[23]

Mignola and Golden later published a *Joe Golem* prequel comic book series expanding on the novel. Both comic and novel gain from the creators' flair for grotesque tales of the supernatural. Unlike most golem tales, the golem in this series isn't the weirdest character in his story.

DESTROYERS

While most protector golems possess the potential to turn destructive, most destructive golems are usually partly protective. Their goal is justice, but like Marvel's Punisher, they're ruthless in the way they achieve it. Other golems are pure destroyers, wanting nothing but to wreak havoc on their targets.

In Barbara Anson's novel *Golem,* paraplegic IT professional David Demneck is initially grief-stricken when his father, a rabbi, dies accidentally on Halloween. When David learns Rabbi Demneck electrocuted himself changing a fuse, he refuses to believe his father would do that on the Sabbath. Even after David's computer research shows a multiyear pattern of local religious leaders dying on Halloween, the police dismiss his talk of murder. They also refuse to listen when David tracks down the Satanic cult responsible.[24]

David uses his computer to digitize his father's Kabbalistic texts and isolate the key ritual elements for creating a golem. Although David doesn't believe in the magic, taking antidepressants on top of his regular painkillers leaves him so addled he carries out the rituals without being aware of it. David sets his creation on the cult's trail, but to his horror, it begins killing the cultists.

David's efforts to stop the murders leads to his death, despite the golem's efforts to save him. The guilt-ridden golem erases the *e* on its forehead, uncreating itself. *Golem* is the paperback equivalent of a low-budget movie, but surprisingly knowledgeable about golem lore. David, unfortunately, is a self-pitying, bitter disability stereotype that undercuts the book's strengths.

Pete Hamill's *Snow in August* takes place in a small Catholic community in post–World War II Brooklyn. Rabbi Judah Hirsch, a Czech immigrant, recruits tween Michael Devlin one Friday evening as his "Sabbath goy," turning on lights so the rabbi doesn't have to break the Sabbath. A friendship grows between them, with Michael teaching Hirsch American ways and the rabbi sharing his knowledge of the wider world. That includes tales of Judah ben Loew and his golem, whom Michael compares to the superheroes he's read about in comics.[25]

Unfortunately, Michael's made an enemy of a local street gang, which assaults both Michael and Hirsch, putting them in the hospital. Michael learns the gang plans to torch the synagogue and the Jewish neighborhood. Fortunately, Hirsch brought the magic talisman for creating the Golem of Prague with him when he came to the United States. Michael uses the talisman to create a golem. It summons up the snowstorm of the title to trap the gang inside a local saloon. The golem then attacks with a violence that feels more like revenge for their past crimes than a desire to prevent future ones. Despite Hamill seeding the golem's appearance with Hirsch's stories, it comes close to a *deus ex machina* in what's otherwise a realistic story about a deep but unlikely friendship.

The third issue of *The Scorpion*, by Gabriel Levy and Jim Craig, pits the eponymous New York superhero against a golem. Neo-Nazis led by the Golden Fuhrer kidnap Rabbi Akibah, a Czech immigrant, and his daughter. The Fuhrer saw Akibah send a golem against the Nazis during the occupation of Czechoslovakia (Akibah's own creation, not the classic Golem of Prague). He now wants the rabbi to use his magic to resurrect some of Nazi Germany's finest military strategists. Akibah can't raise the dead, but fakes it while reactivating his golem, which he brought with him from Europe.[26]

The golem charges across New York to save the Nazis' captives. The Scorpion tries futilely to destroy it until he realizes they're allies. That changes when the golem reaches the Nazis' underground bunker and Akibah snaps, ordering the golem to murder the Golden Fuhrer's forces. The golem's rampage ends up flooding the bunker and drowning the Nazis. Ultimately, the Scorpion saves the rabbi and his daughter. It's a mediocre story that came out right before the publisher, Atlas Comics, went under.[27]

In *The Monolith* by Jimmy Palmiotti, Justin Gray, and Phil Winslade, New York drug addict Alice inherits her namesake grandmother's house. She hopes to hide there from the brutal pimp Prince. Alice is horrified to find someone walled up in the basement alive. Grandmother Alice's diary reveals that after mobsters murdered her sweetheart, Peter, she helped a local rabbi create a golem, mixing Peter's blood in with the clay. The golem avenged Peter's death and cleaned crime out of the neighborhood, then began punishing anyone who got even slightly out of line. To end the killing, Grandmother Alice got the golem drunk, then bricked it up in the basement.[28]

When Prince finds Alice, she and her best friend Tilt free the golem. It almost kills Prince but Alice, fearful of the police investigating, convinces the golem to spare him (one of Prince's other enemies conveniently kills him). Subsequent stories alternated between Grandmother Alice's experiences with the golem in the past and the golem in the present renewing his war on crime, with Alice trying to rein in his ruthless side. Like *Ragman*, *Monolith* deals with a world of low-life street crime, but it's a considerably bleaker, more violent world. Overall, it's a less entertaining one.

Scott Barkman and Alex Leung's *Golem* opens in Sarajevo in 1992, when troops execute the Kabbalist Srojan's best friend in front of him. Srojan creates a golem to avenge her and protect other innocents, sculpting it with a belligerent, intimidating face. Unfortunately, Srojan is an inept mystic: his ritual creates Golem with a soul, free will, and the ability to speak. Golem takes revenge for its creator, but with no mercy or regard for collateral damage. When Srojan protests, Golem sneers that Srojan should have known that neither justice nor revenge come cheap.[29]

Twelve years later, during the U.S. occupation of Iraq, Golem resumes his war on warmongers. This time Srojan brings a team of magically powered superheroes to stop his creation. Srojan tells Golem that he's become a weapon of mass destruction, doing so much damage he should never be deployed. The sorcerer successfully binds Golem, but they both know that this is only a temporary solution. Setting *Golem* in real-world war situations where right and wrong aren't as clear-cut as in World War II adds to the story. The creators' discussion of when violence is justified is more interesting here than when a golem tackles street punks, drug dealers, or Nazis.

Jonathan and Jesse Kellerman's novels *The Golem of Hollywood* and *The Golem of Paris* portray the Golem of Prague as an executioner, not a protector. Shortly after alcoholic LAPD detective Jacob Lev meets the mysterious, beautiful Mai, he's suddenly transferred from a dead-end assignment to LAPD's Special Projects. Investigating a severed head left in a back alley, Lev identifies the head as belonging to a notorious, uncaught serial killer. Was the man killed in revenge for his crimes? Or, given that he appears to have worked with others, did one of his partners eliminate him as a loose end?[30]

This plotline alternates with a plot thread concerning Asham, the sister to Cain and Abel. After Cain kills Abel, Asham kills herself and Cain rather than marry him. Centuries later, her spirit returns to the mortal world, where it becomes the lifeforce powering the Golem of Prague. Holding the parchment with the name of God in her mouth, Asham is unable to speak without the parchment falling out. Eventually, however, the golem's grotesque body is remodeled into a beautiful female form with the parchment repositioned in her vagina. Her memory gone, Asham takes the name Mai.

Lev learns that Special Projects are members of the half-angel, immortal Nephilim. They brought about the golem's creation and use Mai to execute evildoers, keeping her clay form in the Prague synagogue between killings. During one of her periodic escapes, Mai discovered one of the serial killers attacking a woman outside the synagogue. She executed him, then learned about his partners from his memories. This led to her beheading the second killer in LA. Mai's attracted to Lev because he's a descendant of the Maharal; Special Projects hopes to use him as bait to recapture Mai. At the end of the second book, however, Mai remains free, though Russian agents hoping to learn the secrets of her creation are also hunting her.[31]

Jonathan Kellerman has had a long, successful career as a mystery novelist. The two Golem books, however, are a strange mishmash of serial killer thriller, multigenerational family drama, and Jewish mysticism. They don't work on any level.

Patricia Brigg's *Silence Fallen* is part of her series about Mercy Thompson, a werecoyote with the ability to see and communicate with ghosts. In the opening chapters, Bonarata, overlord of Europe's vampires, abducts Mercy to Prague. It's part of an elaborate plan also involving her allies and her partner, the werewolf Adam. Mercy escapes Bonarata but falls into the clutches of another, far more dangerous cabal of vampires.[32]

Mercy also meets the spirit of the Golem of Prague, which she identifies as a manitou, an Earth-spirit the Maharal somehow bound into clay. The golem wants to destroy the vampires, but to regain physical form it needs Mercy to drain energy from Prague's other ghosts. With the ghosts' consent, Mercy does so. The golem annihilates the vampires, but then turns on the rest of Prague, regarding anyone who isn't a Jew as the enemy. Fortunately, Mercy manages to reclaim the ghostly energy and, with her allies' help, destroy the vampire. The golem here has only a marginal connection with the original legend. As this is the tenth book in the series, it works better if the reader's already a fan.

A couple of novels give readers a golem that's purely, utterly destructive, with no redeeming features. In *The Golem's Eye* by Jonathan Stroud, a golem makes a string of terrorist attacks on London, which in this alternate timeline is ruled by tyrannical magicians. The mastermind behind it is a government official who hopes the failure of his superiors to stop the destruction will enable him to rise to a higher rank. It's part of Stroud's excellent juvenile series, the Bartimaeus trilogy.[33] In *The Journals of Professor Guthridge* by

Kyt Wright, the occultist Guthridge investigates a series of murders targeting immigrants. It turns out the men were members of an East-European revolutionary movement who sold out their fellows when they were imprisoned. Now a Kabbalist has arrived in London, using a golem to execute the men for their betrayal. It's a competently written story, ruined by hand-waving away Guthridge raping his lover in retaliation for flirting with another man.[34]

ARTIFICIAL LIFE FORMS

The artificial life form—android, robot, AI—that yearns to understand or become part of humanity is a classic speculative fiction archetype. Golem characters adapt well to this trope.

The golems in Terry Pratchett's Discworld novel *Feet of Clay* are an excellent example. Mute clay figures (they communicate by writing), they're animated by a script placed in their hollow skulls. The script instructs them to serve their master and work hard, and they need neither sleep nor food. The only time they take off work is when they have a holy day. That makes it puzzling when golems in the city of Ankh-Morpork are implicated in a series of murders; violence simply isn't in them. Neither is suicide, but several golems have destroyed themselves out of some shame they refuse to explain.[35]

It turns out that the golems have used the rituals that created them to create a golem king. The script in his head includes "Rule us wisely," "create peace and justice for all," "teach us freedom," and more inspiring thoughts. Rather than creating the Messiah the golems hope for, the king has snapped under the unattainable goals.

During the investigation, one of the city police places a new script—"You are your own master"—in the brain of the golem Dorfl. The concept of being responsible solely to himself petrifies Dorfl, but he eventually allies with the police and helps bring down the golem king. In the aftermath, he goes to work for the city watch, planning to use his earnings to buy golems from their current owners, implant the new idea in their heads, and so liberate his people peacefully. Dorfl reappears as a supporting character in further novels.

While golems in some stories are happier serving others, Pratchett's creations, despite their programming, are not satisfied as slaves. The golem tendency to work unceasingly, even to the point of causing disaster, is explained here as a way of subverting their employers without defying them. With this, Pratchett gets in snarky social commentary about how the oppressed find ways to rebel. He does an excellent job twisting standard golem tropes.

In Lisa Goldstein's *The Alchemist's Door*, the British occultist John Dee and Rabbi Judah ben Loew join forces to protect one of the Lamed Wuvniks, thirty-six individuals whose righteous lives help God keep the world stable.

The unidentified individual lives in the Prague Ghetto, and Roman Emperor Rudolph II believes by killing the Wuvnik, he will be able to destabilize and remake reality. The Maharal creates the golem Yossel to protect the ghetto, but finds that like Pratchett's golems, it wishes to choose its own life: learning to read, marrying, having a conventional life instead of existing as an automaton. At the climax, a demon offers Yossel humanity if he kills the Wuvnik. Instead, Yossel chooses the greater good, allowing ben Loew to unmake him and thwart the demon. It's one of the best fantasy stories using the Maharal as a character and weaving in other elements of Jewish folklore.[36]

In Jonathan Auxier's *Sweep: The Story of a Girl and Her Monster*, the golem, Charlie, is formed from a ball of soot that comes to life to protect Nan, a young Victorian chimney sweep. Like many artificial life forms in speculative fiction, Charlie has a child's fascination in the world; everything from people's customs to animals to the London buildings enthralls him. Nan learns that her mentor, the Sweep, created Charlie before his death so that she would have a protector. With Charlie's help, Nan organizes a protest that wakes up the public to the suffering child sweeps endure. At the climax, Charlie sacrifices his life to save Nan. It's a sweet story, though changing Charlie to a genie, fae, or a magically animated statue wouldn't change the plot.[37]

Sweep and *Feet of Clay* are unusual in assuming free will is a good thing in golems. Most golem stories assume that the world is better off if the golem doesn't make its own choices. This resembles long-standing fears of computers acquiring genuine artificial intelligence and promptly turning on humanity. Ted Chiang's short story "72 Letters" tackles a different fear: the golem's menace isn't that it's a rogue AI but that it might automate people out of a job.[38]

In Chiang's setting, the Kabbalistic rituals that create the golem are to the modern art of "nomenclature" as alchemy was to chemistry. Nomenclature creates mindless automatons at great cost. Manufacturer Robert Stratton has refined the art so that he can mass-produce cheap, affordable automatons, providing an affordable alternative to child labor. Human workers in the automaton industry see his system as a threat to their careers and refuse to work for Stratton.

The Royal Society pressures them into collaborating in return for Stratton's working on the society's project. The scientist Fieldhurst has discovered humanity will become sterile in a few generations. With Stratton's help, he hopes to apply nomenclature to human embryos in ways that will restore human fertility. Then Stratton discovers Fieldhurst also plans to exploit the research to keep the working-class population down, ensuring the dominance of the upper classes. Stratton must find a way to thwart Fieldhurst, save humanity, and dodge a killer hired by the workers who still oppose his plans for mass golem production. It's an excellent story—as in most of his writing, Chiang sees the ideas he plays with from a totally different angle.

Marge Piercy's *He, She and It* tells two parallel stories of two artificial life forms. One is the Golem of Prague; the other is the cyborg Yod of Tikva, a Jewish town in a dystopian near-future America. When technician Shira Shipman returns to Tikva, she discovers her mother's neighbor Avram Stein has created Yod to defend the community. In the second plotline, the Maharal creates the golem Joseph to defend the Jews of Prague. Unlike the legend, Joseph has the power of speech to help him pass for human.[39]

Both Joseph and Yod struggle to define the difference between defender and destroyer. They don't kill randomly, but they don't hesitate to kill, even if they can defeat an adversary without bloodshed. Joseph dreams of marrying the Maharal's granddaughter, Chava, and living as a man. Yod and Shira fall in love, and Yod comes to hate his role as a warrior. Neither tale ends happily. The rabbi uncreates Joseph out of fear of his destructive side; Yod blows himself up along with Avram's laboratory to prevent anyone creating more cyborgs.

As one might guess from Avram's last name, the story draws on *Frankenstein* as well as golem legends. Yod is the more interesting of the two artificial men, with a stronger storyline; Piercy's version of the Golem of Prague is less engaging and memorable than Goldstein's, or Frances Sherwood's *The Book of Splendor* (see the next section).

LOVERS AND CHILDREN

In some golem fiction, the heart of the narrative isn't the golem's actions as much as the connections the golem forms with others. For example, "Puttermesser and Xanthippe," one section of Cynthia Ozick's *The Puttermesser Papers,* focuses on the relationship between the novel's protagonist, New York Jewish woman Ruth Puttermesser, and her golem surrogate daughter. It's engaging, absurd, and very much a New York story.[40]

At this point in her life, Puttermesser is a mid-level office drone in the New York Department of Receipts and Disbursements. Life is good until the new R&D commissioner demotes Puttermesser to put one of his cronies in her place. On top of that, Puttermesser's lover, Rappoport, dumps her for reading in bed when he's ready to make love. Frustrated, Puttermesser goes to sleep dreaming of how much better her life and her city could be. Sleepwalking, she collects soil from the plant pots around her apartment and forms it into a golem. Puttermesser wants to call her Leah, but the golem insists on Xanthippe, the name of Socrates' wife.

In addition to caring for her mother-creator, Xanthippe, acting out Puttermesser's fantasies, gathers enough signatures to qualify her as an independent candidate for mayor. After Puttermesser's victory (Ozick, tongue-in-cheek, assures readers that the details of the campaign are unimportant to the story), Ruth transforms the city into a clean, orderly, law-abiding community. Xanthippe, however, is growing larger and beginning to express Puttermesser's more physical desires. The golem sleeps with Rappoport, then seduces the men of her mother's administration, without regard for their marital status. As she yields to desire, the city relapses into its old ways. Puttermesser uncreates her daughter, with regret, and has the decomposed remains scattered as topsoil in the city's parks.

In Helene Wecker's *The Golem and the Jinni*, a corrupt Kabbalist creates Chava, a female golem, as wife for a lonely Jew emigrating to America. The man dies on the crossing leaving Chava independent, something she finds terrifying. Unlike Pratchett's golems, Chava is happiest serving others; without a master, she finds herself reacting empathically to the needs of everyone around her. After she arrives in New York, a kindly rabbi helps her find a new life working in a bakery. Here, her impulse to work nonstop is a plus: there are always new customers needing new baked goods, so there's never a need to stop working.[41]

Then Chava meets and becomes friends with Ahmad, a jinni released in New York after centuries of imprisonment. Like Chava, Ahmad is working to build a new life; unlike Chava, who cherishes service and obedience, Ahmad's worldview exalts freedom and independence. Even so, their outcast status among humans leads to a friendship. When the Kabbalist who created Chava arrives in New York and seeks to enslave them both, the bonds between the two supernatural beings help them triumph. The book won a Nebula Award for Best Novel as well as a Mythopoeic Award for Best Adult Fantasy. A sequel followed several years later.

In the graphic novel *The Scent of May Rain* by Mark O. Stack, Rae Epstein, and Kaylee Rowena, the golem Esther forms multiple relationships over the course of a century. A widowed Jewish American professor creates her in the 1920s as a mother for his daughter, Judith. He believes a female golem will serve as a role model, combining the strength Judith longs for with the stereotypically female traits the professor wants his daughter to develop. Esther becomes a devoted caregiver to Judith but suffers under the professor's bullying. After they see a lesbian-themed Jewish play, or instance, Esther refuses to share the professor's outrage. He orders her to walk home from the theater while he drives back alone.[42]

By World War II, the professor has died, Judith has married, and Esther, at Judith's suggestion, is fighting the fascists to protect the Jews of Europe. There she meets Patricia, a woman fighting the Axis as the superhero War

Nurse. Patricia doesn't see any need for male supervision, which fascinates Esther. War Nurse christens Esther's superhero identity as Amazon (presumably a reference to Wonder Woman's Golden Age origin as a clay figure given life).

Judith's later death leaves Esther, like Wecker's Chava, adrift. Judith's grandson Craig convinces Esther to take up her Amazon identity again and use her influence to help bring peace to the world. At first Esther delights in her new role. Then she comes to see Craig has pushed her back into being a caregiver, this time nurturing the world. Esther walks away and gives up trying to pass for human. She's still adrift until she meets Patricia again—like Esther, no older than when they first met—and realizes exactly what and who she wants.

Just as Pratchett's golems become a metaphor for enslaved workers, Esther—one of speculative fiction's few female golems—represents generations of women struggling to find their own role in the world despite being under a man's thumb.

Frances Sherwood's *The Book of Splendor* takes us back to Prague, the Maharal, and his golem Yossel, though this only makes up one strand of Sherwood's historical novel. Here, Yossel's story arc is defined not by protecting Jews but by his relationship with Rochel, the teenaged wife of thirty-something shoemaker Zev.[43]

An illegitimate child of rape, Rochel is a walking scandal in the community's eyes. Marrying Zev, a decent and loving man, is her only option for living a normal life, but she's still unhappy in the marriage. With the mute golem, however, Rochel finds it easy to share her feelings and thoughts. She and Yossel fall in love, but Rochel eventually begins to fall in love with her husband as well. When Zev has to flee Prague under the threat of pogroms, Yossel helps Rochel to reach her husband, setting aside his own feelings. Yossel then asks the Maharal to uncreate him, which the rabbi reluctantly does. *Book of Splendor* is a well-executed historical novel. However, Sherwood hints early on that there's a dark force tainting Yossel's creation. That never pays off.

Alice Hoffman's *The World That We Knew* starts in 1941 Berlin as Hannah, a Jewish widow, resolves to send her daughter Lea to the relative safety of France. Fearful of the risks to a girl traveling alone, Hannah pays Ettie, a Kabbalist's daughter, to create a female golem as companion for Lea. The golem, Ava, has *emet* on her arm rather than her forehead, to avoid drawing too much attention.[44]

Ava and Lea head off to France, as does Ettie, who joins the resistance. The book explores the lives and relationships of all three women, with Ava serving as a surrogate caregiver for Lea, often resented, sometimes loved. Ava herself forms a bond with a heron, which with its nonhuman wisdom sees her for what she is. Ettie dies heroically, the heron gets shot, but Lea and Ava survive the war. Like Sherwood's Yossel, Ava begs Lea to destroy her rather than allow an inhuman thing to continue walking the earth. Unlike ben Loew, Lea refuses to kill Ava, an act of compassion that brings the golem to full humanity. Like *Scent of May Rain*, Hoffman makes a good use of the golem to capture the complexity of women's lives.

FACING THE HOLOCAUST

Writing in *Slate*, Adam Kirsch suggests the Holocaust, and the need for a Jewish protector, may have encouraged the growing number of golem stories since World War II.[45] Golem stories set during the Holocaust show little hope that a golem can make a difference; neither Ragman nor Jacob Goldstein can stop the liquidation of the Warsaw Ghetto. The most that can be hoped for is that one or two individuals, like Alice Hoffman's Lea, escape death with a golem's help. In this tradition, Harry Turtledove's short story "In This Season" has a golem appear at a Jewish family's home in World War II Poland on the last night of Hanukkah. The golem sacrifices itself to help the family escape to Allied territory, but that changes nothing for the rest of Poland's Jews.[46]

The Golem's Voice, a graphic novel by David G. Klein, opens in Prague as the Mendel family—Anna and sons Yoakim and Yakov—board a train for the camps. When a chance of escape appears, Anna tells her sons to run; Yoakim gets shot but Yakov hides in a nearby synagogue, where he discovers the Golem of Prague. Yakov can't revive the inert figure, but the spirit of the Maharal transports the boy to a hidden camp of Jewish fugitives outside the city. There, Yakov successfully makes a new golem, which protects the fugitives and derails a death-camp train. When the Nazis close in, Yakov sacrifices himself to save an old woman. The golem gives up its own life force to restore him, revealing that it was Yoakim's spirit inside the golem. At the end of the war, Yakov learns the train the golem derailed was the one deporting his mother. As a result, she survived, and they reunite. It's heartwarming, but the story relies heavily on ben Loew's spirit performing miracles to move the plot along.[47]

Breath of Bones by Steve Niles, Matt Santoro, and Dave Wachter has a golem save an entire Jewish village. The story opens with Noah, a soldier in World War II, making the apparently fatal decision to cover his platoon's retreat. The story flashes back to a Jewish village a few years earlier; Noah's father has gone off to fight against the German invaders and Noah knows he won't return. When a British fighter plane crashes near the village, Noah insists on taking the man to safety and hiding him, despite the risk of German retaliation if they find him.[48]

Some Nazis do find him and summon reinforcements to annihilate the village. Noah's grandfather sacrifices his life to create a golem, which proves to be all-protector: it smashes the Nazi forces when they attack the village but won't hunt them down afterwards. Ultimately it does destroy the Germans to save Noah's life, then dissolves back into mud. The story returns to the present as Noah, pinned down, begins shaping mud into a human form. . . . It's a well-done graphic novel.

Other Holocaust golem stories are more pessimistic. Voros, the Red Magician of Lisa Goldstein's eponymous novel, creates a golem in the 1930s to fight against the coming nightmare, but a local rabbi uses his own magic to destroy it. The rabbi doesn't want to believe the dooms Voros has seen. Despite his skepticism and Voros's magic, the Holocaust comes.[49]

In Michael Chabon's *The Amazing Adventures of Kavalier and Klay*, the pre-war rabbis of Prague worry that once the Nazis occupy the city, they'll steal the Golem of Prague as they have other antiquities. While some hope their champion will arise to defend the city, the final decision is to send the Golem elsewhere. Stage magician Bernard Kornblum finds a way to smuggle him out along with teenager Josef Kavalier, who's hidden in a false compartment in the golem's crate. The golem ends up in Lithuania while Kavalier makes it to the United States and his cousin Sammy Klay. Together Kavalier and Klay (whose story reflects the history of Superman creators Jerry Siegel and Joe Shuster) break into the comics business. Their first unsuccessful superhero is based on the golem; then they find success with a character called the Escapist.[50]

Years later, the crate holding the golem arrives at Kavalier's house. When he opens the box, there's nothing inside it but mud; taken from its home, the golem has lost its life force. The golem managed to inspire Kavalier and Klay's comics creations, but in the real world it is no longer a champion. Both Chabon's and Goldstein's stories are excellent, but the golem only forms a minor part of each tale. Chabon's story, taking place primarily in the United States, is much less bleak and depressing.

Thane Rosenbaum's *The Golems of Gotham* takes the bleakest view, arguing that it's pointless to tell stories where one or two or even a few dozen people survive; the Holocaust's meaning lies in death, not survival. Protagonist Oliver Levin is a successful mystery novelist suffering massive writer's block. His daughter, Ariel, hopes to help him by creating a golem and animating it with the spirits of his parents, Holocaust survivors who committed suicide before she was born. She combines letters in the ritual using an alphanumeric code based on the numbers in her grandparents' camp tattoos.

This summons their ghosts but also those of Primo Levi, Jerzy Kozinsky, and other writers who, having survived the Holocaust, later killed themselves.[51]

The "golems" create chaos in Manhattan with their mystical powers. Smoke reminds them of the camp crematoriums, so they eliminate all its sources. The New York Yankees' pinstripe outfits remind the ghosts of their camp wear, so they bleach them. They also eliminate tattoos as antithetical to Jewish law and painful reminders of the camps. Later they destroy all copies of *Schindler's List* and other Holocaust films they dislike. Oliver becomes unblocked but to his agent's dismay, starts writing a serious novel about the Holocaust. The golems realize that not only have more genocides happened—so much for Never Again—but some people even deny the reality of the Holocaust. Oliver at one point contemplates suicide but eventually gains understanding of how the Holocaust has damaged his life. He and Ariel unconvincingly find peace of mind and the golems depart.

Rosenbaum's golems make a useful metaphor for real-world Holocaust survivors. They also invoke the Jewish legend of the dybbuk, ghosts who possess the living to find closure, and serve as avatars of the Holocaust trauma that haunts later generations. Rosenbaum makes some excellent points, such as the hollowness of "never again!" declarations. Much of what the novel says, however, is unconvincing or trite, such as great art only coming from great suffering. The book's humor fits awkwardly with the tragic aspects. In one chapter Ariel gives the ghosts physical form to run wild in New York; then Rosenbaum announces at the end of the chapter that none of the events happened. It's less amusing than it's meant to be.

WHAT HAS YET TO BE WRITTEN

Writing in 2002, Kirsch suggested the golem has spread into American popculture because the concept strikes so many contemporary chords. Superhero. Weapon of mass destruction. Monster. Robot. Slave. Outcast. As is clear from the stories discussed here, the golem is flexible enough to comment on almost anything: war, New York politics, women's changing roles. That's no small accomplishment, but Kirsch worries whether that's a good thing: "The golem, like the Hanukkah holiday, is a minor part of Jewish history that is being overinflated simply because it fits in so neatly with modern, American appetites." [52]

That was in 2002. Multiple stories have appeared since then. In many of them, *golem* serves as a generic word for any magically animated automaton, as in *The Golem in My Glove Box*. Kavalier and Klay couldn't sell a golem comic book, but multiple real-world creators have done so successfully.

Will increasing use and familiarity drain the legend of the golem of its power? As in Chabon's novel, will removing the golem from its home in Jewish mysticism and folklore destroy it? Only time, and future fantasy tales, will reveal the answer.

NOTES

1. Marge Piercy, *He, She and It* (New York: Fawcett, 1991).

2. Editor, "Letters to the Golem," *Strange Tales & Golem* #177, Dec. 1974, 30.

3. Moshe Idel, *Golem* (Albany: State University of New York Press, 1990), 9–47.

4. Idel, 47–73.

5. Idel, 47–73.

6. Idel, 251–256.

7. Edan Dekel and David Gantt Gurley, "How the Golem Came to Prague," *Jewish Quarterly Review* 103, no. 2 (2013): 243.

8. Dekel and Gurley, 243–244.

9. Dekel and Gurley, 245.

10. Gustav Meyrink, *The Golem* (Great Britain: Dedalus Books, 1915).

11. Brian Cronin, "Who Was the First Jewish Superhero?" *CBR.com,* Feb. 9, 2019, www.cbr.com/first-jewish-superhero.

12. Len Wein (w) and John Buscema (a), "There Walks the Golem," *Strange Tales* #174 (New York: Marvel, June 1974), 2–3.

13. Wein and Buscema, 14–27.

14. Mike Friedrich (w) and Tony DeZuniga (a), "Black Crossing," *Strange Tales & Golem* #176 (New York: Marvel, Oct. 1974), 11–23.

15. Mike Friedrich (w) and Tony DeZuniga (a), "There Comes Now Raging Fire," *Strange Tales & Golem* #177 (New York: Marvel, Dec. 1974), 23.

16. Roy Thomas, Bill Mantlo (w) and Bob Brown (a), "The Thing Goes South," *Marvel Two-in-One* #11 (New York: Marvel, Nov. 1975), 1–31.

17. Friedrich and DeZuniga, "Raging Fire," 1–2.

18. Roy Thomas (w) and Frank Robbins (a), "The Golem Walks Again," *The Invaders* #13 (New York: Marvel, Feb. 1977), 13–31.

19. Keith Giffen (w and a), Robert Loren Fleming (w) and Pat Broderick (a), "Bones of the Defenseless," *Ragman #1* (New York: DC Comics: Oct. 1991), 15–28.

20. Keith Giffen (w and a), Robert Loren Fleming (w) and Pat Broderick (a), "A Ragged Revenge," *Ragman #2* (New York: DC Comics: Nov. 1991), 1–6.

21. Keith Giffen (w and a), Robert Loren Fleming (w) and Pat Broderick (a), "The Folktale," *Ragman #3* (New York: DC Comics: Dec. 1991), 4–28.

22. Keith Giffen (w and a), Robert Loren Fleming (w) and Pat Broderick (a), "Shreds," *Ragman #6* (New York: DC Comics: March 1992), 16–18.

23. Mike Mignola (w) and Christopher Golden (a), *Joe Golem and the Drowning City* (Milwaukie, OR: Dark Horse, 2012).

24. Barbara Anson, *Golem* (New York: Leisure Books, 1978).

25. Pete Hamill, *Snow in August* (New York: Little, Brown & Co., 1997).

26. Gabriel Levy (w) and Jim Craig (a), "Night of the Golden Fuhrer," *The Scorpion* #3 (New York: Atlas Comics, July 1975), 3.

27. Levy and Craig, 17–20.

28. Jimmy Palmiotti, Justin Gray and Phil Winslade, *The Monolith* (Berkeley: Image, 2012).

29. Scott Barkman and Alex Leung, *Golem* (Studio 407, 2012).

30. John Kellerman and Jesse Kellerman, *The Golem of Hollywood* (New York: Penguin, 2013).

31. John Kellerman and Jesse Kellerman, *The Golem of Paris* (New York: Penguin, 2015).

32. Patricia Briggs, *Silence Fallen* (New York: Ace, 2017).

33. Jonathan Stroud, *The Bartimaeus Trilogy Book Two: The Golem's Eye* (New York: Hyperion Books, 2004).

34. Kyt Wright, *The Journals of Professor Guthridge* (USA: Blkdog Publishing, 2020).

35. Terry Pratchett, *Feet of Clay* (New York: Harper Collins, 1996).

36. Lisa Goldstein, *The Alchemist's Door* (New York: Tor Books, 2002).

37. Jonathan Auxier, *Sweep* (New York: Abrams Books, 2018).

38. Ted Chiang, "72 Letters" in *Vanishing Acts,* ed. Ellen Datlow (New York: Tor Books, 2000).

39. Marge Piercy, *He, She and It* (New York: Alfred A. Knopf, 1991).

40. Cynthia Ozick, *The Puttermesser Papers* (New York: Alfred A. Knopf, 1997).

41. Helene Wecker, *The Golem and the Jinni* (New York: HarperCollins, 2013).

42. Mark O. Stack, Rae Epstein and Kaylee Rowena, *The Scent of May Rain* (Weekend Warrior Comics, 2020).

43. Frances Sherwood, *The Book of Splendor* (New York: W. W. Norton, 2002).

44. Alice Hoffman, *The World That We Knew* (New York: Simon & Shuster, 2019).

45. Adam Kirsch, "Does the World Need Another Golem Novel?" *Slate,* Aug. 6, 2002, slate.com/culture/2002/08/does-the-world-need-another-golem-novel.html.

46. Harry Turtledove, "In This Season." In *Christmas Bestiary,* edited by Martin Greenberg (New York: DAW Books, 1992).

47. David G. Klein, *The Golem's Voice* (USA: Now What Media, 2015).

48. Steve Niles and Matt Santoro (w) and Dave Wachter (a), *Breath of Bones* (Milwaukie, OR: Dark Horse Books, 2014).

49. Lisa Goldstein, *The Red Magician* (New York: Pocket Books, 1992).

50. Michael Chabon, *The Amazing Adventures of Kavalier and Klay* (New York: Random House, 2000).

51. Thane Rosenbaum, *The Ghosts of Gotham* (New York: HarperCollins, 2002).

52. Kirsch, "Does the World Need Another Golem Novel?"

WORKS CITED

Anson, Barbara. *Golem*. New York: Leisure Books, 1978.

Barkman, Scott (w) and Alex Leung (a). *Golem*. Studio 407, 2012.

Bloch, Chayim. *The Golem: Mystical Tales from the Ghetto of Prague*. New York: Rudolph Steiner Publications, 1972.

Briggs, Patricia. *Silence Fallen*. New York: Ace Books, 2017.

Chabon, Michael. *The Amazing Adventures of Kavalier and Klay*. New York: Random House, 2000.

Chiang, Ted. "72 Letters." In *Vanishing Acts,* edited by Ellen Datlow. New York: Tor Books, 2000.

Friedrich, Mike (w) and Tony DeZuniga (a). "Black Crossing." *Strange Tales* #176. New York: Marvel Comics, 1974.

Friedrich, Mike (w) and Tony DeZuniga (a). "There Comes Now Raging Fire." *Strange Tales* #177. New York: Marvel Comics, 1974.

Giffen, Keith (w and a), Robert Loren Fleming (w) and Pat Broderick (a). *Ragman*. New York: DC Comics, 1991–1992.

Goldstein, Lisa. *The Alchemist's Door*. New York: Tor Books, 2002.

Goldstein, Lisa. *The Red Magician*. New York: Pocket Books, 1992.

Hoffman, Alice. *The World That We Knew*. New York: Simon and Shuster. 2019.

Idel, Moshe. *Golem: Jewish Magical and Mystical Traditions on the Artificial Anthropoid*. Albany: State University of New York Press, 1990.

Kellerman, Jonathan and Jesse Kellerman. *The Golem of Hollywood*. New York: Penguin, 2013.

Kellerman, Jonathan and Jesse Kellerman. *The Golem of Paris.* New York: Penguin, 2015.

Klein, David G. *The Golem's Voice*. Now What Media, 2015.

Levy, Gabriel (w) and Jim Craig (a). "Night of the Golden Fuhrer," *The Scorpion* #3. New York: Atlas Comics, July 1975.

Meyrink, Gustav. *The Golem*. Translated by Mike Mitchell. Great Britain: Dedalus, Ltd., 1915.

Mignola, Mike (w) and Christopher Golden (a). *Joe Golem and the Drowning City*. Milwaukie, OR: Dark Horse, 2012.

Mignola, Mike (w) and Christopher Golden (a). *Joe Golem, Occult Detective.* Milwaukie, OR: Dark Horse, 2015–2017.

Naquin, R. L. *Golem in My Glove Box*. Toronto: Carina Press. 2014.

Niles, Steve, Matt Santoro (w) and Dave Wachter (a). *Breath of Bones: A Tale of the Golem.* Milwaukie, OR: Dark Horse Books, 2013.

Ozick, Cynthia. *The Puttermesser Papers*. New York: Alfred A. Knopf, 1997.

Palmiotti, Jimmy (w) and Justin Gray (a). *The Monolith*. Berkeley: Image, 2012.

Piercy, Marge. *He, She and It*. Alfred A. Knopf: New York, 1991.

Pratchett, Terry. *Feet of Clay*. New York: Harper, 1996.

Rosenbaum, Thane. *The Ghosts of Gotham*. New York: Harper Collins, 2002.

Sherwood, Frances. *The Book of Splendor*. New York: W. W. Norton, 2002.

Stack, Mark O. (w) and Rae Epstein (a). *The Scent of May Rain*. Weekend Warrior Comics, 2020.

Stroud, Jonathan. *The Bartimaeus Trilogy Book Two: The Golem's Eye*. New York: Hyperion, 2004.

Thomas, Roy, Bill Mantlo (w) and Bob Brown (a). "The Thing Goes South," *Marvel Two-in-One* No. 11. New York: Marvel Comics, 1975.

Turtledove, Harry. "In This Season." In *Christmas Bestiary,* edited by Martin Greenberg, 126–150. New York: DAW Books, 1992.

Wecker, Helene. *The Golem and the Jinni.* New York: HarperCollins, 2013.

Wein, Len (w) and John Buscema (a). "There Walks the Golem," *Strange Tales* #174. New York: Marvel Comics, 1974.

Wright, Kyt. *The Journals of Professor Guthridge.* Blkdog Publishing, 2020.

Chapter Three

"The Golem Was Built to Go to War"

The Golem in TV Fiction

Mara W. Cohen Ioannides

The golem presents an intriguing monster motif for modern fantasy script writers. The Jewish superhero created to protect Jews is first mentioned in the Hebrew Bible. Much later, the golem in popular culture dates back to the beginning of the twentieth century. The idea that humans can create a living being designed specifically as a form of protection is certainly an ideal creature for a fantasy story. Because the golem comes with a mythology and a particular cultural group, there is a draw for a specific set of viewers that only makes it more appetizing for script writers. However, these script writers are not always accurate in their portrayal. This chapter examines the golem character in various popular culture television shows of both cartoon and live performance. By doing so, we will understand how this superhero has devolved to fit the times and the misinterpretations non-Jewish writers have of the character.

GOLEM'S HISTORY

The golem is a mythological creature whose creation formula first appears in the *Sefer Yetzirah* (*Book of Creation*). In the Talmud, the Babylonian Talmudist Rabbah bar Nachmani "created a man" (Sanhedrin 65b) through the use of the *Sefer Yetzirah*. The earliest published account of how to create a golem comes from Rabbi Eleazar of Wormes (1176–1238) in his book *Perush al Sefer Yetzirah* (*Commentary on the Book of Creation*). It is Rabbi Eleazar who promulgates the legend that by inscribing certain letters on a clay model one can create a golem. The word *golem* is an interesting choice of term. In Talmudic Hebrew, it means embryo and in Modern Hebrew, cocoon.[1] Considering that the golem is a being without a soul, just as embryos are defined in Judaism, the choice of terminology is perfect.

However, it is the legend of a Rabbi Judah Lowe of Prague, aka the Maharal, that is most vividly recited. The folktale recounts the Maharal creating a golem to protect the Jews of Prague during a Blood Libel in the late 1500s. There are different endings to this folktale: one tells that the Maharal forgot to deactivate the golem on Shabbat and another tells that the golem actually fell in love. In either case, disaster struck, and the golem had to be permanently destroyed. Jakob Grimm made an entry in his 1808 *Zeitung für Einsiedler* (*Journal for Hermits*) about this folk character, although he associates it with Polish Jews,[2] despite it being Rabbi Eleazar's story. The early novel *Isabella von Aegypten: Kaiser Karl des Fünften erste Jugendliebe* (*Isabella of Egypt: Emperor Charles the V's First Childhood Love*), published in 1812 by Achim von Arnim, presents the golem as a woman.[3] It was not until the mid-1800s that the legend becomes solidly associated with Prague,[4] perhaps Berthold Auerbach's novel *Spinoza: Ein historischer Roman* (*Spinoza: An Historical Novel*) in 1837 is the first.[5] A recurrent theme is that the golem has no emotion and no intelligence; it simply follows orders.

During the early part of the twentieth century, the golem stories became popular again. One of the top-selling versions was Rabbi Yudle Rosenberg's, which appeared in 1909 as *Nifle'ot Maharal 'im ha-golem* (*Book of Wonders of the Maharal with the Golem*). While the author claimed it was based on a book by the Maharal's son, it is, in fact, a fabrication.

The golem is created in 1580, in Rosenberg's folktale, by three men: Rabbi Liva of Prague, Isaac ben Sampson Ha-Cohen, and Jacob ben Khaim-Sassoon Ha-Levi. These three men "drew his [the golem's] face in the earth, and his arms and legs, the way a man lies on his back."[6] Then Isaac circled the figure and recited a formula, followed by Jacob doing the same. The rabbi carrying a Torah scroll circled the golem. Finally, the three recited, "And the Lord G-d formed man of the dust of the ground and breathed into his nostrils the breath of life; and man became a living soul."[7] Then the rabbi directed the golem what to do and he did it, although the golem could not speak. The rabbi named him Joseph.[8] Once the flare-up of pogroms had abated, Rabbi Liva decided to end the life of the golem. He gathered his two acolytes and reversed what they had done to create him, and he returned to clay.[9] This version was reproduced by Mikhah Yosef Berdyczewski in *Mehor Yehudah* (*Fountain of Judah*) and Chiam Block in a book later translated in English as *The Golem: Legends of the Ghetto of Prague*.[10]

Gustav Meryink wrote a serial version, *The Golem,* that was published in its complete form in 1915 and sold 200,000 copies.[11] Paul Wegener turned Gustav Meyrink's serial, later novel, of 1913–1914 into a trilogy of silent movies in 1920. Only *Der Golem, wie er in die Welt kam* (*The Golem: How He Came into the World*) has survived.[12] In 1951, the first color movie with a golem, *Císařův pekař a pekařův císař* (*The Emperor and the Golem*), was released in Czechoslovakia.[13] In 1967, the horror film *It!* or *Anger of the Golem* was released in Britain. Roddy McDowell starred as Arthur Prim, a Judah Lowe–like character, who creates a golem for his own purposes. Golems of course, crept back into children's culture.[14]

The critic and Columbia University's Center for American Studies faculty Adam Kirsch argues that "Since Cynthia Ozick's *The Puttermesser Papers* in 1998, golems have found their way into novels of every type—comic and tragic, allegorical and magic-realist. It's possible that this is nothing more than a fad, the literary equivalent of Hollywood's enthusiasm for Kabbalah, but the golem population explosion also suggests that the ancient legend has become a way to explore some very modern problems."[15]

Many scholars presume that Mary Shelley's Frankenstein monster is a golem,[16] though Rabbi Byron Sherwin, professor at The Spertus Institute of Jewish Learning and Leadership, disagrees with this, instead suggesting that Shelley's monster influenced the golem stories that followed.[17] Scholars, such as Cathy S. Gelbin at the University of Manchester, and Sherwin see the golem in the modern period as "a global signifier of the Jews" and a study of "the misuse of science."[18] Authors Rachel Swirsky and Matthew Kressler both agree that this post-Holocaust use of golems as defenders of Jews has become a trope in Jewish fiction.[19] Kressel stretches the golem imagery to include the Cylons in *Battlestar Galactica* and Hal 9000 in *2001.*[20]

POPULAR TELEVISION SHOWS
THAT INCLUDE GOLEMS

Golems became popular on television at the end of the twentieth century. The first modern TV show that includes a golem is *Gargoyles* (1994–1997). Greg Weisman, the producer, wanted *Gargoyles* to be a series of morality tales.[21] Jordan Calhoun, editor of *Black Nerd Problems* website and an avid fan, notes that "more than anything else, race and xenophobia were themes on the forefront [of the series]. Craftily woven throughout the series, tolerance, courage, and integrity were taught."[22] This is very much a show about inclusion and what it is like to be "other." Gary Sperling, who wrote this 1995 episode "Golem,"[23] "felt he had an affinity for the subject matter and because his brother, a rabbi, was able to advise him on things like the Hebrew, etc."[24]

Weisman really believed that "the parallels of Golem to Gargoyle are obvious, and the main reason why I felt we HAD to do this episode."[25] They both protect the underdog.

Almost immediately Golems became common in television pop culture. A 1996 episode of *The Real Adventures of Johnny Quest*, "Rock of Rages," has the Quest team traveling to the Czech Republic to investigate a golem. Lance Falk, the writer of this episode, admits that the title of the episode is supposed to echo the Jewish Hannukah song "Rock of Ages"[26] that recalls the protection that God has always given the Jewish people. He also did research on the golem mythology, and that is why the story is set in Prague.[27]

The next year *X-Files* included an episode about a golem. The premise of the *X-Files* is the Federal Bureau of Investigation (FBI) has a division that investigates paranormal and supernatural phenomena. Special Agents Fox Mulder and Dana Scully follow these reports trying to find the truth. In the 1997 "Kaddish" (which is the name for the Jewish prayer of mourning), Isaac Luria, a Hassidic shopkeeper, is murdered, but when one of the suspects turns up dead later with Luria's fingerprints, Mulder and Scully are called in to investigate. Eventually Mulder finds a copy of the *Sefer Yetzirah* (the Book of Creation, traditionally the instructions for creating a golem) near Luria's grave.[28] Howard Gordon, the script writer, feels this episode personally. His mother had relatives who survived the Holocaust and came to the United States, and he grew up in a Reform Jewish family. He sees his "characters . . . as a reflection" of himself.[29]

One cannot discuss golems without mentioning the longest-running show on television: *The Simpsons* and its episode "Treehouse of Horror XVII," broadcast in 2006. Here Krusty the Clown has inherited a golem that looks amazingly like the 1915 depiction in *Der Golem*. Bart Simpson, a fan and hero of the series, steals it and uses it defend himself from bullies.[30]

In the 2010 episode of the show *Sherlock*, based on the novels by Sir Arthur Conan Doyle, Sherlock Holmes encounters an assassin who goes by the name "Golem." "The Great Game" is not about Golem, or a golem, but rather the first encounter between Holmes and his nemesis, James Moriarty.[31] Mark Gatiss's naming of the assassin Golem has to do with a Czech theme that runs through the show.

Haven is a 2012 series based on the Stephen King novel *The Colorado Kid*. An FBI agent, Audrey Parker, is sent to the town of Haven, Maine, to work with the chief of police, Nathan Wuornos. The two discover that people in town who have committed violent crimes but are not found guilty because of legal loopholes are being killed in a manner related to their crimes. The perpetrator is the White Woman who moves at superspeed and has super strength. Finally, Parker and Wuornos discover that the White Woman, is the animated figure of Lady Justice that hung in the courthouse.[32]

Sleepy Hollow is a 2013 show about Ichabod Crane, originally conceived by Washington Irving, who is revived 250 years after the American Revolution. The creators of the series, Roberto Orci and Alex Kurtzman, wanted to build from "elements [that are familiar to audiences] to allow for a dense, rich, relatable experience."[33] While the golem, by now a scifi and fantasy regular, is not a major character in television and film, it has made regular appearances and so is familiar, if not a horror favorite. In this series, Crane has a son, Jeremy, and in the episode "The Golem," the golem represents Jeremy's pain in not having his father.[34]

The premise of the television show *Grimm* that began in 2011 is a twist on the Grimm Brothers' fairy tales. Here the fantastic creatures, like werewolves and ogres, that appear in the fairy tales are real, but only the descendants of the Grimm family can see them in their bestial form; regular humans only see them in their human form. The typical mission of a Grimm is to kill these beasts, but our hero, Police Officer Nick Burkhardt, decides there are good and bad supernaturals and he should help the good and punish the bad. In the 2014 episode "Dyin' on a Prayer," the Jewish woman Sara Fisher contends with her alcoholic violent ex-husband, Keith, who is a Seigbarste, an ogre-like beast. She, however, knows nothing of Keith's supernatural self. Rabbi Ben Fisher, Sara's brother, is concerned that his abusive ex-brother-in-law will kill his sister. The police seem incapable of stopping Keith; thus, he takes the only action he can think of—he creates a golem.[35]

The plot of *Supernatural* is that the brothers Sam and Dean Winchester hunt evil throughout the world in the twenty-first century. Their golem appears in a 2013 episode. It was created in the 1940s by Rabbi Isaac Bass to save Jews from Nazi necromancers. Bass leaves this golem to his grandson Aaron who, however, has used the pages of the secret book of instructions about controlling the monster, for marijuana smoking. This golem is sentient and even complains that "the boy [Aaron] knows nothing, observes none of the mitzvahs, labors on sabbath, dines on swine . . . he's no rabbi."[36]

Trollhunters, a 2016 product from DreamWorks, is the story of Jim Lake Jr's adventures as the defender of humans and trolls. There are two episodes with golems; the first, "Mudslinging,"[37] and the second, "Blinkey's Day Out,"[38] were both released on December 23, 2016. In these episodes the golem is created by Angor Rot, a soulless antagonist who hunts trollhunters like Lake, by carving a fetish. This fetish then takes the form of whatever he is buried in. Only by removing the fetish from the golem and breaking it is the golem destroyed.

Dennis Heaton, executive producer, calls *The Order* "a horror-comedy."[39] This provides an interesting forum for a golem. In "Hell Week, Part Two," the golem Clay, one of the main character Jack's roommates, ponders his existence in a very adolescent way. He is a creation of a secret magical society's member to destroy members of the same society. While he normally appears as a human, when he is called to be destructive, he turns into a "mud monster."[40]

RESCULPTING THE GOLEM

The development or de-evolution of the golem in television can be seen in the way that the story of the creation of the golem is provided in these shows. Much of what is included has to do with how much the writers and producers know about Judaism and the golem story, along with what they felt was important for their story.

Rather than explain what a golem is, Sperling in his 1995 episode of *Gargoyles* does a flashback to Rabbi Judah Lowe's initial activation of the golem where the rabbi speaks these words in Hebrew:

של גוף תהיה חים דנפש כחוכמה הכנס ולהים קוס

[Arise and give life: gather spiritual wisdom the life soul will be body of][41]

and then folds the sheet and places it in the golem's mouth. The golem's eyes glow and he is activated. Rabbi Lowe states: "You have been given the breath of life for a purpose to protect our community" and the golem stomps through 1580 Prague, killing those who attacked the Jews.[42] When Max writes the words he heard in his head, he wears a *tallit* as if the words are holy or to emphasize that this is a Jewish act. When Brod's team steals both the golem and written words, so that Halcyon Renard can transfer his soul into the creature, Renard recites these words:

נא להביא נשאר לגוף היא אדמה

[I beseech you to take my soul to this body of earth][43]

Renard becomes evil and through Max learns to accept his death; his soul leaves the body of the golem and Max removes the paper from the golem's mouth.[44] This story follows Rosenberg's story rather well: the recitation of a prayer, feeding the golem a Hebrew prayer, having the golem go awry, and then removing the prayer to end its existence. The care taken in the details is amazing, especially for a thirty-minute cartoon. The faithful interpretation from Rosenberg's words to the visuals of *Gargoyles* shows Sperling's knowledge of the mythology and concern for being accurate. The impact on the viewer is intense; it is more of a history lesson than a piece of fiction.

Just like Sperling's description, Falk's interpretation of this creature in *Johnny Quest* is close to the Rosenberg mythology, although abbreviated. Dr. Quest tells his team to "bring a stone giant to life . . . use this wand [schriv] to carve a mystic symbol into the creature's forehead bringing it to life."[45] He continues by explaining the legend: "A seventeenth-century rabbi created this creature to protect his people from religious persecution."[46] The creature is ultimately destroyed when Johnny Quest shoves a stick into the golem's head. The golem crashes to the ground and breaks into small pieces.[47] Here, we have the story shortened to its basics and the destruction of the golem by the destruction of the infinity symbol, ∞, in its head.

Gordon, who wrote the 1997 *X-Files* "Kaddish," twisted the golem, albeit not as much as others that come later, but does abandon Rosenberg's folktale. However, Mikal Koven rightly argues that "this *X-Files* episode keeps well within the tradition of Ashkenazi golem legends."[48] Here, the golem is created by Ariel, Luria's wife, in the form of Luria, quite a step from the vague man-like creature with a modern feminist twist. The golem possesses the soul of Luria and so adds a dimension to the original character that is outside the mythology. When Ariel erases the "Shem" (ש) from the golem's hand, he disintegrates.[49] This is another change from the mythology. This change of the hand tattoo emphasizes the Holocaust theme and the tattoos those interred in the camps wore,[50] which is another theme in the story where Ariel's father is a Holocaust survivor. It is a fine presentation of Gelbin's claim that "the golem [is] a reawakening of Jewish life after the Shoah."[51] This is more of the golem that Kessler and Swirsky remark is the post-Holocaust golem created to save the Jewish community or a Jew. There is also a hint of a soul for the golem as the golem Luria remembers some of his love for Ariel; thus, we are on the cusp of staying true to the mythology and straying from the story.

In *The Simpsons,* Bart Simpson learns from Krusty that the golem will "perform any task written on paper and placed in its mouth."[52] While *The Simpsons* is a tongue-in-check examination of society, it continues the path of redefining the golem myth. This recreation of the golem is pure Simpson-esque and appropriate for the new century, where acceptance of others is the new theme. Peter Gaffney, the writer, is Jewish[53] and his knowledge of this Jewish myth is clear. Bart and his sister learn that the golem "feel[s] so guilty" for all the murders he committed because while commanded to do so, he is also a moral creature.[54] In an effort to make this golem become good and feel better about himself, the Simpson family creates a female golem out of a modeling compound that marries the original golem.[55] In this way, the evil golem is destroyed and Gaffney adheres to one of the mythological end-ings of the golem.

In *Sherlock*, Holmes tells his companion, Dr. John Watson, an extraordi-narily short version of the tale, that the golem is "a Jewish folk story [that tells of] a gigantic man made of clay. . . . The Golem squeezes the life out of his victims with his bare hands."[56] What we see here is that someone has adopted the name of the creature that it imitates; Golem is paid to kill a person, in other words, doing someone's command to destroy something the owner feels threatens them. The recounting is accurate, but the presentation is not. However, it is clear to the audience that Golem is a caricature of the Jewish folktale legend; he is *not* a golem.

In *Grimm*, the rabbi dons a *tallit* and *kippah*, what the non-Jewish public views as the required garb for any Jewish ritual. Then he places a jar filled with clay and a scroll on his desk. He opens the scroll, grabs some clay from the jar, and recites in Hebrew: "Lord G-d of all the earth, guide your hand . . . and cast your protection on the blood of my blood."[57] The scene fades. Next, we see Keith storming from Sara's house. He steps into a puddle and is engulfed by a golem. The mud literally rises up in a shape reminiscent of a person and covers Keith, suffocating him by filling every orifice.[58] Thus, this golem has no permanent shape, as the mythology includes, but is amorphous until needed. The rabbi insists that to stop the golem a paper with the letter *Shem* (ש) must be "put . . . inside the golem's mouth." Without more explana-tion, he simply says, "it means 'the name of G-d.'"[59] In most simple fashion, Ben Fisher is almost correct. While this is not the human form the Maharal presents as the golem, it does offer a monster that defends its creator.

Parker and Wuornos in *Haven* explain that "your Lady Justice might be a golem . . . [who] exist in folklore but become real when unleashed by a troubled person. [They] are usually made of dirt or clay, designed to do its master's bidding. They're dangerous, indestructible."[60] This is distinctly not golem-esque. The only part of this that is is an inanimate human figure that comes to life. There is no master; there is no intended creation. One could see *Haven's* golem as Galatea, Pygmalion's wife who was a statue that came to life, rather than a golem. She is not made from earth, nor was her creation purposeful, as she was created by a person's subconscious. These two points are significant to a golem.

In *Sleepy Hollow,* Jeremy was raised in an orphanage in the late 1700s. He shows the symptoms of being a witch and so he is whipped to remove the devil from him. Some of his blood splatters on a doll that is "awakened" with a drive to protect Jeremy.[61] There are clearly golem-like aspects to this crea-ture: it is something inanimate that is animated, and its purpose is to protect his creator. However, Jewish mythology has a golem created out of clay with prayer. It has to be a purposeful act on the part of the creator. Ichabod kills the golem/doll with a glass stake.[62] Again, this is not a traditional way to kill a golem. It is far more reminiscent of a vampire. Both of these are steps in the degeneration of the golem myth.

The golem in *Trollhunters* is created by a human and has no soul, but what is interesting here is that the golem is used as a weapon by the forces of evil to destroy the forces of good, not as a protector of the underdog. This is another step from the original folktale. Additionally, it is created by a fetish that absorbs the shape of the surrounding materials, rather than is crafted specifically of mud.

Sam Winchester in *Supernatural* understands that "the golem was built to go to war" and "classically they are not even supposed to speak."[63] The villain gains control of the golem by removing a scroll from his mouth; Aaron Bass gains control of the golem by adding his name to the scroll and replacing it in the golem's mouth. Rabbi Elliot B. Gertel, of Congregation Rodefei Zedek in Chicago, finds "this episode of *Supernatural* appropriately and effectively employs these genres to highlight the abiding evils of fascism and anti-Semitism and the need to be vigilant against them."[64]

The Order is a bit unusual because the description of a golem's creation is explained as: "[a] centuries-old magic used to make anthropomorphic . . . the golem is created from clay, mud, or metal. Its matter bestows life with a magic word etched on the forehead. The word is what keeps the golem alive."[65] What is not explained is that this is Jewish magic or what the word is. However, on the golem's forehead is "אמת."[66] It is only at the end of the episode that Jack realizes that Clay is a golem when he finds clay dust on Clay's side of the room. Jack destroys Clay by wiping the "אמת"[67] off his forehead. However, this word is never translated or explained; it is *emet*—truth.

CONCLUSION

Elizabeth Roberts Baer in *The Golem Redux* sees reinterpretations of the golem as part of "the expectation that each age will renew, adapt, and redeem the stories of the past."[68] Our golem spectrum flows from *The Gargoyles'* golem that follows the traditional description of a creature made of earth that is animated by a prayer and defends the underdog, to the golem in *Johnny Quest* that has the same creation story but is unanimated by destroying a symbol on its head. A more egalitarian version of the golem appears in the *X-Files* that is created by a woman in the shape of her dead husband to defend the Jewish community. The writer for *Grimm* sticks to the folktale, except that this golem doesn't have a permanent form; instead it morphs from the mud near the victim. *Supernatural*'s golem is a stone creature that is used to defend the one who possesses the scroll. Even the parody of a golem in *The*

Simpsons sticks very much to the folktale, only wavering because the golem is not destroyed but provided status as a person.

The golems in *Trollhunters* and *Order* stand on the balance of true golem and a being that has some loose relationship to a golem. The *Trollhunters'* golem is a fetish that absorbs some part of its surrounding to become animated. *The Order*'s golem appears to be human until it is needed by its owner, and even in its human form it leaves behind a clay trail.

At what point is a golem not a golem? *Haven*'s White Woman is neither made from earth nor created with intent, and so the degeneration or the co-opting of the word *golem* has moved beyond the pure sense of the creature has been reinterpreted. The golem in *Sleepy Hollow* that is made from the blood of a witch and a doll has crossed the line. Here there is no intent to create an individual for self-defense and there is no dirt involved.

The use of the word *golem* for creatures that are golem-like simply because they kill to protect their master or master's cause or because they are made of dirt has watered down the image of a golem. Part of the golem is the physical nature of the creature that it is bound to the Earth because it is made of earth. Another part is the motivation of its master, which is good, though through ignorance the actions become dangerous. Thus, those stories, here like *Johnny Quest* and *The Order*, where the golem is activated to aid in nefarious plans, are misinterpreting the purpose of the golem, which was to protect the unprotected. These morphs of the golem are interesting, and to see the devolvement of the golem from this clay semi-sentient being created to provide protection to an inanimate object that becomes animated to help its master is fascinating and disheartening, but the need to glom onto the word *golem* shows the power that this creature has for writers and viewers.

Three of the shows presented here do just that: *Gargoyles*, *X-Files*, and *Grimm*. Even though these shows are not about Jews, the episodes where golems are present are stories about Jews defending themselves as a community, as in *Gargoyles*, or themselves, as in *Grimm*.

Mikel J. Koven, professor of film studies at the University of Wales, Aberystwyth, argues that with "adaptations of folklore into popular culture, little attention is paid to the actual belief traditions within the lore itself."[69] This does not entirely show to be true. What we see in this chapter is the digression of the golem into something that is not a golem at all—from *Gargoyles'* pure golem to *Haven*'s Galatea-golem. Weisman believes that "from a cartoon standpoint . . . *Gargoyles* was . . . ahead of its time."[70] In fact, in many ways it was a pure interpretation of the folk narrative that clearly matches the folktale of Rosenberg: a person in need creates a creature from earth to defend them. The golem has become part of American folk tradition and science fiction trope. It has "come to symbolize the Other, the person or nation that is not understood" in popular culture.[71] The golem was originally created as a defender of the minority, not as a representative of it. Is this appropriate? Could not a *Marvel* superhero, like Captain America, fulfill this niche need of defender of American values?

NOTES

1. Byron L. Sherwin, "Golems in the Biotech Century," *Zygon* 42, no. 1 (2007): 138.

2. Edan Dekel and David Gantt Gurley, "How the Golem Came to Prague," *The Jewish Quarterly Review* 103, no. 2 (2013), 242–243.

3. Dekel and Gurley, 243.

4. Dekel and Gurley, 242.

5. Dekel and Gurley, 246.

6. Yudle Rosenberg, "The Golem or The Miraculous Deeds of Rabbi Liva." *The Great Works of Jewish Fantasy & Occult*, ed. Joachim Neugroschel (New York: Stonehill Pub. Co., 1976), 172.

7. Rosenberg, 172–173.

8. Rosenberg, 173.

9. Rosenberg, 224.

10. Hillel J. Kisval, "Golem Legend," *The YIVO Encyclopedia of Jews in Eastern Europe* (New York: YIVO, 2010), yhivoencyclopedia.org/article.aspx/ Golem_Legend.

11. "Myrink's The Golem: Where Fact and Fiction Collide," *The Guardian*, January 30, 2014, www.theguardian.com/books/booksblog/2014/jan/30/the-golem-gustav -meyrink-books.

12. *Der Golem, wie er in die Welt kam*, written and directed by Henrik Galeen and Paul Wegener, PAGU, 1920.

13. *Cisařův pekař a pekařův císař [The Emperor and Golem]*, director Mrating Fric, written by Jirí Brdecka, Ceskoslovenský Státní Film, 1952.

14. *It!* written by Herbert J. Leder, Gold Star Films Ltd., 1967.

15. Adam Kirsch, "Idol Worship: Does the World Need Another Golem Novel?" *Slate*, August 6, 2002, www.slate.com/articles/arts/culturebox/2002/08/idol_worship .html.

16. Emmanuel Buzay, "Le Golem: Généalogie et postérité d'une figure paradigmatique du post-humanisme," *Contemporary French & Francophone Studies* 22, no. 3 (2018): 353; Jane P. Davidson, "Golem—Frankenstein—Golem of Your Own," *Journal of the Fantastic in the Arts* 7, no. 2/3 (1995): 229.

17. Sherwin, 136.

18. Cathy S. Gelbin, "Towards the Global *Shtetl*: Golem Texts in the New Millennium," *European Review of History* 18, no. 1 (2011): 9.

19. Jack Dann, Rachel Swirsky, and Matthew Kressel, "Turns out a Jewish Blessing Inspired the Vulcan Salute," *Geeks Guide to the Galaxy*, October 17, 2015, www .wired.com/2015/10/geeks-guide-matthew-kressel/.

20. Dann, Swirsky, and Kressel.

21. Greg Weisman, "'I Knew It Was Something Special': An Exclusive Interview with Gargoyles Creator Greg Weisman," *Black Nerd Problems*, 2017, blacknerdproblems.com/i-knew-it-was-something-special-an-exclusive-interview-with-gargoyles-creator-greg-weisman.

22. Jordan Calhoun, "Gargoyles Was the Most Important Cartoon of My Pre-Intellectual Black Childhood," *Black Nerd Problems*, 2017, blacknerdproblems.com/gargoyles-was-the-most-important-cartoon-of-my-pre-intellectual-black-childhood.

23. *Gargoyles*, season 2, episode 27, "Golem," directed by Frank Paur, written by Gary Sperling, December 14, 1995.

24. Greg Weisman, "Chapter XXXXI: 'Golem,'" *Greg's Ramblings, Gargoyles: A Station Eight Fan Web Site*, August 26, 2002, www.s8.org/gargoyles/askgreg/rambles.php.

25. Weisman, "Chapter XXXXI."

26. Lance Falk, "Rock of Rages," *Questfan*, 22 July 2009, questfan.com/Page/Rock_of_Rages.html.

27. Falk.

28. *The X-Files*, season 4, episode 15, "Kaddish," directed by Kim Manners, written by Howard Gordon, February 16, 1997.

29. Howard Gordon, "*Homeland* and *24* Creator Howard Gordon on Terror, Tyranny, and TV as Art." *Tablet*, September 30, 2013, www.tabletmag.com/jewish-arts-and-culture/146747/homeland-howard-gordon.

30. *The Simpsons*, season 18, episode 4, "Treehouse of Horror XVII," directed by David Silverman and Matthew C. Faughnan, written by Peter Gaffney, November 5, 2006.

31. *Sherlock*, series 1, episode 3, "The Great Game," directed by Paul McGuigan, written by Mark Gatiss, aired November 7, 2020, on BBC One.

32. *Haven*, season 3, episode 15, "Double Jeopardy," directed by Nisha Ganatra, written by Nora Zuckerman and Lilla Zuckerman, aired October 19, 2012, on SyFy.

33. Roberto Orci and Alex Kurtzman, "Executive Producers Alex Kurtzman and Roberto Orci Talk *Sleepy Hollow*, a New Version of Ichabod Crane, Making the Mythology Accessible, and More," interview by Christina Radish. *Collider*, September 16, 2013, collider.com/sleepy-hollow-alex-kurtzman-roberto-orci-interview/.

34. Alex Kurtzman, "Emmy Watch: 'Sleepy Hollow' EP Alex Kurtzman on the Epic Reveal," interview by Mandi Bierly, *Entertainment Weekly*, June 16, 2014, www.ew.com/article/2014/06/16/sleepy-hollow-finale-reveal-alex-kurtzman.

35. *Grimm*, season 4, episode 4, "Dyin' on a Prayer," directed by Tawnia McKiernan, written by Sean Calder, November 14, 2014. NBC.

36. *Supernatural*, season 8, episode 13, "Everybody Hates Hitler," written by Ben Edlund, aired February 6, 2013, on The CW.

37. *Trollhunters: Tales of Arcadia*, season 1, episode 15, "Mudslinging," directed by Rodrigo Blaas, written by Marc Guggenheim, December 23, 2016. Netflix.

38. *Trollhunters: Tales of Arcadia,* season 1, episode, 17, "Blinky's Day Out," directed by Elaine Bogan, written by A. C. Bradley, aired December 23, 2016, on Netflix.

39. Dennis Heaton and Shelley Eriksen, "SDCC 2019: Chatting *The Order* with Eps Dennis Heaton and Shelley Eriksen," interview by Marissa and Amrie, *My Take on . . . ,* October 17, 2019, www.mytakeontv.com/2019/10/17/sdcc-2019-chatting-the -order-with-eps-dennis-heaton-and-shelley-eriksen/.

40. *The Order,* season 1, episode 2, "Hell Week, Part Two," directed by David Von Ancken, written by Shelley Eriksen, March 7, 2019. Netflix.

41. *Gargoyles.*

42. *Gargoyles.*

43. *Gargoyles.*

44. *Gargoyles.*

45. *The Real Adventures of Johnny Quest,* season 2, episode 2, "Rock of Rages," written by Lance Falk, aired September 28, 1996 on Cartoon Network.

46. *The Real Adventures of Johnny Quest.*

47. *The Real Adventures of Johnny Quest.*

48. Mikel J. Koven, "'Have I Got a Monster for You!': Some Thoughts on the Golem, *The X-Files* and the Jewish Horror Movie." *Folklore* 111 (2000): 221.

49. *The X-Files.*

50. Koven, "Have I Got a Monster for You!" 224.

51. Gelbin, 9.

52. *The Simpsons.*

53. Peter Gaffney. "Peter Gaffney Chats about MTV, A&E, The History Channel, Nostalgia as Medication on Television, and so much more!" Interview with Clayton Howe, *Entertainmentx,* August 26, 2018, www.iheart.com/podcast/269 -entertainmentx-30076609/episode/peter-gaffney-chats-about-mtv-ae-30078206.

54. *The Simpsons.*

55. *The Simpsons.*

56. *Sherlock.*

57. *Grimm.*

58. *Grimm.*

59. *Grimm.*

60. *Haven.*

61. *Sleepy Hollow,* season 1, episode 10, "The Golem," written by Mark Goffman and Jose Molina, December 9, 2013, FOX.

62. *Sleepy Hollow.*

63. *Supernatural.*

64. Elliot B. Gertel, "A Golem on Supernatural," *Congregation Rodefei Zedek,* April 10, 2013, www.rodfei.org/a_golem_on_supernatural.

65. *The Order.*

66. *The Order.*

67. *The Order.*

68. Elizabeth Roberts Baer, *The Golem Redux: From Prague to Post-Holocaust Fiction* (Detroit: Wayne State University Press, 2012), 184.

69. Mikel J. Koven, "The Folklore *Files*: In(corp)orating Legends in *The X-Files.*" In *The X-Files and Literature: Unweaving the Story, Unraveling the Lie to Find the Truth,* ed. Sharon R. Yang (New Castle: Cambridge Scholars Publishing, 2007), 92.

70. Greg Weisman, "Gargoyles Was Nearly the Center of a Vast Disney Cinematic Universe," interview by Tasha Robinson, *Polygon*, May 14, 2020, www.polygon .com/disney-plus/2020/5/14/21249881/gargoyles-animated-series-disney-plus-greg -weisman-interview-oj-simpson-goliath-chronicles.

71. Lewis Glinat, "Golem! The Making of a Modern Myth," *Symposium*, summer 2001: 84.

WORKS CITED

Baer, Elizabeth Roberts. *The Golem Redux: From Prague to Post-Holocaust Fiction.* Detroit: Wayne State University Press, 2012.

Bradley, A. C., writer. *Trollhunters: Tales of Arcadia.* Season 1, episode, 17, "Blinky's Day Out." Directed by Elaine Bogan. Aired December 23, 2016, on Netflix.

Buzay, Emmanuel. "Le Golem: Généalogie et postérité d'une figure paradimatique du post-humanisme," *Contemporary French & Francophone Studies*, 22, no. 3 (2018): 353–361.

Calder, Sean, writer. *Grimm*, season 4, episode 4, "Dyin' on a Prayer," Directed by Tawnia McKiernan. Aired November 14, 2014, on NBC.

Calhoun, Jordan. "Gargoyles Was the Most Important Cartoon of my Pre-Intellectual Black Childhood." *Black Nerd Problems*, 2017, blacknerdproblems.com/gar-goyles-was-the-most-important-cartoon-of-my-pre-intellectual-black-childhood.

Dann, Jack, Rachel Swirsky, and Matthew Kressel. "Turns Out a Jewish Blessing Inspired the Vulcan Salute," *Geeks Guide to the Galaxy*, October 17, 2015. www .wired.com/2015/10/geeks-guide-matthew-kressel.

Davidson, Jane P. "Golem—Frankenstein—Golem of Your Own." *Journal of the Fantastic in the Arts* 7, no. 2/3 (1995): 228–243.

Dekel, Edan, and David Gantt Gurley. "How the Golem Came to Prague." *The Jewish Quarterly Review* 103, no. 2 (2013): 241–258.

Edlund, Ben, writer. *Supernatural.* Season 8, episode 13, "Everybody Hates Hitler." Directed by Phil Sgriccia. Aired February 6, 2013, on the CW.

Eriksen, Shelley. *The Order.* Season 1, episode 2, "Hell Week, Part Two." Directed by David Von Ancken. Aired March 7, 2019, on Netflix.

Falk, Lance, writer. *The Real Adventures of Johnny Quest.* Season 2, episode 2. "Rock of Rages." Aired September 28, 1996, on Cartoon Network.

Falk, Lance. "Rock of Rages." *Questfan*, 22 July 2009, questfan.com/Page/Rock_of_ Rages.html.

Fric, Martin, dir. *Císařův pekař a pekařův císař [The Emperor and Golem].* Written by Jiří Brdecka, Československý Státní Film, 1952.

Gaffney, Peter, writer. *The Simpsons.* Season 18, episode 4, "Treehouse of Horror XVII." Directed by David Silverman and Matthew C. Faughnan. Aired November 5, 2006, on Fox.

Gaffney, Peter. "Peter Gaffney Chats about MTV, A&E, The History Channel, Nostalgia as Medication on Television, and So Much More!" By Clayton Howe,

Entertainmentx, August 26, 2018. www.iheart.com/podcast/269-entertainmentx -30076609/episode/peter-gaffney-chats-about-mtv-ae-30078206.

Gatiss, Mark, writer. *Sherlock.* Series 1, episode 3. "The Great Game." Directed by Paul McGuigan. Aired November 7, 2020 on BBC One.

Gelbin, Cathy S. "Towards the Global *Shtetl*: Golem Texts in the New Millennium." *European Review of History* 18, no. 1 (2011): 9–19.

Gertel, Elliot B. "A Golem on Supernatural." *Congregation Rodefei Zedek*, April 10, 2013, www.rodfei.org/a_golem_on_supernatural.

Glinat, Lewis. "Golem! The Making of a Modern Myth." *Symposium* (summer 2001): 84.

Gordon, Howard, writer. *The X-Files.* Season 4, episode 15, "Kaddish." Directed by Kim Manners. Aired February 16, 1997, on Fox.

Gordon, Howard. "*Homeland* and *24* Creator Howard Gordon on Terror, Tyranny, and TV as Art." *Tablet*, September 30, 2013, www.tabletmag.com/jewish-arts-and -culture/146747/homeland-howard-gordon.

Guggenheim, Marc, writer. *Trollhunters: Tales of Arcadia.* Season 1, episode 15, "Mudslinging." Directed by Rodrigo Blaas. Aired December 23, 2016, on Netflix.

Heaton, Dennis, and Shelley Eriksen, "SDCC 2019: Chatting *The Order* with Eps Dennis Heaton and Shelley Eriksen." By Marissa and Amrie. *My Take on . . . ,* October 17, 2019, www.mytakeontv.com/2019/10/17/sdcc-2019-chatting-the-order -with-eps-dennis-heaton-and-shelley-eriksen.

Kirsch, Adam. "Idol Worship: Does the World Need Another Golem Novel?" *Slate*, August 6, 2002. www.slate.com/articles/arts/culturebox/2002/08/idol_worship .html.

Kisval, Hillel J. "Golem Legend." *The YIVO Encyclopedia of Jews in Eastern Europe.* New York: YIVO, 2010. yhivoencyclopedia.org/article.aspx/Golem_Legend.

Koven, Mikel J. "The Folklore *Files*: In(corp)orating Legends in *The X-Files*." In *The X-Files and Literature: Unweaving the Story, Unraveling the Lie to Find the Truth.* Edited by Sharon R. Yang, 91–104. New Castle: Cambridge Scholars Publishing, 2007.

Koven, Mikel J. "'Have I Got a Monster for You!': Some Thoughts on the Golem, *The X-Files* and the Jewish Horror Movie." *Folklore* 111 (2000): 217–230.

Kurtzman, Alex. "Emmy Watch: *Sleepy Hollow* EP Alex Kurtzman on the Epic Reveal." By Mandi Bierly. *Entertainment Weekly*, June 16, 2014. www.ew.com/ article/2014/06/16/sleepy-hollow-finale-reveal-alex-kurtzman.

Leder, Herbert J., dir. and writ. *It!* Gold Star Films Ltd., 1967.

"Myrink's *The Golem*: Where Fact and Fiction Collide," *The Guardian*, January 30, 2014. www.theguardian.com/books/booksblog/2014/jan/30/the-golem-gustav -meyrink-books.

Orci, Roberto, and Alex Kurtzman. "Executive Producers Alex Kurtzman and Roberto Orci Talk *Sleepy Hollow*, a New Version of Ichabod Crane, Making the Mythology Accessible, and More." By Christina Radish. *Collider*, September 16, 2013, collider.com/sleepy-hollow-alex-kurtzman-roberto-orci-interview.

Rev. of "Kaddish." *Cinefanastique*, 1997: 59.

Rosenberg, Yudle. "The Golem or The Miraculous Deeds of Rabbi Liva." In *The Great Works of Jewish Fantasy & Occult*. Edited by Joachim Neugroschel, 162–228. New York: Stonehill Publ. Co., 1976.

Sherwin, Byron L. "Golems in the Biotech Century," *Zygon* 42, no. 1 (2007): 133–144.

Sleepy Hollow, season 1, episode 10, "The Golem," written by Mark Goffman and Jose Molina, Aired December 9, 2013, on Fox.

Sperling, Gary, writer. *Gargoyles.* Season 2, episode 27, "Golem." Directed by Frank Paur. Aired December 14, 1995, on ABC.

Wegener, Paul, and Henrik Galeen, dir. and writ. *Der Golem.* 1915, Deitsche Bioscop.

Weisman, Greg. "Chapter XXXXI: 'Golem.'" *Greg's Ramblings, Gargoyles: A Station Eight Fan Web Site*, August 26, 2002. www.s8.org/gargoyles/askgreg/rambles.php.

Weisman, Greg. "Gargoyles Was Nearly the Center of a Vast Disney Cinematic Universe." Interview by Tasha Robinson. *Polygon*, May 14, 2020, www.polygon.com/disney-plus/2020/5/14/21249881/gargoyles-animated-series-disney-plus-greg-weisman-interview-oj-simpson-goliath-chronicles.

Weisman, Greg. "'I Knew It Was Something Special': An Exclusive Interview with Gargoyles Creator Greg Weisman." *Black Nerd Problems*, 2017. blacknerdproblems.com/i-knew-it-was-something-special-an-exclusive-interview-with-gargoyles-creator-greg-weisman.

Zuckerman, Nora, and Lilla Zuckerman, writers. *Haven.* Season 3, episode 15, "Double Jeopardy." Directed by Nisha Ganatra. Aired October 19, 2012, on SyFy.

Chapter Four

The Origins of *Superman*

An Unlikely Window into the Jewish American Experience

Matthew Diamond

Who hasn't heard of Superman? Superman has been and continues to be one of the most popular and iconic superheroes worldwide since the 1930s. Most people can probably provide an accurate summary of Superman's origin: Kal El is the last son of the dying planet, Krypton, who is sent away by his parents for his own safety. He then crash-lands on Earth to be raised by a loving Kansas family that teaches him good old American values. Once Superman realizes that he possesses special abilities, he looks a little more closely at his past, converses with mysterious images of his previous relatives, and then decides to take it upon himself to rescue and protect others from his previous planet's fate.[1]

It's a captivating story that appeals to a wide and diverse international audience. Arguably, that's because the story homes in on themes that readers love: being the chosen one, putting community above oneself, having traditional values, and discovering how a nurturing family breeds good people—the type of people who choose to protect and serve instead of seeking personal gain.

What most audiences may not know is that the story of Superman and of the parallel stories of his creators are very Jewish in their roots. Editor Zeddy Lawrence puts it well when he says, "It may not be true in all cases, but it's a pretty good rule of thumb. If the word 'man' appears at the end of someone's name, you can draw one of two conclusions: a) they're Jewish, as in Goldman, Feldman, or Lipman; or b) they're a superhero, as in Superman, Batman, or Spider-Man."[2]

First of all, Clark Kent's origin and abilities are eerily similar to those of characters from the Torah. Additionally, some readers claim that Superman is actually an allegory for the immigrant experience. More directly, the hero's earliest adventures involved defending the downtrodden from antifascist and anti-Semitic doctrines. Post-Holocaust analyses have also drawn similarities to the kindertransport in Germany during World War II. Beyond all this, of course, the two men who envisioned the Kryptonian superhero were two nice Jewish boys from Cleveland. Regardless of which lens is used to analyze Superman, there's a plethora of compelling evidence indicating that he's more of a mensch than a Kryptonian.

JERRY AND JOE'S VISION: SUPERMAN AS A PRODUCT OF HIS CREATORS

Joseph Schusterowitz was born in Canada in July of 1914. His parents, Ida and Julius, were both Russian immigrants.[3] Ida and her sister Bessie had fled Russia to escape the pogroms that were rampant in their country during the early 1900s.[4] Joe's family started off in Toronto but was forced to move often during the Great Depression. The Schusterowitzs eventually relocated to Cleveland in 1924, when Joe was ten.[5]

By age fourteen, Joe was sure he wanted to be an artist, despite his mother's insistence that he be a doctor instead. Joe collected newspapers and comic strips for years and eventually started working on his junior high newspaper drawing cartoons.[6] Accounts of Joe during this time in his life describe him as short and skinny. In Joe's own words, he was "mild-mannered, wore glasses, was very shy with women."[7] As a result, Joe was often dissatisfied with his appearance, so he exercised often and read magazines about "Physical Culture" or strongmen.[8]

One strongman in particular who Joe focused on was the acclaimed Joseph Greenstein, better known as the Mighty Atom.[9] The Mighty Atom's exploits remain legendary to this day. He could break chains wrapped around him by merely expanding his chest. He was also known to bend iron bars or horseshoes with his teeth. The Atom could even bend half-inch rolled steel rods into heart shapes and drive nails through wood with his bare hands.[10] Greenstein became something of a local hero after singlehandedly fighting off a gang of Nazis who were terrorizing his neighborhood.[11] Greenstein was also only 5' 4," which Joe could appreciate.

This strongman was of even greater interest to teenage Joe because he was also a Jewish man who left Eastern Europe to escape anti-Semitism.[12] The Mighty Atom was also well known for heroic acts in which he actively fought against prejudice. One legendary and possibly embellished story features the

Mighty Atom strolling along the streets of New York City. According to the story, the Atom saw a meeting place for the Nazi Bund party that displayed a sign saying "No Dogs or Jews Allowed." Upon seeing the sign, the strongman crossed the street to buy a baseball bat from a nearby general store. Then he crossed the street a second time with his new sports memorabilia in tow and proceeded to express his own views of the Nazi party on the window behind the sign.[13]

When the teenage Joe Shuster read about the feats of strongmen like the Mighty Atom, and other comic strip heroes like Buck Rogers, he wished that he could be more like them. Joe idealized these iconic heroes, and he fantasized about being as strong, fearless, and successful at righting the world's wrongs as they were.[14] Cartoonist Jerry Robinson notes that Joe Shuster was "very shy, very reserved, very unassuming. He was short and had glasses. You'd never know he was the co-creator of Superman."[15] The alter ego of the character he helped create would end up mirroring himself.

Jerome "Jerry" Siegel was born in October of 1914 in Cleveland, Ohio. His parents, Michel and Sarah Siegel, were both Lithuanian immigrants who were a tailor and a seamstress, respectively. Jerry was the youngest of six children and he spent a great deal of time trying to catch up to his older siblings.[16] Jerry was also a little socially awkward and had troubling fitting in. So, from an early age, he knew what it was like to be victimized.[17] Decades later Jerry could still recall being ridiculed on the playground with chants like, "Siegel, Seagull, Bird of an Eagle!"[18] School didn't really get better for Jerry as he got older. His grades were mostly D's and F's, and he was constantly late to class.[19]

Because Jerry found reality so hard, he would often retreat into fantasy and fiction in his spare time. Much like Joe, Jerry started collecting comic strips and science fiction magazines, hoping to read about heroes who possessed some of the qualities that he aspired to have.[20] Since Jerry also enjoyed radio shows and movies, he became fascinated with characters like Zorro, Tarzan, Robin Hood, and John Carter.[21] (The superhero genre had not yet been invented, but pulp action heroes were their popular precursor.) One of Jerry's favorite quotes came from the young literary sleuth Seck Hawkins: "A quitter never wins; a winner never quits."[22]

Siegel would later recount from this period of his life, "I am lying in bed counting sheep when all of a sudden it hits me. I conceive a character like Samson, Hercules, and all the strong men I ever heard of rolled into one. Only more so."[23] He adds, "You see, Clark Kent grew not only out of my private life, but also out of Joe's. . . . As a high school student, I thought that someday I might become a reporter and I had crushes on several attractive girls who either didn't know I existed or didn't care I existed. It occurred to me: what if I was real terrific? What if I had something special going for me, like jumping over buildings or throwing cars around or something like that? Maybe then they would notice me."[24]

As he got older, Jerry also became more and more interested in science fiction and began saving up his money to buy magazines like *Science and Invention*.[25] When Jerry was fifteen, his household began to know him for constantly clicking away on his typewriter. He would need to sneak it out of his bedroom at night so he wouldn't wake his sleeping brother with his typing.[26] Jerry would busy himself writing letters to the editors of his magazines asking questions or requesting that one of his works be entered in one of the publisher's story contests.[27] At this point, Jerry's ideas weren't getting very far, but that wouldn't last much longer.

Jerry and Joe met in high school when they were seated together alphabetically during one of their classes. They hit it off almost immediately once they realized their mutual interests and similar backgrounds.[28] One author described the moment: "In the early 1930's in a scary school, these boys became best friends over recognition of some kind of weird future they were both only beginning to imagine."[29] They began frequently spending time together outside school, working on stories and submissions for their school newspaper or magazine publishers. Siegel explains: "Joe and I had certain inhibitions . . . which led to wish-fulfillment which we expressed through our interest in science fiction and our comic strip. That's where the dual-identity concept came from, and Clark Kent's problems with Lois. I imagine there are a lot of people in this world who are similarly frustrated. Joe and I both felt that way in high school, and he was able to put the feeling into sketches."[30]

It would be a while still until the idea for Superman as we know him today took shape. Jerry and Joe's first comic together was called "Interplanetary Police," reminiscent of Buck Rogers. Jerry and Joe also had a comic strip in their school newspaper that featured a wisecracking detective solving mysteries a la Dick Tracy.[31] Their self-published fanzine *Science Fiction* (Jan 1933) contained their "The Reign of Superman." In it, Bill Dunn, a homeless man, turns into a bald megalomaniac villain. Drugs give him telepathy as well as gradually increasing mental powers. Dunn then interrupts a peace conference while seeking global domination. At last, his powers vanish, and he heads back into the night.[32] Critic Adam Nemett describes it:

The first Superman was evil. In the 1933 comic, "The Reign of the Superman," two Cleveland Jews, Jerry Siegel and Joe Shuster, envisioned their initial Superman as a bum plucked from the breadline and transformed into a telepathic supervillain. But, according to Siegel, once he saw the plight of Jews in Nazi Germany, he decided he wanted to "help the masses, somehow." So, Superman was transformed from an evil tyrant to a savior.[33]

Unfortunately, it took a tragedy to bring the creators' vision to full clarity. In 1932, Jerry's father, Michel, was working one evening in his tailor shop when three men walked in. One of the men asked to try on a suit, and then walked out of the store without paying for it. Michel protested, but one of the other men blocked his path. Michel suffered a heart attack from the stress of the situation and died.[34] The reason why the Siegels' store was targeted remains a mystery, but it was notable that their tailor shop was one of the only Jewish businesses left in the downtown Cedar Central area. Jerry was seventeen at the time.[35] Jerry's wife, Joanne—the future model for Lois Lane—would later say the death of Jerry's father had a lot to do with the creation of Superman as a hero.[36]

Siegel later wrote a story about flying to the rescue of a man being held up at gunpoint by an armed robber with a painfully clear link to his dad. Jerry Siegel actually used his own looks as the basis for Superman and would strike poses in his own home about how Superman should look in the comic books. Joe Shuster refreshed the character a bit from Seigel himself while using a Jewish model for inspiration. While on vacation he met a man named Stanley Weiss, son of Jewish immigrants, who after showing pictures of his dad at a young age, was the man Shuster had in mind when creating Superman. The sketches of Weiss's dad, striking resemblance to Superman, are still on exhibit at the Center for Jewish History in New York.[37]

THE CRUSADER AGAINST INTOLERANCE: SUPERMAN AS A DEFENDER OF THE WEAK

The Talmud makes reference to a "shapeless mass" known as the golem. According to Ashkenazi lore, one could mold the golem out of clay and use either the spoken or written name of God to give it sentience. The golem could then be directed to help the people of the community with manual labor or defense. Supposedly these creations have physical strength far superior to that of an average man. In one popular story, Rabbi Judah Loew ben Bezalel, the Maharal of Prague, created such a being to protect his community from outside forces during Easter of 1580 when a Jew-hating priest was trying to incite violence.[38]

It can be suggested that Superman's creators envisioned him as their "golem" in the abstract sense. Granted Superman didn't take an actual physical form until decades later, but through the use of Jerry's writing and Joe's art, he took on a life of his own in the minds of readers. The Man of Steel served a very similar purpose to the golem of Prague in that he protected the innocent from those who would do them harm by using his superhuman abilities.

In New York of the time, Jews couldn't get jobs in traditional book publishing or many other industries. However, the new comic book field, invented by Jewish creator Max Gaines, was hiring. Al Jaffee, later of *Mad Magazine,* comments, "We couldn't get into newspaper strips or advertising: ad agencies wouldn't hire a Jew. One of the reasons we Jews drifted into the comic-book business is that most of the comic-book publishers were Jewish. So, there was no discrimination there."[39] Detective Comics (later DC Comics), specifically, was created by Jewish publishers Harry Donenfeld and Jack Liebowitz. It was the first comic book of all-new material built around a single genre, and delighted fans.[40] As it prepared to launch in 1937, teen editor Sheldon Mayer told his boss Max Gaines about Superman. Gaines sent it to DC.[41] Together with Meyer, all the comics publishers mentored the young creator duo of Jerry and Joe. "The comic book industry was really created by Jews," says Gerald Hartman, a renowned expert and collector of World War II era comic books, "because they couldn't get jobs in certain industries such as advertising or illustration art due to antisemitism. As a result, they came up with their own medium that really appealed to the masses."[42]

Superman first debuted as the version we know and love in *Action Comics* #1, published in 1938. This was arguably the first superhero comic. The American public had its fair share of heroes at the time, but they had never seen anything quite like this. This character was a powerful, capable, and confident hero, but he could also be gentle, kind, and humble. He epitomized the ideals of masculinity without any of the toxicity. He also embodied American values of family and standing up for the downtrodden, but he was adopted and born on a different planet that was now long gone. Needless to say, Superman's popularity soared and eventually inspired television shows, movies, cartoons, and a whole Golden Age of comic book heroes.[43]

Part of the reason why Superman grew to popularity so quickly was because Jerry and Joe wrote about real-world events that affected everyday people. "Superman! Champion of the oppressed. The physical marvel who had sworn to devote his existence to helping those in need," *Action Comics* #1 narrated.[44] In the first comic, Superman saves a wrongfully accused woman from execution, then threatens and beats an abusive spouse. After this, he saves Lois from violent goons who bully her on the dance floor and carry her off. When a senator tells a crooked lobbyist, "Before any remedial steps can be taken, our country will be embroiled with Europe," Superman saves his country from war.[45] Clearly, Superman subscribes to the Jewish value of saving lives and repairing the world.

One of Superman's earliest adventures features a mining accident similar to a real accident that occurred in Athens, Ohio, in 1930.[46] In the second year after Superman's debut, his adventures included realistic stories that readers could relate to like helping an orphan go on a treasure hunt, stopping a former boxer from committing suicide and encouraging him to believe in himself again, shutting down illegal gambling dens, and even just rescuing people from car crashes.[47] He exposed corrupt big businessmen, forcing them to stop exploiting workers and shut down their dangerous practices.

However, as the world's perspective shifted in the late 1930s, Superman's focus began to shift as well:

> Once World War II began, the Jewish creators of the comic book industry suddenly found themselves with a burning desire to help their coreligionists suffering in Europe and a medium that allowed them to influence public opinion. "Comic book artists thought it was important to get America to join the war so they tried to shift public opinion," says Hartman. "They changed the bad guy nemesis of their comic superheroes to axis spies and the population starts to believe that there's a Nazi spy around every corner and that America should align with the allies. The Jewish American artists wanted to accelerate the process and save their brethren."[48]

When the Nazi regime began to assert dominance in Europe in the late 1930s, Jerry and Joe saw an opportunity to expand Superman's repertoire. He went from addressing domestic issues and local crime to combating the spreading fascist ideals. In fall 1939, Superman intervenes to stop war profiteers from selling a deadly gas to the fake European country of Borogravia. When he sends a dirigible falling to its doom, audiences must have recalled the *Hindenburg* disaster of two years before. He ends the comic forcing the two leaders to negotiate and in a biblical twist, threatening to collapse the pillars of the hall and bring the building down if they won't reconcile. As Clark Kent, he departs through the celebrating crowd, musing, "And to think that just a few minutes ago, these happy people were under the dread shadow of war."[49] This too is a fantasy, of Superman ending the European war that was endangering the Jews.

One comic strip that debuted in 1940, almost two years before the United States entered the conflict against Nazi Germany as allies of the Soviet Union, featured Superman picking up Hitler, Mussolini, and Hirohito, then dropping them off at the World Court for Judgment. A particularly famous panel from that strip shows Superman holding up a struggling Hitler saying, "I'd like to land a strictly Non-Aryan sock on your jaw."[50] Here, he specifically casts himself as non-Aryan, rejecting Hitler's lies of superiority even as the champion of the little guys reveals himself as actually superior. It should be noted, however, that DC Comics was avoiding taking sides—this comic was commissioned by *Look Magazine*, *Life*'s largest competitor at the time.

In *Action Comics* #22–23 (March 1940), Germany's invasion of Poland is reenvisioned as "the armed battalions of Toran unexpectedly swoop down upon a lesser nation, Galonia."[51] While carefully not taking sides, Superman fights to save a neutral passenger liner and rescue "thousands of lives."[52] He ends by shaking the military leader in question upside down until he confesses, leaving his own people to dismiss him for war crimes. The next issue reveals that the true culprit, stirring up conspiracies behind the scenes "for evil purposes," is Lex Luthor in his first appearance.[53] Despite his schemes to set countries against one another and then take over, an armistice is triumphantly declared.

Still, as the war approached, Superman continued to fight oppression internationally and suggestively. In *Superman* #8 (Feb 1941), the criminal in the espionage story resembles Hitler. Meanwhile, the covers joined the war, even when the content had nothing to match: *Superman* #12, he marches arm in arm with an American soldier and sailor, while on *Action Comics* #43 (Dec 1941), he flies toward a parachuting Nazi clearly wearing a swastika. On *Superman* #13, he takes out a German submarine. "These Jews did what they could in the only way they knew how," reflects Hartman. "In many cases they were teenagers, and they were putting themselves at risk by depicting this message. That's because before Pearl Harbor there were many Americans who were fascists and these people targeted Jewish artists and publishers. So they fought the war in their way."[54]

Superman #10 (May–June 1941) shows Clark and Lois attending the fictional Dulkian American Sports Festival only to then find out that it's a thinly veiled "anti-American demonstration," as Lois insists.[55] This issue can be interpreted as an allegory for the 1936 Berlin Olympics as well as Superman battling the Nazi party, and the clues are abundant: the Dulkian athletes strike a pose reminiscent of "Heil Hitler." The Dukalian consul, named Karl Wolff, also insists that his country's sports stars definitively show "that we Dukalians are superior to any other race or nation! Proof that we are entitled to be the masters of America!"[56] Once Superman uncovers the threat, he then makes himself known and challenges the anti-American demonstrators to prove their superiority. Of course, he beats them in every sports contest.

Joe and Jerry were careful not to be too overt in including pro-Jewish rhetoric in their works, but the German SS certainly took notice. One German newspaper, *The Black Corps*, called out the writers by name, saying in a 1941 rebuttal:

We really ought to ignore these fantasies of Jerry Israel Siegel. . . . The daring deeds of Superman are those of a Colorado beetle. He works in the dark, in incomprehensible ways. He cries "Strength! Courage! Justice!" to the noble yearnings of American Children. Instead of using the chance to encourage really useful virtues, he sows hate, suspicion, evil, laziness, and criminality in their young hearts.[57]

Jerry and Joe could hardly believe that the fictional character they came up with in high school was now performing acts that personally offended the German Gestapo.

The day after the Japanese attack on Pearl Harbor on December 7, 1941, the United States officially declared war on Japan. Just a few days later on December 11, Germany and the rest of the Axis powers declared war on the United States. At this point, superheroes fighting Nazis were much less controversial. More propaganda followed, even in comics without inside content about the war effort. The cover of *Superman* #17 shows Superman grabbing Adolf Hitler and Prime Minister of Japan General Hideki Tojo by their collars,[58] while *World's Finest Comics* #9's cover shows Superman, Batman, and Robin throwing baseballs at the faces of Axis leaders Hitler, Mussolini, and Tojo above a banner that says, "Knock out the Axis with Bonds & Stamps."[59] On the cover of *Superman* #26, Superman is defeating the Nazi propagandist Joseph Goebbels and Radio Berlin.[60]

Superman war comics were complicated by his incredible might—he was strong enough to win the entire war, but that would be unrealistic for the real-life conflict in which so many were embroiled. The first, in a February 1942 newspaper, saw Clark Kent passing the physical but failing the eye exam (another nod to his creator Shuster, who did likewise, while Siegel was drafted in 1943[61]). Back at work, Clark wrote, "The United States Army, Navy, and Marines are capable of smashing their foes without the aid of a superman! Hm-mm. Perhaps I could be of more use to my country working right here at home, battling the saboteurs and fifth columnists who will undoubtedly try to wreck out production of vital war materials."[62] He rallied those at home to the same, even as he voiced his support for an American war in which he could not save the day. In another newspaper comic, "Cadet Training," Superman helps a young man study and train to pass his army entrance qualifications, even as the comic demonstrates and urges readers to do likewise. It concludes with Clark explaining, "Young men of every race, religion, and social level . . . truly a democratic army . . . all animated by one determined desire . . . to crush the Axis threat."[63] At least as Clark he could cheer on the egalitarian side of the war effort.

Still, he found ways to participate. In the Sunday newspaper comics, he fulfilled soldiers' requests in "Superman's Service for Servicemen."[64] He sold war bonds and attended rallies, stopped spies and saboteurs. In *Superman* #18, Nazis use a simulated Nazi invasion in America as a cover for the real thing. This story hit close to home in more ways than one, as the creators emphasized the destructiveness of anti-Semitic gatherings. The "Izan Athletic Club," a group of young men who practice the Nazi salute before they load their guns with real bullets and shoot Clark and then plan to murder others, represent the American Bund and similar groups that subscribed to Hitler's deadly ideology.[65] In *Superman* #25, he once again battles Nazism close to home, with the swastika-wielding "101% Americanism Society."[66] Likewise, the newspaper comic "The Committee for a New Order" has Lois hypnotized into delivering a talk for this society, as many Americans must have felt their neighbors had been. "If you think those mysterious broadcasts of yours will sway public opinion in the United States against democracy, you're badly mistaken!" she thunders, only to find the schemers don't believe their own propaganda and are only stealing funds.[67]

Sometimes he did get to Europe, though often with fantastical adventures that cast his story as otherworldly. Still, these took the time to satirize Hitler and the Germans. "Only the warped, fiendish minds which conceived the bombing of Poland, the execution of innocent millions, the crushing of peaceful nations, could have launched the most terrible horror of the war," explains the cover of *Superman* #20, in which he battles giant squids. Meanwhile, Hitler is seen having heavily accented tantrums and screaming "off mit der head!"[68] He ends this comic executing his own soldiers in his rage. Likewise, *Superman* #22 pits Hitler against the Squiffles, the mythic gremlins known to destroy U.S. army parts. Hitler once again looks foolish, as he calls attention to his failures: he can't sleep for thinking "of our reverses on the Russian front—of America's growing war industries."[69] When the Squiffles arrive to bargain with him, he says they look revolting, and they say the same of him. As he cowers under the covers, he soon rallies and eagerly promises them an unspecified favor—a pitfall in all of fairy tales. These "demons," as the text suddenly names them, end the story taking Hitler's soul—a moment that emphasizes his pure evil.[70]

At last, in the March 1945 newspaper comics, with the war nearly won, Superman visits Goering, Goebbels, and Hitler in the heart of Berlin. They are so pathetic that they dress as Superman, desperate to pick the side of the winners. They also tell him his fury at them is meaningless, since, as Hitler explains, "Ve haff too many *other* things to frighten us."[71] "Anything would be better than breathing the same foul air as you Ratzis," Superman zings back.[72] Hitler ends the arc literally chewing rugs in his panic. Throughout the war, he and his cruelty toward innocents were mentioned repeatedly, as were the dangers of prejudice, but the Jews themselves went unseen. In an America in which Jewish film and comics creators were accused of writing in their own interests, they fought for their cause in the arts, but only obliquely. Author Harry Brod notes, "The story's appearance in an official army publication was designed to boost morale by picturing Nazis as buffoons and removing any remaining vestiges there might be of the Nazi aura of invincibility or being super soldiers, fostering American identification with the invulnerable Superman we've got on our side."[73]

Decades later in 1998, *Superman: The Man of Steel* #80–82, by Louise Simonson and John Bogdanove, was published for the character's sixty-year anniversary. The three-issue trilogy features Clark going undercover in Poland to infiltrate a concentration camp in Nazi Germany. While disguised among Jews, he witnesses firsthand the horrible treatment of prisoners. Superman is then able to able to take Nazi supplies, stop a cattle car before it reaches Treblinka, and fight beside the Jewish resistance at the Warsaw Ghetto.[74] Even long after the original creators had passed away, the original legacy of Superman to protect the weak and mistreated was never forgotten.

THE ÜBER-MENSCH: SUPERMAN AS A CONGLOMERATION OF JEWISH FOLKLORE

Before even taking Superman's deeds into account, the Jewish influence on his character is hard to ignore. Beginning with the most obvious parallel: Superman's origin is essentially Moses's reskinned with a science fiction backdrop. Valerie Estelle Frankel notes that "Superman has been repeatedly compared to Moses for his origin story, as his parents enclosed their baby in a tiny ship and sent him away to foreigners for safety. He's the outsider, come to practice the Jewish value of repairing the world."[75]

Both Moses and Superman are last sons of a dying culture that are placed in vessels as babies to save their lives. Both are sent on perilous journeys that resulted in them being found and raised by caring parents who keep them as their own. Frankel continues with, "Is it just chance that he is sent from an old world, Krypton, that is about to explode, to a new one, Earth (which could readily be seen as standing for Europe, on the verge of self-destruction, and America, with its promise of new life)."[76] Then, many years after their lives are saved, both Superman and Moses find out about their true origins and begin to realize that they have special abilities they can call upon. Finally, both men begin to embrace their destiny as saviors of the downtrodden once they speak to mysterious figures who tell them that they have a grand destiny.

Samson, the Torah's version of Hercules, is another figure that contributed to Superman. The text in Leviticus details God coming to Samson's parents before he's born to tell them that they will bear a son who will be a Nazirite—dedicated to God from birth. When Samson reaches adulthood, he is described as having superhuman strength that allows him to kill thirty Philistines in a fit of rage and a thousand more when he uses an animal skull.[77] The hero may have also inspired the concept of Kryptonite in that he has one major weakness: he will lose all of his super abilities if his hair is ever cut. Samson also bears similarities to Superman in that he pursues the Philistinian woman Delilah instead of a fellow Israelite, much like how Clark pursues the human Lois Lane. Ultimately, Samson's greatest act turns out to be one of self-sacrifice when he's betrayed by his lover and is forced to bring down the temple where he's being held prisoner.[78] This act kills all of the remaining Philistines and rids the Israelites of their enemy forever. Superman eventually must make a similar sacrifice himself to rid the world of superpowered alien Doomsday.

There are some telling clues of the ethnic origins when diving into the etymology of Superman's Kryptonian side. Krypton is described as a very classist society where families are divided into houses, much like ancient Israeli tribes were. Superman comes from the House of El and his birth name is Kal-El; El is a suffix in some of Judaism's most popular names such as Isra-el, Samu-el, and Dani-el, as well as angel names. El is also one of the Hebrew words for God. Kal is similar to the Hebrew words for voice or vessel. So, a loose translation for Superman's original name would be *Vessel of God.*[79]

Superman's iconic catchphrase, "Truth, Justice, and the American Way," has a counterpart in the Mishnah, the codification of Jewish oral traditions. The line reads, "The world endures on three things: justice, truth, and peace."[80] The teachings of the Kabbalah, Jewish mysticism, speak of a need to perform Tikkun Olam ("repairing the world") to bring it closer to the harmonious state for which it was created. Another interpretation of Superman is that his original world was broken due to lack of harmony, and he came to Earth with the intent to help repair this one.

There are some uniquely American Jewish ties to Superman's story as well. Superman could be considered, "the ultimate foreigner, escaping to America from his intergalactic shtetl and shedding his Jewish name for Clark Kent, a pseudonym as transparently WASPish as the ones Jerry had chosen for himself."[81] Cartoonist Jules Feiffer explains, "Superman was the ultimate assimilationist fantasy, the mild manners and glasses that signified a class of nerdy Clark Kents was in no way our real truth. Underneath the shmucky facade there lived Men of Steel! Jerry Siegel's accomplishment was to chronicle the smart Jewish boy's American dream. . . . It wasn't Krypton that Superman really came from: it was the planet Minsk or Lodz or Vilna or Warsaw."[82] Superman was, in the words of critic Arie Kaplan, "the supreme stranger in the strange land and thus the supreme metaphor for the Jewish experience."[83]

Author Stephen J. Whitfield, who's written extensively about Jewish American culture in the twentieth century, has this to say:

> Omnipotent and beneficent, Superman is like a god. In America the man of steel is an outsider who succeeds in a new world. He does so by applying his superhuman powers in a way that Jews typically wished others to behave—by

helping the weak. Superman is an idealized gentile who honors his elderly foster parents' pleas to use his awesome, heroic potentiality "to assist humanity," to rescue the oppressed rather than dominate them. He is episodically engaged in repair of the world. Superman is no Nietzschean Übermensch; instead, he is a sort of New Dealer. Conceived during the presidency of Franklin D. Roosevelt, to whom Jews showed deeper loyalty than did any other ethnic voting bloc, Superman signified the yearning to protect the vulnerable and to stimulate the confidence-building efforts at nationalist recovery. That is why he reliably fights for "truth, justice, and the American way." In his humanitarian acts, he is more effective than the golem who protects the Jews of Prague; the benefactor that Siegel and Shuster fantasized into being is less parochial and thus more democratic as well.[84]

The Clark Kent alter-ego might be described by some Yiddish grandmas as a nebbish. He's created a public persona of a very timid or submissive man who's easily pushed around by others. This was an unfortunate stereotype of Jewish men of the 1930s, but it stemmed from a real struggle that many of them faced; most Jewish men were in the minority at school or work and felt like they needed to create different identities when they were out with others and could only be themselves at home. The comedian Jerry Seinfeld once referred to Superman as his Jewish brother-in-arms.[85] As Frankel notes:

> The Superman/Clark Kent dual identity symbolizes "passing" or assimilation, since the hero's "true" identity must ever remain "secret." The true self, of course, is magical. Superheroes' secret identities with two sets of names and abilities feel quite Jewish. The Clark Kent persona is chosen so the alien or exotic princess can assimilate and blend in with American culture. Frequently, there's ambiguity in the hero's "otherness" as the hero wishes to lose this difference, then finally takes pride in it.[86]

Jerry Siegel would later acknowledge in his memoir that he was strongly influenced by the anti-Semitism he saw and felt when writing *Superman*. He was very proud of the reaction Berlin had to his anti-Nazi superhero. But Jerry repeatedly states that what he did the most was write about the world he grew up in.[87] Cleveland was a neighborhood that was 70 percent Jewish at the time Jerry and Joe met. It had Yiddish theaters, twelve Orthodox synagogues, and only one place to buy pulp fiction magazines. It was a setting where skinny, glasses-wearing juveniles were bullied for how they looked or where they came from, hoping that one day they could be seen as smart, strong, and confident pinnacles of the American way. It's hard to get more Jewish than that.

THE FIRST OF HIS KIND: SUPERMAN AS AN ENDURING LEGACY FOR FUTURE WRITERS AND SUPERHEROES

In 1996, DC Comics writers released a miniseries known as *Kingdom Come*. This was meant to be an Elseworlds story depicting a grim future for the Justice League in which a group of overly violent heroes take to the streets killing supervillains that they deem too dangerous. Superman is one of the heroes who refuses to take part in this brand of justice and decides to retreat into his Fortress of Solitude while the new wave of heroes run amok. However, when the younger vigilantes inadvertently cause a tragedy, Superman is forced out of retirement to re-form the Justice League and confront the new generation of heroes that have never worked with him before.[88]

There's a scene about halfway through the story that depicts several panels of the younger heroes having a party. Superman unceremoniously crashes through the wall, destroys all the alcohol, and then proceeds to chastise the new group about how irresponsible they've been. He states that heroes have rules, and they need to act in a certain way.[89] Superman then goes on to say that heroes who plan to join up with the new Justice League "will be expected to be as responsible as [they] are powerful. [They'll] be expected to behave better."[90] This speech leaves the crowd so moved that one of them states that she felt like she was just asked to be the thirteenth disciple and would follow Superman to Apokolips if needed.[91]

Much like in *Kingdom Come*, many others would go on to follow the path that Superman laid out. Jerry, Joe, and their creation helped pave the way for hundreds of other characters for years to come. They also inspired many other Jewish writers and artists to create their own characters that protected the weak and upheld American ideals. Jack Kirby and Joe Simon created Captain America in 1941 to do a similar task to Superman's: combat Nazi rhetoric and protect American values.[92] Stan Lee was the face of Marvel Comics for almost forty years, and, working with Jack Kirby, he was known for creating characters that tackled real-world issues of bigotry and prejudice like the X-Men and the Thing. Both Bob Kane and Bill Finger were Ashkenazi writers living in the Bronx, and they created Batman, a tragic figure who sought to overcome his own personal demons by fighting injustice wherever he found it.[93]

Superman at his core character design offers hope. He offers the promise of a future where people with means and ability are kind, respectful, and helpful to those who need it. He gives people the permission to be themselves and reinvent their image as they see fit. He embodies the Jewish ideals of Tzedakah (charity), Mitzvot (good deeds), and Tikkun Olam (repairing the world) both in his conception and how he acts. Hartman argues that many Jewish ideas are expressed in the early comics. "Truth, justice and the American way is really a Jewish ideal. This is another way of expressing *Torah, avodah,* and *gemilut chassadim*—Torah, service, and acts of loving kindness."[94] Clearly, even though Superman is an unlikely window into the Jewish American experience, his story can teach something to everyone.

NOTES

1. Jerry Siegel (w) and Joe Shuster (a). *Action Comics Vol 1* #1 (New York: DC Comics 1938), 1.

2. Harry Brod, *Superman Is Jewish?* (New York: Free Press, 2012), 9.

3. Brad Ricca, *Super Boys: The Amazing Adventures of Jerry Siegel and Joe Shuster—The Creators of Superman* (New York: St. Martin's Press, 2013), 9.

4. Ricca, 10.

5. Ricca, 12.

6. Ricca, 12.

7. Jerry Siegel, Joe Shuster, and Joanne Siegel, "Of Superman and Kids with Dreams" interviewed by Tom Andrae, Geoffry Blum, and Gary Coddington, *NEMO: The Classic Comics Library*, issue #2, August 1983, pages 6–19, superman.nu/seventy/interview.

8. Ricca, 122.

9. Ricca, 123.

10. "Joseph Greenstein." In *Sideshow and Other Carnival Curiosities*, ed. Jessica Firpi (Orlando, FL: Ripley Publishing, 2020), 50.

11. "Joseph Greenstein," 50

12. "Joseph Greenstein," 50.

13. Ricca, 123.

14. Ricca, 124.

15. Arie Kaplan, *From Krakow to Krypton: Jews and Comic Books* (Philadelphia: The Jewish Publication Society, 2008), 15.

16. Ricca, 18.

17. Larry Tye, *Superman: The High-Flying History of America's Most Enduring Hero* (New York: Random House, 2012), 4.

18. Tye, 5.

19. Tye, 4–5.

20. Ricca, 44.

21. Ricca, 44.

22. Ricca, 45.

23. Ron Goulart, *Great History of Comic Books* (Chicago, IL: Contemporary Books, 1986), 84.

24. Goulart, 84–85.

25. Ricca, 22.

26. Ricca, 23.

27. Ricca, 24.

28. Ricca, 40.

29. Ricca, 32.

30. Siegel, Shuster, and Siegel, interview.

31. Ricca, 44.

32. Kaplan, 10.

33. Adam Nemett, "Only We Can Save Us: A Brief History of Jewish Superheroes, Real and Fictional." *Jewish Book Council,* November 1, 2018. www .jewishbookcouncil.org/pb-daily/only-we-can-save-us-a-brief-history-of-jewish-superheroes-real-and-fictional.

34. Tye, 6.

35. Ricca, 55.

36. Cassandra Burris, "Origin Story: The Creation of Superman," *Ohio History Connection*, December 1, 2017. www.ohiohistory.org/learn/education/resource -roundup/december-2017/the-creation-of-superman.

37. Joe Connors, "Superman: Our Jewish Hero," *Anfield Index,* December 1, 2016. anfieldindex.com/geek/comics/superman-jewish-hero.

38. Alden Oreck, "Modern Jewish History: The Golem," *Jewish Virtual Library*, 2021. www.jewishvirtuallibrary.org/the-golem.

39. Brod, 2.

40. Valerie Estelle Frankel, *Jewish Science Fiction and Fantasy through 1945* (Lanham, MD: Lexington, 2021), 169.

41. Kaplan, 7–8.

42. Richard Rabkin, "Superman vs. the Nazis: How Comics Influenced American Public Opinion," *Aish,* September 15, 2018, www.aish.com/j/as/Superman-vs-the -Nazis-How-Comics-Influenced-American-Public-Opinion.html

43. Samantha Nelson, "Superman Doesn't Need Fixing Because He's More Relevant than Ever." *Polygon,* October 29, 2020, www.polygon.com/comics/2020/10/29 /21540112/superman-powers-overpowered-clark-kent-problem-comics.

44. Siegel and Shuster, *Action Comics #1*, 4.

45. Siegel and Shuster, *Action Comics #1*, 14.

46. Oreck.

47. Oreck.

48. Rabkin.

49. Jerry Siegel (w) and Joe Shuster (a), *Superman Vol. 1 #2*, 1939, in *Superman Chronicles Vol. 2* (New York: DC Comics, 2007), 83.

50. Jerry Siegel (w) and Joe Shuster (a), "How Superman Would End the War," 1940, in *Superman: Sunday Classics,* ed. Roger Stern (New York: Sterling, 2006), 189.

51. Jerry Siegel (w) and Joe Shuster (a), *Action Comics Vol. 1 #22*, 1940, in *Superman Chronicles Vol. 3* (New York: DC Comics, 2007), 18.

52. Siegel and Shuster, *Action Comics Vol. 1 #22*, 28.

53. Jerry Siegel (w) and Joe Shuster (a), *Action Comics Vol. 1 #23*, 1940, in *Superman Chronicles Vol. 3* (New York: DC Comics, 2007), 44.

54. Rabkin.

55. Jerry Siegel (w) and Joe Shuster (a), *Superman Vol. 1* #10, 1941, in *Superman: The War Years*, ed. Roy Thomas (New York: Chartwell Books, 2015), 116.

56. Siegel and Shuster, *Superman* #10, 117.

57. Ricca, 183.

58. Jerry Siegel (w) and Joe Shuster (a), *Action Comics Vol 1* #17 (New York: DC Comics 1938), 1.

59. Jerry Siegel (w) and Joe Shuster (a), *World's Finest Vol 1* #9 (New York: DC Comics 1943), 1.

60. Jerry Siegel (w) and Joe Shuster (a), *Action Comics Vol 1* #26 (New York: DC Comics 1939), 1.

61. Thomas, Roy. *Superman: The War Years* (New York: Chartwell Books, 2015), 198.

62. Jerry Siegel (w) and Wayne Boring (a), *Superman* daily newspaper comic strip Feb 16–19, 1942, in *Superman: The War Years,* ed. Roy Thomas (New York: Chartwell Books, 2015), 149.

63. Jerry Siegel (w) and Joe Simon (a), *Superman* daily newspaper comic strip #178–183, 1943, in *Superman: Sunday Classics*, ed. Roger Stern (New York: Sterling, 2006), 185.

64. Thomas, 198.

65. Jerry Siegel (w) and John Sikela (a), *Superman Vol 1* #18. 1942, in *Superman: The War Years,* ed. Roy Thomas (New York: Chartwell Books, 2015), 154.

66. Jerry Siegel (w) and Ira Yarbrough (a), *Superman Vol 1* #25. 1943, in *Superman: The War Years,* ed. Roy Thomas (New York: Chartwell Books, 2015), 241.

67. Jerry Siegel (w) and Joe Simon (a), *Superman* daily newspaper comic strip #86–103, 1941 in *Superman: Sunday classics,* ed. Roger Stern (New York: Sterling, 2006), 101.

68. Jerry Siegel (w) and John Sikela (a), *Superman Vol 1* #20. 1942, in *Superman: The War Years,* ed. Roy Thomas (New York: Chartwell Books, 2015), 170.

69. Jerry Siegel (w) and Sam Citron (a), *Superman Vol 1* #22. 1943, in *Superman: The War Years*, ed. Roy Thomas (New York: Chartwell Books, 2015), 201.

70. Siegel and Citron, *Superman Vol 1* #22, 211.

71. Unknown (w) and Wayne Boring (a), *Superman* daily newspaper comic strip #281, Mar. 11–25, 1945, in *Superman: The War Years*, ed. Roy Thomas (New York: Chartwell Books, 2015), 288.

72. Unknown and Boring, #282, 290.

73. Brod, 71.

74. Louise Simonson (w) and Jon Bogdanove (a), *Superman: The Man of Steel Vol 1* #80–82 (New York: DC Comics, 1998).

75. Frankel, 171.

76. Brod, 5.

77. Elana Roth, "The Story of Samson," *My Jewish Learning*, September 18, 2017, www.myjewishlearning.com/article/the-story-of-samson

78. Roth.

79. Tye, 65–66.

80. *Etz Chayim Torah and Commentary* (The Rabbinical Assembly, 2001).

81. Tye, 66.

82. Paul Levitz, *The Golden Age of DC Comics 1935–1956* (New York: DC Comics, 2013), 97.

83. Kaplan, 14.

84. Stephen J. Whitfield, "Declarations of Independence: American Jewish Culture in the Twentieth Century." In *Cultures of the Jews: A New History,* ed. David Biale (New York: Schocken Books, 2002), 1110.

85. Tye, 66.

86. Frankel, 171.

87. Gabe Friedman, "The Tragic Tale of Superman's Jewish Creators, Told in Graphic Novel Form," *The Times of Israel,* October 6, 2018, www.timesofisrael.com /the-tragic-tale-of-supermans-jewish-creators-told-in-graphic-novel-form.

88. Mark Waid (w) and Alex Ross (a), *Kingdom Come* (New York: DC Comics, 1997), 11–54.

89. Waid, 82.

90. Waid, 82.

91. Waid, 83.

92. Burris.

93. Joe Meadow, "The Jewish Origins of Batman," *The Jewish Chronicle,* March 30, 2019. www.thejc.com/lifestyle/arts/the-jewish-origins-of-batman-1.496184.

94. Rabkin.

WORKS CITED

Brod, Harry. *Superman Is Jewish?* New York: Free Press, 2012.

Burris, Cassandra. "Origin Story: The Creation of Superman." *Ohio History Connection,* December 1, 2017, www.ohiohistory.org/learn/education/resource -roundup/december-2017/the-creation-of-superman.

Etz Chayim Torah and Commentary. The Rabbinical Assembly, 2001.

Frankel, Valerie Estelle. *Jewish Science Fiction and Fantasy through 1945.* Lanham, MD: Lexington, 2021.

Friedman, Gabe. "The Tragic Tale of Superman's Jewish Creators, Told in Graphic Novel Form." *The Times of Israel,* October 6, 2018, www.timesofisrael.com/the -tragic-tale-of-supermans-jewish-creators-told-in-graphic-novel-form.

Goulart, Ron. *Great History of Comic Books.* Chicago: Contemporary Books, 1986.

"Joseph Greenstein." In *Sideshow and other Carnival Curiosities*, edited by Jessica Firpi, 49–51. Orlando, FL: Ripley Publishing, 2020.

Kaplan, Arie. *From Krakow to Krypton: Jews and Comic Books.* Philadelphia: The Jewish Publication Society, 2008.

Levitz, Paul. *The Golden Age of DC Comics 1935–1956.* New York: DC Comics, 2013.

Meadow, Joel. "The Jewish Origins of Batman." *The Jewish Chronicle,* March 30, 2019. www.thejc.com/lifestyle/arts/the-jewish-origins-of-batman-1.496184.

Nelson, Samantha. "Superman Doesn't Need Fixing Because He's More Relevant than Ever." *Polygon*, October 29, 2020, www.polygon.com/comics/2020/10/29 /21540112/superman-powers-overpowered-clark-kent-problem-comics.

Nemett, Adam. "Only We Can Save Us: A Brief History of Jewish Superheroes, Real and Fictional." *Jewish Book Council,* November 1, 2018. www.jewishbookcouncil .org/pb-daily/only-we-can-save-us-a-brief-history-of-jewish-superheroes-real-and -fictional.

Oreck, Alden. "Modern Jewish History: The Golem." *Jewish Virtual Library.* Edited by Geoffry Wigoder and David Bridger. American–Israeli Cooperative Enterprise, 2021. www.jewishvirtuallibrary.org/the-golem.

Rabkin, Richard. "Superman vs. the Nazis: How Comics Influenced American Public Opinion," *Aish,* September 15, 2018. www.aish.com/j/as/Superman-vs-the-Nazis -How-Comics-Influenced-American-Public-Opinion.html.

Ricca, Brad. *Super Boys: The Amazing Adventures of Jerry Siegel and Joe Shuster— The Creators of Superman.* New York: St. Martin's Press, 2013.

Roth, Elana. "The Story of Samson." *My Jewish Learning*, September 18, 2017, www .myjewishlearning.com/article/the-story-of-samson.

Siegel, Jerry (w) and Joe Shuster (a). *Action Comics Vol 1* #1. 1938. *Superman Chronicles Vol. 1.* New York: DC Comics, 2006.

Siegel, Jerry (w) and Joe Shuster (a). *Action Comics Vol 1* #22. 1940. *Superman Chronicles Vol. 3.* New York: DC Comics, 2007, 17–30.

Siegel, Jerry (w) and Joe Shuster (a). *Action Comics Vol 1* #23. 1940. *Superman Chronicles Vol. 3.* New York: DC Comics, 2007, 32–44.

Siegel, Jerry (w) and Joe Shuster (a). "How Superman Would End the War." 1940. In *Superman: Sunday Classics, Strips 1–183, 1939–1943,* edited by Roger Stern, 186–190. New York: Sterling, 2006.

Siegel, Jerry (w) and Joe Shuster (a). *Superman* daily newspaper comic strip #86– 103, 1941. In *Superman: Sunday Classics, Strips 1–183, 1939–1943,* edited by Roger Stern, 88–105. New York: Sterling, 2006.

Siegel, Jerry (w) and Joe Shuster (a). *Superman* daily newspaper comic strip #178– 183. 1943. In *Superman: Sunday Classics, Strips 1–183, 1939–1943,* edited by Roger Stern, 185. New York: Sterling, 2006.

Siegel, Jerry (w) and Joe Shuster (a). *Superman Vol. 1* #2. 1939. In *Superman Chronicles Vol. 2.* 62–85. New York: DC Comics, 2007.

Siegel, Jerry (w) and Joe Shuster (a). *Superman Vol. 1* #10, 1941, in *Superman: The War Years*, edited by Roy Thomas, 116–128. New York: Chartwell Books, 2015.

Siegel, Jerry (w) and John Sikela (a). *Superman Vol. 1* #20. 1942. In *Superman: The War Years,* edited by Roy Thomas, New York: Chartwell Books, 2015, 168–181.

Siegel, Jerry (w) and John Sikela (a). *Superman Vol. 1* #18. 1942. In *Superman: The War Years,* edited by Roy Thomas, 152–164. New York: Chartwell Books, 2015.

Siegel, Jerry (w) and Ira Yarbrough (a). *Superman Vol. 1* #25. 1943. In *Superman: The War Years,* edited by Roy Thomas, 240–251. New York: Chartwell Books, 2015.

Siegel, Jerry (w) and Sam Citron (a). *Superman Vol. 1* #22. 1943. In *Superman: The War Years*, edited by Roy Thomas, 200–211. New York: Chartwell Books, 2015.

Siegel, Jerry (w) and Wayne Boring (a). *Superman* daily newspaper comic strip Feb 16–19, 1942. In *Superman: The War Years,* edited by Roy Thomas, 149. New York: Chartwell Books, 2015.

Simonson, Louise (w) and Jon Bogdanove (a). *Superman: The Man of Steel Vol. 1* #80–82. New York: DC Comics, 1998.

Thomas, Roy. *Superman: The War Years.* New York: Chartwell Books, 2015.

Tye, Larry. *Superman: The High-Flying History of America's Most Enduring Hero.* New York: Random House, 2012.

Unknown (w) and Wayne Boring (a). *Superman* daily newspaper comic strip #280–282, Mar 11–25, 1945. In *Superman: The War Years,* edited by Roy Thomas, 288–290. New York: Chartwell Books, 2015.

Waid, Mark (w), and Alex Ross (a). *Kingdom Come.* New York: DC Comics, 1997.

Whitfield, Stephen J. "Declarations of Independence: American Jewish Culture in the Twentieth Century." In *Cultures of the Jews: A New History,* edited by David Biale. 1099–1146. New York: Schocken Books, 2002.

Chapter Five

Bats and Mitzvahs

Judaism in Modern Batman *Comics*

Jonathan Sexton

Much has been written on the influence of Judaism and Jewish creators on Golden Age comics from the 1940s and 1950s. From Roy Schwartz's suggestion of the parallels Superman shares with Moses and Samson[1] to the oft-made joke that Captain America is a golem, anyone passingly familiar with the history of superhero comics and Judaism is aware of the connection. Superheroes, after all, are Jewish American culture.

It is odd, then, that there are so few discussions on the current state of Judaism in superhero comics. What exists is largely focused on Marvel, in particular X-Men and Spider-Man. If, as author Simcha Weinstein suggests, Batman is shaped by creators Bob Kane's and Bill Finger's Jewish anxiety of urban dangers and sense of justice from the mid-twentieth century,[2] then what is the state of the character in the 2000s and 2010s? Is Batman still Jewish?

In some ways *Batman* is more Jewish—both as a character and a franchise—than it was in the Golden Age. Harley Quinn (Harleen Quinzel) was created for the animated series episode "Joker's Favor" in 1992, modeled after her actress—Jewish comedian Arleen Sorkin. Harley Quinn was established as Jewish herself in *Batgirl Adventures* #1 in 1997[3] and debuted in main continuity during *No Man's Land* in 1999.[4] Kate Kane, a reboot of the Batwoman character Kathy Kane from 1956, appears on the page in 2006, and has a defining arc in 2009 written by Jewish writer Greg Rucka. In 2013, *Batwoman* #25 makes her the maternal cousin of Bruce Wayne (Batman), thereby making Batman himself halachically Jewish. Kate comes with her own cast of characters, either Jewish or ambiguously so—her father Jacob, her stepmother Catherine, her sister Beth (Alice), and her cousin Bette (Flamebird). Similarly, Ragman (Rory Regan), a minor character from the

1970s, was reimagined in the early 1990s as a Jew living in Gotham City and has remained one since. Most recently, DC released the young adult graphic novel *Whistle: A New Gotham City Hero*, featuring a Jewish titular character. Originally written as an Elseworld (that is, a universe separate from the mainline comics) like *Batgirl Adventures* and *Bombshells*, Whistle cameoed in *Teen Titans Academy* #8 two months later.[5]

But as explicitly Jewish characters make their way onto the page, the Judaism in the writing dwindles. Kate Kane's Judaism started out prominent in her early appearances in the 2000s but falls to flavor text in her 2017 solo. Neither Kate nor Harleen nor Bruce keep kosher, and holidays besides Hanukkah are rarely mentioned. None of these characters are given Jewish love interests. The 2020 movie *Birds of Prey (and the Fantabulous Emancipation of One Harley Quinn)* went so far as to erase Harley Quinn's Judaism entirely, making her Catholic.

THE EVOLUTION OF BATWOMAN

The most notable Jewish character in Batman is Batwoman—the alter ego of Katherine "Kate" Kane, a lesbian discharged from West Point under Don't Ask, Don't Tell.[6] She has appeared in more than three hundred issues, with lead roles in story arcs of *Detective Comics* in 2009 and 2016 and first a mini-series and later multiple ongoing solo series as Batwoman. Kate Kane debuted in DC Comics title *52* #7 (2006).[7] *52* was a weekly series that ran for one year, covering the events in the time skip between the events *Infinite Crisis* and *One Year Later*. Geoff Johns, Grant Morrison, Greg Rucka, and Mark Waid all worked on *52* and no singular writer was credited for each individual story. Instead, the entire issue was credited to all four writers, though Jewish writer Greg Rucka has since been credited with Kate's creation.

Kate is established as Jewish during her fourth appearance, in *52* #33. "Kate made a big deal out of [Hanukkah],"[8] her ex-girlfriend Renee Montoya's narration says, alongside a panel of an unlit menorah with seven branches rather than the nine seen on holiday menorahs. "Cooked latkes and even laid out jelly doughnuts for dessert [. . .]. Kate said she did it because that's how her family celebrated Hanukkah, at least before her father remarried."

Immediately, the entire storyline begins to take on a different cast. In addition to Kate Kane and her relationship with Renee Montoya, *52* creates one of Batwoman's most well-known villains, the Religion of Crime. The Religion of Crime is a cult that views the biblical figure Cain as a prophet, with four lessons of crime—deceit, lust, greed, and murder. With Kate's Judaism now established, the Religion of Crime reads not as a thoughtless attempt at satire of organized religion, but as a dramatic extension of Christianity and its rejection of Jewish tradition. When she hears of a prophecy relating to her death at the hands of the Religion of Crime, Batwoman declares in *52* #28, "I've always felt that people should take responsibility for their actions . . . not excuse them by denying there was any choice in the matter."[9] A page later she pointedly tells a member of the cult that she is "working off a different text."

This rejection of a destined fate echoes the difference in Jewish thought from Christian theology, especially the Calvinist Protestantism common to the United States. In Devarim (Deuteronomy) 30:19, HaShem impresses upon the Israelites the importance of mitzvot: "I call heaven and earth to witness against you this day: I have put before you life and death, blessing and curse. Choose life—if you and your offspring would live."[10] This verse has long been interpreted as saying that mortals have free will, and Jewish philosophers have sought to solve the contradiction of HaShem's infinite knowledge with mortal choice through limiting the knowledge of HaShem or limiting the amount of choice in mortal action.[11]

Calvinism, by contrast, removes the choice entirely. In *the Humble Advice of the Assembly of Divines* John Calvin writes: "GOD from all eternity did by the most wise and holy Counsell of his own Will, freely, and unchangeably ordain whatsoever comes to pass." He reinforces this further on, saying that a person can only have free will to do good once they have converted to Christianity. "Man by his fall into a state of sin, hath wholly lost all ability of Will to any spirituall [*sic*] good accompanying salvation."[12]

This dichotomy remains present in Rucka's depiction of Kate Kane in *Detective Comics*. Here the Religion of Crime returns, now led by the villain Alice, depicted in *Detective Comics* #857 as wearing a long white veil that suggests Catholic depictions of the Virgin Mary.[13] In *Detective Comics* #859, a cult member named Abbot says that although his faith faltered when Batwoman continually survived, he came to believe that the prophecy referred not to her death, but to the death of Alice[14]—soon revealed to be Kate Kane's sister, Beth. Abbot, named for the head of a Christian monastery, is deemed a heretic for his doubt that Batwoman was the one prophesied to die. In the face of adversity, the dogmatic Religion of Crime cannot accept questions or wrestle with faith.

Batwoman's Judaism shows up in this arc as well, both in thematic as well as material ways. In a flashback to her origin in *Detective Comics* #860, upon seeing the costume her father, Jacob, designed for her, Kate says, "red and black . . . *gevurah*, the pillar of severity . . . the colors of *war*."[15] Gevurah here refers to one of the Sefirot, forces that, in Kabbalistic thought, "intervene between the infinite, unknowable God ('Ein Sof') and our created world."[16] Gevurah or Din is the Sefira of strength, and is also associated with judgment, might or power, justice, and restraint—all things particularly important to

Kate. The significance of this dialogue is twofold: not only does Greg Rucka invoke Kabbalistic symbolism through Batwoman's costume, but Batwoman herself is educated in Judaism enough to immediately make the connection. The same issue has Kate's stepmother Catherine telling Kate her family didn't expect her home until the High Holy Days—another indication of Kate's observance of Judaism, and a retroactive continuity change (retcon) of the implication from *52* #33 that Jacob married a gentile and lost connection with Judaism.

When Jacob agrees to help Kate become Batwoman, he tells her "Define the terms of victory. Because if victory means bringing your mother and sister back, then you've already lost [. . .] but if the objective is to save just one life . . . to protect one innocent . . . to keep one person from having their life shattered in violence, and come home alive when you're done, then you can prevail."[17] This quote calls to mind the Mishnah, a legal text that is often quoted philosophically. *Sanhedrin* 4:5 discusses the death penalty thus:

> Adam the first man was created alone, to teach you that with regard to anyone who destroys one soul from the Jewish people, i.e., kills one Jew, the verse ascribes him blame as if he destroyed an entire world, as Adam was one person, from whom the population of an entire world came forth. And conversely, anyone who sustains one soul from the Jewish people, the verse ascribes him credit as if he sustained an entire world.[18]

The importance of preserving life and refusing to kill is emphasized frequently in modern *Batman* comics, with many storylines—especially in the 2000s—asking where the line is drawn. In 2001's *Batgirl* #19, Batgirl, then Cassandra Cain, intervenes at the lawful execution of a criminal, believing his death to be immoral.[19] Much of Devin Grayson's work on *Nightwing*—Dick Grayson's post-Robin identity—is devoted to this subject, with Nightwing feeling so guilty over allowing one villain to kill another that he attempts to turn himself in for murder in *Nightwing* #100 and later abandons the moniker of Nightwing in shame.[20]

Batman himself is famous for his "no killing" rule, which dates to 1941, two years after his debut. In *Batman* #4, Batman tells Robin as they duel pirates, "Remember, we never kill with weapons of any kind!"[21] The extent to which this rule is enforced differs by author, era, and character. In the Golden Age, Batman was content to let villains and criminals die by accident. In recent years, more writers have shown him intervening here as well.

This rule is generally followed by other members of Batman's team, and sometimes characters more loosely associated with Batman. Initially, Kate is included in this, with her preventing Renee Montoya from shooting a suspect in *52* #11.[22] In 2009's *Detective Comics* #857 when Jacob warns Batwoman not to kill Alice, saying, "Batman rule in effect," to which she replies, "I'm always on the Batman rule, sir."[23]

In the 2010s, Kate's unwillingness to kill disappears, corresponding with a shift away from her Jewish roots in favor of gentile writers focusing on her military background. In *Detective Comics* #973, published in early 2018 and written by James Tynion IV (background unknown), Batwoman kills Clayface, who has reformed from villainy but lost control of his powers.[24] Although she does so in order to save Cassandra Cain (now going by Orphan), Batman puts her on mock-trial in *Detective Comics* #975, seeking opinions from the rest of the team, who condemn her for her actions.

In 2017, Batwoman was given her second solo series, *Batwoman* Volume 3, which ran for eighteen issues and ended in mid-2018. James Tynion IV cowrote the first six issues with Marguerite Bennett, after which Bennett took over as sole writer. The closest the series reaches toward a conversation about Kate's Judaism comes in *Batwoman* #1, when the minor character Rafael comments on her Judaism in their first meeting despite no textual or visual indication that he is Jewish. The exchange is uncomfortable: "What? Turning up your nose because you're worried it isn't kosher, or because there isn't a proof on the bottle?" and "The tattoos . . . usually throw people off."[25] The scene references an interview Tynion gave six months earlier, in October of 2016: "She would have been flying to every corner of the world. It was the idea that Kate Kane could walk into the seediest bar in the seediest neighborhood in Cairo, and the bartender would know her name and her drink."[26] Without the context of this interview, the comic on its own feels nightmarish to a Jewish reader—not only is the lone and currently defenseless Kate instantly recognized as a Jew for no given reason, in the same breath she is mocked for her potential observance of Judaism.

In the other seventeen issues of *Batwoman,* her Judaism is only mentioned three more times, each in passing. In *Batwoman* #9 she tells a hallucination caused by the villain Scarecrow that, "I don't need anymore sacraments, buddy—I'm Jewish."[27] Later in the same issue she corrects a comment about Batman buying her Christmas presents with "Hanukkah." This follows *Batwoman* #8, in which she clumsily ends a layout of battle tactics with "Fershtay?"[28] the Yiddish for "understand," while speaking to a gentile character.

Batwoman doesn't stop at minimizing its protagonist's Judaism but toes the line with outright anti-Semitism. In *Batwoman* #14 Alice, Batwoman's villainous sister, declares, "I was always so good with drugs and potions and poisons"[29] as she explains her plans to unleash a new lab-created virus using Batwoman as a patient zero. Published in 2018, the issue was two years before COVID-19, but already history shows anti-Semitism related Jews to pandemics such as the medieval Black Death. Four years on in the era of COVID-19 denial and conspiracies, the story has aged extremely poorly.[30]

Batwoman #16, published six months after *Detective Comics* #975, references Clayface's death. When Batwoman declines to agree to Batman's suggestion that she place Alice in Arkham Asylum and demands a say in her treatment as her sister, Batman tells her, "Clayface was strike one. This is strike two."[31] When she hits three strikes, he says, "you'll never be Batwoman again." The message from these two issues is clear: Batwoman cannot exist on her own terms. Batwoman is a hero at the whim of Batman.

Batman has carried tension with other heroes who kill as well, most notably his former apprentice Red Hood. With Red Hood, however, much of the conflict comes from Red Hood's push for Batman to kill and whether or not Red Hood is allowed to operate in Gotham. But Batwoman leaving Gotham grants her no freedom—when she does so, she does so at the will of Batman, such as in *Batwoman* #1 when she is tasked by him with the specific mission of taking down an arms dealer.[32] In some ways, this feels like another fallback on the part of the writers onto her military background: Kate Kane wants to serve, and she does so as Batwoman, following the orders of Batman. Judaism is not a primary factor in the way she thinks or acts.

JEWISH ETHICS AND PHILOSOPHY IN *BATMAN*

In 2013's *Batwoman* #25, a retcon establishes Bruce's mother, Martha Kane, as the sister of Kate's father, Jacob.[33] The issue, set during the funeral of Martha and Jacob's brother Phillip, would have a great deal more impact had the writer and artist not apparently forgotten that Jacob Kane is Jewish.

Phillip is given a Christian burial in a Christian cemetery, filled with cross-shaped gravestones and a conspicuous absence of kippot. The reception is held at Wayne Manor, with Bruce raising a toast to Phillip immediately before sending his guests—including Jacob, Phillip's brother and the only direct mourner—on their way due to an approaching storm.[34] There are no siddurim, no mention of kaddish or shiva, no wishes for the deceased's memory to be a blessing.

Funerals are a common occurrence in *Batman*, with so many characters shaped by the loss of loved ones. The previously mentioned *Detective Comics* #975 shows the funeral of Kate's mother, where several men wear kippot and Kate and Bruce are both shown throwing dirt on the unseen casket.[35] 2016's *Detective Comics* #939 seems confused about Martha Wayne's funeral: the service is held in an unspecified building with the Gothic architecture typical of Gotham, no heads are covered, and a portrait of Martha is displayed alongside both a menorah and flowers. Eight-to-ten-year-old Bruce sits alone until Kate asks if she can join him.[36]

Something about *Batwoman* #25 feels especially egregious, though, not only in the absence of indicators of Judaism, but in the seeming absence of any mourning at all. Jacob is smiling when he meets Kate at the airport. He is the one driving to the reception as Kate contemplates a turn of phrase heard on the radio. When Kate tells him she wants to patrol the streets that night, he tells her she's a civilian for the weekend.[37] No acknowledgment is made of the fact that, so soon after the murder of his brother—in Jewish tradition, only two days—Jacob's only remaining immediate family is telling him she is about to throw herself into danger. Were it not for a line referring to Kate's "Uncle Phil," a reader could easily be left with no impression of Jacob and Phillip as siblings.

This strait-laced, silenced form of mourning reminds one far more of white American Christian mourning practices than Jewish ones. While Jewish mourning is divided into strict segments with rules dictating that the siblings—and children, spouse, and parents—of the deceased receive support and allow themselves to grieve, white American Christian tradition demands the opposite. After the burial, mourning is over. A funeral is held, and the family moves on. White American Christian culture looks down on those who show their grief and disdains male displays of emotion in general.

These ideals are reflected in the characterization of modern Batman. In the Golden Age and even into the 1990s, Batman was portrayed as a detective first and fighter second, and comics were willing to show him as a loving father. The 2000s and especially the 2010s by contrast have seen Batman become characterized more as a brawler closed off to everyone except, perhaps, his love interest.

1987's *Batman* #410, 1995's *Robin Annual* #4, and 2021's *Robin & Batman* #1–3 all portray origins or training periods for Batman's sidekick and ward, Robin—a role filled by Jason Todd in *Batman* #410 and Dick Grayson in the others. The difference in how Batman, his role as a vigilante, and his relationship with Robin are treated is clear. In *Batman* #410, Jason is taught how to fight, but his physical prowess is not given more importance than his intelligence. The issue seems deliberate in its wording, with the Batcave described as "a school with a single pupil," and Batman himself as "a teacher who thrives upon hand-to-hand combat while insisting violence is merely a 'tool' to be used 'judiciously and without joy.'"[38]

Robin Annual #4 shows Batman as both fighter and detective, but also as an adult with compassion toward children. Dick describes him as a "guardian angel,"[39] and the first interaction between the pair of characters is when a worried Batman asks Dick where his shoes are. As in *Batman* #410, the soon-to-be Robin learns detective skills like forensics and criminology as well as martial arts, and the conflict hinges upon clues being uncovered to catch a criminal. Notably, Bruce does not take Dick in with the intention of training him as a sidekick, but out of empathy. Despite the fact that he sees himself in Dick, he does not push him to take the same path. When Dick asks what will happen to him after they solve his parents' murder, Bruce tells him, "That's up to you. You can go on being my ward or join another foster family [. . .] your future is always up to you."[40] This again references the Jewish ideal of free will, with Bruce refuting the idea that Dick has no choice. During training, Batman remarks, "I see there's a few moves you [Robin] can teach me."[41] The Babylonian Talmud teaches us in Taanit 7a12, "I have learned much from my teachers and even more from my friends, but from my students I have learned more than from all of them."[42] As Rabbi Chanina learned, so too has Batman.

In 2021's *Robin & Batman* this characterization is largely gone. The villain, Killer Croc, directly attacks Batman and Robin, with no emphasis on the intellectual mystery as to his identity or search for his whereabouts. In *Robin & Batman* #1, Alfred comments that he expects Bruce to say Dick "needs to be a soldier,"[43] a statement Bruce admits to believing and one that is repeated through the miniseries. Robin's training is entirely combat based, focused on physical abilities and strategy. Batman is unconcerned with Robin's intellectual education, saying in *Robin & Batman* #3 that he can stay home from school, and that "This [being Robin] is more important than whatever they're teaching him at Gotham Academy."[44] Batman only expresses affection when trying to convince Robin to leave him behind after he is captured by Killer Croc during the climax.[45]

This shift in Batman, the emphasis on violence over investigation, mirrors the more literal militarization of Batwoman and shifts Batman from a portrayal of masculinity in line with traditional Judaism to one in line with the dominant white Christianity of America. Traditionally in Judaism, men are less likely to be portrayed as heroic warriors than they are in Christianity. Bereshit (Genesis) 25 contrasts hunter Esav with his trickster brother Yaakov, who tricks his brother out of his birthright. Judaism understands this to be right, that Yaakov, as the "mild man who stayed in camp"[46] should be considered the greater of the two sons despite his younger birth and is the third Jewish patriarch. Even King David is equally known for his music and psalms as he is for slaying the giant Goliath.

Other aspects of Jewish masculinity contrast similarly. Pirkei Avot (Ethics of Our Fathers) 4:1 tells us that the person who is "mighty" is the person "who controls his passions,"[47] and reminds us of Proverbs 16:32, "He that is slow to anger is better than the mighty, and he that ruleth over his spirit than he that takes a city."[48] Jewish masculinity values not only scholarly prowess, but patience and self-restraint. Batman, who once saw violence as an unfortunate but necessary tool, is now one of the more violent heroes to lead a solo title in DC, with writers going so far as to show him hitting his adult children outside of training contexts.[49]

One relatively modern story that stands out in its handling of Batman is "Perpetual Mourning," written and drawn by Ted McKeever (background unknown) and published in the anthology *Batman: Black and White* in 1996, the year after *Robin Annual* #4. The short story features Batman performing an autopsy on a murdered woman with narration describing his thought process and investigation as he does so. This approach allows the typically stoic Batman to reveal his motivations and emotions about his work.

"Does the individual count for nothing?" Batman asks. "Are we only preserving the general features of humanity? The broad brushstrokes?"[50] With this line, he calls forth the same Mishnah Jacob Kane does in *Detective Comics* #860: "anyone who sustains one soul from the Jewish people, the verse ascribes him credit as if he sustained an entire world."[51] To Judaism, and to Batman, the individual's life is worth an entire world.

After explaining his observations of the corpse, Batman says, "People think I'm a knight. A savior. But, in truth, I'm only a vessel to hold the memories of those who've passed on."[52] Here, Batman sets aside comparisons to Jesus and the Christian concept of saviors to identify his purpose as a smaller one, human but holy in its own, very Jewish, way. When he identifies the deceased woman, Batman concludes with this sentiment: "You only have your thoughts and dreams ahead of you. You're someone. You mean something. I'll remember."[53] This line evokes the Jewish ambiguity of the afterlife in preference over a Christian heaven, hell, or "better place." Instead, Batman acknowledges her importance as a human being, and focuses on the memories the living carry of her.

FALSE REPRESENTATION: CHRISTIAN HEGEMONY IN *RAGMAN*

The most obvious place to discuss Jewish theology and spirituality in *Batman* and related comics is the character Ragman. Like Batman, Ragman was originally created by a Jewish writer and artist team, Bob Kanigher and Joe Kubert. In 2010, Kubert said that although he did not set out to create a Jewish character, Ragman was inspired by the Jewish immigrants he saw growing up in the 1930s. "Ragman does have a Jewish background [. . .]. but the motivation was more to create a different kind of superhero. Kanigher came from a similar background to mine. I grew up in the late '20s, early '30s, in Brooklyn, and it was not unusual to have older men, Jews who had just come from Europe, go round with pushcarts or a horse and wagon and collect old clothes. These were people who eked out a living any way they could."[54] Though the original *Ragman* series in 1976 only ran for five issues, the character was revived in the 1990s by Robert Loren Fleming and Keith Giffen, writers of unknown but likely gentile backgrounds.

Parallels can be drawn immediately to Batwoman. Both Batwoman and Ragman were created prior to the Modern Age of comics, are given military backgrounds in their revivals that serve to displace the importance of Judaism in their lives, and are portrayed as less reluctant to kill than gentile heroes. Like Kate Kane's Judaism being canonized by a seven-branched menorah at Hanukkah, the 1990s portrayals of Ragman have missteps, as the lore described in both the 1991 miniseries *Ragman* and his sparse appearances in *Batman* is based in Christocentric thought. Spirits of the dead form Ragman's magical cloak and suit, with each new soul taking its place as a singular patch. Through his appearances it is repeatedly emphasized that the cloak is powered by "evil souls," with Rory Regan, the current wearer, constantly struggling not to give into the ghosts' thirst for violence.

More issues come from Ragman's backstory, told first in *Ragman* #3 in 1991 and again in *Batman* #551 in 1997. In sixteenth-century Prague, the golem, "a monster, a creature with no soul"[55] was replaced by the Ragman, a "human agent" wearing a costume created with the same spell that created the golem. Little explanation is given for the reason behind the replacement, only that the rabbis of Prague were "uneasy about being defended by a soulless monster."[56] The "living costume" was then inherited by Rory's father, Jerzy Reganiewicz, who wore it during World War II and fought in the Warsaw Ghetto Uprising. Jerzy later immigrated to the United States and anglicized his name to Gerry Regan.

The golem is one of the most commonly used and recognizable aspects of Jewish folklore due to its appropriation by broader fantasy. In its fundamentals a golem is a creature of clay or stone brought to life with holy words, used for protection or menial labor. It has been appropriated all over fantasy, from the more or less direct adaptation of the folktale in the *X Files* episode "Kaddish" to games like *Dungeons & Dragons*, where the term becomes synonymous with a magical robot. In *Ragman,* this symbol of Jewish survival in the face of adversity is portrayed as untrustworthy due to its lack of a human soul.

The golem may make the rabbis "uneasy," but the Ragman suit outright breaks halacha. Vayikra (Leviticus) 19:31 states, "Do not turn to ghosts and do not inquire of familiar spirits, to be defiled by them,"[57] and repeats in 20:6, "And if any person turns to ghosts and familiar spirits and goes astray after them, I will set My face against that person and cut him off from among his people."[58] The Talmud explains that this may refer to two types of communication with the dead, or that a necromancer who raises the dead and a medium who speaks to the dead are addressed in the same verse. Tractate Keritot (Excisions) 3b:28 further says that "[a sorcerer] such as this, who gathers demons together, is included in the category of a necromancer [. . .]."[59] Though Jewish text and folklore have stories of interactions with the dead, from Saul consulting the ghost of Samuel to stories of the dybbuk, it is generally done as a last resort, and is not empowering to the living Jew.

Even beyond this thematic dissonance, portrayals of Ragman in the 1990s ask us to set aside Jewish concepts of souls, evil, and the dead. *Batman* #551 refers to the dead spirits powering the suit's magic as "evil souls,"[60] a concept more in line with Calvinist ideas of souls as predestined for evil than Jewish theology. Unlike the Calvinism from which American Christianity is descended, Jewish theology not only denies predestination but also the treatment of a person as wholly good or wholly evil. Each person has both a yetzer hara and a yetzer tov—an inclination and capacity for evil and an inclination and capacity for good. Judaism attempts to guide us toward our yetzer tov (good inclination), and views sin as a misstep, separate from ritual impurity.

The 2017 reboot of Ragman's origin takes this even further. Here the suit is not only tied to demons from the hell of the greater DC universe, but according to *Ragman* #1 contains "ruah tum'ah,"[61] translated literally but spiritually incorrectly as "unclean spirits"[62] in *Ragman* #3. This phrase makes no sense for multiple reasons, the most obvious being that "ruah tum'ah" is singular. On a deeper level, it also creates an association of uncleanliness or impurity—tum'ah—with evil that does not exist in Judaism. To be tum'ah not evil; it is merely a state of being, occurring at such times as menstruation or after coming into contact with the dead. The correlation of impurity with evil comes from Christian thought, not Judaism.

The Ragman of the 1990s fell short in other, more cultural ways as well. In *Ragman* #3 an old friend of Rory's father's from the Warsaw Ghetto provides exposition. The unnamed rabbi knew Gerry only as Jerzy and finds the idea of a Jew changing his name ridiculous. "Jerzy Reganiewicz?" he exclaims. "That was his true name! Do you think 'Regan' is a name fit for Jews?"[63] Given the long history of Jewish immigrants changing their names and the implication that Gerry's "true" name was not his Hebrew name or his English call name, but a Polish name, the scene reads more as a gentile writer impressing his idea of what a "Jewish name" looks like than a Jew expressing surprise. More humorously, in scenes featuring the golem the word *emet* is consistently written in the Latin alphabet, not the Hebrew alphabet.

Even more glaring mistakes are found in his appearances in *Batman*. *Batman* #551 includes a scene where reporter Vesper Fairchild interviews a "hate crimes expert," David Levy, on anti-Semitism. The character claims that "Jews have been persecuted throughout history, expelled or exiled from one country after another." After Vesper's prompting him with "the

diaspora?" he continues, "originally from *Babylon*, and then *Egypt*,"[64] implying that Jews were expelled from those places in that order. In fact, Babylon
conquered ancient Judea and forcefully removed Jews to Babylon after the
destruction of the First Temple.

Worse yet, having lost control of the Ragman suit in *Batman* #552, Rory
cries for Batman to "scorch the evil souls straight to Hell! Destroy the
Ragman forever! Free me of the rags and send the souls where they belong!"[65]
His demand to send them to hell is the most glaring example of Christian
ideas dripping into his stories thus far. Later in the same issue Rory declares
that the out-of-control souls in the suit are trying to kill a man, but "the deed
will be on my soul!"[66] a direct inversion of the Jewish belief that the dead
receive partial credit for acts they inspired the living to do—and far from the
biggest worry that would be on Rory's mind. The same issue features a rabbi
referring to "God's revealed law as found in the Pentateuch,"[67] ignoring the
additions of oral tradition, and addressing Rory as "my son" as a Catholic
priest would.

And yet, like Batwoman, Ragman only grows worse in the 2010s. The
2017 reboot not only aligns the suit of souls with demons from hell, but also
says in *Ragman* #4 that the suit was summoned and worn by a Christian
knight in the Crusades.[68] In this version, all connection to the golem is lost,
but so is all connection to Judaism. Although a token effort to keep Rory's
religion is made, the series implicitly endorses Christian mythology as correct. Ragman's suit and enemies are born of hell. In *Ragman* #5, he allies with
Ystin, a knight of Camelot.[69] Here, the suit of souls was sealed in a "temple"
somewhere in Israel until Rory, a U.S. Marine, uncovered it.[70]

Like the 1990s run of *Ragman* before it, the 2017 comic has erased a symbol of Jewish protection and replaced it with evil. Rory's history as a Marine
is far more important to the 2017 story than his Vietnam veteran status was to
the stories published in the 1990s. In this he shares a commonality with Kate
and Bruce, his Judaism lessened in favor of a culture and ideal that Christian
America can more easily understand—and write about.

Similarly frustrating is Whistle, advertised as "DC Comics' first [super-
hero] to be explicitly created as Jewish in 44 years."[71] *Whistle: A New Gotham
City Hero* is a graphic novel written by the secular Jewish writer E. Lockhart,
which debuted on September 7, 2021—the first day of Rosh Hashanah, a day
that kept observant Jews from supporting the book at launch.[72] The book features Willow Zimmerman as Whistle, the secular Jewish daughter of a Jewish
studies professor. Though Willow says her mother is more observant, the closest to ritual observance the book shows for either character is when Willow
goes to synagogue to think.[73] Instead, the main aspect of Judaism discussed
in *Whistle: A New Gotham City Hero* is Tikkun Olam, meaning "repairing

the world." Tikkun Olam is a phrase that is frequently interpreted by Reform Judaism as promoting social activism, as it is in *Whistle: A New Gotham City Hero* and is an aspect of Jewish philosophy that is easily accessible to gentile readers. The prioritization of Tikkun Olam allows *Whistle: A New Gotham City Hero* to work on "easy mode" rather than prioritizing a Jewish audience or encouraging gentile readers to work to understand Judaism on a deeper level. As a side effect, the relation of Whistle's Judaism to her superheroics feels shallow and unexplored, rather than giving her a meaningful philosophy with which to wrestle or connect to the reader.

In an early scene, Willow buys a treif sandwich at Rosen Brothers Delicatessen, despite dialogue later stating that Rosen Brothers closes on Shabbat.[74] To the reader familiar with kosher dining, this disconnect causes the presentation to fall flat, destroying both connection to the characters and the emotional resonance of the scene.

Both *Ragman* and *Whistle: A New Gotham City Hero* center working class characters, with Rory Regan owning a pawn shop in a slum and Willow Zimmerman struggling to pay her mother's medical bills and fighting against gentrification.[75] This is a welcome contrast to Kate Kane's wealth as well as the stereotype of the wealthy Jew in gentile perception, and reflects the reality that 16–20 percent of Jewish households in the United States earn less than $30,000 a year and a higher percentage have trouble making ends meet.[76] A 2011 study found that 32 percent of Jews in New York live at or near poverty. Of these, 42 percent were older adult households and 17 percent were Ultra-Orthodox.[77] Willow and Rory do not represent the bulk of real-world impoverished Jews. They are both secular Jewish outliers in their communities—both exist separately from other Jews who would provide context and perspective on both Jewish poverty and the main characters' approaches to Judaism. While showing a new friend around Gotham, Willow says the area where she lives "used to be an all-Jewish neighborhood,"[78] but the only Jews in the book besides Willow and her mother are the background characters who run Rosen Brothers. Although *Whistle: A New Gotham City Hero* draws on Lockhart's relationship with Judaism, reading it feels like a missed opportunity to broaden the current range of Jews shown in superhero comics, especially given the lack of supporting Jewish characters in the book.

HISTORICAL JUDAISM IN ELSEWORLDS

Other stories about Jewish characters from *Batman* comics have been published as Elseworlds, comics set outside of main continuity. This allows writers to explore possibilities without affecting the main brand of the character. The 1997 story "Berlin Batman," published in *Batman Chronicles* #11 and written and drawn by gentile writer Paul Pope, depicts Batman as a Jew living in Nazi Germany.[79] The 2015 series *DC Comics: Bombshells*—an alternate history of World War II starring the female characters of DC—adds several characters to the list of potential Jews: featuring not only Harley Quinn and Batwoman, but also Andrea Gruenwald (an adaptation of Andrea Beaumont, here known as Reaper), along with several non-Batman characters like Zatanna Zatara (Zatanna), Rachel Roth (Raven), and Miriam Batzel (an adaptation of Mary Batson, here going by Miri Marvel). Indeed, this willingness to explore possibilities of representation in Elseworlds extends not only to Jewish characters but other groups as well. *Bombshells* also features a Cuban Lois Lane who falls in love with Supergirl, a scene implying Black Canary is trans, and a Zatanna who is both Jewish and Romani.

But the simple presence of Jewish characters does not mean they are written well. "Berlin Batman" takes the premise of Batman as a bat-themed vigilante who witnessed his parents' murder as a child and transplants the original 1939 story to Berlin in the same year. Instead of a mugging gone wrong, Baruch Wane's family is killed in an anti-Semitic attack, after which he vows to "avenge their deaths" and "spend the rest of [his] life warring on all criminals."[80] As an adult, he is a cubist artist viewed as an eccentric layabout who rarely leaves his home in "one of the most exclusive districts in Berlin."[81] Komissar Garten, an adaptation of Gotham's police commissioner and Batman's friend Jim Gordon, tells Baruch that he should socialize more, and even goes as far as to suggest that he paint a portrait of Adolf Hitler.

Garten's exchange with Baruch regarding his artwork also minimizes both the censorship and the anti-Semitism of Nazi Germany. When Baruch responds to Garten's suggestion saying that he is "not a political artist" and names Pablo Picasso as an inspiration, Garten disdains him not for his modern cubist work, but for taking inspiration from a Spaniard. In fact, it was a supposed Jewish influence that contributed to the Nazis' concept of "Degenerate Art." Nazis believed that modern art promoted pacifism and "contained Jewish and Communist influences that could 'endanger public security and order.'"[82] In 1937, four years after the Reich Chamber of Culture was founded to regulate German art, an exhibition of "Degenerate Art" opened in Munich. It featured artwork by Jewish and modernist artists (including Picasso himself), described as "how sick minds viewed nature."[83]

In reality, all the events of "Berlin Batman" would have been impossible without extensive papers falsifying not only Baruch's identity, but a family history. By the end of 1938, Nazi Germany required Jews to register their property, prohibited Jews from operating businesses or attending both public school and university, and barred them from social areas and certain districts.[84] After the Kristallnacht pogrom in November 1938, nearly ten thousand Jews were imprisoned at the Buchenwald concentration camp outside

Weimar.[85] Beginning in February 1939, Germany required Jews to surrender their valuables to the German state.[86]

By 1939, anti-Semitism would have been pushing on every aspect of Baruch's life, as his property, business, movements, access to social services, and ability to interact with gentiles were heavily restricted. The notion of his wealth shielding him is a false one and particularly problematic; the myth of Jewish wealth allowed Nazi Germany to justify the confiscation of Jewish property beginning in 1938 and 1939. Baruch would not have been able to easily pass as a gentile, either. The Nuremberg Race Laws defined a Jew not by religious status but by family history. In January 1938 Germany forbade Jews from changing their names, and in October passports belonging to Jews were declared void until stamped to indicate the owner as Jewish.[87]

In "Berlin Batman" none of this context is given to Baruch's life. Aside from his name (Hebrew for "blessing") and his parents' murder, little indication is given of Baruch's Judaism. Narration describes Baruch as "the strongest, smartest, most precocious child in his whole class" as a child, adding, "He noticed the others resented him more for this than for being a Jew."[88] Anti-Semitism seems to exist not as a constant, threatening presence, but as a one-off motivator for Baruch.

"Berlin Batman" goes even further to erase Nazi censorship. When Batman stops the Berlin police from confiscating the property of the historical Jewish economist Ludwig von Mises, he thinks, "once they catalogue all the books and notes in von Mises's library, they'll ship everything to some storehouse to rot!"[89] Historically, the Nazi party had been hosting book burnings since 1933.[90]

"Berlin Batman" whitewashes the crimes of Nazi Germany, showing a world where anti-Semitism and totalitarianism are limited to active war and the days of the Final Solution. It does so with no artistic purpose, depicting neither a realistic (or, at least, as realistic as one can get with superheroes) picture of Jewish life in Nazi Germany nor an optimistic world of what could have been. This downplaying of anti-Semitism, even in a story written at the height of grimdark Batman, contributes to a persistent myth that the Holocaust was an unpreventable tragedy with no greater context in Jewish history. It is, every panel and speech bubble, an irresponsible story.

In contrast to "Berlin Batman" and its attempt at imitating the somewhat darker, if pulpy, tones of Golden Age comics, *DC Comics: Bombshells* (inspired by a line of collectible pinup statues) attempts an optimistic alternate history where the United States has already entered the war in 1940. The series was published digitally from 2015 to 2017 and written by Marguerite Bennett, who later went on to work on the comic *Batwoman* and features several superheroines from different teams—most notably for our purposes Batwoman, Raven, and Miri Marvel. In a conversation with fans in 2019,

Marguerite Bennett said, "DC was incredibly supportive for all the places that I wanted to go [. . .] getting into the much darker and less 'rally round the flag' American history version of the war."[91]

Not all readers agree. One Jewish blogger said in her review of the first eighteen of one hundred digital issues, "the 'What If' nature of the book becomes a strange idyllic 1940's that chooses to face and ignore the World War II era [. . .] the actual Holocaust, racial and LGBTQ inequities, the internment of Japanese Americans, the darkness of this period is largely avoided. This is only exacerbated by the fact that while everyone loves punching Nazis, the actual Big Bad is an otherworldly creature."[92] Though the series later features scenes in the Berlin Jewish Quarter[93] and the sequel series mentions Japanese American internment camps,[94] the subjects of death and genocide are mostly avoided, and *Bombshells* remains light in tone until the very end.

Like "Berlin Batman," *Bombshells* often seems to downplay the anti-Semitism in Nazi Germany. In *DC Comics: Bombshells* #11 Harley Quinn—later revealed to be Jewish, as she is in main continuity—immediately leaves London for Germany when she hears her lover the Joker is alive there.[95] Two issues later, Kate Kane enters Berlin as a spy at a formal party—without an alias.[96] When Kate is taken prisoner by the villain Brother Night in *DC Comics: Bombshells* #29, he tells her, "I do not want you to die, Fraulein Kane. You are far more useful alive than as a vessel for the Tenebrae,"[97] referring to the supernatural beings he summons that inhabit the bodies of the dead. "The Tenebrae care nothing for race, for love, for the divisions of nations. They serve whomever pays them in flesh." This choice to displace the human evil of racial hatred and center a supernatural evil that kills blindly is a choice that erases the harm of anti-Semitism and the specific and very real harm done by Nazi Germany. The suggestion that Nazism harms non-Romani gentiles as much as it does Jews and Romani allows those gentiles to set aside their own anti-Semitism and anti-Romanyism.

Other scenes in *Bombshells* seem more like mistakes. When Kate fights Brother Night, she tells him, "When you are a memory, detested, despised by everything to ever come after—we will still be here. We survived Egypt and we survived Masada."[98] A rousing speech, were it not for the fact that the siege of Masada ended in mass suicide with only two survivors. What Kate means here is that Judaism survived the Roman occupation of Judea, but her invocation of Masada reflects *Bombshells*' refusal to engage with the uglier aspects of Jewish history.

Another, more cultural mistake is seen in issue #49. When the heroines stoke a rebellion in the Berlin Jewish Quarter, Harley Quinn says to a man, presumably another Jew, "Molotov cocktails from sacramental wine—this is probably incredibly offensive, isn't it?" and receives the reply, "God will understand."[99] The concept of a special sacramental wine to be used only for religious purposes is a Catholic one—for Jews, what matters is not any particular state the wine is in, but that it be made from a vine-grown fruit to be used for Kiddish.

This is not to say that *Bombshells* is entirely without merit. The same issue also depicts a Shabbat dinner and candlelighting, portraying both the spiritual and communal aspects of the ritual. The young Miriam Batzel reminds Kate of the stories of Jewish resistance and strong Jewish women, mentioning the Four Matriarchs Sarah, Rebecca, Rachel, and Leah, along with Deborah, Judith, and her own namesake, Miriam. She also walks Kate through one of the prayers, correcting her pronunciation of the Hebrew names: "Yesmich [Elokim] keSarah Rivka Rachel veLe'ah." "Yesmich [Elokim] ke . . . keSerach" "KeSarah Rivka Rachel veLe'ah."[100] One Jewish reviewer notes of this scene, "The sound Kate gravitates towards is more or less synonymous with Hebrew. The 'ch' is a . . . how do I put this . . . like you're clearing your throat, but from the back of your top pallet. A guttural sound. Most people who don't grow up with it have difficulty . . . making that sound, similar to the rolling 'r' in Spanish."[101] This scene portrays Judaism not as a weakness or as completely lost to the assimilated Kate, but as a feeling of home that she naturally returns to in time of burden. Though Zatanna and Harley Quinn are also present in the Jewish Quarter, they don't join the scene to make their own connection to Judaism.

Miriam goes on to tell Kate, "The Reich, they want me to hate that I am a Jew. But I am proud. What they think is a shameful thing is what makes me strong."[102] The sentiment of Judaism as a source of strength echoes in larger ways through the story. In the next issue, Miriam invokes the names of Shiphrah, Huldah, Abigail, Zipporah, Asaneth, and Miriam, and quite literally finds power from them when she transforms into the superhero Miri Marvel with the acronym of their names—SHAZAM.[103]

With Miriam's help, the Jewish Quarter is evacuated. Together she, Zatanna, and Raven cast a spell transporting not only the heroines but the Jews in Berlin to the coast of France, where Aquawoman delivers them to refuge in Atlantis. In issue #53, Aquawoman splits the sea to allow the heroines and refugees passage to the underwater city in a scene that deliberately evokes the parting of the Red Sea by Moses—complete with enemy soldiers chasing them and being held off by Zatanna and Poison Ivy as Batwoman, Raven, and Harley Quinn rush everyone else toward safety.[104]

Miriam is a supporting character and largely disappears from the series after this, but in *DC Comics: Bombshells* #79 we learn the backstory of another Jewish heroine, the sorceress Raven. In main continuity, Raven of the Teen Titans is the daughter of Trigon, a demon intent on taking over the world. In *Bombshells,* he is reimagined as a horned mountain spirit and

Raven's mother, Azaria, as the daughter of a rabbi. Raven says of her parents, "My father was a monster, but my mother's love made him a man. [. . .] my mother believed that love redeemed . . . that love saved. That in their love of me I had saved them both."[105] Despite her father being a rabbi, Azaria espouses Christian philosophy in her belief of redemptive love and an emphasis on being "saved." Christian writer Melva Henderson describes this belief: "Redemptive love is the highest form of love. It recognizes that judgment is due, but instead releases mercy [. . .]. One walking in redemptive love isn't consumed with what they receive in return when they choose to forgive someone. They view their willingness to release love as an offering or investment, leaving the return on their investment to God."[106]

In contrast to redemptive love, Judaism places the emphasis not on the person offering forgiveness but on the one seeking it. The Mishnah Yoma 8:9 teaches us, "With regard to one who says: I will sin and Yom Kippur [the Day of Atonement] will atone for my sins, Yom Kippur does not atone for his sins. Furthermore, for transgressions between a person and God, Yom Kippur atones; however, for transgressions between a person and another, Yom Kippur does not atone until he appeases the other person."[107] Teshuvah—repentance—consists not only of remorse and seeking forgiveness but, more crucially, undoing harm already done and no longer committing harm.

More harmful Christian ideas leak into Raven's writing elsewhere in *Bombshells*. In most of his designs Trigon has horns or antlers—here, a pair of horns reminiscent of a Cashmere goat. The collectible statue that inspired the design for Raven in *Bombshells* features a blue headband with a pair of short blue horns. For most of the comic this headband is purely ornamental, and in some scenes, we see Raven without it, revealing her bare and entirely human-looking head. At times, however, Raven releases her full power—once while under a curse and again later of her own will—and grows massive horns longer than the span of her shoulders, such as in *DC Comics: Bombshells* #96 and #97.[108] This design is particularly frustrating given that in other comics where she is written as a gentile, Raven is rarely given horns or antlers, instead showing her demonic nature through oddly colored skin, hair, and eyes.

Like many anti-Semitic myths, the "horned Jew" is an old one. Artists like Michelangelo sculpted the shared figure Moses with horns in the sixteenth century, but in isolated areas the myth persists into the twenty-first century. In 2015—two years before *DC Comics: Bombshells* #96 was published—writer Esther Mendelsohn wrote, "I think I was the first Jew to set foot in the quaint Yorkshire village where I studied since, oh, 1922? Although no one actually asked me, I did get many suspicious glances in the direction of my curly black hair (perfect for concealing horns . . .). Only once, though, did someone have the courage to actually sneak up on me and run her fingers quickly across my scalp, saying nervously—'just checking, just checking!'"[109] Anecdotally I've heard stories of Jews being asked about their horns as recently as the 1990s, and in rural areas all across the United States including Texas and New England. Although *Bombshells* removes the direct connection of Jews as demons by making Raven's father, Trigon, a nature spirit, it still contributes to the demonization of Jews by giving Raven horns.

In all its one hundred issues, *DC Comics: Bombshells* only gives a single moment of Jewish ritual to its characters—the Shabbat dinner. Its host, Miriam Batzel, the learned and observant Jew, is a supporting character beside the starring Wonder Woman, Batwoman, Zatanna, Aquawoman, and Supergirl. Zatanna is established as Jewish and Romani in *DC Comics: Bombshells* #18, but her relationship to neither culture is given any weight.[110] Instead, it is treated as a reason for her to be blackmailed and in hiding. In one scene, in *DC Comics: Bombshells* #53 a Nazi calls her a "little Jew-Gypsy bitch."[111] The willingness to use the derogatory "Gypsy" (after Zatanna identifies herself using the word *Romani* in #18) alongside the self identifier "Jew" leads the reader to one of three conclusions: *Bombshells* is either minimizing anti-Romanyism, unwilling to show anti-Semitism, or views the word *Jew* on level with the word *Gypsy*. Andrea Gruenmont is a minor character, but she shares issues with Zatanna and Raven—like Baruch of "Berlin Batman," her Judaism acts as a motivator for her to fight the villainous Nazis and has no meaning beyond that.

Not only do "Berlin Batman" and *Bombshells* minimize their characters' Judaism, but it is also notable that they share the setting of World War II. Through Elseworlds and universe travel Batman characters have been in stories with dozens of settings—the Wild West, the 853rd century, the Golden Age of Sail, medieval-esque fantasy worlds, and even an alternate history where the American Revolution never happened. Out of all of these worlds, the two to most prominently feature Judaism are both set during World War II. This reflects and reinforces the gentile perception of the Holocaust as the only time Jewish history is worth studying and the only time anti-Semitism was prominent. There are no Batman stories about the Spanish Inquisition, the Jewish Enlightenment, or Radhanite merchants of the Middle Ages. In stories set in such times, our presence is absent, a quietly gaping hole in the gentile view of Judaism.

CONCLUSION

This gap in the gentile writing of Judaism applies to cultural aspects as well. When examining the Jewish influence on Golden Age–era comics and stories like "Perpetual Morning"—which have no explicitly Jewish characters—in contrast to stories like *Batwoman* and *Ragman*, one trend becomes clear: comic books allow the presence of Jews disconnected from their heritage or Judaism disconnected from its members. The same holds true for other cultural groups. Nightwing's Romani heritage is mentioned so little that I have seen fans claim canon was changed when a writer used it for flavor text. Cassandra Cain seems deliberately designed to be accessible to white writers as she was raised exclusively by her white father, with her mother spending decades on the page before being specified as Chinese. These characters and their failures emphasize the need for diversity not only in writers but also in artists and editors. Although the push for diverse voices in both the novel and comic book industries continues, the gentile view of Judaism as a religion with little consequence on perspective or everyday life leaves us behind. Comic books are a collaborative medium, and an educated Jew in any position on a creative team can help create a more authentic and meaningful story. This could include a writer mentioning the High Holy Days, an artist drawing a mezuzah, or an editor catching a mistake. Moreover, the industry must foster a culture where members of a creative team work together and are comfortable correcting mistakes and hiring outside consultants.

Still, even in a world of Christianized superheroes, there remains hope: in *Detective Comics* #1033,[112] the last issue published in 2020, Bruce Wayne visits Alfred Pennyworth's grave, and, on the headstone of a gentile buried in a Christian cemetery, sets a stone as in Jewish tradition. For one moment, in one issue, for one writer, Batman is Jewish.

NOTES

1. Roy Schwartz, *Is Superman Circumcised?* (Jefferson, NC: McFarland, 2021), 22.

2. Simcha Weinstein, *Up Up and Oy Vey* (Fort Lee, NJ: Barricade Books, 2006), 14.

3. Paul Dini (w) and Rick Burchett (a), "Oy to the World," *Batgirl Adventures* #1 (New York: DC Comics, 1997).

4. Paul Dini (w) and Yivel Guichet (a), "Harley Quinn," *Batman: Harley Quinn* #1 (New York: DC Comics, 1999).

5. Tim Sheridan (w) and Mike Norton (a), "The Haunting of Titans Tower," *Teen Titans Academy* #8 (Burbank: DC Comics, 2021).

6. Greg Rucka (w) and J. H. Williams III (a), "GO, Part Two," *Detective Comics* #859 (New York: DC Comics, 2009).

7. Geoff Johns, Grant Morrison, Greg Rucka, and Mark Waid (w), and Keith Giffen and Ken Lashley (a), "Going Down," *52 #7* (New York: DC Comics, 2006).

8. Geoff Johns, Grant Morrison, Greg Rucka, and Mark Waid (w), and Keith Giffen and Ken Lashley (a), "The Most Wonderful Time of the Year," *52 #33* (New York: DC Comics, 2006).

9. Geoff Johns, Grant Morrison, Greg Rucka, and Mark Waid (w), and Keith Giffen and Ken Lashley (a), "Beyond the Black Stump," *52* #28 (New York: DC Comics, 2006).

10. Deut. 30:19, *Tanakh: The Holy Scriptures* (Philadelphia: Jewish Publication Society, 1985).

11. "Free Will in Judaism 101," *My Jewish Learning*, accessed January 25, 2022, www.myjewishlearning.com/article/free-will-in-judaism-101.

12. John Calvin, *The Humble Advice of the Assembly of Divines* (Edinburgh: Evan Tyler, 1647).

13. Greg Rucka (w) and J.H. Williams III (a), "Elegy, Part Four: Rubato!" *Detective Comics* #857 (New York: DC Comics, 2009).

14. Rucka and Williams, "GO, Part Two."

15. Greg Rucka (w) and J. H. Williams III (a), "GO, Part Three," *Detective Comics* #860 (New York: DC Comics, 2009).

16. "The Ten Sefirot of the Kabbalah," *Jewish Virtual Library*, accessed January 25, 2022, www.jewishvirtuallibrary.org/the-ten-sefirot-of-the-kabbalah.

17. Rucka and Williams, "GO, Part Three."

18. Sanhedrin 4:5 (William Davidson Edition, Sefaria, 2017).

19. Kelley Puckett (w) and Damion Scott (a), "Nobody Dies Tonight," *Batgirl* #19 (New York: DC Comics, 2001).

20. Devin Grayson (w) and Mike Lilly (a), "The Ride's Over," *Nightwing* #100 (New York: DC Comics, 2004).

21. Bill Finger (w) and Bob Kane (a), "Blackbeard's Crew and the Yacht Society," *Batman* #4 (New York, Detective Comics, Inc, 1940).

22. Geoff Johns, Grant Morrison, Greg Rucka, and Mark Waid (w), and Keith Giffen and Ken Lashley (a), "Batwoman Begins!" *52* #11 (New York: DC Comics, 2006).

23. Rucka and Williams, "Elegy, Part Four."

24. James Tynion IV (w) and Jesús Merino (a), "Fall of the Batmen, Finale," *Detective Comics* #973 (Burbank: DC Comics, 2018).

25. Marguerite Bennett and James Tynion IV (w) and Steve Epting (a), "The Many Arms of Death, Part 1: Sinnerman," *Batwoman* #1 (Burbank: DC Comics, 2017).

26. Jesse Schedeen, "Detective Comics Writer Reflects on the Fate of Red Robin Tim Drake," *IGN*, October 25, 2016, www.ign.com/articles/2016/10/25/detective-comics-writer-reflects-on-the-death-of-red-robin-tim-drake.

27. Marguerite Bennett (w) and Fernando Blanco (a), "Stay High," *Batwoman* #9 (Burbank: DC Comics, 2017).

28. Marguerite Bennett (w) and Fernando Blanco (a), "Wonderland," *Batwoman* #8 (Burbank: DC Comics, 2017).

29. Marguerite Bennett (w) and Fernando Blanco (a), "The Fall of the House of Kane, Part Two," *Batwoman* #14 (Burbank: DC Comics, 2018).

30. Henry Abramson, "History Shows That Epidemics Can Carry Dangerous Side Effects for Jews: Deadly Anti-Semitism," *JTA,* March 6, 2020. www.jta.org/2020/03/06/opinion/history-shows-that-epidemics-can-carry-dangerous-side-effects-for-jews-deadly-anti-semitism.

31. Bennett, Marguerite (w) and Blanco, Fernando (a), "The Fall of the House of Kane, Finale," *Batwoman* #16 (Burbank: DC Comics, 2018).

32. Bennett, Tynion, and Epting.

33. Marc Andreyko (w), Trevor McCarthy, Andrea Mutti, Patrick Oliffe, and Jim Fern (a), " . . . Or High Water," *Batwoman* #25 (New York: DC Comics, 2013).

34. Andreyko, et al.

35. James Tynion IV (w) and Álvaro Martínez Bueno (a), "The Trial of Batwoman," *Detective Comics* #975 (Burbank: DC Comics, 2018).

36. James Tynion IV (w) and Álvaro Martínez Bueno (a), "Rise of the Batmen, Part Six: The Thin Red Line," *Detective Comics* #939 (Burbank: DC Comics, 2016).

37. Andreyko, et al.

38. Max Allan Collins (w) and Dave Cockrum (a), "Two of a Kind," *Batman* #410 (New York: DC Comics, 1987).

39. Chuck Dixon (w) and Jason Armstrong (a), "Year One," *Robin Annual* #4 (New York: DC Comics, 1995).

40. Dixon and Armstrong.

41. Dixon and Armstrong.

42. Taanit. 7a:12.

43. Jeff Lemire (w) and Dustin Nguyen (a), "Chapter 1," *Robin & Batman* #1 (Burbank: DC Comics, 2021).

44. Jeff Lemire (w) and Dustin Nguyen (a), "Chapter 3," *Robin & Batman* #3 (Burbank: DC Comics, 2022).

45. Lemire and Nguyen, "Chapter 3."

46. Gen. 25.27.

47. *Pirkei Avot* 4:1, "The Sayings of the Jewish Fathers: Gorfinkle 1913" (Cincinnati: Bloch, 1913).

48. Prov. 16, "The Sayings of the Jewish Fathers: Gorfinkle 1913" (Cincinnati: Bloch, 1913).

49. Scott Snyder (w) and Greg Capullo (a), "The Talons Strike!" *Batman* #7 (New York: DC Comics, 2012).

50. Ted McKeever, "Perpetual Morning," *Batman: Black and White* #1 (New York: DC Comics, 1996).

51. Sanhedrin 4:5.

52. McKeever.

53. McKeever.

54. "Is It a Bird? Is It a Plane? No, It's a Jewish Superhero," *The JC,* November 26, 2010, www.thejc.com/culture/features/is-it-a-bird-is-it-a-plane-no-it-s-a-jewish-superhero-1.19667.

55. Robert Loren Fleming (w) and Keith Giffen (w and a), "The Folktale," *Ragman* #3 (New York: DC Comics: 1991).

56. Doug Moench (w) and Kelley Jones (a), "Suit of Evil Souls," *Batman* #551 (New York: DC Comics, 1997).

57. Lev. 19:31.

58. Lev. 20:6.

59. Keritot (Excisions) 3b:28.

60. Moench and Jones, "Suit of Evil Souls."

61. Ray Fawkes (w) and Inaki Miranda (a), "Return Fire," *Ragman* #1 (Burbank: DC Comics, 2017).

62. Ray Fawkes (w) and Inaki Miranda (a), "S.N.A.F.U.," *Ragman* #3 (Burbank: DC Comics, 2017).

63. Fleming and Giffen, "The Folktale."

64. Moench and Jones, "Suit of Evil Souls."

65. Doug Moench (w) and Kelley Jones (a), "The Greatest Evil," *Batman* #552 (New York: DC Comics, 1997).

66. Moench and Jones, "The Greatest Evil."

67. Moench and Jones, "The Greatest Evil."

68. Ray Fawkes (w) and Inaki Miranda (a), "Cavalry," *Ragman* #4 (Burbank: DC Comics, 2018).

69. Ray Fawkes (w) and Inaki Miranda (a), "Hearts and Minds," *Ragman* #5 (Burbank: DC Comics, 2018).

70. Fawkes and Miranda, "Return Fire."

71. Julian Voloj, "Whistle, Gotham City's Latest Superhero, Is Jewish. It's a Full-circle Moment for the Comics Industry," *Jewish Telegraph Agency*, September 17, 2021, www.jta.org/2021/09/17/culture/whistle-gotham-citys-latest-superhero-is -jewish-its-a-full-circle-moment-for-the-comics-industry.

72. "Introducing the Villains of E. Lockhart's *Whistle: A New Gotham City Hero*." *DC Comics,* August 27, 2021. www.dccomics.com/blog/2021/08/27/exclusive-first -look-at-the-villains-of-e-lockharts-whistle-a-new-gotham-city-hero.

73. E. Lockhart (w) and Manuel Preitano (a), *Whistle: A New Gotham City Hero* (Burbank: DC Comics, 2021).

74. Lockhart and Preitano.

75. Lockhart and Preitano.

76. Jonathan Hornstein, "Jewish Poverty in the United States: A Summary of Recent Research," *FedWeb,* 2019, cdn.fedweb.org/fed-42/2892/jewish-poverty-in-the-united-states%2520Weinberg%2520Report.pdf

77. Hornstein, 7.

78. Lockhart and Preitano.

79. Paul Pope, "Berlin Batman," *Batman Chronicles* #11 (New York: DC Comics, 1997).

80. Pope.

81. Pope.

82. "'Degenerate' Art," *United States Holocaust Memorial Museum,* June 8, 2020, encyclopedia.ushmm.org/content/en/article/degenerate-art-1.

83. "'Degenerate' Art."

84. "Antisemitic Legislation 1933–1939," *United States Holocaust Memorial Museum*, accessed February 10, 2022, encyclopedia.ushmm.org/content/en/article/ antisemitic-legislation-1933–1939.

85. "Buchenwald," *United States Holocaust Memorial Museum*, accessed February 10, 2022, encyclopedia.ushmm.org/content/en/article/buchenwald.

86. "Antisemitic Legislation 1933–1939."

87. "Anti-Jewish Legislation in Prewar Germany," *United States Holocaust Memorial Museum*, accessed February 9, 2022, encyclopedia.ushmm.org/content/en/article/anti-jewish-legislation-in-prewar-germany.

88. Pope.

89. Pope.

90. "Book Burning," *United States Holocaust Memorial Museum,* accessed February 10, 2022, encyclopedia.ushmm.org/content/en/article/book-burning.

91. Marguerite Bennett, "Live Q&A w/ Comic Writer Marguerite Bennett, Monday 10/28 2:30–3:30 pm PST!" Clubs & Eents/Q&As, *DC Universe Infinite forum,* October 28, 2019, community.dcuniverseinfinite.com/t/live-q-a-w-comic-writer-marguerite-bennett-monday-10–28–230pm-pst/101079/45?page=3.

92. "Bombshells: Enlisted," *Reading Art* (blog), April 8, 2021, readingartreviews.wordpress.com/2021/04/08/bombshells-enlisted.

93. Marguerite Bennett (w) and Sandy Jarrell (a), "The Battle of Berlin Part 1," *DC Comics: Bombshells* #49 (Burbank: DC Comics, 2016).

94. Marguerite Bennett (w) and Marguerite Sauvage (a), "American Soil Part 1" *Bombshells United* #1 (Burbank: DC Comics, 2017).

95. Marguerite Bennett (w) and Mirka Andolfo (a), "Combat Part 2," *DC Comics: Bombshells* #11 (Burbank: DC Comics, 2015).

96. Marguerite Bennett (w) and Ming Doyle (a), "Combat Part 4," *DC Comics: Bombshells* #13 (Burbank: DC Comics, 2015).

97. Marguerite Bennett (w) and Marguerite Sauvage (a), "Allies and Enemies Part 8," *DC Comics: Bombshells* #29 (Burbank: DC Comics, 2016).

98. Bennett and Sauvage, "Allies and Enemies Part 8."

99. Marguerite Bennett (w) and Sandy Jarrell (a), "The Battle of Berlin Part 1," *DC Comics: Bombshells* #49 (Burbank: DC Comics, 2016).

100. Bennett and Jarrell.

101. Griffin, "Jewish Reclamation, Batwoman, and Bombshells," *The Fandomentals,* August 23, 2016, www.thefandomentals.com/jewish-reclamation-batwoman-bombshells.

102. Bennett and Jarrell.

103. Bennett and Andolfo, "The Battle of Berlin Part 2."

104. Marguerite Bennett (w) and Mirka Andolfo (a), "The Battle of Berlin Part 5," *DC Comics: Bombshells* #53 (Burbank: DC Comics, 2016).

105. Marguerite Bennett (w) and Mirka Andolfo (a), "The Death of Illusion Part 1," *DC Comics: Bombshells* #79 (Burbank: DC Comics, 2017).

106. Melva Henderson "Redemptive Love," Justbetweenus.org, Just Between Us Magazine, accessed March 10, 2022 justbetweenus.org/christian-relationship-advice/healthy-relationships/redemptive-love/

107. Mishna Yoma 8:9.

108. Marguerite Bennett (w), Laura Braga and Aneke (a), *DC Comics: Bombshells* #96–97 (Burbank: DC Comics, 2017).

109. Esther Mendelsohn, "Orthodoxy at University," *Aish*, July 5, 2015, aish.com/orthodoxy-at-university.

110. Marguerite Bennett (w) and Maria-Laura Sanapo (a), "Combat Part 9," *DC Comics: Bombshells* #18 (Burbank, DC Comics, 2015).

111. Bennett and Andolfo, "The Battle of Berlin Part 5."

112. Peter Tomasi (w) and Brad Walker (a). "Shut Out the Light," *Detective Comics* #1033 (Burbank: DC Comics, 2020).

WORKS CITED

Abramson, Henry. "History Shows That Epidemics Can Carry Dangerous Side Effects for Jews: Deadly Anti-Semitism." *JTA*, March 6, 2020. www.jta.org/2020/03/06/opinion/history-shows-that-epidemics-can-carry-dangerous-side-effects-for-jews-deadly-anti-semitism.

"Anti-Jewish Legislation in Prewar Germany." *United States Holocaust Memorial Museum.* Accessed February 9, 2022. encyclopedia.ushmm.org/content/en/article/anti-jewish-legislation-in-prewar-germany.

"Antisemitic Legislation 1933–1939." *United States Holocaust Memorial Museum.* Accessed February 10, 2022. encyclopedia.ushmm.org/content/en/article/antisemitic-legislation-1933–1939.

Bennett, Marguerite. "Live Q&A w/ Comic Writer Marguerite Benett, Monday 10/28 2:30–3:30 pm PST!" Clubs & Eents/Q&As. *DC Universe Infinite Forum,* October 28, 2019. community.dcuniverseinfinite.com/t/live-q-a-w-comic-writer-marguerite-bennett-monday-10–28–230pm-pst/101079/45?page=3

Bennett, Marguerite (w) and Fernando Blanco (a). "Stay High," *Batwoman* #9. Burbank: DC Comics, 2017.

Bennett, Marguerite (w) and Fernando Blanco (a). "The Fall of the House of Kane, Part Two," *Batwoman* #14. Burbank: DC Comics, 2018.

Bennett, Marguerite (w) and Fernando Blanco (a). "Wonderland," *Batwoman* #8. Burbank: DC Comics, 2017.

Bennett, Marguerite (w) and Marguerite Sauvage (a). "Allies and Enemies part 8," *DC Comics: Bombshells.* Burbank: DC Comics, 2016.

Bennett, Marguerite (w) and Marguerite Sauvage (a). "American Soil Part 1," *Bombshells United* #1. Burbank: DC Comics, 2017.

Bennett, Marguerite (w) and Maria-Laura Sanapo (a), "Combat Part 9," *DC Comics: Bombshells* #18 (Burbank: DC Comics, 2015).

Bennett, Marguerite (w) and Ming Doyle (a) "Combat Part 4," *DC Comics: Bombshells* #13 Burbank: DC Comics, 2015.

Bennett, Marguerite (w) and Mirka Andolfo (a). "The Battle of Berlin Part 2," *DC Comics: Bombshells* #50. Burbank: DC Comics, 2016.

Bennett, Marguerite (w) and Mirka Andolfo (a). "The Battle of Berlin Part 5," *DC Comics: Bombshells* #53. Burbank: DC Comics, 2016.

Bennett, Marguerite (w) and Mirka Andolfo (a). "Combat, Part 2," *DC Comics: Bombshells* #11. Burbank: DC Comics, 2015.

Bennett, Marguerite (w) and Mirka Andolfo (a). "The Death of Illusion Part 1," *DC Comics: Bombshells* #79. Burbank: DC Comics, 2017.

Bennett, Marguerite (w) and Sandy Jarrell (a). "The Battle of Berlin Part 1," *DC Comics: Bombshells* #49. Burbank: DC Comics, 2016.

Bennett, Marguerite, James Tynion IV (w), and Steve Epting (a). "The Many Arms of Death, Part 1: Sinnerman." *Batwoman* #1. Burbank: DC Comics, 2017.

Bennett, Marquerite (w), Laura Braga and Aneke (a). *DC Comics: Bombshells* #96–97. Burbank: DC Comics, 2017.

"Book Burning." *United States Holocaust Memorial Museum.* Accessed February 10, 2022. encyclopedia.ushmm.org/content/en/article/book-burning.

"Buchenwald." *United States Holocaust Memorial Museum.* Accessed February 10, 2022. encyclopedia.ushmm.org/content/en/article/buchenwald.

Calvin, John. *The Humble Advice of the Assembly of Divines.* Edinburgh: Evan Tyler, 1647. quod.lib.umich.edu/cgi/t/text/text-idx?c=eebo2;idno=A96226.0001.001

Collins, Max Allan (w) and Dave Cockrum (a). "Two of a Kind." *Batman* #410. New York: DC Comics, 1987.

"'Degenerate' Art." *United States Holocaust Memorial Museum.* June 8, 2020. encyclopedia.ushmm.org/content/en/article/degenerate-art-1.

Dini, Paul (w) and Rick Burchett (a). "Oy to the World," *Batgirl Adventures* #1. New York: DC Comics, 1997.

Dini, Paul (w) and Yvel Guichet (a). "Harley Quinn," *Batman: Harley Quinn* #1. New York: DC Comics, 1999.

Dixon, Chuck (w) and Jason Armstrong (a). "Year One," *Robin Annual* #4. New York: DC Comics, 1995.

Fawkes, Ray (w) and Inaki Miranda (a). "Cavalry," *Ragman* #4. Burbank: DC Comics 2018.

Fawkes, Ray (w) and Inaki Miranda (a). "Hearts and Minds," *Ragman* #5. Burbank: DC Comics 2018.

Fawkes, Ray (w) and Inaki Miranda (a). "Return Fire," *Ragman* #1. Burbank: DC Comics, 2017.

Fawkes, Ray (w) and Inaki Miranda (a). "S.N.A.F.U.," *Ragman* #3. Burbank: DC Comics, 2017.

Finger, Bill (w) and Bob Kane (a). "Blackbeard's Crew and the Yacht Society," *Batman* #4. New York, Detective Comics, Inc, 1940.

Fleming, Robert Loren (w) and Keith Giffen (w and a). "The Folktale," *Ragman* #3. New York: DC Comics: 1991.

"Free Will in Judaism 101." *My Jewish Learning.* Accessed January 25, 2022. www.myjewishlearning.com/article/free-will-in-judaism-101.

Grayson, Devin (w) and Mike Lilly (a). "The Ride's Over," *Nightwing* #100. New York: DC Comics, 2004.

Griffin. "Jewish Reclamation, Batwoman, and Bombshells." *The Fandomentals,* August 23, 2016. www.thefandomentals.com/jewish-reclamation-batwoman-bombshells.

Henderson, Melva. "Redemptive Love." *Just Between Us Magazine,* accessed March 10, 2022. justbetweenus.org/christian-relationship-advice/healthy-relationships/redemptive-love.

Hornstein, Jonathan. "Jewish Poverty in the United States: A Summary of Recent Research." *Fedweb,* 2019. cdn.fedweb.org/fed-42/2892/jewish-poverty-in-the-united-states%2520Weinberg%2520Report.pdf

"Introducing the Villains of E. Lockhart's *Whistle: A New Gotham City Hero.*" *DC Comics*, August 27, 2021. www.dccomics.com/blog/2021/08/27/exclusive-first-look-at-the-villains-of-e-lockharts-whistle-a-new-gotham-city-hero.

"Is It a Bird? Is It a Plane? No, It's a Jewish Superhero." *The JC,* November 26, 2010. www.thejc.com/culture/features/is-it-a-bird-is-it-a-plane-no-it-s-a-jewish-superhero-1.19667.

Johns, Geoff, Grant Morrison, Greg Rucka, and Mark Waid (w), and Keith Giffen and Ken Lashley (a). "Batwoman Begins!" *52* #11. New York: DC Comics, 2006.

Johns, Geoff, Grant Morrison, Greg Rucka, and Mark Waid (w), and Keith Giffen and Ken Lashley (a). "Beyond the Black Stump," *52* #28. New York: DC Comics, 2006.

Johns, Geoff, Grant Morrison, Greg Rucka, and Mark Waid (w), and Keith Giffen and Ken Lashley (a). "Going Down," *52* #7. New York: DC Comics, 2006.

Johns, Geoff, Grant Morrison, Greg Rucka, and Mark Waid (w), and Keith Giffen and Ken Lashley (a). "The Most Wonderful Time of the Year," *52* #33. New York: DC Comics, 2006.

JPS Tanakh: The Holy Scriptures. Philadelphia: Jewish Publication Society, 1985.

Lemire, Jeff (w) and Dustin Nguyen (a). "Chapter 1," *Robin & Batman* #1. Burbank: DC Comics, 2021.

Lemire, Jeff (w) and Dustin Nguyen (a). "Chapter 3," *Robin & Batman* #3. Burbank: DC Comics, 2022.

Lockhart, E. (w) and Manuel Preitano (a). *Whistle: A New Gotham City Hero.* Burbank: DC Comics, 2021.

McKeever, Ted. "Perpetual Morning," *Batman: Black and White* #1. New York: DC Comics, 1996.

Mendelsohn, Esther. "Orthodoxy at University." *Aish,* July 5, 2015. aish.com/orthodoxy-at-university.

Moench, Doug (w) and Kelley Jones (a). "The Greatest Evil," *Batman* #552. New York: DC Comics, 1997.

Moench, Doug (w) and Kelley Jones (a). "Suit of Evil Souls," *Batman* #551. New York: DC Comics, 1997.

Pope, Paul. "Berlin Batman," *Batman Chronicles* #11. New York: DC Comics, 1997.

Puckett, Kelley (w) and Damion Scott (a). "Nobody Dies Tonight," *Batgirl* #19. New York: DC Comics, 2001.

Rucka, Greg (w) and J. H. Williams III (a). "Elegy, Part Four: Rubato!" *Detective Comics* #857. New York: DC Comics. 2009.

Rucka, Greg (w) and J. H. Williams III (a). "GO, Part Three," *Detective Comics* #860. New York: DC Comics, 2009.

Rucka, Greg (w) and J. H. Williams III (a). "GO, Part Two," *Detective Comics* #859. New York: DC Comics, 2009.

"The Sayings of the Jewish Fathers: Gorfinkle 1913." Translated and edited by Joseph I. Gorfinkle. Cincinnati: Bloch, 1913. Project Gutenberg, 2005. www.gutenberg .org/cache/epub/8548/pg8548.html.

Schedeen, Jesse. "Detective Comics Writer Reflects on the Fate of Red Robin Tim Drake." *IGN,* October 25, 2016. www.ign.com/articles/2016/10/25/detective-com-ics-writer-reflects-on-the-death-of-red-robin-tim-drake.

Schwartz, Roy. *Is Superman Circumcised?* Jefferson, NC: McFarland, 2021.

Sheridan, Tim (w) and Mike Norton (a). "The Haunting of Titans Tower," *Teen Titans Academy* #8. Burbank: DC Comics, 2021.

Snyder, Scott (w) and Greg Capullo (a). "The Talons Strike!" *Batman* #7. New York: DC Comics, 2012.

Steinsaltz, Adin Een-Israel, ed. and trans. *William Davidson Talmud.* Sefaria, 2017. www.sefaria.org/Mishnah_Sanhedrin.4.5?ven=William_Davidson_Edition.

"The Ten Sefirot of the Kabbalah." *Jewish Virtual Library.* Accessed January 25, 2022. www.jewishvirtuallibrary.org/the-ten-sefirot-of-the-kabbalah.

Tomasi, Peter (w) and Brad Walker (a). "Shut Out the Light," *Detective Comics* #1033. Burbank: DC Comics, 2020.

Tynion IV, James (w) and Álvaro Martínez Bueno (a). "Rise of the Batmen, Part Six: The Thin Red Line," *Detective Comics* #939. Burbank: DC Comics, 2016.

Tynion IV, James (w) and Álvaro Martínez Bueno (a). "The Trial of Batwoman," *Detective Comics* #975. Burbank: DC Comics, 2018.

Tynion IV, James (w) and Jesús Merino (a). "Fall of the Batmen, Finale," *Detective Comics* #973. Burbank: DC Comics, 2018.

Voloj, Julian. "Whistle, Gotham City's Latest Superhero, Is Jewish. It's a Full-circle Moment for the Comics Industry." *Jewish Telegraph Agency,* September 17, 2021. www.jta.org/2021/09/17/culture/whistle-gotham-citys-latest-superhero-is-jewish -its-a-full-circle-moment-for-the-comics-industry.

Weinstein, Simcha. *Up Up and Oy Vey.* Fort Lee, NJ: Barricade Books, 2006.

Chapter Six

Have Onscreen Superheroes Lost Their Faith?

Considering Marvel, Magneto, the Arrowverse, and Harley Quinn

Valerie Estelle Frankel

Basically, all DC and Marvel superheroes, when each studio first started, were created by Jews. Superman, Batman, Black Canary, Green Lantern, Sheena (as well as equally famous villains like Lex Luthor, the Joker, and Catwoman), and then at Marvel Captain America, Spider-Man, the Fantastic Four, the X-Men, and all the Avengers.

However, Jews were trying to blend in and minimize difference. While some characters, especially the X-Men, demanded rights for minorities, they didn't identify as Jewish. A rare exception was *Sergeant Fury and the Howling Commandos*, which included Izzy Cohen on the diverse team. In one of the most memorable instances of covert then overt Judaism, the Thing strongly resembles his creator, Jack Kirby. He's a true outcast using humor to cope and using occasional Yiddishisms. Still, that's as far as it goes.

Decades later, writer Karl Kessel and penciler Stuart Immonen created the *Fantastic Four* comic "Remembrance of Things Past" in 2002, in which the character reveals his Judaism. On being asked if he's ashamed of being a Jew, "Nah, that ain't it," the Thing responds. "Anyone on the Internet can find out, if they want. It's just . . . I don't talk it up, is all. Figure there's enough trouble in this world without people thinkin' Jews are all monsters like me."[1] "However, the realworld reason probably has more to do with the usual conventions of comics until roughly the 1990s, where religion, politics, and other controversial topics were studiously avoided," notes Andrew Alan Smith in *Working-Class Comic Book Heroes*."[2]

Following this pattern, most characters who were introduced as Jewish showed up around the eighties or later: Harley Quinn,[3] Batwoman, Atom Smasher, Seraph, Sy-Borg, Alice Cohen and the Monolith, Doctor Manhattan, Nite Owl, Nyssa Al Ghul, the Hayoth, Dust Devil (DC) (with a few more in *Bombshells* continuity), Kitty Pryde, Moon Knight, Justice, Legion, Sabra, Wiccan, Mettle, Dominic Fortune, Screaming Mimi, Volcana, White Tiger (Kasper Cole), Steve Rogers's girlfriend Bernie Rosenthal, and possibly Magneto's children (Marvel) and other lines' Masada, Fathom, Reuben Flagg, Prime, The Tick's sidekick Arthur, and Sublime. Of course, there are also alt-universe counterparts, family, and occasional friends or even rabbis.

Other preexisting characters "came out" around this time or later, when writers decided the established heroes had Jewish-sounding names or backgrounds: Magneto, Bobby Drake,[4] Colossal Boy, Doc Samson, Ragman, Green Lantern (Hal Jordan), Doctor Fate, Firestorm (Martin Stein), Mr. E, and Sasquatch.

Fast forward to the twenty-first century. The superhero boom is enormous. Films and TV are churning out superheroes as never before. Besides the original creators, there are Jewish writers, directors, and actors throughout the stories. But Jewish characters . . . not so much.

The Arrowverse, as it's often called, including CW shows *Arrow, The Flash, Supergirl, Black Lightning, Legends of Tomorrow,* and *Batwoman,* has a reasonable number of Jews. These include Arrow's love interest and computer expert Felicity Smoak, Rory Regan the Ragman, Professor Stein, and Kate Kane (who, since Batwoman is Batman's cousin and canonically Jewish in comics, has always had fans speculating whether Batman is Jewish too).

Penguin and Sy-Borg on the *Harley Quinn* cartoon (DC Universe/HBO Max, 2020–) are identified as Jewish, complicated by their clichéd villainy. Harley herself, here and on the big screen, has given up any sign of Jewishness, though the cartoon establishes that she was raised in the faith.

Marvel, if it seemed possible, has fewer. There's Magneto. Gertrude Yorke, and presumably her parents, in the Hulu show *Runaways.* Peter B. Parker in *Spider-Man: Into the Spider-Verse* suggests it in his wedding but not dialogue. The Thing, Bobby Drake, and Kitty Pryde, appearing in a number of films, give no indicator either way.

There have been many sensitive and thoughtful Jewish episodes in speculative television: most memorably, Commander Ivanova on *Babylon 5* sits shiva for her father, guided by Theodore Bikel (who inquires whether space fish is kosher). *Penny Dreadful: City of Angels* parallels the rising anti-Semitism of the thirties with the Chicano experience. Simon, a Jewish teen vampire on *Shadowhunters,* spends Yom Kippur hiding his condition from his concerned family even as he struggles with the issue of atonement. Identifiably Jewish characters appear in films from *Spaceballs* to *Independence Day*—to say nothing of Indiana Jones's quest for the Ark of the Covenant. The opportunity is present. However, Jewish moments are scattered and underplayed in this recent era of the onscreen superhero.

MARVEL

The 2018 film *Spider-Man: Into the Spider-Verse* has a flashback to Peter B. Parker and Mary Jane Watson's wedding in which Peter steps on a glass.[5] This suggests (though does not make definitive) that Peter is Jewish, or at least the Peter of his universe. As the writer describes:

> It was just something that I wanted to do. It was kind of a running joke that we had, was me insisting that Peter Parker was Jewish, but we're not really saying—first of all, we're not really saying Peter Parker is Jewish. It could be that MJ is Jewish in this universe. It could be that in an alternate universe, Buddhists step on glass. We don't know. It's an alternate universe. But I mean, I guess when I thought about Stan Lee and Forest Hills and Peter Parker . . . I thought for 15 frames, we can do this.[6]

As less than a minute of Jewish representation, it works as a salute to Spider-Man's creators and his own coding, as he hails from Forest Hills, famously reflects Stan Lee's teen experience, throws in Yiddishisms, and suffers constantly from guilt in the post-Holocaust era.[7]

The 2022 *Moon Knight* series on Disney+ gives its hero multiple marginalizations as a man suffering from dissociative identity disorder with blackouts and trauma, haunted by an Egyptian moon god in London, played by Guatemalan-born Oscar Isaac. (Isaac's Cuban father apparently has Jewish roots that helped supply his middle name of Isaac—his full legal name is Óscar Isaac Hernández Estrada.[8]) The show does address Jewishness with a shiva scene with kippot, despite fans' fears that, with so many other characteristics to explore, this aspect would be left out. Moreover, all these identities combine to offer intersectionality—emphasizing that Jews can have widely varied individualities with many needs to address.

The beloved Hulu teen show *Marvel's Runaways* (2017–2019) features Gertrude Yorkes, who keeps her comics' Jewishness, as do her parents. (The premise is that a group of misfit teens all discover their parents are evil and go on the run, so this series balances the Jewish heroes and villains.) Gertrude is a purple-haired feminist rebel, embracing politics and underdog causes. When one teen insists a bad guy was just following orders, Gert retorts, "Isn't that what the Nazis said?"[9] Her parents are the laughable, awkward hippies of the group, passing around stinky homemade cheese and negotiating awkwardly with the children. In episode four, Alex quips that if they worship the Giborim,[10] he'll be spared the Yorkes' Passover brisket, suggesting that the Yorkes host them all for an unappealing seder.[11] Unlike other onscreen Jewish superheroes, Gert has a romance implied to be within the tribe, as Chase Stein has a suggestive last name. While his religion isn't discussed, he's a jock and popular kid, deconstructing Jewish clichés. By contrast, she's a rebellious feminist intellectual, like many famous Jews. This subtle representation seems to be one almost all Jewish superheroes have going. As critic Noah Bertlasky notes:

> *The Punisher* carries this dynamic to almost parodic extremes in its first season. Just about every major character in the series is Jewish. That includes Joe Bernthal as the Punisher/Frank Castle and Ben Barnes as antagonist Billy Russo. It also includes Amber Rose Revah, whose mother is of Polish-Jewish ancestry, and who plays Dinah Madani, a member of Homeland Security. If these Jewish actors played Jewish characters, *Punisher* would provide strikingly diverse Jewish representation. Frank is a working-class bruiser, oozing testosterone and integrity with a face that looks like a "rough road," as one character quips in the second season. Billy Russo is a slick pretty boy with a ruthless core. Madani is a determined crusader traumatized by violence. She's also a Jewish woman of color—a group almost never represented in the media or entertainment. If these Jewish actors played Jewish characters, "Punisher" would provide strikingly diverse Jewish representation.[12]

Of course, they aren't cast as such—Madani's Iranian American, and Frank is Italian American. Billy's heritage is unstated. As such, the Jewish character is mostly a stereotype, while the toughness and variety go to non-Jews. Punisher in fact is juxtaposed against the Christian fanatic John Pilgrim, suggesting Punisher's own faith is a reflection of this one. The one character identified as Jewish is David Lieberman (Ebon Moss-Bachrach), a government computer programmer who's funny, intense, and brave. He functions as the moral center of the team. As Bertlasky concludes, "He also, though, plays into a lot of stereotypes about nerdy, intellectual unmasculine Jewish men— his nickname is Micro."[13] With all these characters, removing the Judaism and falling into clichés predominate.

MAGNETO

Magneto is the most famous of the Jewish super-characters, though he didn't begin that way. Stan Lee invented him as a simple villain with magnet powers. When the X-Men were reinvented a decade later to be more multi-cultural, they were soon given to Chris Claremont, "a British-born artist and writer whose mother is Jewish, and who was deeply influenced by his work on a kibbutz at which he saw the film *Judgment at Nuremberg,* which moved him deeply."[14] In a description of the *X-Men* series in 1982, Claremont stated: "What we have here, intended or not, is a book about racism, bigotry, and prejudice [. . .]. It's a book about outsiders, about people who are beyond the pale, so to speak [. . .] a story about downtrodden, repressed people fighting to change their situation." As he added, "The Jewish situation is the most obvi-ous genocidal example in the human experience."[15] As Claremont describes, many experiences combined to create Magneto:

> The prosecuting character, Richard Widmark, shows documentary footage of the liberation of Dachau. And I remember in the dining hall, and it was the first time in my life that I ever understood the concept of silence as an active force. It wasn't just the absence of sound, it was all the sound in the room being sucked away. Emotionally. Because, as with the last scene of *Schindler's List,* where you're sitting there watching the movie for three hours, safe in the artifice that this is a movie, that these are actors, it's all special effects, that no matter what Spielberg is doing, you're safe because it's all make-believe. But the minute you get that last scene with the survivors, and the surviving members of the principal cast walking by Oskar Schindler's grave, and putting the stones down, . . . I mean, I was shattered watching it. I couldn't stop crying for about 10 minutes. Because the fourth wall is gone. You then have to sit there and realize that every-thing you have seen happened to these real people. And that you have to accept the reality that what you saw is just a pale reflection of what must have been. Because . . . we know how it ended. When it happened for them, they didn't. And that moment in Israel was sort of epiphanic, in the sense of, "How can you try to convey that?" You know, is there any way to try to convey that—from my own limited experience—to my audience?[16]

A new backstory appeared, in which Magneto and Xavier met in Israel, where they were working with Holocaust survivors. Now Magneto's trauma has taught him why he can never trust humanity. "In the differing responses of Magneto and Professor X to humanity's anti-mutant agitation, one can see the clashing reactions of any minority group to persecution," notes Henry Gonshak in *Hollywood and the Holocaust.*[17] As Claremont adds, "And once I sort of found that point of departure for him, the rest of it all fell into place. Because it allowed me to turn him into a tragic figure, in that his goals were totally admirable. He wants to save his people! His methodology was defined by all that had happened to him."[18]

Most importantly, this Jewishness was not incidental but the source of his origins and motivations. Accordingly, the films, which generally deemphasize religion, depict his origin twice in *X-Men* (2000) and *X-Men: First Class* (2011). The latter also offers a flashback of Hannukah as Erik's cherished memory.[19] In many viewers' first encounter with the X-Men, in indeed, the start of the superhero film renaissance in 2000, a frightened child reaches for his family and warps the gates. "This is the viewer's first introduction to the world of the X-Men—a young Jewish boy in a concentration camp who also happens to be a mutant. More than any other way of potentially introducing the X-Men to movie audiences, this opening scene clearly establishes the thematic connection between the X-Men as a persecuted minority and the Holocaust," explains Rachel Elizabeth Mandel in "From Maus to Magneto: Exploring Holocaust Representation in Comic Books and Graphic Novels."[20] Magneto is not sweet and sentimental like Anne Frank but angry enough to be deadly. Having been shaped in the camps, he uses his power to save his new community from oppression.

In the original film, Magneto has learned to distrust authority, and Congress's campaign against those who are different is all too familiar to him. As he insists, "Mankind has always made laws to protect itself from what it doesn't understand. Laws like your Mutant Registration. . . . Trust me . . . it is only a matter of time before mutants will be herded into camps."[21] As it happens, he's proved right, since armed soldiers invade the school in the sequel and have hunted mutants almost into extinction by *Days of Future Past.* Magneto, his number from Auschwitz on his arm, remarks, "I've heard these arguments before. It was a long time ago."[22] This sentence clearly evokes the prologue and also criticizes modern government programs of marginalization and bigotry. "To Magneto (Ian McKellen), Kelly's registration drive is a replay of the initial steps taken by the Nazis against Holocaust victims such as himself. The lesson Magneto has drawn from his Holocaust experience is that humanity is inherently, irredeemably evil," Gonshak observes.[23] His plan to make the lawmakers into mutants has some logic (in a fantasy of many oppressed people who must wish the tables were turned). However, as Wolverine points out, Magneto is killing innocents to achieve his goal. There is no simple solution to ending prejudice.

In the third film, *X-Men: The Last Stand,* Magneto refuses to get a mutant pride tattoo since he's already been marked in the camps. Once again, his experiences drive his actions, this time with a mutant cure plot:

Mutant Theatre Organizer: This cure is voluntary. Nobody is talking about extermination.

Eric Lensherr: No one ever talks about it. They just do it. And you go on with your lives, ignoring the signs all around you. And then, one day, when the air is still and the night has fallen, they come for you.

Mutant Theatre Organizer: [interrupting] Excuse me, but . . .

Eric Lensherr: It's only that you realize, while you were talking about organizing and committees, the extermination has already begun. Make no mistake, my brothers. They will draw first blood. They will force their cure upon us. The only question is, will you join my brotherhood and fight, or wait for the inevitable genocide? Who will you stand with—the humans . . . or us?[24]

Accordingly, Magneto leads an army to destroy the cure, whoever gets caught in the way. Once again, his methods are violent, but his predictions prove terrifyingly true. His story resonates with viewers of many backgrounds, asking how one should respond to being deprived of rights by the government meant to protect them.

The prequel redeems Magneto by not making him the film's villain. As Gonshak notes, "Merely by dramatizing the early friendship of Magneto and Professor X, *First Class* generates sympathy for Magneto, who is thus portrayed as an inherently good mutant gone bad. Moreover, supplying Magneto with an evil nemesis—the diabolical Shaw—renders his character far more appealing than he is in the first film, where Magneto's only enemy is the noble Professor X."[25]

X-Men: First Class shares the opening sequence at Auschwitz with a gate-bending scene. After he thus displays his mutant powers, Erik is taken to Nazi scientist Dr. Schmidt, a Dr. Mengele analog. He becomes a victim of Schmidt's sadistic experiments to the point where Schmidt murders Erik's mother in front of him, triggering the powers.[26] While the Holocaust is a motive in the first film, this time it's a significant subplot as Erik seeks revenge against Schmidt in the present. He also hunts down and executes Nazi war criminals, having established the justification. Erik finally kills Schmidt over Xavier's protestations, turning from heroism to revenge. With this, he dons the helmet, turning into Magneto.

In *Days of Future Past*, a handful of mutants are kept alive in internment camps, and of these, the last X-Men and their former enemy Magneto concoct a desperate plan to send a single hero back in time and reverse what is happening. In Claremont's comic, it's the tellingly Jewish Kitty Pryde; in the film, it's the more classically heroic Wolverine. If this is the mutant Holocaust prevented, Jewish Kitty's saving her people is a clearer analogy. Further, the original comic emphasizes that, despite Magneto's determination, he and his people have created the very dark future they sought to prevent, even as they failed to teach the next generation what to watch for.[27] Through her experience, Kitty truly understands the terrors of the past, which she can harness to create a better future. Kitty of the comics succeeds, but "the fact that even when this task is completed, the future is uncertain demonstrates the real-world complexity of the issue and the difficulty of changing the many factors that lead to a situation like the Holocaust."[28] As the characters point out that other racists might rise, the comic emphasizes the need for constant vigilance.

The film depicts a more generic apocalypse with fewer Holocaust parallels. Still, the mission—of stopping Mystique from committing a murder that will trigger anti-mutant reprisals—is very reminiscent of the Reichstag Incident. As Professor X pleads with her to find a better path, he shows that the future can be changed through *bechirah*—free will and *teshuva*—repentance. This leaves a Jewish sensibility more subtle but still evident.

In *X-Men: Apocalypse,* Magneto returns to Auschwitz and blasts it into tiny pieces, discovering his power but also making a statement. At the same time, Erik asks, as the Jewish people often did: "Where were you? When my father and mother were slaughtered in this place?"[29] Of course, this continues the poignancy of his onscreen struggle. Apocalypse, the supervillain offering him increased power, calls himself "Elohim" as well as Shen and Ra. As he adds, "I've been called many names over many lifetimes." Nonetheless, all his followers, including Erik, eventually name him a false god and turn on him. False religion may offer power but not enlightenment.

Neither Magneto actor is Jewish, and with no acknowledgment of Kitty or Bobby's religion, this leaves basically the only explicitly Jewish onscreen superhero a villain. Magneto is important, but a balance would be nice.

HARLEY QUINN

In three movies so far, Margot Robbie's Harley never suggests Jewishness by dialogue, flashback, or décor. In her adult cartoon (2019–) Harley finally identifies as Jewish in episode ten, "Bensonhurst," and waves a menorah as candelabra around in "Riddler U" (2.02). Penguin, however, offers a Jewish episode much earlier. Arielle Kaplan notes in her review, "Voiced by Kaley Cuoco and written by Jewish showrunners Justin Halpern, Patrick Schumacker, and their non-Jewish colleague Dean Lorey, we first get a taste of what I'll call 'ironic anti-Semitic comedy' in the second episode of *Harley Quinn.*"[30]

Harley crashes the Penguin's bucktoothed nephew's bar mitzvah at the Gotham Mint, to which most supervillains have been invited. The theme is money, and bags of money are given out as party favors. In fact, the Penguin isn't canonically Jewish. As Kaplan notes, "So the writers went out of their way to reinvent his roots as a money-hungry, hooked-nose super Jewish villain."[31] What's more, Harley could have joked that Penguin was giving Jews a bad name, thus steering the imagery in a different direction instead of leaving it apparently true. Instead, she doesn't say a word. On *Reddit,* Halpern addressed enraged Jewish fans and made this statement:

We honestly thought all of those jokes were super-villain related jokes. Stealing the bag of money, etc. In retrospect I can definitely see where people could infer something different than that, but in the room, five Jewish writers all sat and wrote those jokes and it didn't ring any bells for us.[32]

Mrs. Cobblepot chirps that while she knows everyone at the bar mitzvah is evil, she'd like Harley to watch the bad language (as the lady not only identifies as both Jewish and evil but confirms all their friends are evil too). The Penguin, meanwhile, takes the opportunity to initiate his nephew: "Hey, everybody, let's give it up for Joshua's bar mitzvah, huh? It was very special for me. It was when I realized it was my dream to become a crime lord. Aw. So today, I force that dream on to you." Penguin has planned a mock bank robbery with an improv team and also hands the nephew an umbrella gun to shoot Harley and prove his manhood. Of course, Joshua is too frightened to do it, especially when Harley psyches him out and reveals his lies about his dating prowess to the room. "You're right. I'm not ready," he wails.

His mom chides, "I told you we should've gotten him the dollhouse like he asked, Oswald."

Joshua protests, "It's not a dollhouse! It's an army base with sound effects of real screams and it's the only thing I wanted!"[33] Such a toy is childish and nerdy with a young villain's urge for violence. More stereotypes thus emerge. Certainly, those who attend bar mitzvahs can find humor in the outrageous theme, geeky immature boys, and parody of a manhood ceremony. Still, the actual tropes used don't play well. Poison Ivy ends the episode ignominiously by having to kiss all the gawky thirteen-year-old boys. Further, Joshua appears again, as in episode ten he puts a hit out on Harley out of an immature desire for revenge. All this makes for a violent and over-literal manhood ceremony, along with uncomfortable stereotypes about finances.

At last, Harley's Jewishness is established in episode ten. Her dad is shown as an Irish mobster (another stereotype), while Harley's mom, Shannon, is a stereotypical Jewish mom from Brooklyn who wants her daughter to stop "suckin face with that *goyishe* clown" and marry a Jewish doctor.[34] Harley argues that she *is* a Jewish doctor, but apparently that's not good enough. This one is more clichéd than offensive, but it means Harley's only real Jewish culture shown is negative and judgmental. Elias Rosner notes in his review:

Every single clue up until this moment says that this exchange should never have happened in the way that it did; Harley's mom should be so assimilated that the Joker himself, rather than his non-jewishness, should be the problem. She should not be spouting off the most stereotypical Jewish mother lines out there, with Yiddish no less. While I did laugh, and have played on this trope myself before, *I* don't sit in isolation the way this line does. The joke, which should be just another piece in the theme of parent/child conflict, and a touchstone for NY Jewish comedy, instead reads as incongruous to what we have been led to believe about these characters.

Harley's mom's usage of "*Goyishe*" indicates they are not as cut off as was established; you have to be connected enough, aware enough, to some aspect of the culture to casually drop that Yiddish instead of just saying non-Jew, but that is literally the only marker of Judaism beyond stereotypes in that house. We get a "you never call" but no references to, say, the high holidays, which in my experience would be the bigger insult.[35]

The article goes on at some length on how this line, delivered in a house with no Jewish books, ritual items, or decorations, in a family that cremates their dead son, is very jarring. A family with no trace of Jewish practice, including in its funeral ceremonies, is unlikely to revert to century-old Yiddish while protesting intermarriage.

Instead, the focus of the episode is on Harley rejecting everything her parents stand for; her choosing of Joker and the rejection of her heritage being an extension of that, the latter of which runs into the aforementioned Frankenstein's Monster: what is there to reject if there is nothing there? Harley is not actively rejecting the Judaism of her parents because, aside from one singular moment, it simply doesn't exist.[36]

Harley might have pointed out how hypocritical it is to only value Jewish marriage (which her mother skipped out on) amid so little Jewish practice. This would even explain her lack of Jewish activity through the show. However, she doesn't, and another opportunity for discussion slips by.

Another member of Harley's crew is Sylvester "Sy Borg" Borgman, the elderly Yiddish-accented landlord voiced by Jason Alexander. He is indeed a cyborg (though his once-impressive government technology is now falling apart). Unlike in the comics, he's been made the unscrupulous landlord (another incidental but painful stereotype). His villainy is more hapless, as he finds Harley and her friends in comas and, assuming it's a suicide that will bring down his property rates, plans to incinerate them all. Sy calls his friend Golda. She comes over and suggests they burn the apartment down and take the insurance money, like he's done before, adding, "A little Jewish Lightning never hurt anyone."[37] They laugh. On Reddit, Halpern defends "Jewish lightning": "It was something someone's Jewish grandpa used to say, and it felt like this weird old-timey phrase that for sure is antisemitic, but when appropriated by a Jewish character and written by Jewish writers, felt to us like it was more of a Mr. Burns type joke."[38] Sy and Golda dance around the furnace chanting about cremation. Surely, Boomer-age characters would be more sensitive to Holocaust imagery. As Halpern adds:

> It's a fine line for sure, and for people who felt it crossed that line, I wouldn't want to invalidate those feelings. . . . I can tell you that a big part of being Jewish and dealing with anti-Semitism for me and the other writers, is being able to be self-deprecating and poke fun at ourselves, because in a way that feels empowering and takes the power out of the hands of people who hate Jews.[39]

Certainly, self-deprecating Jewish jokes are a staple, particularly from the Mel Brooks/Woody Allen era. Today, however, the culture has largely moved on from self-aware racist jokes, and the internet was quick to protest.

The characters wake just in time, and Harley holds this over his head to get the rent decreased. Sy eagerly joins her team as it makes him feel alive, though he's often late for everything. He's a former CIA agent and, as it turns out, so was his sister . . . who's been kept in the basement of this abandoned shopping mall because she got turned into an octopus creature, as episode eight reveals. After some denial, Sy finally admits that there "may be a giant tentacle monster in the basement."[40] He lets her out and she destroys the city in an explosion of rage. Once again, the joke here aligns to painful stereotypes, as Rosner notes: "Octopi tend to be used as a symbol of strangulation or control, usually around a globe. It is an age-old symbol that has been used to represent everything from Standard Oil to Stalinism to American Imperialism to, you guessed it, Jews."[41] Further, the sister's illogical, infuriated destruction seems another moment of unreasoning villainy.

Finally, Clayface, a shapeshifting actor, gets in on the Jewish jokes: When distracting the wolf from Red Riding Hood, he disguises himself as "Grandfather Wolf" with a heavy Yiddish accent, prompting Dr. Psycho to ask, "Why is your wolf Jewish?"

"I took a swing," Clayface responds.[42] Considering that Disney's actual Big Bad Wolf was condemned for anti-Semitism, this seems a mark of criticism at them. On the other hand, the original fairytale has anti-Semitic tropes, and Clayface's assuming such a wolf should be Jewish is not a good look for the character, either. All in all, it's a long list of anti-Semitic jokes and tropes for almost the only Jewish superhero show.

DC'S ARROWVERSE

The CW's *Arrow* (2012–2020) has more Jews than are typical for superhero television. Arrow's love interest, Felicity Smoak, earns her wedding by telling off Arrow's alt-world Nazi version. She insists that her grandparents didn't survive the Holocaust for her to stand aside for Nazis in the crossover adventure "Crisis on Earth X."[43] "I hate Nazis" all the heroes chorus when swastikaed villains invade the wedding.[44] At the same time, the atrocities are minimized in favor of shorthanding the villainy. The Earth-X version of Felicity, condemned to a concentration camp in striped pajamas and an authentic yellow star, appears unkempt but fails to convey the actual horrors of the Holocaust. Nazis are convenient villains, with Felicity's heritage giving her added fierceness, but the story skims over the true brutality.

In season five, Ragman joins. In another Holocaust echo, he was the only survivor of a catastrophe that leveled his city . . . and gave him his powers. As he tells villains, "I am the very last living soul of Havenrock . . . and I carry with me a message from all those souls you killed."[45] Despite his anger, he gives up on vengeance to save Arrow's life. When Arrow asks him why, he hesitates. "I don't know. I think it's what my father would have wanted me to do. He saved my life. On Genesis Day, he . . . wrapped me in these rags, said they were ancient, from the time of Devarim, that they would protect me from the fire. And they did. So you see why I have to avenge him."[46]

Adding painful complications for the characters, Felicity caused the tragedy—sacrificing the town by diverting a missile from a more populated target. The show offers this as a source of tension between them. When Rory finds out, he quits, explaining that he's too disturbed by the past to work alongside her, a philosophy many can see reflecting the feelings of some post-Holocaust Jews for the Germans. In episode four, "Penance," Felicity comes to Rory and points out, "Your father was a Gulf War veteran, 2nd Battalion, 1st Marines, but that's not what made him a hero, was it? . . . He wore your rags, his father before him, whose name was also Rory. That's a big legacy to live up to."[47] This salutes the history of the comics as well as Jewish immigration. After some soul-searching, Rory dramatically returns and saves the day. He bargains with Felicity that they both need to give up their guilt.

The difficulty with this character is that he doesn't get more conflict or depth than this initial difficulty. He's a nice character, one who doesn't defy Arrow or turn traitor. He counsels the others on morality from a place of comfortable certainty. However, this lack of conflict doesn't give him much of anywhere to go. Providing a little religious diversity, he lights a menorah in the Christmas episode, "What We Leave Behind" (5.09)—though Felicity does not.[48] The show frames him as a faith warrior, especially during his exit. In "Bratva" (5.12), he stops another nuclear explosion with his rags, insisting he can contain it because "I have faith." Afterward, Felicity greets him with "Oh my God," and Rory quips, "He always gets all the credit," saluting his religion once more.[49] This heroic act wipes out his rags' powers and, after a half-season, he departs. Between the character's minimal arc and his quick departure, there's a lesson that devotion to God is moral but not entirely welcome among the superheroes. Felicity, of Jewish heritage but not practice, is more of an insider.

DC's Legends of Tomorrow has another understated Jew. Nobel Prize–winning physicist Martin Stein with two PhDs joins his powers with a young Black man to create the two-person superhero Firestorm. This split between abstract brain and muscular brawn offers clumsy dual stereotypes, of course. Stein is often out of touch, and when he's given command (deferring to historical characters' expectations for the older white man), he freezes in indecision and quickly passes on the job. When he's finally shot by a Nazi in his third season and then sacrifices himself for his partner, he's buried in a coffin with a Jewish star.

Martin Stein appears observant, as he's even licensed as a rabbi—"My father made me become a rabbi before he would send me to MIT," he notes in "Fast Enough," where he performs a wedding but skips the Hebrew.[50] Like Rory, Martin celebrates Hannukah during the Christmas episode. This involves an ugly Hannukah sweater and a mad race for the last "Cuddle Me Beebo" toy—he joins in on holiday materialism as "Hannukah Oh Hannukah" plays in a lighthearted sequence.[51]

The same franchise added *Batwoman* in 2019. Kate Kane, Batwoman in season one, was reimagined in 2006 comics as a Jewish lesbian and Batman's cousin.[52] The show mentions her Jewishness, though rarely. Like Magneto, a trauma massively defines the character. In this case, it's the car crash that killed her mother and twin sister—on the day Kate and Beth had their bat mitzvahs. This symbolically makes the ceremony a true rite of passage. The crash (though not the ceremony) is shown in a flashback in "Off with Her Head" (1.15), as their mother wishes them Mazel Tov and gives them birth-stone necklaces.[53] However, even with her family members as main characters, Kate's religion rarely appears. The heroine is recast in season two, with a new backstory. In a final send-off, at Kate's funeral, the attendees wear torn ribbons, and her father wears a kippah. They all say "may her memory be a blessing."[54]

DC'S BIG SCREEN TWIST

While heroes on the big screen have never mentioned their Jewishness, Jewish actors often play non-Jewish heroes: "Gal Gadot (Wonder Woman) and Scarlett Johansson (Black Widow) are both Jewish actors with high-profile superhero roles, for example. The fact that their characters aren't Jewish just underlines the extent to which white Jews are treated like any other white ethnic group," Bertlasky notes.[55] In 2017, this changed, as in *Justice League*, Flash specifically mentions he's Jewish when he first meets Batman. His actor, Ezra Miller, is Jewish and apparently ad-libbed the line.[56] This is a new invention, not one supported by the comics, though it is of the character. Bertlasky observes:

> Flash, to some degree, supports this idea that heroes can't be Jewish. The most famous version of Flash in the comics wasn't Jewish; he was a blond, gentile police scientist named Barry Allen. The film's Jewish version is less advanced in his career; he's down on his luck and his dad's in prison. He's also younger, smaller and notably less confident. Miller plays the character with a bit of Woody Allen self-deprecation and a bit of Mel Brooks/Jerry Seinfeld fast talk. He's the Yiddish comic relief.[57]

In the film, Barry is uncertain about heroism—when he admits he's never tried, Batman must talk him into the role.

Likewise, Wonder Woman is not Jewish in the comics (and, unusually among Golden Age superheroes, was not invented by Jews, either). Still, Gal Gadot's identity as Miss Israel (2004), who served in the army as a combat trainer and posts in support of Israel on social media, has linked the identities in many viewers' minds.

Though *Wonder Woman* (2017) is a World War I film, it strongly resonates with Jewish history. Germans are painted as the enemy, engaged in a conquering war that will take over the world. When they invade Diana's island, and American soldier Steve Trevor describes how they're killing civilians, Diana proclaims, "It's our sacred duty to defend the world and I wish to go."[58] This is the Jewish value of Tikun Olam, repairing the world by intervening on the side of good. Diana leaves literal paradise to, as she says, "fight for those who cannot fight for themselves." When she adds "Who will I be if I stay?" viewers hear an echo of Hillel's "If not me, who? If not now, when?"

Diana hopes the war is a matter of manipulation, and she can free both sides. As she believes, the Germans "will be good men again, and the world will be better."[59] In the time leading to World War II, how much must Jews, suddenly forbidden work and bullied by their neighbors, have whispered this at night—these are our friends. We are citizens. Why are they turning against us? Surely soon they'll come to our senses. Surely there must be a limit, a stopping point to the persecution.

When Diana arrives at the front, she beholds atrocities. Though she tries over and over to help, Steve Trevor and his friends hustle her past fleeing families, broken wagons, dying soldiers. She stares at the camera, anger marring her face. Over and over, Steve insists that helping individuals will detract from the great mission. However, insistence on the "big picture" has always meant a lack of compassion. Focused on winning the war, America spent World War II refusing to liberate the concentration camps or even spare a single bomb for the train tracks.

When a woman with a baby huddled in the trenches reaches out and tells Diana her people have been killed and enslaved, Diana feels the call to intervene. Though Steve Trevor tells her, "We can't save everyone," she refuses to stop for his talk of the bigger picture.[60] Like Jews wish more people had done with the victims of the camps, she charges across hell to rescue them.

When Steve Trevor tells Diana the poisoned gas is designed to kill civilians, Diana is horrified. "What kind of weapon kills innocents?" she asks.[61] World War I certainly killed and displaced civilians, but it was the Second World War that specifically *targeted* civilians with gas-filled trucks and gas chambers. Her plaintive plea for rationality, for an end to the madness, reaches through all the eras of history.

When she walks into a gassed village, she sees the people lying dead on the ground, terrorized by the German army and its villainous leaders. She looks ready to cry, and blames Steve, desperate to have someone to condemn for the atrocity. When he argues, she decides that the war isn't one of German sinners and Allied saints. "It's corrupted all of you."[62] Indeed, the racism and disregard for life stretched far beyond Nazism to the point of neo-Nazis among the countries that once battled Germany. As revealed by their Native American friend called Chief (Eugene Brave Rock), no one has clean hands here.

Diana finally reaches General Ludendorff and stabs him "in the name of all that is good." He has become a supersoldier with near-magical power, the Nazi ubermensch ideal. However, killing him ends nothing—the war rages on. Steve tries to comfort her, telling her he wishes there was just one man to kill in order to end man's brutality. Certainly, many tried to assassinate Hitler. But even after his death, the Pacific war raged on, and repairing all the hatred was a long time in coming. As with World War II, there's perseverance and sacrifice, but no easy solution.

Ares tempts Diana, not with domination, but with a world of peace and green trees, the world the Jews sing about every Shabbat. As he unmasks Doctor Poison, showing Diana the banality of evil, the scientists in their labs who created more efficient ways to kill, Wonder Woman doesn't give in to hatred or despair. Gazing at Steve Trevor's sacrifice, she achieves a state of perfect love for even flawed humanity. "You're wrong about them. They're everything you say, but so much more." This realization parallels Anne Frank's, even surrounded by despair and the threat of death—

In spite of everything I still believe that people are really good at heart. I simply can't build up my hopes on a foundation consisting of confusion, misery, and death. I see the world gradually being turned into a wilderness, I hear the ever approaching thunder, which will destroy us too, I can feel the sufferings of millions and yet, if I look up into the heavens, I think that it will all come right, that this cruelty too will end, and that peace and tranquility will return again.[63]

Wonder Woman, who believes this too, also understands she must battle every day, to make the world she wants.

FINAL THOUGHTS

Clearly, though there are a few Jewish superheroes on the small screens, they do little with the religion or culture. On the big screen, there are fewer still. Magneto's Judaism is rooted in the Holocaust, giving him a very strong association but leaving him, a scarred villain, as nearly the only example. Flash and Wonder Woman, ironically not canonically Jewish or invented by Jews, do more to further the Jewish experience. As Bertlasky concludes, "When Jewish people are heroes, they're not seen as Jewish; when they're seen as Jewish, they often aren't heroes. Jewish people made Superman, Captain America, Batman, and the Avengers. But the culture that loves them still can't quite see us at the center of our stories."[64]

NOTES

1. Karl Kessel (w) and Stuart Immonen (a), "Remembrance of Things Past," *Fantastic Four* #56 (New York: Marvel, 2002), 28.

2. Andrew Alan Smith, "Jack Kirby the Not-So-Secret Identity of the Thing." In *Working-Class Comic Book Heroes: Class Conflict and Populist Politics in Comics,* ed. Marc DiPaolo (Mississippi: University Press of Mississippi, 2018), 197.

3. Only on her mother's side, but she's declared herself Jewish in several comics.

4. With Jewish and Catholic parents at least.

5. *Spider-Man: Into the Spider-Verse,* directed by Peter Ramsey, Bob Persichetti, and Rodney Rothman, 2018. (Culver City, CA: Sony Pictures Home Entertainment, 2019), DVD.

6. Max Evry, "Interview: Spider-Man: Into the Spider-Verse Directors," *Coming Soon, December 12, 2018.* www.comingsoon.net/movies/features/1017643-cs -interview-spider-man-into-the-spider-verse-directors

7. Jordan Hoffman, "Is Spider-Man Jewish?" *Times of Israel,* June 13, 2012, www .timesofisrael.com/is-spider-man-jewish.

8. Noah Dominguez, "*Moon Knight* Explores the Character's Jewish Heritage, Promises Head Writer," *CBR,* March 29, 2022, www.cbr.com/moon-knight-explores -marc-spector-jewish-faith-disney-plus-marvel.

9. *Marvel's Runaways,* season 1, episode 5, "Kingdom," directed by Jeffrey W. Byrd, written by Rodney Barnes and Michael Vukadinovich, aired December 5, 2017. Hulu.

10. The Giborim are the villains' extradimensional benefactors in this series, named for and likely identified with the children of the biblical Nephilim.

11. *Marvel's Runaways,* season 1, episode 4, "Fifteen," directed by Ramsey Nickell, written by Tamara Becher-Wilkinson, aired November 28, 2017. Hulu.

12. Noah Bertlasky, "Netflix's *The Punisher* Is a Reminder That Unlike Jewish Creators, Jewish Superheroes Remain a Tough Sell in Hollywood," *NBC,* January 22, 2019, www.nbcnews.com/think/opinion/netflix-s-punisher-reminder-unlike-jewish -creators-jewish-superheroes-remain-ncna961491.

13. Bertlasky, "Punisher."

14. Stephen E. Tabachnick, *The Quest for Jewish Belief and Identity in the Graphic Novel* (Tuscaloosa: University of Alabama Press, 2014).

15. Quoted in Rachel Elizabeth Mandel, "From Maus to Magneto: Exploring Holocaust Representation in Comic Books and Graphic Novels," Syracuse University Honors Program Capstone Projects. Paper 846 (2015), 7.

16. Arie Kaplan, *From Krakow to Krypton: Jews and Comic Books* (Philadelphia: The Jewish Publication Society, 2008), 117.

17. Henry Gonshak, *Hollywood and the Holocaust* (Lanham, MD: Rowman & Littlefield, 2015), 264.

18. Kaplan, *Krakow*, 120.

19. *X-Men: First Class,* directed by Matthew Vaughn. (Beverly Hills: Twentieth Century Fox Home Entertainment, 2011), DVD.

20. Mandel, 25.

21. *X-Men*, directed by Bryan Singer (Beverly Hills: Twentieth Century Fox Home Entertainment, 2000), DVD.

22. *X-Men.*

23. Gonshak, 263.

24. *X-Men: The Last Stand*, directed by Bryan Singer (Beverly Hills: Twentieth Century Fox Home Entertainment, 2006), DVD.

25. Gonshak, 268.

26. *X-Men: First Class.*

27. Chris Claremont (w) and John Byrne (w and a). "Days of Future Past," *The Uncanny X-Men* #141–142 (New York: Marvel, 1981).

28. Mandel, 12.

29. *X-Men: Apocalypse.*

30. Arielle Kaplan, "For a Show About a Jewish Anti-Hero, *Harley Quinn* Sure Has a Lot of Anti-Semitic Tropes." *Hey Alma,* 31 July 2020. www.heyalma.com/for -a-show-about-a-jewish-anti-hero-harley-quinn-sure-has-a-lot-of-anti-semitic-tropes.

31. Kaplan, "For a Show."

32. Kaplan, "For a Show."

33. *Harley Quinn,* season 1, episode 2, "A High Bar," directed by Matt Garofalo, Ben Jones, and Frank Marino, written by Jane Becker. December 6, 2019, HBO Max.

34. *Harley Quinn,* season 1, episode 10, "Bensonhurst," directed by Ben Jones and Colin Heck, written by Laura Moran, January 31, 2020, HBO Max.

35. Elias Rosner, "Jews in DC and the Uncomfortable Anti-Semitism of One *Harley Quinn," Multiversity Comics, January 1, 2021* www.multiversitycomics.com/longform/jews-dc-uncomfortable-harley-quinn/

36. Rosner.

37. *Harley Quinn,* season 1, episode 5, "Being Harley Quinn," directed by Juan Meza-Leon, written by Adam Stein. December 27, 2019, HBO Max.

38. Arielle Kaplan, "For a Show About a Jewish Anti-Hero, 'Harley Quinn' Sure Has a Lot of Anti-Semitic Tropes." *Hey Alma,* 31 July 2020. www.heyalma.com/for-a-show-about-a-jewish-anti-hero-harley-quinn-sure-has-a-lot-of-anti-semitic-tropes.

39. Kaplan, "For a Show."

40. *Harley Quinn,* season 1, episode 8, "L.O.D.R.S.V.P.," directed by Matt Garofalo, Ben Jones, and Frank Marino, written by Tom Hyndman, January 17, 2020, HBO Max.

41. Rosner.

42. *Harley Quinn,* season 1, episode 12, "Devil's Snare," directed by Juan Meza-Leon, written by Jane Becker, February 14, 2020, HBO Max.

43. *Legends of Tomorrow*, season 3, episode 8, "Crisis on Earth-X, Part 4," directed by Gregory Smith, story by Marc Guggenheim and Andrew Kreisberg, teleplay by Phil Klemmer and Keto Shimizu, aired November 28, 2017, in broadcast syndication. Warner Brothers, 2018, DVD.

44. *Supergirl*, season 3, episode 8, "Crisis on Earth X Part 1," directed by Larry Teng, story by Andrew Kreisberg and Marc Guggenheim, teleplay by Robert Rovner and Jessica Queller, aired November 27, 2017, in broadcast syndication. Warner Brothers, 2018, DVD.

45. *Arrow,* season 5, episode 2, "The Recruits," directed by James Bamford, written by Speed Weed and Beth Schwartz, aired October 12, 2016, in broadcast syndication. Warner Brothers, 2017, DVD.

46. *Arrow,* "The Recruits."

47. *Arrow,* season 5, episode 4, "Penance," directed by Dermott Downs, written by Brian Ford Sullivan and Oscar Balderrama, October 26, 2016.

48. *Arrow,* season 5, episode 9, "What We Leave Behind," directed by Antonio Negret, written by Wendy Mericle and Beth Schwartz, aired December 7, 2016, in broadcast syndication. Warner Brothers, 2017, DVD.

49. *Arrow,* season 5, episode 12, "Bratva," directed by Ben Bray, written by Oscar Balderrama and Emilio Ortega Aldrich, aired February 8, 2017, in broadcast syndication. Warner Brothers, 2017, DVD.

50. *The Flash,* season 1, episode 23, "Fast Enough," directed by Dermott Downs, story by Greg Berlanti and Andrew Kreisberg, teleplay by Gabrielle Stanton and Andrew Kreisberg, aired May 19, 2015, in broadcast syndication. Warner Brothers, 2015, DVD.

51. *Legends of Tomorrow*, season 3, episode 9, "Beebo the God of War," directed by Kevin Mock, written by Grainne Godfree and James Eagan, aired December 5, 2017, in broadcast syndication. Warner Brothers, 2018, DVD.

52. Geoff Johns, Grant Morrison, Greg Rucka, and Mark Waid (w), and Keith Giffen and Ken Lashley (a), "Going Down," *52* #7 (New York: DC Comics, 2006).

53. *Batwoman,* season 1, episode 15, "Off with her Head," directed by Holly Dale, written by Natalie Abrams, aired March 15, 2020, in broadcast syndication. Warner Brothers, 2020, DVD.

54. *Batwoman,* season 2, episode 9, "Rule #1," directed by Michael Blundell, written by Nancy Kiu and Maya Houston, aired March 28, 2021, in broadcast syndication. Warner Brothers, 2021, DVD.

55. Noah Bertlasky, "With *Justice League,* Now There's a Jewish Superhero Played by a Jewish Actor on the Big Screen." *Washington Post, November 17, 2017.* www .washingtonpost.com/news/acts-of-faith/wp/2017/11/17/with-justice-league-now -theres-a-jewish-superhero-played-by-a-jewish-actor-on-the-big-screen.

56. Bertlasky, "Punisher."

57. Bertlasky, "Justice League."

58. *Wonder Woman,* directed by Patty Jenkins (Burbank, CA: Warner Bros. Home Entertainment, 2017), DVD.

59. *Wonder Woman.*

60. *Wonder Woman.*

61. *Wonder Woman.*

62. *Wonder Woman.*

63. Anne Frank, *The Diary of a Young Girl: The Definitive Edition* (New York: Doubleday, 1995), 328.

64. Bertlasky, "Punisher."

WORKS CITED

Abrams, Natalie, writer. *Batwoman.* Season 1, episode 15, "Off with Her Head." Directed by Holly Dale. Aired March 15, 2020, in broadcast syndication. Warner Brothers, 2020, DVD.

Balderrama, Oscar, and Emilio Ortega Aldrich, writers. *Arrow.* Season 5, episode 12, "Bratva." Directed by Ben Bray. Aired February 8, 2017, in broadcast syndication. Warner Brothers, 2017, DVD.

Barnes, Rodney, and Michael Vukadinovich, writers. *Marvel's Runaways.* Season 1, episode 5, "Kingdom." Directed by Jeffrey W. Byrd. Aired December 5, 2017. Hulu.

Becher-Wilkinson, Tamara, writer. *Marvel's Runaways.* Season 1, episode 4, "Fifteen." Directed by Ramsey Nickell. Aired November 28, 2017. Hulu.

Becker, Jane, writer. *Harley Quinn.* Season 1, episode 2, "A High Bar." Directed by Matt Garofalo, Ben Jones, and Frank Marino. Aired December 6, 2019.

Becker, Jane, writer. *Harley Quinn.* Season 1, episode 12, "Devil's Snare." Directed by Juan Meza-Leon. Aired February 14, 2020.

Berlanti, Greg, and Andrew Kreisberg, story, teleplay by Gabrielle Stanton and Andrew Kreisberg. *The Flash.* Season 1, episode 23, "Fast Enough." Directed by Dermott Downs. Aired May 19, 2015, in broadcast syndication. Warner Brothers, 2015, DVD.

Bertlasky, Noah. "Netflix's *The Punisher* Is a Reminder That Unlike Jewish Creators, Jewish Superheroes Remain a Tough Sell in Hollywood." *NBC,* January 22, 2019. www.nbcnews.com/think/opinion/netflix-s-punisher-reminder-unlike-jewish-cre-ators-jewish-superheroes-remain-ncna961491

Bertlasky, Noah. "With *Justice League*, Now There's a Jewish Superhero Played by a Jewish Actor on the Big Screen." *Washington Post*, November 17, 2017. www .washingtonpost.com/news/acts-of-faith/wp/2017/11/17/with-justice-league-now -theres-a-jewish-superhero-played-by-a-jewish-actor-on-the-big-screen.

Claremont, Chris (w) and John Byrne (w and a). "Days of Future Past," *The Uncanny X-Men* #141–142. New York: Marvel, 1981.

Dominguez, Noah. "*Moon Knight* Explores the Character's Jewish Heritage, Promises Head Writer." *CBR,* March 29, 2022. www.cbr.com/moon-knight-explores-marc -spector-jewish-faith-disney-plus-marvel.

Evry, Max. "Interview: Spider-Man: Into the Spider-Verse Directors." *Coming Soon*, December, 12, 2018. www.comingsoon.net/movies/features/1017643-cs-interview -spider-man-into-the-spider-verse-directors

Frank, Anne. *The Diary of a Young Girl: The Definitive Edition.* New York: Doubleday, 1995.

Godfree, Grainne, and James Eagan, writers. *Legends of Tomorrow.* Season 3, episode 9, "Beebo the God of War." Directed by Kevin Mock. Aired December 5, 2017, in broadcast syndication. Warner Brothers, 2018, DVD.

Gonshak, Henry. *Hollywood and the Holocaust.* Lanham: MD, Rowman & Littlefield, 2015.

Hoffman, Jordan. "Is Spider-Man Jewish?" *Times of Israel,* June 13, 2012. www .timesofisrael.com/is-spider-man-jewish.

Hyndman, Tom, writer. *Harley Quinn.* Season 1, episode 8, "L.O.D.R.S.V.P." Directed by Matt Garofalo, Ben Jones, and Frank Marino. Aired January 17, 2020.

Jenkins, Patty, dir. *Wonder Woman.* Burbank, CA: Warner Bros. Home Entertainment, 2017. DVD.

Johns, Geoff, Grant Morrison, Greg Rucka, and Mark Waid (w), and Keith Giffen and Ken Lashley (a). "Going Down," *The New 52* #7. New York: DC Comics, 2006.

Kaplan, Arie. *From Krakow to Krypton: Jews and Comic Books.* Philadelphia: The Jewish Publication Society, 2008.

Kaplan, Arielle. "For a Show About a Jewish Anti-Hero, *Harley Quinn* Sure Has a Lot of Anti-Semitic Tropes." *Hey Alma*, July 31, 2020. www.heyalma.com/for-a-show -about-a-jewish-anti-hero-harley-quinn-sure-has-a-lot-of-anti-semitic-tropes.

Kessel, Karl (w) and Stuart Immonen (a). "Remembrance of Things Past," *Fantastic Four* #56. New York: Marvel, 2002.

Kiu, Nancy, and Maya Houston, writers. *Batwoman.* Season 2, episode 9. "Rule #1." Directed by Michael Blundell, Aired March 28, 2021, in broadcast syndication. Warner Brothers, 2021, DVD.

Kreisberg, Andrew, and Marc Guggenheim, story, teleplay by Robert Rovner and Jessica Queller. *Supergirl.* Season 3, episode 8. "Crisis on Earth X Part 1." Directed by Larry Teng. Aired November 27, 2017, in broadcast syndication. Warner Brothers, 2018, DVD.

Kreisberg, Andrew, and Marc Guggenheim, story, teleplay by Phil Klemmer and Keto Shimizu. *Legends of Tomorrow.* Season 3, episode 8, "Crisis on Earth-X, Part 4." Directed by Gregory Smith. Aired November 28, 2017, in broadcast syndication. Warner Brothers, 2018, DVD.

Mandel, Rachel Elizabeth, "From Maus to Magneto: Exploring Holocaust Representation in Comic Books and Graphic Novels." Syracuse University Honors Program Capstone Projects. Paper 846. 2015. surface.syr.edu/cgi/viewcontent. cgi?article=1847&context=honors_capstone.

Mericle, Wendy, and Beth Schwartz, writers. *Arrow*. Season 5, episode 9, "What We Leave Behind." Directed by Antonio Negret. Aired December 7, 2016, in broadcast syndication. Warner Brothers, 2017, DVD.

Moran, Laura, writer. *Harley Quinn*. Season 1, episode 10, "Bensonhurst." Directed by Ben Jones and Colin Heck. Aired January 31, 2020.

Ramsey, Peter, Bob Persichetti, Rodney Rothman, dir. *Spider-Man: Into the Spider-Verse*. 2018. Culver City, CA: Sony Pictures Home Entertainment, 2019. DVD.

Rosner, Elias. "Jews in DC and the Uncomfortable Anti-Semitism of One *Harley Quinn*." *Multiversity Comics*, January 1, 2021. www.multiversitycomics.com/ longform/jews-dc-uncomfortable-harley-quinn.

Singer, Bryan, dir. *X-Men: The Last Stand*. Beverly Hills: Twentieth Century Fox Home Entertainment, 2006. DVD.

Singer, Bryan, dir. *X-Men*. Beverly Hills: Twentieth Century Fox Home Entertainment, 2000. DVD.

Smith, Andrew Alan. "Jack Kirby the Not-So-Secret Identity of the Thing." In *Working-Class Comic Book Heroes: Class Conflict and Populist Politics in Comics,* edited by Marc DiPaolo, 191–205. Mississippi: University Press of Mississippi, 2018.

Stein, Adam, writer. *Harley Quinn*. Season 1, episode 5, "Being Harley Quinn." Directed by Juan Meza-Leon. Aired December 27, 2019.

Sullivan, Brian Ford, and Oscar Balderrama, writers. *Arrow*. Season 5, episode 4, "Penance." Directed by Dermott Downs. Aired October 26, 2016, in broadcast syndication. Warner Brothers, 2017, DVD.

Tabachnick, Stephen E. *The Quest for Jewish Belief and Identity in the Graphic Novel*. Tuscaloosa: University of Alabama Press, 2014. eBook Collection, EBSCOhost.

Vaughn, Matthew, dir. *X-Men: First Class*. Beverly Hills: Twentieth Century Fox Home Entertainment, 2011, DVD.

Weed, Speed, and Beth Schwartz, writers. *Arrow*. Season 5, episode 2, "The Recruits." Directed by James Bamford. Aired October 12, 2016, in broadcast syndication. Warner Brothers, 2017, DVD.

Chapter Seven

Making a Jewish Case for Ferenginar

Redeeming Star Trek's *Worst Archetypes*

Miriam Eve Mora

Are the Ferengi Space Jews? If so, are they an insulting stereotype based on the worst of anti-Semitic propaganda? I always bristle when asked this question, both as a scholar of Jewish history and anti-Semitism, and as a lifelong *Star Trek* superfan. I defensively loathe the question, feeling protective of my love of *Star Trek* and the universalist messages it sends, and my unwilling but truthful agreement that yes, indeed, a Ferengi sure would look like a Jew to a Nazi. The connection between the Ferengi species and a classic anti-Semitic Jewish stereotype is a logical one, but as Mr. Spock reminds us, "Logic is the beginning of wisdom . . . not the end."[1] I contend that the Ferengi indeed became Space Jews quickly after their inception (and that denial of this connection is intellectually indefensible), and that the showrunners, writers, costumers, and designers found a trope that worked and ran with it, regardless of their intention or full awareness of the consequence. I also contend, however, that *Star Trek: Deep Space Nine* (*DS9*) redeemed the Ferengi from this negative stereotype by focusing on the development of characters and Ferengi society, and through processes of political, social, and religious reform that mirrored more positive realities of Jewish life and history. The evolution of Ferengi is that of societal reform, and what the *Trek* universe originally misconstrued as flaws in a race of peoples are proven to be religious holdouts from an age past, one capable of modernization for what is otherwise a highly advanced and impressive society.

In the following pages I show that by the time *DS9* began, enough similarities and connections had manifested to make it clear that many viewers perceived the Ferengi as Space Jews, whether intentional or not. I further argue that the creators of *DS9* reworked the Ferengi race to transcend the negative stereotype, without trying to change what had already been established. This transformation, from an insulting Jewish stereotype to a respectable, compassionate, and Federation-worthy alien race, does not merely redeem the Ferengi from their negative reflection of anti-Semitic myths: it does so in a uniquely Jewish way. I present three arguments in the following pages: first, that the Ferengi *are* Space "Jews," as they are nearly perfectly in-line with *negative* stereotypes of Jews; second, that the Ferengi are not *real* Space Jews, as the realities of Ferengi society are antithetical to actual Jewish life; and lastly, that the solution to the problem of such insulting Ferengi depictions as Space Jews was to make them *more* like *real* Jews. By recognizing, not erasing, the connection the Ferengi presented to Jewish stereotypes, the writers of *DS9* were able to transform an anti-Semitic archetype into a positive one. A Jewish solution to an unfortunately Jewish problem.

FERENGI ARE SPACE JEWS . . .

Let us first examine the ways in which the Ferengi did come to embody the anti-Semitic archetype of Jews in Space and consider what it tells us about the content makers and their intentions. As consumers of media, we must recognize that no elements seen on screen merely fell in front of the camera without someone making a decision to have it there. Someone designed Ferengi noses, teeth, and earlobes. Someone cast them with Jewish actors. Someone gave them direction. Someone determined that the Ferengi culture should be every bit of what it was. Without statements confirming or denying intention by most of the series' content creators, we must take the Ferengi as *Star Trek* has presented them, and accept that we are getting a mixed bag, but that nothing (including anti-Semitic portrayals written by Jews) is by accident.

The initial appearance of the Ferengi in "The Last Outpost" (1.05) in the first season of *Star Trek: The Next Generation* (*TNG*), establishes them as a fairly despicable race, driven by greed, dishonest practice, and misogyny. They also appear ludicrous and animalistic, moving like monkeys, arms waving, fingers twitching, bodies hunched.[2] Worf immediately calls them "pigmy cretins," as they jump on his back, gnawing at him like sharp-toothed macaques.[3] This portrayal did not need to be consistent. Before their first contact, they were a species known to the Federation only by reputation. They were described as an advanced society and appeared piloting a ship with impressive design and technology equal or superior to that of the Federation. According to Armin Shimerman, who played one of the first Ferengi onscreen in the episode, "What we were told about the Ferengi and what we ended up with were like night and day. The Ferengi were going to be the new Klingons. They were never meant to be a comical race; they were meant to be ferocious and menacing."[4] The initial episode informed viewers that Federation databases compared them to the Yankee traders of the eighteenth and nineteenth century, and assumed they were governed by the worst aspects of capitalism. This description might have been the precursor to a great variety of alien species, presenting physically and behaviorally in any number of ways. The way the species appeared and behaved, however, presented phenotypical and behavioral characteristics reminiscent of the most rabid anti-Semitic stereotypes.

Though no *Star Trek* writer has given public indication that this visual recalling of *Jews* was intentional, *TNG* coproducer Herb Wright did make clear that their very earliest influence was, in fact, based on a caricature of a Jew that most experts agree is an anti-Semitic one.[5] He explained, in an interview in *Star Trek: The Magazine,* that in his initial description of the species to the design team, Shakespeare's Shylock had served as an inspiration for the visual appearance of the Ferengi.[6] The Ferengi were originally conceived by *Star Trek* creator Gene Roddenberry, who has been accused of anti-Semitism by several actors and writers who worked with and for him across the many *Star Trek* series, about and long before the Ferengi introduction in *The Next Generation.*[7]

The superficial similarities to Jewish archetypes cover nearly everything distinctive about their phenotypical traits and are also the elements most closely connected to anti-Semitic depictions of Jews, particularly those propagated in Nazi Germany. These include that the Ferengi are short and have strange, oversized noses; big ears; visibly large brains; distinctive head coverings; dark-circled, beady eyes; dark/orange skin; oversized (and thus eternally clenched) teeth; and blue fingernails. These align closely with those characteristics ascribed to Jews by the so-called "racial science" of the late nineteenth and early twentieth centuries. It was said, for example, that Jews had oversized ears; large, hooked noses; short stature; abnormal intellect and cunning (and therefore discernable results in craniometry); square fingernails; dark skin; clenched teeth; and beady or twitchy eyes.[8] Even the strangeness of blue Ferengi fingernails recalls not only the assumption that Jews had square nails, but also the curiosity of Jewish practice surrounding fingernails, which were often clipped in a specific order and the nail parings disposed of as dead human flesh (to be buried or burned).[9] There are other attributes that anti-Semites have claimed Jews possess that do not appear in the Ferengi (horns, tails, devilish odor, and even the belief in Jewish male menstruation), but the overlap is damning.

The behavioral similarities were similarly unflattering. In the *TNG* pilot, *Enterprise* crew discuss that the Ferengi are suspected of cannibalism, another shared trait with anti-Semitic blood libel accusations (the charge that Jews require the blood of Christian children to make Passover matzo). Their obsession with wealth also shows their distance from Starfleet and humanity, as they explain of humans, "They are demented. Their values are insane. . . . They adorn themselves with gold, a despicable use of a valuable metal."[10] Further, the first look at the mysterious Ferengi arrives from their Daimon in very close focus on the viewscreen of the *Enterprise*, head features prominent. His observation that "The ugliness of the human was not an exaggeration" calls attention to his own appearance and his off-putting social nature.[11] In spite of all of these features, they do not manifest as fierce or frightening in "The Last Outpost." They are weakly conniving villains here and in "The Battle" (1.09), but after the first season, they become comical in their schemes.

The Ferengi are, until *DS9* (and in the iterations of *Star Trek that* followed), the consummate Schlemiel, always comically foolish, clumsy, or unfortunate in circumstance. Riker maliciously sends them finger-puzzles in "The Outpost," and gets released from confinement by needling the Ferengi with his superior ability at chess in "Ménage à Troi" (3.24). In "Rascals" (6.07), four children defeat them. In their single appearance in *Star Trek: Enterprise*, "Acquisition" (1.19), they are quickly taken in by false promises of a vault on the ship, deceived by three members of the crew, and easily defeated. But they are not depicted as cute or benign, in spite of their humorous foolishness. They are unabashedly greed-driven and covetous, pushy, and uncouth, deeply misogynistic and patriarchal, clannish and exclusive, and lustful toward women of all species. The depiction of Jewish men as lusting after gentile women is an old trope, but a distinctive one that the Ferengi tend to mimic. The representation of Jewish men as seducers of Aryan women in Nazi propaganda depicted Jews as lecherous, but not particularly masculine, even when sexual conquest was assumed.[12] These qualities of hypersexuality, sensuality, and seduction pertained more often to women in the mid-twentieth century and were considered feminine characteristics, not manly, by the Nazis and their ilk.[13]

It does not help their case that most of the actors hired to play featured Ferengi characters are, themselves, of Jewish descent. This includes the most notable Ferengi actors, such as Armin Shimerman (Letek, DaiMon Bractor, and Quark), Aron Eisenberg (Nog), Max Grodénchik (Rom, Gint, Par Lenor, Sovak), Wallace Shawn (Grand Nagus Zek), and Cecily Adams (Ishka), as well as many lesser-known featured Ferengi.[14] The character Ishka was initially played by comedian Andrea Martin, who has repeatedly spoken about how often she's assumed to be Jewish, though she is actually of Armenian descent, explaining "I don't think I said I was Jewish. It is just that no one knew I was Armenian, and it was easy for people to assume it."[15] Whether

Andrea Martin was assumed Jewish by producers or audiences, the name chosen for her character, *Ishka*, is close enough to the Hebrew word for woman, *ishah,* to put viewers with minimal knowledge of the language onto the Ferengi-as-Jews bandwagon. Similarly, the political leader of the Ferengi people holds the title of *Nagus*, which though not as strong a similarity, is still reminiscent of the Hebrew *nasi,* the title given to the political ruler of Judea in Ancient Israel.[16]

Further, Shimerman as an alternate Quark appears, unburdened by his Ferengi prosthetics, as Herbert Russoff, a lefty communist writer in the episode "Far Beyond the Stars" (6.13). This episode implies the Jewishness of his character more heavily than any other appearance of a named, speaking character on *Star Trek*. It also acknowledges the existence of Jews, showing two Orthodox Jews on the streets of New York, which no other iteration of *Star Trek* has done.

BUT THEY AREN'T REALLY SPACE JEWS . . .

The essential characteristics of Ferengi society that are definitively *not* Jewish are just as significant as those above that connect the Ferengi to anti-Semitic depictions of Jews. It is easy to see a fictional race that was created to be unlikeable (the Ferengi were, after all, supposed to be villains in *TNG*), and highlight their characteristics as similar to any number of groups that have already been represented as villains in the past. Tanya S. Osensky, for example, explains in her book on height discrimination that the short stature of the Ferengi is a defining characteristic showing that they were never meant to be taken seriously—an insult to short people as much as to Jews.[17] The same language is often used to abuse several distinct groups, which otherwise have very little in common. However, in addition to the visual and behavioral comparisons enumerated above, a number of similarities have been routinely cited as evidence of the Jewish–Ferengi connection, regarding the societal structure of the Ferengi homeworld and spiritual life. The Ferengi are controlled by a complex religious–legal system, the 285 Rules of Acquisition, that governs every aspect of their lives in "ten thousand years of Ferengi tradition."[18] Viewers and critics have often compared this set of regulations to the 613 mitzvot (commandments) extracted from the Torah.[19] Aside from having a rigid number of rules interpreted and debated for thousands of years by Ferengi scholars, the Rules of Acquisition themselves bear no resemblance to the 613 commandments.

The rules were not extracted from a holy text in order to frame religious life. They were written by the first Grand Nagus, Gint, and done so largely as a marketing scheme (having numbered the very first law 162, in order to increase demand for the first 161).[20] The effect of some of the rules, in fact, are in direct opposition to some of the most important Jewish laws. For example, rule 266 states, "When in doubt, lie," and rule 52, "Never ask when you can take," actually violates the Ten Commandments.[21] Rabbi Yonassan Gershom, however, argues that the existence of the Ferengi and their behavior were, in a way, a giant Jewish joke, but an in-joke, created by Jewish *Star Trek* writers like Ira Behr. Yes, the Ferengi play out like an anti-Semitic cartoon reminiscent of Nazi propaganda, but the punchline, he insists, is that although the Ferengi spoof Jewish stereotypes, they are antithetical to actual Jewish life. "Unfortunately," he explains, "the general public is not familiar enough with the authentic Jewish teachings to recognize a parody when they see one."[22]

The distinctions between the Jewish religion and the religious–legal system created for the Ferengi on *Star Trek* are not, however, one great insider joke for Jewish creators and viewers of the shows. The similarities and notable differences are more easily explained by the simple fact that the species was largely created by Jewish writers who had varying levels of Jewish knowledge, had internalized anti-Semitic caricatures as villains, and whose goal for the species, as explained by Gene Roddenberry, was to be an embodiment of one of humanity's worst features: capitalistic greed. Riker concludes their first encounter with a smugly superior "I find them very much as we were several hundred years ago. . . . But we can hardly hate what we once were. They may grow and learn."[23] The Ferengi are not Jews, point for point. They see no value in education, which Jews hold as not only valuable, but sacred. Jews forbid the mutilation of the bodies of their deceased, while the Ferengi sell off pieces to be distributed at the time of their deaths.

One of the most unattractive qualities of the Ferengi is their extreme misogyny, a characteristic that some have argued is yet another parallel to Jewish culture, as a patriarchal society. For example, Ross S. Kraemer, professor of religious studies at Brown University, wrote that the exclusion of women from making profit in Ferengi society is "reminiscent of traditional exclusion of women from Judaism's most culturally valued activity—the study of the Torah."[24] It is not written into the Rules of Acquisition that women are not permitted to make profit, but an additional legal practice (and one that makes little sense, given the Ferengis' objectivist societal structure).[25] Similarly, Ferengi women are required to sign, when entering a marriage, a "Waiver of Property and Profit," giving up all rights to property. This has been compared to the legal/financial contract for Jewish marriage, the *ketubah*. However, the purpose of a *ketubah* is to protect the bride, establishing the groom's financial obligation to her. Jewish women, quite unlike Ferengi, were often the primary breadwinners in Jewish families, and were explicitly permitted to do so religiously. Proverbs 31:16 says of the virtuous woman: "She considers a field and buys it; with her profits she plants a vineyard."[26] This is an important distinction, as it is not merely a fact of Jewish life, but one of the distinctive features that made Jewish assimilation in the United States more difficult, as an aberration of American gender roles. The ultimate sign of success for Jewish men was to have the ability to spend their time studying Torah, not making profits. The only people insisting that Jewish men value money above all else are those espousing anti-Semitic theories of malevolent power and conspiracies of global financial control.

Beyond the distinction of gender there are significant behavioral traits in Ferengi society that are antithetical to Jewish society. Traditional Jewish women wear modest dress, the Orthodox favoring long dresses and hair coverings (if married). The Ferengi women, by contrast, are not permitted clothes at all. Over the course of the shows, only two Ferengi females appear, and both are aberrant Ferengi women. One is Pel, a Ferengi female posing as a man to work at Quark's bar (in a plot reminiscent of *Yentl*); the other is Quark's mother, Ishka, a feminist lawbreaker, determined to undermine the status quo.[27]

OKAY. YEAH. MAYBE THEY ARE SPACE JEWS. BUT MAKE THEM SPACE MENSCHES.

Over the course of the seven seasons of *Deep Space Nine*, the Ferengi evolve, from an anti-Semitic caricature to a reforming religious culture learning to adapt in a larger universe. That they are Jewish is actually emphasized in *Deep Space Nine*, the only show to try to redeem the Ferengi. This Jewish emphasis, as with all *Star Trek* series to date, is a silent one. As discussed above, it is reasonable to assume that the makers of *Star Trek* who wrote, cast, directed, and visualized the Ferengi unintentionally fell into an anti-Semitic trope, without awareness of what they had created until it was already well established. *DS9* showrunner Ira Steven Behr, who is Jewish himself, explained that he was not a fan of the Ferengi, thought including one on *DS9* as a main character was a mistake, and was not at all excited at the prospect of writing for the Ferengi.[28] This was his attitude until he decided to change the Ferengi, to write them (particularly Rom and Quark) as twentieth-century humans, with dysfunction and behaviors to match pre-utopian human society. He has not responded to the Space Jew accusation, but the ways in which he redeemed the Ferengi by relating their development and plotlines to Jewish history and culture used the Space Jew trope in which the species was already entrenched to draw them out of their deplorable status. In essence, Behr made the Ferengi far more Jewish than they had ever been. However, until Behr and his cowriters began to change them, the Ferengi had been a reflection only of negative stereotypes, not any sort of representation of Jews with all of their complexities and diversity.

One of the most significant ways in which Ira Behr grew the Ferengi from stereotype to representation was in the episode "Family Business" (3.23), in which Rom and Quark are called home to Ferenginar, a planet that, previous to this episode, did not exist. The Ferengi were, in the early years of *TNG*, described as a roaming race without a home, recalling the myth of the "wandering Jew." According to the *Star Trek: The Next Generation Officer's Manual*, "Federation sociologists speculate that the original homeworlds of the Ferengi may have become exhausted, forcing the race to reach for the stars to replenish their lost resources."[29] By giving the Ferengi a homeworld, Behr and fellow writer Robert Hewitt Wolfe negated the "wandering Jew" element of Ferengi culture. Further, the constant rain, mushroomy buildings, and purple skies are not reminiscent of ancient Palestine or modern-day Israel. As the series continues, the culture adds different legalistic allusions as Nog references "Ferengi bylaws, section 105, subparagraph 10" (evocative of a twentieth-century contract), and Ferenginar has a Ferengi Bill of Opportunity, evocative of the American Bill of Rights.[30] With this new world, the creators build a better Ferengi culture and history, aligning with more positive reflections of Jews.

Ishka: The Jewish Mother/The Feminist

In the aforementioned episode, "Family Business," audiences are introduced to Ishka (known by her sons Rom and Quark as "Moogie"). Ishka is a more complex character from the moment of her introduction than most with so little screen time. She appears in only five episodes spanning five seasons.[31] Ishka fits the most dominant stereotype of Jewish mothers as smothering, pushy, controlling, nagging, loud, interfering, and manipulative. She responds to Quark's "Moogie, leave me alone," with "I'm your mother, I can't leave you alone!"[32] She coddles Rom (the nice Jewish boy), softening in his presence, and acquiescing to remove her clothes (as Ferengi females are traditionally unclothed) and sharpen his teeth, pre-chewing his food, and generally babying him upon his return home. The dichotomy of the two sons is a nearly perfect representation of the stereotypical tension between Jewish mothers and sons, though the aspects of the son are split across two personalities: one is an eternally infantilized mama's boy, the other resentful of his overinvolved mother's attention. The similarity of the relationship between Jewish sons and their mothers and that of the Ferengi is perfectly demonstrated in the two parts of the 31st Rule of Acquisition, "Never make fun of a Ferengi's mother," which Ira Behr's book *Legends of the Ferengi* eventually concludes, "insult something he cares about instead."[33]

But Ishka embodies an additional Jewish characteristic that goes beyond the mother stereotype and reflects the history of Jewish women in political activism. She is an early feminist agitator, pushing for full equality under Ferengi law, and with aspirations for brighter futures for Ferenginar. "I predict," Ishka says, "that one day, a female will enter the Tower of Commerce, climb the forty flights of stairs to the Chamber of Opportunity, and take her rightful place as Grand Nagus of the Ferengi Alliance."[34] Ishka clearly believes that Ferengi females, like human women, "belong in all places where decisions are being made," as did Jewish feminist jurist Ruth Bader Ginsburg, or author Betty Friedan (also Jewish) when she wrote, "Who knows what women can be when they are finally free to become themselves?"[35] As a Ferengi fighting for equal rights in practice and under the laws of the Rules of Acquisition, Ishka agitates for political, religious, and social reform, all written unquestionably into the scripts as correct and overdue.[36] She insists on earning profit, adding, "It's about pride. And knowing that I'm just as capable of earning profit as any male."[37] She still reflects some negative stereotypes about Jewish women—she is pushy, aggressive, loud, and opinionated. However, she is also a heroic character, of sorts. Embodying the Jewish activist, Ishka's fight for equal rights, through her relationship with Grand Nagus Zek, spearheads the reforms that by the end of the series have begun to transform the Ferengi into a more admirable, Federation-worthy species.

Zek: The Jewish Reformer

Grand Nagus Zek, played by Wallace Shawn, is a key character in the dramatic reformation of Ferengi society and religion, and the restoration of the Ferengi as Space Jews. In fact, his modifications to the Rules of Acquisition and the Laws of Ferenginar signify one of the most Jewish elements of the Ferengi story: a reform movement taking the species through a modernization process.

In the episode "Ferengi Love Songs" (5.20), the role of Ferengi men as merely dominant harassers of Ferengi women is broken with the romance between Zek and Ishka. Throughout the remaining series, Zek, due to Ishka's influence, leads a modernizing movement to alter the course of Ferengi history. He begins with amending the Ferengi Bill of Opportunity to allow females the right to wear clothes and make profit, and continues instituting reforms like progressive income tax, wage subsidies for the poor, retirement benefits, and health care.[38] Zek enacts these changes not only because he loves and listens to Ishka, but because his exposure to other worlds and peoples through trade and diplomacy has exposed him to more ideas and cultures, and he sees a new future for his people. Rabbi David Phillipson, an early pioneer of the Reform Jewish movement, mused that "the Jew has always been susceptible to the influences at work in the environment in which he has chanced to be. His mind is singularly open to the thought-waves that permeate his intellectual surroundings." Zek reflects a similar openness in his exposure to Ishka and the Federation.[39] Zek himself is not a visionary and does not change his own feelings about being a Ferengi, his greed and obsession with profit, or his lecherous treatment of women (as shown with Leeta, Rom's fiancée), but he reasons and listens to reason. Zek is no Moses Mendelssohn, but he acts as one, bringing Ferengi practice before the bar of reason. In so doing, he opens up the rigid rules of Ferengi society to modernize through enlightenment, reform, and progress.

Rom: The Nice Jewish Boy/Socialist Agitator

The most common positive stereotype of the modern Jewish man is a gentle, timid, studious, and delicate *nice Jewish boy*. Though these can and are seen as positive traits, it is also reflective of the anti-Semitic tendency to emasculate Jewish men when compared with those in the dominant masculine hegemon of European or American society. Rom is the consummate nice Jewish boy. Though he is initially introduced as a blundering shlamazel (a classic unfortunate fool or loser), Behr and his fellow writers develop his character, and he proves himself highly intelligent and capable, with a mind for mechanics and scientific theory. In "Heart of Stone" (3.14), Nog insists, "My father is a mechanical genius. He could've been chief engineer of a starship if he'd had the opportunity. But he went into business, like a good Ferengi."[40] The more the character of Rom develops, the more he becomes this Jewish archetype. His relationship with his mother is that of the nice Jewish boy, defining her role as the "one person in my life who's always been there for me. Who's never too busy to listen, who reassures me when I'm scared, comforts me when I'm sad, and who showers me with endless love without ever asking anything in return."[41]

Rom embodies Jewish representation in another way, by engaging in collective bargaining and leading a union strike (a cultural taboo for Ferengi). Jews have long been associated with the labor movement, and by writing Rom into the position of leader of the movement, *DS9* writers empower his character in a historically Jewish way. The history of the American labor movement, while not an exclusively Jewish narrative, is a substantial part of the story of Jewish acculturation in the United States. And in Rom's case, engaging in this tradition becomes a substantial part of his own story as an acculturating Ferengi. While leading his strike, all cowardice vanishes, and Rom becomes a brave, intelligent leader. He researches the history of collective bargaining on Earth, and even quotes Karl Marx's *Communist Manifesto* to Quark: "Workers of the world unite! You have nothing to lose but your chains!"[42] When the union wins, Rom claims his independence from his brother by quitting his job to become a diagnostic and repair technician for the station. In this new position, he completely abandons his previous designation as shlamazel, and for the remainder of the series is depicted as having the expertise and skills necessary for the running of the station and the success of its missions.

Rom doesn't outgrow the nice Ferengi boy stereotype; he is redeemed through it. It is a far more positive depiction of a Ferengi conforming to a Jewish stereotype than his initial introduction, and his character is rewarded for his kindness and goodness with a beautiful Bajoran Dabo girl for a bride, and eventually, with the reigns of the entire Ferengi Alliance, as the new Grand Nagus. Grand Nagus Zek appoints him, praising the very qualities that make him a nice Jewish boy, and a very poor Ferengi, insisting, "A new Ferenginar needs a new kind of Nagus. A kinder, gentler Nagus."[43] In that decision, Zek symbolically casts off the anti-Semitic stereotype that plagued the Ferengi and embraces a much more Jewish character for their future.

Nog: The Masculine Redeemer

An old anti-Semitic canard that fans and critics have claimed shows the Jewish connection to the Ferengi is that of male cowardice and evasion of physical confrontation or violence.[44] The most notable example of this argument has been made about Nog and his character arc as the first Ferengi in Starfleet. Nog is, as the only young Ferengi depicted on the show, the sole example of Ferengi boyhood on the cusp of maturity. At the start of Nog's progression from boy to man, the writers include one of the most blatant references to ascendant Jewish manhood imaginable. When Nog enters Sisko's office to declare his intention to join Starfleet, he presents a bewildered Sisko with a bag of gold-pressed latinum. By way of explanation, he says, "Yesterday I completed the Ferengi attainment ceremony." Grinning hugely, he declares, "I'm an adult."[45] In essence, Nog is presenting Sisko with his bar mitzvah money to buy an apprenticeship. This only serves to strengthen the Jewish–Ferengi connection. His character growth through his experiences in Starfleet (and in the war with the Dominion, particularly), however, shows a determined reclamation of his Jewish–Ferengi masculinity.

Quark is horrified at Nog's decision, insisting, "All it takes is for one impressionable youngster to join Starfleet, and the next thing you know, a whole generation of Ferengi will be quoting the Prime Directive and abandoning the pursuit of latinum. It's the end of Ferengi civilization as we know it."[46] He is at least partially correct, as Nog becomes an entirely new sort of Ferengi. After losing a leg in battle in "The Siege of AR-558" (7.08), Nog returns a war hero. In a 2003 article on the Ferengi and ethnicity in *Star Trek*,

J. Emmett Winn argued that Nog is only able to attain his status as a heroic Starfleet officer by shedding his ethnic/cultural identity. This is, according to Winn, evidence that the Ferengi are irredeemable, as Nog has to "rise above his despised race to embrace the values of the dominant culture," and thus "grows from Ferengi boy to a man who adopts the values of a culture that despises his race."[47] According to this analysis, the valor Nog displayed in combat made a man of him, and less a Ferengi. If a substitution for Judaism, then the argument is that a Jewish character cannot be a man, and so ceases to be a Jew in becoming one. Given the setup for this character progression, I argue this is an unfortunate misreading of the arc, which demonstrates exactly the opposite.

Just two episodes prior, in the episode "Treachery, Faith and the Great River" (7.06), Nog demonstrates that not only in spite of his becoming a Starfleet officer, but in support of it, he is still faithful to the belief system of his people and shows how his understanding of Ferengi culture and spirituality can help Starfleet through faith in the support of the Great Material Continuum. As he negotiates a series of trades to help his superior, Chief Miles O'Brian, to obtain an otherwise impossible demand from Captain Sisko, he contributes to the war effort in a way that a non-Ferengi simply could not. The *DS9* writers, in effect, take the core initial argument for "Space Jews" (the Ferengi as Yankee traders) and show its potential for positive contribution and redemption. And there are, indeed, positive depictions in history and popular media of Jewish traders, peddlers, and merchants that support the argument that this is a far cry from Yankee traders.[48]

Quark: The Jewish Lawyer/The True Believer

Quark, the only Ferengi main character in any *Star Trek* franchise, is a complex one, acting, for a time, as spokesperson for Ferengi culture. As he is the character through which so much knowledge of Ferengi life and law is related, he represents their ideals and practices, making him most closely fit the stereotype of Jewish lawyer. These depictions tend to be greedy, cunning, manipulative, dishonest, and steeped in ideas of legalism. Indeed, Quark is seen manipulating the system as he squares off with Liquidator Brunt, Constable Odo, and his other nemeses, using Ferengi and Federation codes to his advantage.[49] Even when he attempts chivalry to save a woman he loves, he still uses underhanded tricks to save himself, promising Odo, "You do this for me, and I promise you there'll be no more secrets between us. I will tell you about every underhanded deal, every lying scheme, every dirty trick . . . my brother Rom's involved in."[50]

Still, he also has moments growing beyond this. "Profit and Loss" reveals that he sold food to starving Bajorans during the Occupation and fell in love with the principled Cardassian Natima. Because writers were able to give Quark the screentime and plotlines necessary to develop a character complex enough to depict and defend the Ferengi, he serves as both the negative stereotype of Jewish lawyer and the religious true believer. Quark is Ferengi to the core: he deplores violence and has a fierce love of profit; he is duplicitous and dishonest, but maintains a morality (to which he is true) based on his own culture's laws that do not conform to those of the Federation; it is through him that we learn the Rules of Acquisition; and he defends the Ferengi as a species through reasoned argument and explanation of Ferengi law, culture, and history. At the end of the second season, Quark explains to Commander Sisko why the Ferengi are off-putting to human and other Federation characters:

> The way I see it, Humans used to be a lot like Ferengi: greedy, acquisitive, interested only in profit. We're a constant reminder of a part of your past you'd like to forget. . . . But you're overlooking something. Humans used to be a lot worse than the Ferengi: slavery, concentration camps, interstellar wars. We have nothing in our past that approaches that kind of barbarism. You see? We're nothing like you . . . we're better.[51]

Aside from the fact that there is a history of Jews owning enslaved persons (in antiquity as well as in the Americas), his defense could be for the Jewish people, and the mention of concentration camps certainly brings Jews to mind. It is one of his defining moments in *Deep Space Nine*. Quark maintains his position as true believer through to the end, cringing at the reforms that Zek is introducing, and determinedly remaining the traditional Ferengi he had defended to the Federation, the Bajorans, and the Cardassians on the station for so much of his life.

Armin Shimerman, who played Quark, has explained that the Ferengi, to him, are the "other," but not Jews specifically. Shimerman explains, "In America, people ask 'Do the Ferengi represent Jews?' In England, they ask 'Do the Ferengi represent the Irish?' In Australia, they ask if the Ferengi represent the Chinese. . . . The Ferengi represent the outcast . . . it's the person who lives among us that we don't fully understand."[52] It is completely understandable that Shimerman would not acknowledge the Ferengi–Jewish connection, even if he did recognize it.[53] To recognize it publicly would be to endorse the connection and would strongly imply there was intent behind it. He has stated in the past that he felt responsible for setting the standard that defined the Ferengi, as he played one of the first Ferengi that appeared on *The Next Generation*. "The Last Outpost," he explains, "was a disaster. And no one bears the brunt of that mistake more than I do." He made it a goal to rehabilitate the Ferengi, saying, "I didn't put it behind me for years; it was like [the] sword of Damocles hanging over my head. All of my work on *Deep*

Space Nine, for the first four seasons, was me trying to eradicate that original performance from everyone's mind."[54]

THE FUTURE OF SPACE JEWS: WHY DOES IT MATTER?

The Ferengi are not the only species credited with the title *Space Jews*. A search of scholarly articles, as well as internet rants, demonstrates a number of species in sci-fi who have been deemed as such (including the Bajorans as well as Vulcans). But the Ferengi are different, in that *Star Trek* writers accomplish something rarely done in popular media—they adhered to a negative stereotype, recognized it, and used the realities of the insulted group to rectify the offense. Philo-Semitism through telling a more truthful historical Jewish story, as opposed to an offensive stereotype, saved the Ferengi. It is not ideal, of course, as the offensive depictions of Ferengi in other series remain and cannot be fixed. It is also troubling for its continuing support of the co-constitutive nature of stereotyping "good Jews" and "bad Jews," which itself has a long and storied history. However, Ira Behr and his cowriters did an admirable job of rescuing their Space Jews with uniquely Jewish tools, and without ever owning that there was anything intentionally Jewish about the early, unpleasant characterizations of the Ferengi. Whether they did so consciously, or unknowingly, I imagine we will never know. If it was the latter, however, it was extremely lucky for the Ferengi to have Jewish writers like Behr and Berman, who could draw unknowingly from their own knowledge of Jewish life, history, and culture, to create a better Jewish Ferengi.

The Ferengi have not appeared meaningfully in any series since *DS9* (though there are teasers that they will appear as members of the Federation in *Star Trek: Discovery*). If we do see them again, they would be done the most justice by maintaining their identities, not backpedaling away from their Jewish roots. *Star Trek* creators now and into the future have an incredible species to work with: one that has been through as much progress as have the Klingons since their unrecognizable appearances in the original *Star Trek,* and whose relationships with humans and the Federation are as complex and interesting as the Vulcans (particularly through *Star Trek: Enterprise*). It is a rare opportunity in a large franchise with a relatively consistent canon: a species introduced in the worst way that has transcended all expectations, overcome the challenges placed in their way by their fellow characters as well as their creators, and is left a distinct, recognizable minority with a rich and interesting story of acculturation.

NOTES

1. *Star Trek VI: The Undiscovered Country,* directed by Nicholas Meyer (Hollywood, CA: Paramount Pictures, 1991).

2. Apparently following the directorial instruction to "jump up and down like crazed gerbils," according to Armin Shimerman, quoted in Judith Reeves-Stevens and Garfield Reeves-Stevens, *The Continuing Mission: A Tenth Anniversary Tribute* (New York: Pocket Books, 1998), 61–62.

3. *Star Trek: The Next Generation,* season one, episode five, "The Last Outpost," directed by Richard Colla, story by Richard Krzmeien, teleplay by Herbert Wright, aired October 19, 1987, in broadcast syndication, Paramount, 1987, Netflix.

4. "Armin Shimerman Feels Responsible for Failed Ferengi Introduction on *Star Trek: The Next Generation,*" *TrekMovie.com,* March 21, 2018, trekmovie. com/2018/03/21/armin-shimerman-feels-responsible-for-failed-ferengi-introduction-on-star-trek-the-next-generation.

5. The Jewishness of the character, Shylock, is not a debate, though the anti-Semitic intention of Shakespeare in the writing of *The Merchant of Venice* is still discussed in scholarly literature. For a history of the debate on the anti-Semitic intention of Shakespeare's Shylock, see Brandon Ambrosino, "Four Hundred Years Later, Scholars Still Debate Whether Shakespeare's *Merchant of Venice* is Anti-Semitic," *Smithsonian Magazine,* April 21, 2016, www.smithsonianmag.com/arts-culture/why-scholars-still -debate-whether-or-not-shakespeares-merchant-venice-anti-semitic-180958867.

6. Nick Ottens, "Awful Versions of Ourselves: Creating the Ferengi," *Forgotten Trek,* last modified March 5, 2017, forgottentrek.com/the-next-generation/ creating-the-ferengi.

7. See reference to protestations by writer Brannon Bragga about the anti-Semitism of the Ferengi at first filming, as well as analysis by Sheldon Teitelbaum and quotes from Leonard Nimoy about Roddenbery's anti-Semitism and attitudes toward Jews in Teitelbaum's "My Jewish Trek," *Jewish Journal,* March 18, 2015, jewishjournal. com/commentary/opinion/164916.

8. Alain F. Corcos, *The Myth of the Jewish Race: A Biologist's Point of View* (Bethlehem, PA: Lehigh University Press, 2005), 47–48. See page 26 for Corcos's list of characteristics believed to be innate in the Jewish race.

9. Though much of this custom is superstitious rather than religious, it is drawn from the Babylonian Talmud, mentions of which are examined by Dan Ben-Amos in his chapter "On Demons," in *Creation and Re-Creation in Jewish Thought*, ed. Rachel Elior and Peter Schafer (Tübingen, Germany: Mohr Siebeck, 2005), 36. The practice of disposing of one's nail clippings by burial or burning was also observed and noted among American Jewish communities in the early twentieth-century American South. Leah Rachel Yoffie, "Popular Beliefs and Customs among the Yiddish-Speaking Jews of St. Louis, Mo," *The Journal of American Folklore* 38, no. 149 (July–September 1925): 375–399.

10. "The Last Outpost."

11. "The Last Outpost."

12. According to Patricia Szobar, Jewish men consistently found themselves accused by Germans of hyperactive sex drives, described as deviant and animalistic, and as exploiters of Aryan women for their own sexual gratification. Patricia Szobar, "Telling Sexual Stories in the Nazi Courts of Law: Race Defilement in Germany, 1933–1945." In *Sexuality and German Fascism*, ed. Dagmar Herzog (New York: Berghahn Books, 2005), 147.

13. Andrea Dworkin wrote that traditional anti-Semitism habitually portrayed Jews as rapists of Christian women. The sexual nature of this act, she argued, did not make Jewish men more masculine, but dehumanized them—a feature that is also certainly intended in the lecherous nature of the Ferengi. Andrea Dworkin, "The Sexual Mythology of Anti-Semitism." In *A Mensch Among Men: Explorations in Jewish Masculinity,* ed. Harry Brod (Freedom, CA: The Crossing Press, 1988), 119.

14. Available research into the backgrounds of the actors playing Ferengi included many actors self-identified as being of Jewish descent, such as Hélène Udy (Pel), Josh Pais (Gaila), Lee Arenberg (Gral, Prak, and Bok), Peter Marx (Nibor, Reyga, and Birta), and more of the seventy-eight known named Ferengi across all *Star Trek* series.

15. Alin K. Gregorian, "Comedy Legend Andrea Martin Releases New Book," *Mirror Spectator,* October 10, 2014, mirrorspectator.com/2014/10/10/comedy-legend-andrea-martin-releases-new-book.

16. For a history of the Jewish political tradition, see Daniel Judah Elazar and Stuart Cohen, "Introduction," *The Jewish Polity: Jewish Political Organization from Biblical Times to the Present* (Bloomington: Indiana University Press, 1985).

17. Tanya S. Osensky, *Shortchanged: Height Discrimination and Strategies for Social Change* (Lebanon, NH: University Press of New England, 2018), 30.

18. *Star Trek: Deep Space Nine,* season 4, episode 16, "Bar Association," directed by LeVar Burton, story by Barbara J. Lee and Jenifer A. Lee, teleplay by Robert Hewitt Wolfe and Ira Steven Behr, aired February 19, 1996, in broadcast syndication, Paramount, 1996, Netflix.

19. In a seemingly intentional and misguided redirect, *Star Trek: The Magazine* explained (in a small aside within a twenty-page briefing on the Ferengi species) that the religious significance of the Rules of Acquisition was similar to Earth's Christian religion's Ten Commandments. They do not mention that the Ten Commandments are, of course, Jewish, or that the comparison with the Ferengis' 285 rules are at all reminiscent of that unmentioned religion, from which Christianity was drawn. "Briefing: The Ferengi," *Star Trek: The Magazine* #9 (January 2000): 62–82.

20. Ira Steven Behr, *Star Trek Deep Space Nine: The Ferengi Rules of Acquisition* (New York: Pocket Books, 2012), ix.

21. Ira Steven Behr and Robert Hewitt Wolfe, *Legends of the Ferengi: A Collection of Stories, Fables, Folk Songs, Philosophical Meditations and Outright Lies Based on the Ferengi Rules of Acquisition* (New York: Pocket Books, 1997), 50, 153.

22. Rabbi Yonassan Gershom, *Jewish Themes in Star Trek* (Morrisville, NC: Lulu Press, Inc, 2013), 130.

23. "The Last Outpost."

24. Ross Kraemer, "What Happens When You Die?" in *The Religions of Star Trek*, ed. Ross Kraemer, William Cassidy, and Susan L Schwartz (New York: Basic Books, 2009), 126.

25. The only mention of females in the Rules cited on the show is Rule 94: Females and finances don't mix. *Star Trek: Deep Space Nine*, season five, episode 20, "Ferengi Love Songs," directed by René Auberjonois, written by Ira Steven Behr and Hans Beimler, aired April 21, 1997, in broadcast syndication, Paramount, 1997, Netflix.

26. A connection pointed out by Rabbi Yonassan Gershom in *Jewish Themes in Star Trek*, 130.

27. Pel appears in *Star Trek: Deep Space Nine*, season 2, episode 7, "Rules of Acquisition," directed by David Livingston, story by Hilary J. Bader, teleplay by Ira Steven Behr, aired November 6, 1993, in broadcast syndication, Paramount, 1993, Netflix.

28. "Armin Shimerman."

29. *Star Trek: The Next Generation Officer's Manual* (FASA Corp., 1988).

30. "Heart of Stone," and "Ferengi Love Songs."

31. *Star Trek: Deep Space Nine:* "Family Business," "Ferengi Love Songs," "The Magnificent Ferengi," "Profit and Lace," and "The Dogs of War."

32. *Star Trek: Deep Space Nine,* season 6, episode 23, "Profit and Lace," directed by Siddig El Faddil, written by Ira Steven Behr and Hans Beimler, aired May 11, 1998, in broadcast syndication, Paramount, 1998, Netflix.

33. The first part is revealed in *Star Trek: Deep Space Nine,* season 2, episode 3, "The Siege," directed by Winrich Kolbe, written by Michael Piller, aired October 10, 1993, in broadcast syndication, Paramount, 1993, Netflix; Behr, *Legends of the Ferengi*, 32.

34. "Profit and Lace."

35. Betty Friedan, *The Feminine Mystique* (New York: W. W. Norton & Company, 2010), 512.

36. Joyce Antler's recent book, *Jewish Radical Feminism,* demonstrates two branches of Jewish feminist activity, that of Jewish women in the larger liberation movement, and those leading the movement for religious feminism. Her book stresses the importance of activism in defining the Jewish American woman of the twentieth century, in religious life as well as her place in American society. Joyce Antler, *Jewish Radical Feminism: Voices from the Women's Liberation Movement* (New York: New York University Press, 2018).

37. "Family Business."

38. *Star Trek: Deep Space Nine*, season 7, episode 24, "The Dogs of War," directed by Avery Brooks, story by Peter Allan Fields, teleplay by René Echevarria and Ronald D. Moore, aired May 26, 1999, in broadcast syndication, Paramount, 1999, Netflix.

39. Rev. Dr. David Philipson, "The Beginnings of the Reform Movement in Judaism" in *The Jewish Quarterly Review* Volume XV (New York: The Macmillan Company, 1903), 475.

40. "Heart of Stone."

41. "Ferengi Love Songs."

42. "Bar Association."

43. "The Dogs of War."

44. For more on accusations of Jewish male cowardice and evasion of military service, see Miriam Eve Mora, *Carrying a Big Schtick: American Jewish Acculturation and Masculinity in the Twentieth Century*, Wayne State University Press, forthcoming.

45. "Heart of Stone."

46. "Family Business."

47. J. Emmett Winn, "Racial Issues and Star Trek's Deep Space Nine," *Kinema: A Journal for Film and Audiovisual Media* (Spring 2003), 6.

48. From Jewish peddlers selling goods on the road to family-owned stores that grew into American chains like Macy's, Sears, Gimbels, Stern's, and Filene's, Jews have a long history of commerce in the United States. See Leon Harris, *Merchant Princes: An Intimate History of Jewish Families Who Built Great Department Stores* (New York: Harper Collins, 1982).

49. While pressing Odo to end Rom's strike in "Bar Association," for example, he cites Federation standards: "They're blocking access to my place of business, causing a disturbance on the Promenade, and they're probably a fire hazard."

50. *Star Trek: Deep Space Nine,* season 2, episode 18, "Profit and Loss," written by Robert Wiemer, directed by Flip Kobler and Cindy Marcus, aired March 20, 1994, in broadcast syndication, Paramount, 1994, Netflix.

51. *Star Trek: Deep Space Nine,* season 2, episode 26, "The Jem'Hadar," directed by Kim Friedman, written by Ira Steven Behr, June 12, 1994, in broadcast syndication, Paramount, 1996, Netflix.

52. Andrew Whalen, "Are Ferengi Jewish? *Star Trek: Deep Space Nine* Actor Armin Shimerman Answers," *Player.One,* September 2, 2016, www.player.one/are-ferengi-jewish-star-trek-deep-space-nine-cast-quark-armin-shimerman-118548.

53. He had made no statement that acknowledges any connection, aside from the above.

54. "Armin Shimerman."

WORKS CITED

Ambrosino, Brandon. "Four Hundred Years Later, Scholars Still Debate Whether Shakespeare's *Merchant of Venice* is Anti-Semitic." *Smithsonian Magazine,* April 21, 2016, www.smithsonianmag.com/arts-culture/why-scholars-still-debate-whether-or-not-shakespeares-merchant-venice-anti-semitic-180958867.

Antler, Joyce. *Jewish Radical Feminism: Voices from the Women's Liberation Movement.* New York: New York University Press, 2018.

"Armin Shimerman Feels Responsible for Failed Ferengi Introduction on *Star Trek: The Next Generation,*" *TrekMovie.com,* March 21, 2018, trekmovie.com/2018/03/21/armin-shimerman-feels-responsible-for-failed-ferengi-introduction-on-star-trek-the-next-generation.

Bader, Hilary J., story, teleplay by Ira Steven Behr. *Star Trek: Deep Space Nine.* Season 2, episode 7, "Rules of Acquisition." Directed by David Livingston. Aired November 6, 1993, in broadcast syndication. Paramount, 1993, Netflix.

Behr, Ira Steven. *Star Trek Deep Space Nine: The Ferengi Rules of Acquisition.* New York: Pocket Books, 2012.

Behr, Ira Steven, writer. *Star Trek: Deep Space Nine.* Season 2, episode 26. "The Jem'Hadar." Directed by Kim Friedman. June 12, 1994, in broadcast syndication. Paramount, 1996, Netflix.

Behr, Ira Steven and Hans Beimler, writers. *Star Trek: Deep Space Nine.* Season 5, episode 20, "Ferengi Love Songs." Directed by René Auberjonois. Aired April 21, 1997, in broadcast syndication. Paramount, 1997, Netflix.

Behr, Ira Steven and Hans Beimler, writers. *Star Trek: Deep Space Nine.* Season 6, episode 23. "Profit and Lace." Directed by Siddig El Faddil. Aired May 11, 1998, in broadcast syndication. Paramount, 1998, Netflix.

Behr, Ira Steven and Robert Hewitt Wolfe. *Legends of the Ferengi: A Collection of Stories, Fables, Folk Songs, Philosophical Meditations and Outright Lies Based on the Ferengi Rules of Acquisition.* New York: Pocket Books, 1997.

Behr, Ira Steven and Robert Hewitt Wolfe, writers. *Star Trek: Deep Space Nine.* Season 3, episode 14, "Heart of Stone." Directed by Alexander Singer. Aired February 6, 1995, in broadcast syndication. Paramount, 1993, Netflix.

Ben-Amos, Dan. "On Demons." In *Creation and Re-Creation in Jewish Thought*, edited by Rachel Elior and Peter Schafer. Tübingen, Germany: Mohr Siebeck, 2005.

"Briefing: The Ferengi." *Star Trek: The Magazine* #9 (January 2000): 62–82.

Corcos, Alain F. *The Myth of the Jewish Race: A Biologist's Point of View.* Bethlehem, PA: Lehigh University Press, 2005.

Dworkin, Andrea. "The Sexual Mythology of Anti-Semitism." In *A Mensch Among Men: Explorations in Jewish Masculinity*, edited by Harry Brod. Freedom, CA: The Crossing Press, 1988.

Elazar, Daniel Judah and Stuart Cohen. *The Jewish Polity: Jewish Political Organization from Biblical Times to the Present.* Bloomington: Indiana University Press, 1985.

Fields, Peter Allan, story, René Echevarria and Ronald D. Moore, teleplay. *Star Trek: Deep Space Nine.* Season 7, episode 24. "The Dogs of War." Directed by Avery Brooks. Aired May 26, 1999, in broadcast syndication. Paramount, 1999, Netflix.

Friedan, Betty. *The Feminine Mystique.* New York: W. W. Norton & Company, 2010.

Gershom, Rabbi Yonassan. *Jewish Themes in Star Trek.* Morrisville, NC: Lulu Press, Inc, 2013.

Gregorian, Alin K. "Comedy Legend Andrea Martin Releases New Book." *Mirror Spectator,* October 10, 2014, mirrorspectator.com/2014/10/10/ comedy-legend-andrea-martin-releases-new-book.

Harris, Leon. *Merchant Princes: An Intimate History of Jewish Families Who Built Great Department Stores.* New York: HarperCollins, 1982.

Kraemer, Ross. "What Happens When You Die?" In *The Religions of Star Trek*, edited by Ross Kraemer, William Cassidy, and Susan L Schwartz. New York: Basic Books, 2009.

Lee, Barbara J. and Jenifer A. Lee, story, Robert Hewitt Wolfe and Ira Steven Behr, teleplay. *Star Trek: Deep Space Nine.* Season 4, episode 16. "Bar Association."

Directed by LeVar Burton. Aired February 19, 1996, in broadcast syndication. Paramount, 1996, Netflix.

Meyer, Nicholas, dir. *Star Trek VI: The Undiscovered Country,* directed by Nicholas Meyer. Hollywood, CA: Paramount Pictures, 1991.

Mora, Miriam Eve. *Carrying a Big Schtick: American Jewish Acculturation and Masculinity in the Twentieth Century.* Wayne State University Press, forthcoming.

Osensky, Tanya S. *Shortchanged: Height Discrimination and Strategies for Social Change.* Lebanon, NH: University Press of New England, 2018.

Ottens, Nick. "Awful Versions of Ourselves: Creating the Ferengi," *Forgotten Trek,* last modified March 5, 2017, forgottentrek.com/the-next-generation/creating-the-ferengi.

Philipson, Rev. Dr. David. "The Beginnings of the Reform Movement in Judaism." In *The Jewish Quarterly Review* Volume XV. New York: The Macmillan Company, 1903.

Piller, Michael, writer. *Star Trek: Deep Space Nine.* Season 2, episode 3. "The Siege." Directed by Winrich Kolbe. Aired October 10, 1993, in broadcast syndication. Paramount, 1993, Netflix.

Reeves-Stevens, Judith and Garfield Reeves-Stevens. *The Continuing Mission: A Tenth Anniversary Tribute.* New York: Pocket Books, 1998.

Star Trek: The Next Generation Officer's Manual. FASA Corp, 1988.

Szobar, Patricia. "Telling Sexual Stories in the Nazi Courts of Law: Race Defilement in Germany, 1933–1945." In *Sexuality and German Fascism*, edited by Dagmar Herzog. New York: Berghahn Books, 2005.

Teitelbaum, Sheldon. "My Jewish Trek," *Jewish Journal*, March 18, 2015, jewish-journal.com/commentary/opinion/164916.

Whalen, Andrew. "Are Ferengi Jewish? *Star Trek: Deep Space Nine* Actor Armin Shimerman Answers," *Player.One,* September 2, 2016. www.player.one/are-ferengi-jewish-star-trek-deep-space-nine-cast-quark-armin-shimerman-118548.

Wiemer, Robert, writer. *Star Trek: Deep Space Nine.* Season 2, episode 18. "Profit and Loss." Directed by Flip Kobler and Cindy Marcus. Aired March 20, 1994, in broadcast syndication. Paramount, 1994, Netflix.

Winn, J. Emmett. "Racial Issues and Star Trek's *Deep Space Nine.*" *Kinema: A Journal for Film and Audiovisual Media* (Spring 2003).

Yoffie, Leah Rachel. "Popular Beliefs and Customs among the Yiddish-Speaking Jews of St. Louis, Mo." *The Journal of American Folklore* 38, no. 149 (July–September 1925): 375–399.

Chapter Eight

Who Brings the Messiah?

*Klingon Messianism and
Anti-Messianism in* Star Trek: TNG

Ari Elias-Bachrach

With nearly eight hundred TV episodes and ten movies spread over fifty-four years, *Star Trek* is unquestionably one of the most popular and iconic science fiction franchises in entertainment history. Like all good science fiction, it seeks to examine contemporary issues in a fictional frame. Since its inception, *Star Trek* has striven to show an idyllic version of the future as envisioned by its creator, Gene Roddenberry. In fact, Roddenberry, an avowed secular humanist, did not see a role for religion in the future. Several episodes in the original series and early seasons of *The Next Generation* show religion as the crutch of non-advanced societies that humanity has outgrown.[1] After Roddenberry died in 1991, the show began to examine issues of faith and religion in a much deeper and more nuanced fashion. One particular episode, "Rightful Heir," from the sixth season of *Star Trek: The Next Generation* examines the role of human effort in the name of heavenly redemption and has significant parallels in Jewish thought and practice.

In this episode, Worf, the sole Klingon member of the *Enterprise* crew, has a crisis of faith and decides to visit the Klingons' most sacred monastery at Boreth in the hope of having a spiritual experience. The monastery sits on the site where Klingons believe the emperor Kahless will one day return. According to their legends, Kahless was a Klingon who lived fifteen centuries before. He was a great warrior who united the Klingon tribes and played a vital role in the creation of the Klingon Empire. After his death, he became mythologized to the point of reaching near prophetic status in Klingon culture. In fact, Worf tells his son a tale about how Kahless battled his brother for days for telling a lie—using his mythology as a teaching tale. He is said to be waiting for all honored dead in the afterlife, while his enemies await the dishonored dead.[2]

Worf begins with a spiritual crisis after mentoring young Klingons even more isolated from their Klingon heritage than he is. As he tells Captain Picard (after neglecting his duties to throw himself into a private ceremony):

> WORF: They were young. They knew nothing of their heritage. So while I was there, I tried to teach them. Teach them about their people, their culture. I told them our ancient stories, instructed them in our customs, explained our beliefs. And then I told them about Kahless. How he united our people long ago. How he gave us strength and honor, and how he promised to return one day and lead us again.
>
> PICARD: Is that what you're doing here? Trying to recapture those feelings?
>
> WORF: Yes. I was trying to summon a vision of Kahless.
>
> PICARD: It's a pity you didn't try using the holodeck instead of setting fire to your quarters.
>
> WORF: Using the holodeck would not have been appropriate. Everything had to be real if Kahless were to appear. But all this was for nothing. He did not come to me. I gave Toq and the others a belief in Sto-Vo-Kor, the life which lies beyond this life where Kahless awaits us. When I saw the power of their beliefs, I began to question the strength of my own. And I found it wanting.
>
> PICARD: Have you lost your faith in Sto-Vo-Kor?
>
> WORF: To lose something, one must first possess it. I am not sure I ever had a true belief.

His captain sympathetically suggests, "Perhaps you need to immerse yourself in Klingon beliefs in order to discover whether they can hold any truths for you" and sends him to a retreat where he can explore his faith completely, far from the secular world.

Worf goes to the monastery hoping to have a spiritual revelation. Frustrated by his inability to find a spiritual fulfillment, he becomes jealous of another Klingon who has a vision of Kahless. Eventually, Kahless appears to Worf; however, to Worf's surprise, Kahless is not a vision but a real flesh and blood Klingon. Kahless then proclaims that his long-awaited return has occurred. Kahless's return is greeted with excitement by the priests, hostility by Klingon political leaders who do not want to cede political power, and skepticism from a highly conflicted Worf. Even as Worf is slowly won over, not only by evidence but by Kahless's promise of joy and a return to the spiritual side of life, the Klingon leader Gowron arrives to prove Kahless a fraud. He also points out that Kahless will not unite but will rather divide. "It will be war," Gowron insists. "You are not a fool, Worf. Do you really think that every Klingon in the Empire will bend his knee and grovel before this man just because Koroth says he is Kahless?" He refuses to hand over the Empire.

Still, Worf, inspired by this new leader, protests, "You do not understand. Kahless is our future. Only with his help can we revive the pure warriors within ourselves. Listen to him, Gowron. Open your heart. Hear his words. He will restore your faith as he has restored mine. Give him a chance to lift your spirit and cleanse your heart before you take up arms." When Worf's faith is shattered by Kahless failing the most crucial test—losing a fight with Gowron and thus proving he's not actually the greatest warrior of all—Worf realizes that he is not dealing with the true Kahless, and forces Koroth to reveal the truth: Kahless is a clone. The priests at the monastery cloned Kahless from the blood on a sacred relic and programmed his brain to believe he was Kahless to cause his "miraculous" return.

In contrast to some other Klingons, the priests do not consider their actions to be illegitimate. Their leader Koroth even suggests that they were meant to clone Kahless and that their cloning is merely the method by which Kahless always intended to return. "How do you know that this is not the way the prophecy was to be fulfilled? Who is to say that what we did was wrong?" he insists. To borrow a phrase from nineteenth-century Jewish activist Leon Pinsker, the priests believed in auto-emancipation—that they needed to take their redemption into their own hands instead of waiting for a Messiah to come on his own. Not everyone agrees, of course—as word of the cloning spreads, Worf reveals that while many Klingons are ready to follow the Kahless clone, many view this action as illegitimate. Both sides are fervent enough in their views that he fears the issue may plunge the Klingon empire into civil war.

Although the show's writers compared Kahless and his return to Jesus (The man who developed the screenplay, Ron Moore, commented that he worked to try and tone down the Jesus parallels),[3] and previous work has compared the storyline to Christianity,[4] the plot has, perhaps, greater parallels to Jewish thought than Christian. Jews have likewise been waiting for their redeemer for centuries. Jewish tradition maintains that the coming of the Messiah will bring about an era of peace, a return of Jews to the land of Israel, and a rebuilding of the holy Temple in Jerusalem.[5] Like Kahless, the Jewish Messiah is said to be a great warrior who will unite the people, defeat his enemies, and usher in an era of peace and prosperity. The coming of the Messiah is also meant to coincide with the rebuilding of the holy Temple in Jerusalem, bringing back the Jewish people to the land of Israel, and the reestablishment of religious functions that have ceased.[6] Ultimately, the messianic era will lead to the end of war, famine, and human conflict, leading to an era of peace and harmony that in many ways looks like Gene Roddenberry's ultimate vision for the future.[7] While waiting for the Messiah, Jews too have struggled with the balance between passively waiting for a miraculous redemption and actively sparking one via human endeavors. The debate has played out in almost every time and place in which Jews have lived and continues to this very day.

Maimonides includes waiting for the coming of the Messiah in his thirteen principles of faith. Although he does include a recognition that it may be a long wait, he gives no instructions on how one is to wait.[8] Are Jews expected to wait passively, or should they take action to try and hasten the Messiah's coming? If Jews are meant to actively attempt to bring about the Messiah, what actions should be taken? As is the case with most great Jewish philosophical debates, there are thinkers, rabbis, and philosophers on all sides of the issue. There is one strain of thought that follows the passive approach— redemption can only be brought about by heavenly means and human actions are either not needed or actively discouraged. Another strain of thought follows the opposite approach—human action is necessary to bring about redemption and the coming of the Messiah. This debate usually takes place in one of two spheres—religious action and political action.

Many traditional sources indicate that the timing of the messianic redemption rests solely in the hands of heaven. The Talmud strongly discourages one who even tries to calculate when the messianic redemption will occur (despite providing several examples of rabbis who do just that).[9] The Amidah prayer, which is said three times daily, includes a supplication for messianic redemption. Its text suggests two human actions—waiting and hoping. Neither of these verbs suggests deliberate human action, and thus it supports the thesis that only heavenly endeavors can bring about redemption. While many take it for granted that the Messiah will come when Jews are deserving of redemption, the presence of hope in the prayer is explained by some to be indicative that we hope for redemption even if it is unmerited.[10] Judah Loew ben Bezalel, better known as the Maharal of Prague, writes in *Netzach Yisrael*, his work on exile and redemption, that while the redemption from Egypt was due to the merits of our ancestors, the final messianic redemption will only occur when God wills it.[11] Over the years, many have latched on to these ideas to show that human action cannot hasten the coming of the Messiah.

In the "Rightful Heir" story, the Klingon political leader, Gowron, is strongly opposed to Kahless, in part because of the threat his ascension would pose to his political power. At the same time, Worf sees that Kahless makes a valid point that Klingons have lost their joy and spirituality and would benefit from his teaching them directly. As he tells Gowron, "Like many of our people, they need something to believe in, just like I did. Something larger than themselves, something that will give their lives meaning. They need Kahless." Worf ultimately comes up with a viable solution. Kahless is to be given a new title: Emperor. Although not fully explained in the show, the viewer is left to believe that it is similar to the monarchy in present-day England, where the titleholder has no political power but is still an important and very visible figure. In this role, Kahless will not threaten the established political order but can serve as a moral voice to inspire the people. As Worf adds, "Kahless would be a figurehead, but he will have the ability to rally the people, to lead by example, to guide them in spiritual matters. . . . You would have the power to mold the Klingon heart. You could return them to honorable ways according to the original teachings of Kahless which are within you."

This plotline works not only because of the scattered true believers but the majority's feeling of emptiness. Almost all the Klingon characters seem to agree that the citizenry is engaging in immoral behavior, and a powerful voice capable of inspiring individual behavior would be helpful. In many ways, this is an inversion of a common Jewish practice. Many sources indicate that the Messiah will come only when the people act in a manner befitting redemption (although the timing is still under the control of heaven and not earth). Therefore, the thought goes, we should endeavor to perform the commandments (mitzvot) to spark redemption. In this line of Jewish thought, moral behavior will bring about the Messiah, not the other way around.

Numerous sources in the Torah, the Talmud, and rabbinic writings show a clear connection between *teshuva* and the coming of the Messiah.[12] Although usually rendered as repentance in English, *teshuvah* literally means "return." In its religious context, it means a return to God by performing the mitzvot, or religious commandments. Bringing about messianic redemption is a commonly stated motivation when rabbinic personalities encourage Jews to do mitzvot. As Rabbi Moshe Shternbuch, an Israeli Haredi rabbi who has worked extensively to try to make the South African Jewish community more religious, stated in an address in Johannesburg:

> We know that the timing of Moshiach's arrival is dependent upon our good deeds and that the future of the whole world is interwoven with our redemption. Therefore, each person must do his best to improve himself and bring the redemption that bit closer.[13]

In addition to the general precept that mitzvot will lead to the messianic redemption, there are also examples of specific mitzvot that rabbinic sources single out as directly leading to the coming of the Messiah. Among these are observing the Sabbath,[14] studying Torah,[15] giving charity, and having children.[16] However, if God is judging the Jewish people collectively, then individual action is insufficient. Many modern Jewish observance campaigns are based, at least in part, on attempting to hasten the redemption by encouraging large numbers of Jews to perform mitzvot.

Perhaps the best-known mitzvah campaigns of our time are those run by Chabad. The Chabad organization has, since the late 1960s, made an incredible and concerted effort to get more Jews to perform mitzvot. Several of these have focused on the specific mitzvot mentioned above like giving charity, learning Torah, and lighting Shabbat candles (one of the many aspects of observing the Sabbath).[17] However, most of their efforts are more generally targeted at enabling Jews to perform mitzvot they wouldn't otherwise. This often takes the form of getting an individual to do a single act. It is common to see members of Chabad giving out Shabbat candles, or standing on a street corner with a lulav and etrog on Sukkot to entice passersby to take a few minutes to perform that one mitzvah.[18] From the outset, some of their coreligionists have criticized these tactics as too narrowly focused—to the critics, there is little point in getting a non-religious Jew to shake a lulav for two minutes if he will continue to eat non-kosher food and violate Shabbat. Chabad, on the other hand, maintains a strong belief that each mitzvah has value in and of itself. Part of that value is the potential to bring the Messiah. Each mitzvah that a Chabad emissary gets another Jew to do has the potential to bring about the Messiah and the ultimate salvation he will bring.[19] The Lubavitcher Rebbe, Menachem Mendel Schneerson, was fond of quoting a passage in Maimonides' Mishnah Torah that states that one should view the whole world as being in perfect balance between good and bad, and even one single mitzvah could bring about the entire world's salvation.[20][21] As Rabbi Naftali Silberberg, the author of the popular Moshiach 101 series on Chabad. org puts it:

> As such, when discussing how to hasten the Redemption, the most basic answer is quite simple: jump at every mitzvah opportunity that presents itself. You never know which mitzvah—and it can be any mitzvah—will be the proverbial "straw that breaks the camel's back" and brings the Messianic Era.[22]

While it would be an oversimplification to say that messianic zeal is the primary driver of Chabad's outreach activities, it is clear that the desire to bring about messianic redemption is one of the motivations for their tireless efforts to increase the number of mitzvot performed by their fellow Jews.

Of all the mitzvot in the Torah, one of the most enigmatic is the commandment to send away a mother bird before taking the eggs from her nest. Although rarely performed in modern societies, where most eggs come from the grocery store, it is still a requirement should a Jew try to take the eggs from a nest while the mother bird is present. There is a midrash that states that the performance of this mitzvah will bring about various rewards, including hastening the coming of the Messiah.[23] The Zohar, the source of Jewish kabbalistic thought, provides a more esoteric approach that leads to a specific mechanism that connects these two things—a Jew performing this mitzvah will cause God to have compassion upon the Jewish people and bring them out of exile.[24] Despite the fact that almost no one ever needs to fulfill this mitzvah, there are several practical guides to the mitzvah published in English and Hebrew,[25] and an organization set up to help people fulfill this mitzvah themselves.[26] All of these sources, as well as YouTube instructional videos, explain that the person fulfilling the mitzvah doesn't even need to keep the eggs, as most modern people do not need them. Although the Torah assumed that people would be eating the bird's eggs, the modern sources all focus on the performance of the mitzvah for its own sake, and the potential rewards enumerated by the midrash and the Zohar. The attention given to this mitzvah, despite the fact that it should be almost completely deprecated by modern society, is almost all due to the singular fact that people are performing the commandment for the sake of the heavenly rewards they believe that its performance will bring.

Another midrash that relates to the coming of the Messiah that people have seized upon is found in the Talmud. In three places, the Talmud relates that the Messiah will not come until all the souls awaiting their birth have been born, and only then will the Messiah be born.[27] Immediately, Talmudic commentators are divided on how to interpret this. One group thinks that when the conditions for redemption have been met, a miracle will occur that will cause a large number of multiple births, using up all the souls quickly so that the Messiah can be born.[28] A second group interprets this passage differently— that the Jewish people can cause the messianic age to come quickly by having many children.[29] The second group also gets some support from a number of commentators who wonder how a person who is unable to have children can contribute. They note a second Talmudic prescription, that when the people of Israel properly observe two Sabbaths the Messiah will come and conclude that keeping the Sabbath can be the contribution of someone unable to bear children.[30] Although the division between the Talmudic commentators seems to be technical, we can see that underlying it is a fundamental difference in how they see the world. One group of commentators thinks that humankind can, and perhaps should, play an active role in bringing about the messianic age, while another group is of the view that only God can bring it about, and humans cannot force it to come earlier. This same issue divides the Klingons when they are faced with the Kahless clone; they need to decide if mere mortals can take an active role in hastening the coming of their Messiah.

Perhaps the most visible Jewish movement based on the idea of auto-emancipation is not a religious campaign at all, but rather a political one: the Zionist movement. Many of the founders of the modern Zionist movement were not religious. In fact, Leon Pinsker, in his famous pamphlet, makes it clear that his motives are political. Jewish people can never assimilate fully into their surrounding culture, he says, and therefore they need to have a land of their own to be truly free. He even goes as far as to criticize the idea of the coming of the Messiah as enfeebling and detrimental to national aspirations. If Jews are always waiting for the Messiah to come and save them, they do not feel the need to push for national liberation themselves.

> Moreover, the belief in a Messiah, in the intervention of a higher power to bring about our political resurrection, and the religious assumption that we must bear patiently divine punishment, caused us to abandon every thought of our national liberation, unity and independence. Consequently, we have renounced the idea of a nationhood and did so the more readily since we were preoccupied with our immediate needs. Thus we sank lower and lower. The people without a country forgot their country. Is it not high time to perceive the disgrace of it all?[31]

These political Zionists differed from the established religious order in a critical manner—they were no longer waiting for the Messiah to come and bring about the salvation of the Jewish people. Rather, they were taking matters into their own hands and bringing about that salvation, albeit focused on the physical and not the spiritual dimensions, themselves. Max Nordau, cofounder of the World Zionist Organization with Theodore Hertzl, put it like this:

> The new Zionism, which has been called the political one, differs, however, from the old, the religious, the Messianic one, in this, that it disavows all mysticism, no longer identifies itself with Messianism, and does not expect the return to Palestine to be brought about by a miracle, but desires to prepare the way by its own efforts.[32]

Many of these early Zionists, while not supporting a religious agenda, were still pushing for the emancipation and right of self-determination for the Jewish people. However, they inverted what they saw as the previous model. Much like the priests that cloned Kahless, they were tired of waiting for religious salvation brought about from heaven to bring them the physical changes they wanted and instead decided to push for the physical changes themselves.

In parallel to the political Zionist movement, the nineteenth century also saw the beginnings of a religious Zionist movement. One of the earliest religious Zionists was Rabbi Judah Alkalai. In 1840, several non-religious Western Jews had saved several Jews imprisoned in Damascus on blood libel-related charges. Alkalai saw this human action as a precedent for messianic redemption.[33] Further, Alkalai argued for the creation of Jewish colonies in the land of Israel through human effort, basing himself on traditional Jewish beliefs. He even used a Talmudic interpretation to calculate the minimal number of Jews that needed to move to the land of Israel to cause the divine presence to descend from heaven and dwell amongst the Jews in the land of Israel.[34] Another early religious Zionist, Rabbi Zvi Hirsch Kalischer, also encouraged his fellow Jews to bring about redemption by self-help and not wait for heavenly intervention. He believed, "The redemption will begin with the generating of support among philanthropists and with the gaining of the consent of the nations to the gathering of the scattered of Israel into the holy land."[35]

Further, Kalischer believed that human intervention was not just a nicety, but a necessity to bring about the Messiah. Jews would need to move to Palestine, cultivate the land, and create a viable country through hard work and effort. He believed that God would never do such a thing by miraculous means as a test. Humans need to take matters into their own hands and prove their belief in God by beginning the process of redemption. Only afterward would God finish the work by bringing the Messiah.[36] While religious Jews have always prayed for the coming of the Messiah and the return to Zion, this movement, led by the likes of Alkalai and Kalischer, laid out specific earthly steps to take that would lead to redemption. Like the political Zionist movement, they wanted to invert the common order of waiting for heavenly deliverance to bring about physical change, and they decided to take matters into their own hands by pursuing the physical changes first, which they believed would then lead to heavenly deliverance.

No movement, of course, is without its opponents. When the Klingon priests clone Kahless, many others see that as an illegitimate step that is interfering with the natural order. The use of cloning, deemed an unnatural method even within the science fiction show, underscores how artificial an intervention it is, as does the priests' concealment of their act. In short, the skeptics do not believe that auto-emancipation is legitimate and think only a miracle can bring back the real Kahless. So too with Zionism—there is a very strong Haredi anti-Zionist community that does not believe in the legitimacy of the state of Israel or the movement that created it. Rabbi Moshe Shternbuch sums up the modern Haredi anti-Zionist position as such:

> Some see the establishment of the state of Israel per se as the fulfillment of one of the conditions of the coming of Moshiach, but this is nonsensical. . . . Since the State of Israel does not further Jewish life in accordance with the laws set out by the Torah, it has no significance in the eternal scheme.[37]

To Shternbuch and those like him, a modern secular state not governed by Torah law can never fulfill the dream of messianic redemption. In their eyes, only God can bring the true Messiah and cause all the miracles associated with the Messiah. Anything else is a false hope that detracts from the real focus of performing mitzvot and leading a religious life. He completely rejects not only the notion of auto-emancipation as presented by the secular Zionists, but also the messianic notions of the religious Zionists as well.[38]

Shternbuch is, of course, not alone. In 1900, well before the creation of the state of Israel, Rabbi Zadok Hocohen Rabinowitz, better known as Rav Zadok of Lublin, wrote an open letter criticizing the Zionist movement. He includes the standard religious objection that due to the domination of the Zionist movement in his time by non-religious Jews, the movement was not supportive of the religiously observant lifestyle he supported. However, he also went further. He objected to the use of physical force—weapons and an army—to establish a state.[39] This despite the fact that numerous sources paint the Messiah as a mighty warrior who will subdue the Jewish people's enemies by force.[40] Rav Zadok thought that the right to wield military might was something that could only be granted by God, and that until God sent the Messiah, the Jewish people should be relying on God and God alone for their physical protection. These positions put him in direct contradiction to the Zionist movement.

No survey of religious anti-Zionist beliefs would be complete without a discussion of the three oaths. The Talmud describes three oaths taken when the Jews were exiled from their land, which form a central tenet in Jewish religious anti-Zionist beliefs. The Jewish people swore not to ascend to the land of Israel "like a wall," usually interpreted as meaning to immigrate in large numbers or by force. The Jewish people's second oath was to not rebel against the nations of the world. The third one was not to "force the end" (the end refers to the coming of the Messiah). In return, the nations of the world took an oath not to oppress the Jewish people unduly.[41] Many Jewish Hasidic leaders have based their opposition to Zionism on these oaths, which they believe preclude human action to bring about redemption. Rabbi Joel Teitelbaum, the Satmar Rebbe, is perhaps the most influential religious ant-Zionist and the author of VaYoel Moshe, his magnum opus on the three oaths and religious anti-Zionism in general. He explains that the third oath is referring only to physical activity and not prayer. In doing so he finds himself at odds with Rashi's interpretation, although he does find other sources on which to base his claim.[42] As the Munkaczer Rebbe, Chaim Elazar Spira, head of the Munkaczer Hasidic dynasty in the early part of the twentieth century, put it: "One may not rely on any natural effort or on material salvation by human labor. One should not expect redemption from any source other than God."[43] To the people who subscribe to this notion, the three oaths essentially forbade any human activity that would bring about the Messiah. On the contrary, such actions were a violation of the oaths the Jewish people took, and therefore an act against God. Passivity itself has been raised as a religious obligation and, in complete contradiction to the Zionists, any human action is forbidden.[44]

This conflict over Zionism is perhaps the best crystallization of the debate argued by the Klingons because it hinges on the same fundamental issue—whether human activity can play a role in messianic redemption. Opinions on Zionism within the Jewish community range far and wide. There are secular Zionists who want physical freedom, as embodied by the likes of Nordeau and Herzl. There are also religious leaders like Kook, Alkalai, and Kalischer who view Zionism as, if not an absolute religious obligation, at least a positive step as it will help to bring about religious redemption. The Klingon monks who cloned Kahless are probably most analogous to this group—they too view mortal intervention, even shockingly artificial intervention, as necessary if they are to achieve redemption. The last group discussed here is the religious anti-Zionists who, in complete opposition to the religious Zionists, view any human action to bring about messianic redemption as inherently invalid and even detrimental to the cause of messianic redemption as they constitute an act against God. Gowron, when he discovers that Kahless is a clone, scoffs at the very notion of a cloned leader. Even when he's convinced to consider Kahless as Emperor, he quips, "And what will we tell the people about their new Emperor? That he appeared in a cave or a laboratory?" emphasizing how much the people will be revolted by the revelation of an artificially created Messiah. Although *Star Trek* continually displays his political ambitions as more powerful than his religious ones, he instinctively understands that a manmade (or Klingon-made) Messiah would be invalid. In this way, he is very similar to the various religious anti-Zionists who have taken a similar stance on the cause of Zionism.

Since 1967, the state of Israel has had control of the Temple Mount—the location where the first and second holy Temples stood, and the holiest site in Judaism. This has been the cause of much controversy around the issue of whether a third Temple should be built, and it revolves largely around lines similar to what we have already seen. There are political and practical concerns mostly centered around the fact that the Dome of the Rock, sacred to Islam, is now in the place where the Temples formerly stood. Beyond the practical considerations, of course, are the spiritual. Several midrashim state that the third Temple will be miraculously built by God.[45] The medieval biblical and Talmudic commentator Rashi famously explains that the third holy Temple, whose building is either part of or a herald to the messianic era, will descend from heaven completely built.[46] The Zohar goes a step further, stating that due to the fallible nature of its builders, the destruction of the second Temple was inevitable. The third Temple, built by God, will be eternal.[47]

Believing that the third Temple will descend from heaven fully built does raise some problems. The primary objection is the historical one. King

Solomon built the first Temple, and Ezra and Nechemiah the second. Many people wonder why the third would be any different. A famous statement by Maimonides that the nature of the world will not be altered in the messianic age would also seem to preclude a miraculously appearing Temple.[48] Maimonides also includes the building of the Temple in his list of commandments, implying that it is an obligation incumbent upon humans.[49] There are also sources that state that the Temple will be built, presumably by man, before the Messiah comes.[50] Other authorities also spell out this obligation explicitly.[51] There is also the famous dictum that "one does not rely on a miracle," which would seem to spur humans to action rather than wait passively for God to save them.

With conflicting sources providing different possibilities for when, how, and who will build the third Temple, several rabbinic authorities have tried to harmonize them. Some take the tack that the Temple descending from heaven is meant to be a metaphor and not to be taken literally.[52] Rabbi Jacob Ettlinger states that the physical building will be built by man, but the spirituality will descend from heaven, similar to the way a soul enters a body.[53] Rabbi Shlomo Goren, the former chief rabbi of the Israeli Defense Forces, takes a pragmatic approach—if the Temple does descend from heaven then so be it, but if it doesn't, then it is up to man to build it.[54] On the other hand, the religious anti-Zionists take the divine nature of the third Temple as a given, and see no reason for humans to try to construct a building. Joel Teitelbaum describes this explicitly in the introduction to his work *VaYoel Moshe* and adds that the sins of the Zionists are actively preventing the third Temple from being completed in heaven and descending to Earth.[55] While this is but one microcosm of the debate between Zionists and anti-Zionists, we can see how the fundamental issue of whether or not human action should be used to bring about the messianic era underlies the positions of both sides.

Since its founding in 1987, The Israel-based Temple Institute has been actively preparing for the building of the third Temple. The organization has researched the requirements for temple utensils, clothing, and rituals, and even begun construction on many of the implements the Temple will require. In the late 1990s, the Institute began a new project—an attempt to bring a red heifer to Israel that could be used to purify people who intend to enter the holy areas of the Temple. Described in the Torah in Numbers 19, the cow must be completely red, at least three years old, have never worn a yoke, and be subject to certain other restrictions. It is ritually slaughtered and burned, and its ashes are sprinkled on anyone who wants to become pure in order to enter the Temple. The Mishnah reports that there have only been nine red heifers used prior to the destruction of the second Temple. It is said that the tenth red heifer will be slaughtered by the messiah himself, and many people see the birth of a red cow as an indicator that the messiah's coming is close at hand. The Temple Institute worked with an American cattle farmer to produce a red cow. Their methods are oddly reminiscent of those used by the Klingon priests—they are using thoroughly modern technologies like the implantation of frozen Red Angus Cattle embryos from the United States to speed the process along. To date, the Institute has not managed to produce a cow which meets all the technicalities required by Jewish law, but their work continues. As can be expected, their project has been with support and opposition. Some oppose the project because they view the project as "forcing the end." Others support it for precisely the same reason. There is also another group of people who have emerged in on this debate—secular Jewish Israelis who have minimal interest in the debate over humanity bringing about its own salvation, but who are afraid of the consequences of upsetting the political situation in Israel. One liberal *Haaretz* columnist called for destroying a previous red heifer that was born in northern Israel in 1996. The cow eventually had to be placed under armed guard. This position, too, is well represented in the "Rightful Heir" storyline. Many of the Klingons, including Worf, do not want to see the actions of the priests divide the empire. They, like the secular Israelis who took a similar position, realized that the debate had the potential to divide their people and wanted to eliminate the catalyst for any such debate.

The debates in "Rightful Heir" mirror debates in the Jewish community that have been ongoing for centuries. The role that mortals can play in bringing about divine salvation has been a controversial one. Much like the struggle the Klingons have when faced with the cloned Kahless, Jews too have had to decide whether they should actively try to bring the Messiah or wait for God to send him. The Jewish debate has focused largely on the issue of mitzvah observance to bring the Messiah, and Zionist activities to bring about earthly change that will lead to the coming of the Messiah. In both cases there are arguments on both sides of the issue, with some adhering to a more passive approach to waiting, and some adhering to a more active form of waiting designed to end exile quickly. For those who oppose human-initiated redemption, there is also the issue of how to contend with the results once it has already been done. The priests' intervention will be allowed a place in Klingon society. The equivalent to this would be the segments of the Jewish community that, while rejecting the legitimacy of the state of Israel, do continue to take advantage of access to spiritual sites within the land of Israel while continuing to reject Israel's political power.

The compromise that Worf came up with ultimately sees a separation of religion and state, rather than one entirely subsuming the other. While many American Jews take to this framework naturally, as it is one of the foundational principles of the United States, it is still a somewhat alien concept in Israel. In the episode, Kahless and Gowron, representatives of the spiritual and political, each accept the partnership for the good of the people, as each acknowledges the value in the other's leadership. Real life is, of course, more nuanced than what can be conveyed in a single television episode, and while many Jews today are happy to accept a similar partnership, using political power to control religion or religion to control the state is nothing new in Israeli politics. Issues such as whether the state should continue to enforce religious observance through legislation and whether religious courts should continue to hold political power are hot-button issues in Israel today.

The episode's other conclusion is a personal one for Worf—he tells Kahless that after he found and lost his faith, he no longer knows what to believe. Kahless, the voice of spirituality, replies that an artificial creation's existence does not detract from future miracles or faith in a higher power beyond him. Worf's religion is still there for him, as it was before this addition to it: "You doubt the real Kahless will return one day. You doubt that he is still waiting for you in Sto-Vo-Kor. Kahless left us, all of us, a powerful legacy. A way of thinking and acting that makes us Klingon." Further, receiving the same lesson from an artificial creation, a stand-in, is just as valuable as it's the morality that matters, not its source. Kahless concludes, "If his words hold wisdom and his philosophy is honorable, what does it really matter if he returns? What is important is that we follow his teachings. Perhaps the words are more important than the man." An Israel created by the efforts of man, like a third Temple or Messiah created by human intervention if those were made to exist (to say nothing of an artificially created red heifer or other such debated religious elements), will not stop miracles or divine intervention when the time is right. Kahless is suggesting to his opponents that even if they oppose his existence, it does not need to make them lose faith in their own ways. This too mirrors current beliefs within the Jewish community— there are those who maintain, for example, that the state of Israel is the first step toward the coming of the Messiah, and there are those who think that its existence is an affront to God. Kahless seems to be speaking to the Klingon equivalent of the second group and trying to create common ground with them by showing them that they can continue to pray for true redemption, and it does not matter if the Kahless clone is around or not.

NOTES

1. Primary among these are "The Apple," "Who Mourns for Adonis," and "Who Watches the Watchers." For a full treatment of how these episodes treat religion, see Ross S. Kraemer, William Cassidy, and Susan L. Schwartz, *Religions of Star Trek* (Boulder: Westview Press, 2001).

2. *Star Trek: The Next Generation*, season 6, episode 23, "Rightful Heir," story by James E. Brooks, teleplay by Ronald D. Moore, aired May 17, 1993, in broadcast syndication.

3. Edward Gross and Mark A. Altman, *Captains' Logs: The Unauthorized Complete Trek Voyages* (Boston: Little Brown and Company, 1995), 278.

4. Ross S. Kraemer, William Cassidy, and Susan L. Schwartz, *Religions of Star Trek* (Boulder: Westview Press, 2001), 169.

5. Maimonides, Mishnah Torah, Laws of Kings and Wars, chapter 11.

6. Maimonides, Mishnah Torah, Laws of Kings and Wars, chapter 11.

7. Maimonides, Mishnah Torah, Laws of Kings and Wars, chapter 12.

8. Maimonides, commentary on Mishnah Sanhedrin 10:1.

9. Sanhedrin 97b.

10. Chaim Yosef David Azulai, מדבר קדמות, (Lemberg: Israel Elimelech Stenner, 1864), 99.

11. Maharal, Netzach Yisrael 31:3.

12. Deuteronomy 30:3, Yoma 86b, Sanhedrin 97b.

13. Yaakov Rosenes, *Rav Moshe Speaks: An Anthology of Talks by HaRav HaGaon Rav Moshe Shternbuch* (Jerusalem: Jerusalem Writers Guild, 1988), 123.

14. Shemot Rabbah 25:12.

15. Eliyahu Zuta 14, Zohar III: 2701.

16. Yevamot 62a, Eliyahu Zuta 14.

17. "The Ten Mitzvah Campaigns—Chabad.org." *The Rebbe's 10-Point Mitzvah Campaign for Jewish Awareness and Observance.* Chabad. Accessed February 24, 2021. www.chabad.org/library/article_cdo/aid/108410/jewish/The-Ten-Mitzvah -Campaigns.htm.

18. Sue Fishkoff, *The Rebbe's Army* (New York: Shocken Books, 2003), 11.

19. Fishkoff, 49.

20. Maimonides, Mishnah Torah, Laws of Teshuva 3:4.

21. "The Ten Mitzvah Campaigns."

22. Naftali Silberberg, "Particularly Propitious Mitzvot for Hastening the Redemption," *Chabad. Accessed February 24, 2021,* www.chabad.org/library/article_cdo/aid /1128794/jewish/Particularly-Propitious-Mitzvot.htm.

23. Deuteronomy Rabbah, 6:7.

24. Tikkunei HaZohar, Tikun 6, Zohar Chadah, Midrash Ruth, Ma'amar Kan Tzippor.

25. Naftali Weinberger. *Shiluach Hakan, a Practical Guide* (Brooklyn: Feldheim, 2007), Aharon Zakai, שילוח הקן כהלכתו (Jerusalem: Yeshiva Ohr Yom Tov, 2019), and Avraham Ades, ספר שילוח הקן: שו"ע יור"ד סימן רצב עם פסקי גדולי דורינו (Jerusalem, 2015).

26. "The Mitzvah of Shiluach Hakan" *ShiluachHakan.com*, accessed February 23, 2021. www.shiluachhakan.com.

27. Nida 13b, Yevamot 63b, and Avoda Zara 5a.

28. Tosafot on Nida 13b, S.V. Ad Sheyechlu.

29. Shenei Luchot HaBerit, Torah Shebikhtav, Bereshit, Torah Ohr 52.

30. Yismach Moshe, Ki Tisa 10:1. Chatam Sofer on Nida 13b S.V. Ein Ben David.

31. D. S. Blondheim. "Texts Concerning Zionism: 'Auto-Emancipation.'" (Leon Pinsker). *Jewish Virutal Library. Accessed March 12, 2021.* www.jewishvirtuallibrary .org/quot-auto-emancipation-quot-leon-pinsker.

32. Max Nordau, *Zionism and Anti-Semitism* (New York: Fox, Duffield & co., 1905), 16–17.

33. Howard M. Sachar, *A History of Israel: From the Rise of Zionism to Our Time* (New York: Alfred A. Knopf, 2002), 6.

34. Arthur Herzberg, *The Zionist Idea* (Philadelphia: Jewish Publications Society, 1997), 103–105.

35. Sachar, 7.

36. Herzberg, 109–113.

37. Yaakov Rosenes, *Rav Moshe Speaks: An Anthology of Talks by HaRav HaGaon Rav Moshe Shternbuch* (Jerusalem: Jerusalem Writers Guild, 1988), 127.

38. Rosenes, 127.

39. Paul Mendes-Flohr and Jehuda Reinharz, *The Jew in the Modern World* (Oxford: Oxford University Press, 1995), 544–545.

40. Maimonides, *Mishnah Torah*, Laws of Kings and Wars, 11:4.

41. Ketubot 111a.

42. Joel Teitelbaum, *משה וייאל* (Brooklyn: Jerusalem Publishers, 1961), 55–57.

43. Aviezer Ravitzky, *Messianism, Zionism, and Jewish Religious Radicalism* (Chicago: University of Chicago Press, 1996), 47.

44. Ravitzky, 15–16.

45. Tanna d'bei Eliyahu 18, Pesikta Rabbati 28, Midrash Tanchuma 13.

46. Rashi on Sukkah 41a, s.v. Ei Nami.

47. Zohar, I:221a.

48. Maimonides, Mishnah Torah, Laws of Kings and Wars 12:1.

49. Maimonides, Mishnah Torah, Laws of the Chosen Temple 1:1.

50. Jerusalem Talmud, Maaser Sheni 5:2.

51. Sefer HaChinuch, mitzva 95, Ohr HaChaim on Exodus 25:8.

52. Tifferet Yisrael, introduction to Mishnah Middot.

53. Aruch Laner, Sukkah 41a s.v. Ei Nami.

54. Shlomo Goren, *המועדים תורת,* (Tel-Aviv: Avraham Zioni Publishing, 1964), 472.

55. Teitelbaum, 11 *משה וייאל*.

WORKS CITED

Ades, Avraham. דורינו גדולי פסקי עם רצב סימן ד"יור ע"שו: הקן שילוח ספר, Jerusalem 2015.

Azulai, Chaim Yosef David. *קדמות מדבר,* Lemberg: Israel Elimelech Stenner, 1864.

Blondheim, D. S. "Texts Concerning Zionism: 'Auto-Emancipation.'" *Jewish Virtual Library*. Accessed March 12, 2021. www.jewishvirtuallibrary.org/quot-auto-emancipation-quot-leon-pinsker.

Brooks, James E., story, teleplay by Ronald D. Moore. *Star Trek: The Next Generation.* Season 6, episode 23, "Rightful Heir." Directed by Winrich Kolbe. Aired May 17, 1993, in broadcast syndication.

Fishkoff, Sue. *The Rebbe's Army.* New York: Shocken Books, 2003.

Goremberg, Gershom. *The End of Days: Fundamentalism and the Struggle for the Temple Mount.* New York: Oxford University Press, 2002.

Gross, Edward, and Mark A. Altman. *Captains' Logs: The Unauthorized Complete Trek Voyages.* Boston: Little Brown and Company, 1995.

Herzberg, Arthur. *The Zionist Idea.* Philadelphia: Jewish Publications Society, 1997.

Kraemer, Ross S., William Cassidy, and Susan L. Schwartz, *Religions of Star Trek.* Boulder: Westview Press, 2001.

Maimonides. *Commentary in Talmud Bavli—The Classic Vilna Edition.* 1881. New Jersey: Artscroll, 2003.

Maimonides. *Mishnah Torah, Laws of Kings and Wars.* Translated by Eliyahu Touger. Brooklyn, NY: Moznaim, 1998. *Chabad.* www.chabad.org/library/article_cdo/aid/682956/jewish/Mishneh-Torah.htm

Mendes-Flohr, Paul, and Jehuda Reinharz, *The Jew in the Modern World.* Oxford: Oxford University Press, 1995.

"The Mitzvah of Shiluach Hakan," *Shiluach Hakan,* accessed February 23, 2021. www.shiluachhakan.com.

New, David S. *Holy War: The Rise of Militant Christian, Jewish, and Islamic Fundamentalism.* Jefferson: McFarland & Company, 2001.

Nordau, Max. *Zionism and Anti-Semetism.* New York: Fox, Duffield, & Co, 1905.

Ravitzky, Aviezer. *Messianism, Zionism, and Jewish Religious Radicalism.* Chicago: University of Chicago Press, 1996.

Rosenes, Yaakov. *Rav Moshe Speaks: An Anthology of Talks by HaRav HaGaon Rav Moshe Shternbuch.* Jerusalem: Jerusalem Writers Guild, 1988.

Sachar, Howard M. *A History of Israel: From the Rise of Zionism to Our Time.* New York: Alfred A. Knopf, 2002.

Shipler, David K. "2 Jewish Settlers Held in Bus Plot Said to Confess in a Hebron Raid." *The New York Times,* May 3, 1984, sec. A.

Shipler, David K. "Israelis Charged as Terrorists Get Some Support." *The New York Times,* June 12, 1984, sec. A.

Silberberg, Naftali. "Particularly Propitious Mitzvot for Hastening the Redemption." *Chabad,org.* Accessed February 24, 2021. www.chabad.org/library/article_cdo/aid/1128794/jewish/Particularly-Propitious-Mitzvot.htm.

Teitelbaum, Joel. השמ לאיי Brooklyn: Jerusalem Publishers, 1961.

"The Ten Mitzvah Campaigns—Chabad.org." *The Rebbe's 10-Point Mitzvah Campaign for Jewish Awareness and Observance.* Chabad. Accessed February 24, 2021. www.chabad.org/library/article_cdo/aid/108410/jewish/The-Ten-Mitzvah-Campaigns.htm.

Weinberger, Naftali. *Shiluach Hakan, a Practical Guide.* Brooklyn: Feldheim, 2007.

Zakai, Aharon. שילוח הקן כהלכתו Jerusalem: Yeshiva Ohr Yom Tov, 2019.

Chapter Nine

Across Galaxies

How Science Fiction Echoes the Jewish Experience under Colonization

Sarah Katz

With its gritty exploration of galactic expansion and alien species oppressed by human and nonhuman forces alike, the science fiction television series *Star Trek: Deep Space Nine* demonstrates post-colonial sentiment shared by many previously and presently colonized peoples in the real world. In fact, in following multiple species projected to be occupied by humanity in the near-to-distant future, the two renowned science fiction sagas *Star Trek* and *Star Wars* often excel at creating fictional characters as a mirror for the trauma that war, colonization, and occupation have caused among many humans on today's Earth. As a people whom history has framed as both colonized and colonizer, the legacy of the global Jewish community presents a formidable analogy for many of the nonhuman species in both *Star Trek: Deep Space Nine* and the *Star Wars* prequel series.

On perhaps the most morbid level, the ruthless Borg species of *Star Trek: The Next Generation* represents colonization at its worst—conquest. As a hive mind with the sole mission to assimilate all encountered life forms into their community of drones, this fearsome entity embodies possibly the most notable foe ever to face our Federation protagonists. Indeed, thanks to the collective nature of the Borg, a comparison can be drawn to real-world communism, first viewed as a threat on the global scale during World War II and existing today across various contemporary nations such as China, North Korea, and Russia. As the modern state of Israel was established primarily by Jews from the former Soviet Union, Israeli culture started out by clinging to the communal customs of the nations from which they had fled. In fact, while many Jews expressed obvious gratitude at the opportunity to finally settle in the land of their ancestors that would expectedly provide a safe haven from persecution, the tendency of many Israeli founders to bring along the colonial baggage of their former diaspora host cultures led to many of the later accusations of Jews as oppressors in the Jewish State.

Indeed, while overall few Jews ended up remaining in Europe and even the surrounding Middle East following the founding of Israel and increased emigration opportunities to the United States, the collective trauma of colonization, oppression, and pogroms has left a stain on modern Israeli ethos that the United States frequently faces as intermediary the same way the Federation seeks to mediate among post-colonial alien societies. Unfortunately for the Federation, while they repeatedly succeed in vanquishing the Borg in the preceding series *The Next Generation* and opening scenes of *Deep Space Nine*, the latter series delves into the dark underbelly of a society fresh out of occupation—the Bajorans, finally free from the talons of their former technologically advanced Cardassian overlords.

Only distantly familiar with the Borg threat yet intimately entwined with the Cardassian military members and politicians who still visit their home world, the Bajorans often view the Federation's intermediary efforts as intrusive. Despite the fact that the humans and other species working for Starfleet rarely frequent the planet Bajor, the proximity of the space station *Deep Space Nine* to the planet sets many of the native inhabitants on edge, particularly Acting Major Kira Nerys. As a matter of fact, the parallels between the Bajorans and the Jews stand out with such vigor that sometimes distinguishing whether the Bajorans represent the pre-1948 Jews or the contemporary Palestinian Arabs presents a challenge.

THE ALLUSION TO COLONIZATION AND GENOCIDE

In examining which real-world people the Bajorans resemble most, let us begin with a discussion of assimilation. Historically, whether in the Middle East, China, or Europe—Jews living in diaspora have managed to both integrate enough into society for a portion of their communities to attain prosperity as well as maintain their unique identity and traditions enough to still face bigotry from their host nations during surges of ethnic cleansing. By contrast, the Bajorans never had cause to leave their homeland and, therefore, experienced only colonization rather than forced assimilation. In that way, whereas Jews might even be comparable to Borg drones in terms of involuntary adaptation to their host cultures, one could argue that the Bajoran experience of occupation by a foreign people with stronger weapons echoes closer the Palestinian experience under British rule and then Jewish settlement in reestablished Israel.

That said, the Bajoran plight under brutal occupation also evokes another renowned blight on human history in the real world—Nazi Europe, with the ruthless Cardassian labor camps echoing the concentration camps of Hitler's Third Reich. Indeed, the *Deep Space Nine* episode "Duet" captures the tragic impacts of an occupation on both sides.[1] When Kira Nerys must help decide the fate of a former Cardassian overseer, Gul Darhe'el, who contributed to the genocide of her people, she initially puzzles over his true intentions. Despite his claim to have a high-standing military position, this Cardassian's bio scan identifies him as Aamin Marritza, a mere file clerk.

Moreover, Marritza suffers from a rare disease only contractable in the mines of the brutal Gallitep labor camp. As a Gul military leader would have been unlikely to toil in or near the mines, both Kira as well as the station commander Benjamin Sisko swiftly realize that this man is not who he claims to be. Once evidence ascertains that Gul Darhe'el is, in fact, Aamin Marritza, Kira puzzles over why a Cardassian would approach the station specifically seeking punishment for a crime he did not commit.

Indeed, Marritza eventually comes clean regarding this guilt over years of inaction whilst his species tortured the Bajoran people. This confession echoes the many German soldiers and civilians who took part in the atrocities of the Holocaust out of a sense of duty and fear over the consequences of questioning or disobeying the Nazi authority. Furthermore, this guilt-ridden demonstration also serves as a foil for the multiple Nazis and Nazi sympathizers who showed no remorse for their actions, even at their subsequent trials and executions. Indeed, the fact that Marritza aims to act as Cardassian representative for a more inclusive and peaceful Cardassia exhibits an optimism not readily witnessed in former participants of real-world occupation and genocide.

POST-COLONIAL REIDENTIFICATION

As *Deep Space Nine* continues on from a freshly liberated Bajor to a reality in which the Federation has stepped in as protector and mediator between the Cardassians and the Bajoran people, a parallel emerges to the reidentification of Jews who have settled in the new state of Israel following the Holocaust.

The first mirror into post-colonial identification arises in the episode "Sanctuary," in which the Skrreea, a humanoid alien species from the distant Gamma Quadrant, arrive to the station as refugees after their home world becomes uninhabitable.[2] At first, Kira and the presiding Bajoran government jump at the chance to find these immigrants a new home, scouting out for them Draylon II, a nearby hospitable planet in the Alpha Quadrant. However, the leader of the Skrreea party, Haneek, soon realizes upon studying a star map that Bajor is, in fact, their prophesized holy land. Hearing Haneek's request to settle on Bajor alongside the indigenous inhabitants, Kira and the provisional government soon determine that the planet's resources remain too scarce from post-colonial recovery to accommodate another population of millions. In response, Haneek points out that her people are farmers and, as such, can only benefit the Bajorans in recultivating the land ravaged by the Cardassian occupation. Nonetheless, the Bajorans refuse to take on the Skrreean people, and the latter must relocate to Draylon II.

While an initial viewing of this episode may seem to place the Skrreeans in the role of Jewish refugees from both the Middle East and Europe seeking sanctuary in the new Israeli state, a stark difference arises in terms of origin. For instance, whereas the Skrreeans had not only never set foot in the Alpha Quadrant of the Milky Way, let alone on the planet Bajor, the Jewish people have roots in today's Israel extending over three millennia.[3] Indeed, while various skepticism has challenged the ancient Jewish claim to Israel as solely religious—especially regarding Jews of the European diaspora—relics like an Egyptian stele serves as archaeological evidence alongside genetic evidence placing both Ashkenazi and Mizrahi roots in the Levant.[4] On the other hand, the Skrreeans appear to have simply designated a certain planet as their destined home-world with no explanation as to why or how this determination came to be.

Notwithstanding, the Skrreean offer to help the Bajorans till the land brings to mind the first waves of Ashkenazim fleeing Europe for Israel. Similar to the Skrreea, those Jewish refugees also offered the resident Palestinian Arabs help in making the desert bloom.[5]

By contrast, the Skrreea could similarly take on the role of the Palestinian Arabs who immigrated to the region that currently constitutes Israel during the Islamic Caliphate of the 600s. Over the ensuing years, the Jews and Muslims of the region would experience a tumultuous relationship of alternating allyship and enmity, from Ottoman rule to the influx of Jews from Europe under British-ruled Palestine. In particular, the manner in which the Ferengi—whose capitalistic tendencies and exaggerated facial features (ears versus nose) fans often compare to anti-Semitic tropes surrounding Jewish people—quarrel with the Skrreea while the Federation condescends to them both evokes the Orientalist prism through which many Western nations have tended to view both Jews and Palestinians. This portrayal of Skrreea and Ferengi as infantile and barbaric while Bajorans remain the victims of the post-colonial Cardassian shadow reflects a Federation savior's complex stance akin to that of Europe and the United States in many affairs of the contemporary Middle East.

RESISTING NEOCOLONIAL ASSIMILATION

On the subject of assimilation as well as integration by coercion or for purposes of avoiding persecution, perhaps the greatest difference yet appears between the fictional Bajorans and the Ashkenazi Jews. After all, while Jews today whose ancestors fled Europe for both Israel and the United States are widely assumed to have acquired a proximity to whiteness—and, therefore, to the privilege of safety, such adaptation could be viewed as the Ashkenazim "selling out" to the mainstream, a tendency of which Kira Nerys often accuses the Ferengi barkeep Quark in regard to the Cardassians who used to rule the station. Indeed, as opposed to the Ferengi who frequently seem satisfied to go along with whatever will secure their profits under either Cardassian or Federation leadership, the Bajorans never assumed a Cardassian identity. In this way, despite ubiquitous comparisons to the Ashkenazi victims of the Holocaust by scholarship and pop culture alike, having never caved to the need to assimilate, the Bajorans resemble more closely the Mizrahim living under Dhimmitude in Islamic nations prior to the creation of Israel in 1948.[6]

Potentially closer to a more consensual version of the Borg, Ashkenazi assimilation has tended to model itself after the host culture in the areas of cuisine and fashion, whilst retaining various elements of Jewish tradition via holiday customs and language. However, regardless of the various reasons Ashkenazim may have had for needing to assimilate and blend in prior to making Aliyah to Israel, the fact that many carry a sense of Eurocentrism has often cast a negative light on their diaspora community. Whereas Mizrahi Jews have at least, in many cases, retained fully Hebrew surnames as well as a sense of shared culture with contemporary Middle Eastern cultures, the tendency of many American and even Israeli Ashkenazim to cling to that colorism and superiority they learned from their colonizers presents an opportunity for anti-Semites to paint them as "fake Semites."[7] In contrast, Bajorans have never lost their sense of indigenous identity through a desire to adopt proximity to Cardassian society.

Still, one might attribute this discrepancy between the Ashkenazi and Bajoran neocolonial attitudes to the nature of oppression experienced by each community. For instance, whereas the Bajorans remained on their native land during the occupation of their planet, Ashkenazi Jews eventually adapted to white European culture following generations of forced exile in Europe. Similar to the Bajorans, while largely unable to remain in Israel proper, many Mizrahi Jews at least had the opportunity to remain in the Middle East and North Africa, thus retaining proximity to a Levantine identity, which in many circles during contemporary times has come to define their legitimacy as Zionist Jews.[8] Meanwhile, though brutally tortured and subjected to genocide, most Bajorans managed at least to stay on their home world, mean-ing their identity as Bajorans never faced skepticism.

Thus, rather than any one primary parallel to the Jewish experience in *Deep Space Nine*, allusions to the multifaceted plight of the Jews take several dif-ferent forms. Amidst the recent dive into identity politics by American pop culture and media, various *Star Trek*–related discussions have begun focusing on intersectionality—one such thread of discourse involving Jewish allegory in both the Bajorans and Ferengi, the former as colonized and the latter as begrudgingly assimilated. In the case of the Ferengi, from large noses swapped out for massive ear lobes to the fixation on profit to all actors portraying main Ferengi characters being Ashkenazi Jews, the similarities don't exactly fall short. While often viewed as the series' comic relief species, Quark describes how he plays by Federation rules because when he doesn't, "people like [him] are rounded up and shot," making stark reference to the precarious position the Ferengi have held in Cardassian as well as Federation spaces.

Turning from a point in time immediately after occupation to orienta-tion toward a longer-term neocolonial reality, the *Deep Space Nine* episode "Cardassians" captures survivor's guilt in a light found with great abundance among today's American Ashkenazi Jews.[9] Indeed, while the Bajoran spe-cies largely serves as a main allegory for Jews throughout the franchise, this episode stands out in that the Cardassian character of focus actually exhibits a similar type of remorse and resentment to that shared by many Ashkenazim in the West—a sense of white privilege.

Rugal, a young Cardassian war orphan whose high-ranking parents aban-doned Bajor with the end of the occupation, grew up knowing only the Bajoran couple who raised him. As such, he feels only disdain toward his species and the pain they inflicted upon those with whom he grew up. In fact, when Rugal has the opportunity to meet his birth father, he refuses to return to Cardassia with him or even get to know him, consumed by the knowl-edge of the evil his people enacted. While the notion of a German non-Jew raised by Jews would likely present the expected parallel here, Rugal instead demonstrates the shame experienced by many Ashkenazim in contemporary America and Europe regarding the violence committed by the Israeli govern-ment upon Palestinians during bouts of war with the terrorist group Hamas, seen across world news in great abundance.

Moreover, at home in the West where intersectionality prevails in framing Ashkenazim as the "problematic, powerful white Jews," many Ashkenazi youth have built up resentment toward Israel and even many times toward their own diaspora community as shameful blights of white privilege and colorism.[10] Indeed, with a guilt similar to that of Aamin Marritza alongside a lack of experience with any positive aspects of his own species, Rugal adopts a cynicism that reflects the disdain felt by many Western Jewish youth toward the Israel they have come to view as a white colonialist enterprise in the Middle East.

Building upon the darker aspects of war and occupation that *Deep Space Nine* captures with striking aptitude, the neocolonial experience frequently involves instances of terrorism. Oftentimes, the insurgents in question seek to either oust an occupying military force or protest what they view as the remaining presence of a colonial entity. In the case of real-world history, both militants working for the Gazan political group Hamas as well as Jewish Zionist zealots have each assassinated Jewish people. As an echo to such acts of terrorism in our world, the fictional Bajorans must contend with Vedek Winn, an insidious religious leader who—unlike Kira Nerys, who committed acts of terror while fighting for the liberation of her fellow Bajorans from horrific labor camps—orchestrates attacks not only on the secular human schoolteacher Keiko O'Brien but also upon her own fellow religious figures who she feels challenge her position of power in maintaining the Bajoran faith.

Thereby, in light of the apparent colorist, social hierarchies in contemporary Israel coupled with the perceived religious fanaticism of many Israel supporters, the very question of Zionism—or the belief in a Jewish homeland in historical Israel—has proven contentious enough to generate fictional parallels that can paint the Jewish people as either oppressed or oppressor.[11] Returning to *Deep Space Nine*, perhaps the most controversial allegory for the Jewish experience might just come as a reaction to colonization and oppression—in the form of the elusive and powerful Changeling species. Hailing from the mysterious Gamma Quadrant, the origin race of the shapeshifting station security chief Odo constitutes the main antagonist of the series, as the story shifts from the aftermath of the Bajoran–Cardassian conflict to war with the totalitarian threat from the Gamma Quadrant. Indeed, when the Changelings turn out to be the founding species of the mighty Dominion—an interstellar, colonizing force arguably on par with even the Borg—the Federation must form unlikely alliances with the Cardassians, Romulans, and other major races in order to defend the Alpha Quadrant from conquest.

Still, one of the first aspects Odo learns of his people involves the oppression they endured at the hands of "solids," their term for lifeforms that cannot shapeshift. In fact, the very ability to alter shape even arises as a possible evolutionary response to eons of persecution. When turning again to real-world history and the Jewish people, the myth of "changing shape" has long accompanied large noses and a fixation on money in terms of anti-Semitic stereotypes.[12] Echoing Europe's anti-Semitic fairytales that reflect and justify brutal attacks, Odo's first rumors of his people appear in fairytales the "solids" tell of wicked Changelings. Similar to the history of the Changelings, the Jews have a long history rife with trial and tribulation at the mercy of a vast array of other nations. When the leader of the Dominion—the Female

Founder—tells Odo the story of their people, she consistently refers to her species as under threat from non-Changelings. In fact, she often uses these negative experiences to justify the violent actions of her own race against numerous societies across the Gamma Quadrant. After so much persecution, the Changeling leaders of the Dominion, the Founders, have long held a preemptive outlook to dealing with unknown lifeforms. That is to say, they believe in striking first before a newly encountered community can even pose a threat. Similar to the Borg, the Dominion demands all species either submit or be conquered.

Meanwhile, whereas Jews have never sought to conquer or even send religious missions across the globe, many critics of Israel have come to view the Jewish position of power in the world as one of grossly tipped scales. In his well-known book about Western views on the "exoticism" of the East, Palestinian American professor Edward W. Said states, "You cannot continue to victimize someone else just because you yourself were a victim once—there has to be a limit."[13] While applicable to the human tendency to project, these words also apply in the case of Odo's people. Even though the count-less societies they are conquering may have played no part in Changeling suffering, the Founders view such conquest as necessary to preserving their own security. In the case of the Jewish people, once Israel was reestablished as a safe haven for Jews, suddenly the tides took a turn. Despite the fact that the Ashkenazim had just endured the Shoah and Ethiopian Jews, Mizrahim, and Sephardim survived all manner of hardship from devastating famine to prolonged ethnic cleansing, the granting of a Jewish homeland shifted their perceived victimhood into what looked like agency to the rest of the world. Israel's military successes solidified this impression.

Similarly, in *Deep Space Nine*, the Federation, Bajorans, and other "solids" from the Alpha and Beta Quadrants have had no prior contact with or knowl-edge of the Changelings. As such, from their perspective, the Founders' intent on eradicating every perceived threat before any risk becomes viable seems like nothing short of fascist genocide. Indeed, the Founders have even bioen-gineered their soldiers, the Jem'Hadar species, into becoming physiologically addicted to a chemical that forces obedience and imprinting them to worship the Changelings. The Changelings have likewise genetically manipulated the Vorta species for generations, from worship to removing most of their sense of taste to remind them of their humble origins.

With how the tables have turned according to Western perception—and, in many ways, worldwide—regarding Jewish status gone from oppressed to oppressor, the Changeling parallel might not tread too far. After all, whereas the Jews once may have seemed like the ultimate refugees and scapegoats, destined to remain forever exiled from their homeland to live among strang-ers—the reestablishment of Israel has created challenges for the credence of anti-Semitism as a persistent threat. The very existence of a state solely for Jews renders any possibility of Jewish people facing oppression difficult to comprehend for many people. Moreover, just as the Federation and its allies struggle to understand the Founders' need to spread their Dominion across literal galactic quadrants, myriad Israel critics across the real world rail against the Jewish State's hawkish stance toward its Arab neighbors. Indeed, the West Bank settlements often serve as a hotbed of contention for Western spectators such as the United Nations, not to mention Israeli air raids in response to Palestinian terror attacks from the Gaza Strip on Israel's western border.

Perhaps understandably, the younger generation of Jews in the West who have grown up knowing only relative safety with the lack of pogroms suffered by their forefathers have largely come to distance themselves from Israel and, in many ways, the Jewish culture itself. With anti-Israel Jewish groups such as IfNotNow as well as a staggering decrease in the percentage of Jews in the United States identifying as religiously or even culturally Jewish, a recent poll from 2013 demonstrates significant desire to assimilate, likely in response to the prevalent criticism of Israel and the arguably dangerous notion of Jewish privilege in the West.[14] In *Deep Space Nine,* this sort of pressure to conform has been with Odo since before he even knew about his origins. In fact, on the station he shapes his features to resemble his Bajoran discoverer and has unofficially integrated himself into the military hierarchy as a "constable" devoted to justice without species favoritism. As the only shapeshifter among humanoid solids, he soon discovers his long-awaited meeting with his species brings up more questions than answers. Although he has spent all of his conscious existence under both Cardassian military occupation and Bajoran scientific surveillance focusing all of his energy in maintaining a humanoid shape all day every day, his yearning to know his people continues to simmer.

However, once Odo learns the travesties the Founders have wreaked across his native quadrant and how they aim to do the same in the Alpha Quadrant, the need to dissociate from what the Changelings have become largely supersedes his begrudging desire to rejoin his people. Indeed, once the Federation and Cardassians both learn of the impending threat posed by the Dominion, Odo must prove his loyalty more than ever before. In this way, he essentially has to play the role of the "good Changeling" despite the horrid reputation of his people. In the contemporary West, many Jews can relate regarding the non-Jewish skepticism of Israel as well as perceived Jewish power over arenas such as Hollywood, the media, and politics through groups like the American Israel Public Affairs Committee. While such beliefs surrounding Jewish control may hold little truth, these notions all serve to pressure Jewish youth into securing the part of the "good Jew"—one who is loyal to progressive Western values by valiantly opposing oppressive entities, a label often placed upon the Israeli state by large Western media outlets.[15]

The episode "The Die Is Cast" presents perhaps the most visceral depiction of Odo's inherent yearning for his people—a sentiment comparable to the immense nostalgia felt by so many Jews for the historic Land of Israel.[16] Indeed, while the Cardassian spy Elim Garak tortures Odo in a reluctant, pained attempt to extract information regarding the Founders' motives, the security chief opens up perhaps more than ever before. In an agonized confession, he sputters, "I want to go home." When Garak assumes at first that Odo means home to *Deep Space Nine*, the Changeling clarifies with obvious hesitation, "To the Great Link."

The Great Link serves as the joined state of Odo's entire species, a unification both mental and physical that he later admits provides such perfect clarity that he isn't certain he is even ready to rejoin his people. However, regardless of the political obstacles that may lie in his way and particularly in his most desperate moment, Odo cannot deny that connection to the Link. When compared with the cultural and emotional incentive behind Zionism, the Changeling will to both protect their species at all costs and remain tied to each other holds undeniable parallels. Especially following millennia in Egypt to the mercy of the Assyrians and Babylonians to Greco-Roman and Ottoman rule to the eventual tragedy of the Holocaust in Europe, Zionism has become the primary cultural goal for so many Jews in not only uniting with others of the Jewish faith and history but also of finally having a haven that is entirely *theirs*. The devastation of not only needing to adapt to survive for centuries but then being framed as occupiers once they finally returned to Israel exists at the forefront for much of the collective Jewish psyche. Like Odo's people, Jews continue to contend with the price of the very human tendency to long for home.

THE COLONIZED AS "OTHER"

Thus, science fiction often serves as a window for both optimism and cynical transparency with regard to human nature and experience. Continuing along the vein of occupation to the actual otherization of colonized people, we conclude with another massive *Star* franchise, in a Galaxy Far, Far Away. In the *Star Wars* prequel series, the questionably handled Gungan species, indigenous to Naboo, the home planet of Senators Padmé Amidala and Sheev Palpatine, alludes to both the respectively Eastern European and North African Jewish diaspora pidgin languages of Yiddish and Ladino as well as the creation of cinema's "most reviled character," Jar Jar Binks. Clearly the source of much annoyance for Jedi humans—Qui-Gon Jinn and

Obi-Wan Kenobi—Jar Jar has often been compared to a racist caricature of a Rastafarian.[17] If the Bajorans and Ferengi are the weaker "other" next to the "civilized" Federation, the Gungans are depicted as outright, hapless barbarians, colonized by no fault of their own and struggling to remain in secure isolation rather than assimilate to any degree beyond the most basic trade negotiations. If nothing else, while often accused of mocking the Caribbean Black community, the Gungans are also an allegory for any colonized people—either in their homeland or in exile—who have wound up adopting various aspects of the occupying culture in order to continue existing with some semblance of security.

Commonly derailed for his allegedly childlike demeanor and clumsiness, Jar Jar Binks does represent a caricature—one of a colonized, infantile primitive beside the graceful, competent Jedi and humans of Naboo. Referenced often in Edward Said's "Orientalism," this tendency of colonialists to view the colonized as comic relief fodder suits not only the Western stereotype of the pidgin-speaking Jew but also that placed on Muslim Arabs as terrorists.[18] Even in the case of *Star Wars*, the indigenous Jawa and Tusken Raider species of Anakin Skywalker's home world of Tattooine are literally masked brutes who attack all humans daring to venture onto the desert planet. Specifically, in the case of the Jawa, they are said to raid human outposts because they view water irrigated from the dunes as Jawa territory. Moreover, the Raiders serve as brutes who actually trade humans among their tribes. Indeed, the imagery in *Attack of the Clones* of Anakin's white mother tortured and tied up in their tent is a classic Orientalist stereotype.

Perhaps most obviously, the character of Watto, the slaveowner who oversees Anakin and Shmi Skywalker, can be said to represent the "swindler Jew," complete with short stature, obscure foreign accent, and hooked nose. The second film even adds a beard and black hat, exacerbating this allusion. In fact, Watto's trading of the franchise's main character treads dangerously close to insinuation of the conspiracy holding Jews as responsible for the Transatlantic Slave Trade.[19] If anything, the similarity between Jewish and Arab portrayals in Western science fiction shows that, as much as Jews may seem to have attained a formidable sense of whiteness and privilege, non-Jews in the West commonly still regard them with suspicion and continue to associate them with negative traits. Thereby, whether groveling to adapt and assimilate on foreign lands or to survive impending violence in their recent haven of the new state of Israel, many Jewish people still contend daily with the shadow of colonization.

At the end of the day, a people subjected to the power of another society will often seek any means possible to survive. In fact, Jewish history might represent an almost ideal allegory for the journeys of fictional species explored across some of the most popular science fiction and fantasy in the world. After all, while many cultures have undergone displacement and war, the Jews in the many diasporas throughout their long existence as a people have managed to overcome occupation by fellow Middle Eastern nations in ancient times to colonization by European powers to genocide in European lands. To each of these unique and trying experiences, Jewish people have reacted in kind, adapting as they had to and resisting when necessary. In this way, all of the species examined here could represent the Jewish experience at a certain time and place. In terms of eras throughout history—the Bajorans under Cardassian occupation stand to symbolize the Jews at the mercy of the pogroms and Holocaust in Eastern Europe and Nazi Germany, even as an alternate perspective could portray the Cardassians as the Jews and the Bajorans as the Palestinians or even Mizrahim living in Muslim lands. Meanwhile, the Changelings and Ferengi may allude to Jewish people alternating between assimilation and exploitation in order to safely prosper despite a negative reputation in the West.

Whether in the case of the real-world Jews or the fictional Bajorans, Changelings, Gungans, or Ferengi, all colonized peoples respond to occupation in a manner that they deem most likely to keep them safe. The largest fandoms in Western science fiction have excelled at depicting the multitude of forms that the will to survive can assume.

NOTES

1. *Star Trek: Deep Space Nine*, season 1, episode 19, "Duet," directed by James L. Conway, written by Peter Allan Fields, featuring Avery Brooks, Harris Yulin, Nana Visitor, aired June 13, 1993, in broadcast syndication, Paramount, 2003, DVD.

2. *Star Trek: Deep Space Nine*, season 2, episode 10, "Sanctuary," directed by Les Landau, written by Gabe Essoe and Kelley Miles, featuring Aron Eisenberg, Avery Brooks, Cirroc Lofton, Deborah May, Nana Visitor, aired November 28, 1993, in broadcast syndication, Paramount, 2003, DVD.

3. Kenton L. Sparks, *Ethnicity and Identity in Ancient Israel: Prolegomena to the Study of Ethnic Sentiments and Their Expression in the Hebrew Bible* (Ann Arbor, MI: Eisenbrauns, 1998), 96.

4. Tony Frudakis, "Ashkenazi Jews" in *Molecular Photofitting: Predicting Ancestry and Phenotype Using DNA* (New York: Elsevier, 2010). 383.

5. Jonathan Adelman, "The Case for Israel." *Loyola Journal for Civil Discourse—Loyola University New Orleans*, Loyola University New Orleans, October 23, 2003, www.loyno.edu/civildiscourse/journal.

6. Victor Grech, "The Banality of Evil in the Occupation of Star Trek's Bajor." *Early Human Development* 145 (2020): 105016. doi:10.1016/j.earlhumdev.2020.105016.

7. H. D. Kalev, "Colorism in Israel: The Construct of a Paradox," *American Behavioral Scientist* 62, no. 14 (Dec. 2018): 2101–2116. doi:10.1177/0002764218810749.

8. Moshe Behar, "1911: The Birth of the Mizrahi–Ashkenazi Controversy." *Journal of Modern Jewish Studies* 16, no. 2 (2017): 312–331, doi:10.1080/14725886.2017.1 295588.

9. *Star Trek: Deep Space Nine*, season 2, episode 5, "Cardassians," directed by Cliff Bole, written by Gene Roddenberry and Rick Berman, featuring Avery Brooks, Rene Auberjonois, Alexander Siddig.

10. Cynthia Levine-Rasky, "Jewish Whiteness and Its Others." *Journal of Modern Jewish Studies* 19, no. 3 (2020): 362–381. doi:10.1080/14725886.2020.1718342.

11. Orna Sasson-Levy, "A Different Kind of Whiteness: Marking and Unmarking of Social Boundaries in the Construction of Hegemonic Ethnicity." *Sociological Forum*, 28, no. 1 (2013) 27–50. doi:10.1111/socf.12001.

12. Michael Barkun, Culture of Conspiracy Apocalyptic Visions in Contemporary America." In *Culture of Conspiracy Apocalyptic Visions in Contemporary America*, edited by Michael Barkun (Berkeley: University of California Press, 2014), 101–110.

13. Edward. W. Said, *Orientalism* (New York: Penguin Books, 2019).

14. "A Portrait of Jewish Americans," *Pew Research Center's Religion & Public Life Project*, May 30, 2020, www.pewforum.org/2013/10/01/jewish-american-beliefs-attitudes-culture-survey.

15. John Lloyd, "How the Western Media's Middle East Coverage Has Changed," *BBC News*, Sept. 15, 2014, www.bbc.com/news/world-middle-east-29154941.

16. *Star Trek: Deep Space Nine*, season 3, episode 21, "The Die Is Cast," directed by David Livingston, written by Ronald D. Moore, featuring Rene Auberjonois, Andrew Robinson, Avery Brooks, aired May 1, 1995, in broadcast syndication, Paramount, 2003, DVD.

17. Will Brooker, "Readings of Racism: Interpretation, Stereotyping and *The Phantom Menace*," *Continuum: Journal of Media & Cultural Studies* 15, no. 1 (2001): 15–32.

18. Amaya Martin, "Naji Attallah's Crew: Stereotypes of Jews, Arabs, and Americans in Egypt's Most-Watched Ramadan 2012 Soap Opera," *The Levantine Review* 4, no. 1 (2015): 8. doi:10.6017/lev.v4i1.8717.

19. Bruce Gottlieb, "The Merchant of Menace," *Slate,* May 27, 1999, www.slate.com/id/29394.

WORKS CITED

Adelman, Jonathan. "The Case for Israel." *Loyola Journal for Civil Discourse—Loyola University New Orleans*, Loyola University New Orleans, Oct. 23, 2003. www.loyno.edu/civildiscourse/journal.

Barkun, Michael. *Culture of Conspiracy Apocalyptic Visions in Contemporary America.* Berkeley: University of California Press, 2014, 101–110.

Behar, Moshe. "1911: The Birth of the Mizrahi–Ashkenazi Controversy." *Journal of Modern Jewish Studies* 16, no. 2 (2017): 312–331. doi:10.1080/14725886.2017.1 295588.

Brooker, Will. "Readings of Racism: Interpretation, Stereotyping and *the Phantom Menace*." *Continuum: Journal of Media & Cultural Studies* 15, no. 1 (2001): 15–32.

Essoe, Gabe, and Kelley Miles, writers. *Star Trek: Deep Space Nine.* Season 2, episode 10, "Sanctuary." Directed by Les Landau, featuring Aron Eisenberg, Avery Brooks, Cirroc Lofton, Deborah May, Nana Visitor. Aired November 28, 1993, in broadcast syndication. Paramount, 2003, DVD.

Fields, Peter Allan, writer. *Star Trek: Deep Space Nine.* Season 1, episode 19, "Duet." Directed by James L. Conway, featuring Avery Brooks, Harris Yulin, Nana Visitor. Aired June 13, 1993, in broadcast syndication. Paramount, 2003, DVD.

Frudakis, Tony. "Ashkenazi Jews." In *Molecular Photofitting: Predicting Ancestry and Phenotype Using DNA.* Amsterdam: Elsevier, 2010, 383.

Gottlieb, Bruce. "The Merchant of Menace." *Slate,* May 27, 1999. www.slate.com/id/29394.

Grech, Victor. "The Banality of Evil in the Occupation of Star Trek's Bajor." *Early Human Development* 145 (2020): 105016. doi:10.1016/j.earlhumdev.2020.105016.

Kalev, H. D. "Colorism in Israel: The Construct of a Paradox." *American Behavioral Scientist* 62, no. 14 (Dec. 2018): 2101–2116., doi:10.1177/0002764218810749.

Levine-Rasky, Cynthia. "Jewish Whiteness and Its Others." *Journal of Modern Jewish Studies* 19, no. 3 (2020), 362–381. doi:10.1080/14725886.2020.1718342.

Lloyd, John. "How the Western Media's Middle East Coverage Has Changed." *BBC News*, 15 Sept. 2014, www.bbc.com/news/world-middle-east-29154941.

Martin, Amaya. "Naji Attallah's Crew: Stereotypes of Jews, Arabs, and Americans in Egypt's Most-Watched Ramadan 2012 Soap Opera." *The Levantine Review* 4, no. 1 (2015). doi:10.6017/lev.v4i1.8717.

Moore, Ronald D., writer. *Star Trek: Deep Space Nine.* Season 3, episode 21, "The Die Is Cast." Directed by David Livingston, written by, featuring Rene Auberjonois, Andrew Robinson, Avery Brooks. Aired May 1, 1995, in broadcast syndication. Paramount, 2003, DVD.

"A Portrait of Jewish Americans." *Pew Research Center's Religion & Public Life Project*, May 30, 2020. www.pewforum.org/2013/10/01/jewish-american-beliefs -attitudes-culture-survey.

Roddenberry, Gene, and Rick Berman, writers. *Star Trek: Deep Space Nine.* Season 2, episode 5, "Cardassians." Directed by Cliff Bole, written by, featuring Avery Brooks, Rene Auberjonois, Alexander Siddig. Aired October 24, 1993, in broadcast syndication. Paramount, 2003, DVD.

Said, Edward. W. *Orientalism*. New York: Penguin, 2019.

Sasson-Levy, Orna. "A Different Kind of Whiteness: Marking and Unmarking of Social Boundaries in the Construction of Hegemonic Ethnicity." *Sociological Forum* 28, no. 1 (2013): 27–50. doi:10.1111/socf.12001.

Sparks, Kenton L. *Ethnicity and Identity in Ancient Israel: Prolegomena to the Study of Ethnic Sentiments and Their Expression in the Hebrew Bible.* Ann Arbor, MI: Eisenbrauns, 1998.

Chapter Ten

Mandalorian Midrash

Space Jews and Ancient Exegetical Analysis in Star Wars' The Mandalorian

Caleb Horowitz

In the second season finale of Disney's hit *Star Wars* spin-off series *The Mandalorian*, three different Mandalorians face off because none of them respects each other's visions of what it means to be a Mandalorian.[1] One was born on the planet Mandalore and cites ethnic ties to the tribe. Another was a foundling, adopted by a specific sect of Mandalorians with distinctive cultural practices. And the last of them does not care about whether others consider him a "true" Mandalorian but deeply values the Mandalorian armor he inherited. The questions of what it means to be a Mandalorian and who is a Mandalorian are omnipresent throughout the show. Also present is a consistently upheld real-world parallel, which seems only to grow in legitimacy with each episode: Mandalorians as "space Jews." From dabbling in midrash to expounding Jewish moral lessons, *The Mandalorian* answers questions about the religious function of intertextual storytelling, what it means to be a member of an ethnoreligion, and who gets to claim membership in such an ethnoreligious group. This chapter will show how *The Mandalorian* positions itself as a distinctly Jewish text through replicating Jewish history and culture via the history of the titular Mandalorians; performing a midrashic function in relationship to its revered parent text, *Star Wars;* and presenting Jewish ideology through its storytelling.

MANDALORIANS AS JEWS

The argument that Mandalorians in *The Mandalorian* are stand-ins for real-world Jews is certainly not new. Charlotte Gartenberg proposed this parallel in November 2019 after viewing just the pilot episode of the show. In her *Tablet* article, "Is There a Jew Under the Mandalorian's Mask?" Gartenberg sums up the Mandalorian people as "a race of people repeatedly almost decimated by genocide who now live scattered across the galaxy."[2] She further describes their complicated relationship with assimilation: "These rootless cosmopolitans sometimes blend into their new societies. More often, however, they're forced to support themselves by turning to professions their societies despise."[3] Gartenberg draws parallels between society's pressure to engage in bounty hunting and money lending and between the yarmulkes and Mandalorian helmets as cultural dress and identifier.[4] Although bounty hunting is a common part of the *Star Wars* universe, characters frequently regard the profession with disdain. In *The Empire Strikes Back*, even the villainous Admiral Piett responds with revulsion: "Bounty hunters! We don't need that scum."[5] The *Star Wars Visual Dictionary* claims that "the profession [bounty hunting] as a whole is distinguished by outstanding slime."[6]

Finally, Gartenberg concludes that she may be reading too much into the text, but "even if future episodes deliver very little by way of national narratives about a resourceful people struggling for redemption, it's at least nice for us Jewish *Star Wars* fans to no longer be reduced to Watto."[7] However, Gartenberg's intuition proved right, and across the subsequent fifteen episodes of *The Mandalorian*, the exact themes she suggests are further explored. Mandalorians are frequently depicted as resourceful; the entire plot of the first season of the show is about Din Djarin's "redemption" after putting "the child" Grogu in Imperial hands, and, in season two, national narratives about taking back the planet Mandalore versus continuing to live in exile appear alongside questions about who gets to claim a right to Mandalorian armor and what it means to be a Mandalorian.

Although Jewish parallels to Mandalorians already existed in the animated *Star Wars* shows *The Clone Wars* and *Rebels*, *The Mandalorian* amplifies these themes. For instance, the existence of "The Great Purge," a stand-in for the Holocaust, in which many Mandalorians are slaughtered and most of their prized metal, Beskar, is stolen from them, is introduced in the first season. "The Purge" is a clear parallel for Nazi looting of Jewish jewelry and other possessions. In fact, Nazi Germany relied on plunder of Jewish Holocaust victims to fund its military effort,[8] so *The Mandalorian* draws a parallel with the stolen Beskar and the already Nazi-coded Empire. Likewise, season one ends with teasing the central villain's possession of the stolen

Mandalorian Darksaber (familiar from the cartoons), which served as a symbol of Mandalorian unity and pride.[9] Furthermore, this villain, Moff Gideon, references a specific night of brutality during the Purge called "The Night of a Thousand Tears," a *Mandalorian* counterpart to the very real, very brutal "Night of Broken Glass."[10] The horrifying stack of armor pieces from slaughtered Mandalorians in the season one finale similarly echoes the piles of possessions stolen from death camp victims.

Another detail unique to *The Mandalorian*'s depiction of Mandalorians is the introduction of the code or belief system followed by Mandalorians known as "The Way." Jewish religious law, called *halakha,* also translates roughly as "the way." Just as *halakha* is based on Jewish laws and commandments, *mitzvot,* "The Way" appears to be based on a series of structured rules as well, known as "The Way of Mandalore," which the *Star Wars* wiki, Wookiepedia, describes as "a religion followed by orthodox Mandalorians," indicating that fans are seeing the parallels.[11] These rules fell out of mainstream Mandalorian practice, but Din's branch, "The Tribe," members of the group known as the Children of the Watch, tried to revive these ancient practices, such as never taking off one's helmet.[12] The "orthodox" branch of Mandalorians having stricter guidelines about ceremonial headgear makes the Orthodox Jewish comparison almost inevitable.

Not much is currently known about the exact rules of "The Way," although the tenets of "The Way" seem to be based on the "Resol'nare" of the pre-Disney *Star Wars* Legends sources (no longer canon but often used as source material for newer Disney projects).[13] The "Resol'nare" teaches Mandalorians six important actions: "raising the young to seek honor and glory, wearing armor, defending one's self and one's family, supporting one's clan, speaking a common language, and owing fealty to the leader of the clans."[14] Valerie Frankel notes in *Hunting for Meaning in the Mandalorian* that "this list of practices is not identical to 'The Way' of Mando and his clan . . . [but] the Mando'ade might have been adapted into the Way, as the philosophies are similar."[15] Whereas The Children of the Watch appear to follow both "The Way" and additional, stricter rules, it would appear that most Mandalorians just follow "The Way." Whether an individual who refuses to follow "The Way" could be considered a Mandalorian at all is a question the show does not fully answer, although my analysis of the character Boba Fett will attempt to address this gap.

The question of whether Mandalorians constitute a race, ethnicity, or a religion is additionally complicated by differing answers across the old canon, the new canon as established by Disney for the sequel era, and statements within *The Mandalorian*. Mandalorians' repeated appearances in the cartoons show them as a cultural group willing to take in outsiders. Din Djarin claims, "Mandalorian isn't a race. It's a creed."[16] *Star Wars* Legends sources support this claim. In *Imperial Commando: 501st*, Mandalore the Destroyer insists that Mandalore cannot be exterminated: "We're not huddled in one place—we span the galaxy. We need no lords or leaders—so you can't destroy our command . . . We have no species or bloodline—so we can rebuild our ranks with others who want to join us. We're more than just a people or an army . . . We're a culture. We're an idea. And you can't kill ideas."[17] However, the claim that Mandalorians "have no species of bloodline" is complicated by the canon fact that the people originated on the planet Mandalore, a planet to which the current Mandalorian diaspora shows strong cultural ties and longing for return.

When it comes to authorial intent, none of the writers or creators of *The Mandalorian* have publicly acknowledged the Jewish parallels in the show. However, series creator, producer, and writer John Favreau and episode 8 director Taika Waititi are both Jewish, and both have spoken publicly about how their Jewishness shapes their creative output. In a 2011 interview with *Forward*, Favreau described being raised Jewish, being bar mitzvahed, and raising his own children "Jewish by example."[18] He also describes how the "self-deprecating aspect of [his] persona . . . owes a lot to its Jewish roots."[19] Favreau's production company is even called "Golem Creations," named for the Jewish folk creation.[20] In an interview with *The Hollywood Reporter*, Favreau shows his understanding of the golem myth, explaining that he picked the name because "the Golem could be used to protect the village or you could lose control and it rampages. Technology is that way. You have to make sure that you know why and how you are engaging technology."[21] Jewish director Taika Waititi, director of the 2019 episode "Redemption," which contains the line about Mandalorians being "a creed," the first reference to the "Night of a Thousand Tears," and the first appearance of the stolen Darksaber, also directed the Holocaust comedy drama film *Jojo Rabbit* the same year and believed part of the negative reception the film received was a result of critics not realizing he was Jewish.[22] The presence of these Jewish voices in the making of *The Mandalorian* does not inherently make the texts themselves Jewish, nor does it confirm that Mandalorians are a metaphorical or allegorical representation of the Jewish people, but it does contribute to a narrative of larger parallels—parallels that extend to the structure of *Star Wars* storytelling and fandom itself.

Star Wars and Fandom as Religion: Franchise Storytelling and Revisionism

Star Wars as a franchise has a unique relationship to religion beyond that of creating religious parallels in its text. In "Whose Film Is It Anyway?

Canonicity and Authority in *Star Wars* Fandom," John C. Lyden proclaims that "if there is any popular culture phenomenon that can be referred to as 'religion,' it would be the fandom associated with the *Star Wars* films."[23] He notes that a 2001 census of English-speaking countries found a large number of people marked their religion as "Jediism," but, considering our inability to tell how serious the participants were about their answers, this alone is not particularly compelling evidence of *Star Wars* as religion.[24] More importantly, however, "fan activities" related to *Star Wars* bear striking similarities to religious practice; Lyden identifies such "markers" of religion as "communal identity, a system of beliefs and values, myths and ritual practices."[25] The *Star Wars* fandom engages with the *Star Wars* franchise in much the same way as people engage with religion: meeting in conventions to partake in rituals, celebrating their own holidays, maintaining databases full of information (such as Wookiepedia) to clarify and document the "canon," making moral choices based on the teachings in their text, participating in heated arguments about the canon in places such as internet forums, and collecting significant talismans or figurines.

Although *Star Wars* creator George Lucas often manipulated these religious texts he had originally created and made storytelling decisions the fandom disliked, resulting in fan attempts to restore the "original" versions of the first trilogy or corrective fan fiction, such revisionist processes are not foreign to religious texts either. Lyden notes that "the continual process of revising and reinventing . . . texts" is a hallmark of religious practice as well as fandom.[26] Lyden claims that the internet is responsible for this interactivity by which "practitioners [can be] co-creators of their scriptures, and hence [can] share the authority with the 'original' creators of the text,"[27] (783), but this analysis overlooks that revision and reinvention have been staples of religion from the very beginning, from the abundant versions of Greek mythological tales to the Jewish texts known as midrashim, which will be discussed shortly.

Lyden claims that the internet is responsible for killing the notion of the "fixed, static" text and replacing it with the "interactive, continually reinvented" text,[28] but the process of revision, reinterpretation, and re-creation is not unique to the internet at all. The internet has merely allowed fandoms to take part in community practices formerly reserved for religion. In 2022, the lines between fandom and text are even blurrier than they once were. Members of the 501st Legion, a group of Stormtrooper cosplayers dedicated to hyperrealistic re-creations of Stormtrooper and clone armor, were brought in to act in the eighth episode of *The Mandalorian*.[29] *Clone Wars* and *Rebels* creator and *Mandalorian* director Dave Filoni grew up a huge *Star Wars* fan.[30] The current generation of *Star Wars* creators is composed of the very people who grew up in the fandom/religion of *Star Wars* text(s).

Drawing on cultural studies, Lyden notes that "fans interact with popular culture products to create readings of them which may be subversive to the intents of the commercial manufacturers, or at least at odds with them."[31] This becomes complicated when the fans who interact with the text are given the authority to canonize their contributions. A seemingly similar process happens with midrashim, the main Jewish method of exegetical analysis, which will be explored more in the next section. Through midrashim, rabbinical writers recontexualize the Torah without negating it. Midrashim often read like important updates or reinterpretations of texts for the current moment. Feminist and queer midrashim are testament to the changing nature of religious needs and the texts that fulfill these needs. In much the same way, contemporary canonical *Star Wars* material serves a midrashic function in the ways in which it responds to and redefines *Star Wars*.

MIDRASH

The establishment of *The Mandalorian* as a Jewish text, by virtue of its overt Jewish parallels and the impact of Jewishness on its Jewish authors, can be extended to the function of the text itself as a model of Jewish exegesis. Midrash, a Jewish mode of textual interpretation and analysis, attempts to explain, clarify, or even sometimes "solve" parts of *Tanakh* (Jewish Bible), or in particular, the Torah. As *The Encyclopedia of Judaism* describes, midrash fills in gaps in biblical texts, offering "instructive tales woven around biblical or rabbinic figures being used to derive lessons from the bible" filling in motivations and connections along with more modern interpretations.[32]

Midrash falls into two distinct categories, *halakha* and *aggadah*; halakhic midrash deals specifically with Jewish law and religious practice, and aggadic midrash poses ethical and theological questions, which it often answers through parable, allegory, or metaphor. Aggadic midrash occupies a fraught theological space by having seemingly conflicting jobs: to reify the unchanging text of the Torah and to simultaneously expand meaning of the text in new directions. The problems posed by midrashim are quite similar to those posed by literary interpretation. As Alexander Freer puts it in "Faith in Reading: Revisiting the Midrash-Theory Connection," "any discussion of what a text says or does requires paraphrase, but must add something of interest to that paraphrase if it is to be worthwhile. Yet what it adds must have been already implicit in the original, else it is unjustified."[33] In this way, interpreters of literature, much like rabbinical writers of midrashim, must "infinitely expand" and also "preserve" the text.[34] *The Mandalorian*, as a show, plays the triple role of literary interpretation, midrash, and sacred text. It exists in a space in which it responds to the themes of *Star Wars* (religion, power, family, good versus evil) and "fills in gaps" in its parent text, but it also creates new text, which is then endlessly interpreted by fandom.

If *Star Wars* fans tune in to the weekly episode of *The Mandalorian* hoping to have questions answered about how Snoke was made or the First Order came to power before the events of *The Force Awakens*, or what happened to Ahsoka Tano after *Star Wars: Rebels*, or if Boba Fett really died in *Return of the Jedi*, they are more than happy to engage with a literature that, as Daniel Boyarin puts it, "[like] all serious literature is revision and interpretation of a canon and a tradition," that is "in dialogue with the past and with authority which determines the shape of human lives in the present and future."[35] The hallmarks of pop culture franchise storytelling—expanding on minor characters, eking meaning out of small moments in beloved texts, retconning storytelling inconveniences, and leaving exciting ambiguities for fans to puzzle out—are not so different from the hallmarks of midrash. And in much the same way as a reader could enjoy a midrash for the parable and themes within but would ultimately be lost without the context of the Torah, *The Mandalorian* may provide some enjoyment, but ultimately barely functions without the context of the larger *Star Wars* franchise. This storytelling system only works because the original texts were accepted as sacred, as before described. It is only because of a thriving fandom's obsession bordering on religious fanaticism with the central text—the *Star Wars* original trilogy, or, perhaps, even more narrowly, the 1977 film *Star Wars*—and their acceptance of this text as sacred and profound that a show like *The Mandalorian* is allowed to perform a midrashic function.

Midrash and *The Mandalorian*—acting as commentaries on their parent texts, commentaries on commentaries on the parent text, and texts to which commentaries will later be added—are both largely interested in intertextuality. As Susan Handelman puts it, "texts echo, interact, and interpenetrate" and this intertextuality creates a mode of writing that "expresses an attitude towards the text and its interpretation which is fundamental to Jewish thought."[36] Such intertextuality, often reduced to "easter eggs" by fans and "fan service" by critics, plays an important function in creating a midrashic text, a text that both creates and reifies.

Star Wars functions as what Marsha Kinder calls a "commercial supersystem of transmedia intertextuality."[37] As Lincoln Geraghty puts it in "Transmedia Character Building: Textual Crossovers in the *Star Wars* Universe," this mode of storytelling involves the "creation and development of megafranchises . . . through the dispersal of one storyworld across multiple media."[38] He describes this transmedia world as "flexible and reflexive."[39] Much like midrashim, newer *Star Wars* texts engage intertextually with their predecessor texts. Characters like Boba Fett and Thrawn are "transformed and reimagined" over time[40] as the zeitgeist changes and different kinds of stories become culturally relevant. As with midrashic texts, the newer *Star Wars* canon stories are not meant to detract from what came before. As Geraghty puts it, Fett's new origin story in *Attack of the Clones* "in no way devalues what came before"[41] because "new insights into the character do not start his story over again, as with a reboot, but rather add depth to what fans already perceive as a complicated and important backstory."[42] Similarly, the midrash only ever expands and widens its source text, never removing from it, even as it reinterprets. When, in *The Mandalorian* season two premier, it is revealed that Boba Fett is still alive[43] (after his apparent death in *Return of the Jedi*), this development is viewed as an extension of his story (he must not have *actually* died when it seemed like he did). *Return of the Jedi* does not lose its canonical status; rather, the new events of the *Mandalorian* warp around it to reexamine and reexplain.

A MIDRASHIC READING OF
MANDALORIAN'S THEMES

This chapter is primarily concerned with *The Mandalorian*'s Jewishness, so it becomes relevant to examine the show not only as fulfilling a midrashic function in *Star Wars*, but also as functioning as a traditional aggadah midrash for a distinctly Jewish audience. Although claiming seemingly secular texts such as *The Mandalorian* as biblical midrash is unusual, it is not unprecedented. In *Movies and Midrash: Popular Film and Religious Conversation*, Wendy Zierler outlines a technique she calls "inverted midrash," in which, rather than using rabbinical midrashim to extract Jewish truths, she begins with "profound matters that are raised by thoughtful, artistically rendered novels and movies," and brings these matters into context with Judaism.[44] Although this is a tempting model for examining *The Mandalorian*, it would not allow us to treat *The Mandalorian* as the quintessentially Jewish text it is. Whereas Zierler acknowledges the secular or even Christian nature of her texts and extracts from them more universal themes, such as "issues of religious and theological importance: Good and Evil, Truth and Sin, Free Will, Memory, Cleverness versus Simplicity in matters of faith, images and representations of God, patterns of Confession and Repentance, and the religious function of Beauty,"[45] the themes to which *The Mandalorian* points offer much less universality. Although *The Mandalorian* certainly contains secular themes, episode titles like "The Sin,"[46] "Redemption,"[47] and "The Believer"[48] all explicitly point to the Mandalorian protagonist's religion, which is coded as Jewish.

Furthermore, themes that appear secular take on a Jewish twist through the nature of their Jewish framing. For instance, Din Djarin's turn from a bounty hunter to a man chiefly concerned with caring for a child could be seen as a universal exploration of fatherhood or simply the arc of a character becoming a better person through caring about other people. But instead, the show frames the Mandalorian's change of heart as intrinsically linked to this religious belief system and the framework of being a Mandalorian. Helping Grogu find a Jedi master is not merely about Din becoming a better person, but also represents Din fulfilling his religious duty and becoming a better *Mandalorian*. Din may choose to save Grogu rather than giving him to the remnants of the Empire because he is kind, but he frames this act of kindness through his religion. When he reunites with his mentor the Armorer in the final episode of season one, "Redemption," he explicitly atones for his actions in "The Sin."[49] He asks the armorer what "the Child" is, and she tells him, "It is a foundling. By Creed, it is in your care."[50] When Din is skeptical of this command because the Child is a member of a "race of enemy sorcerers," she tells him he has "no choice." He must "reunite it with its own kind." Her justification? "This is the Way."[51] If "The Way" is to be read as a stand-in for *halakha*, the Mandalorian's choice to take the Child (later known as Grogu) with him cannot be read as separate from his religious beliefs and practice. This does not mean Din doesn't care about Grogu, but rather that the ways in which Din cares about things are rooted in his religious tradition. Taking care of Grogu is not just "being a good person." It is an act of *tikkun olam*.

It is tempting to dismiss the concept of *tikkun olam*, too, as universal, a Jewish word for a universal concept. *Tikkun olam*, literally "repairing the world," is not merely secular but also spiritual work. Its originator, Rabbi Isaac Luria, taught that evil relies on light captured from goodness, and that biblical Adam was given the mission, now passed to humanity, to heal the world: "If he were to obey God's commands, and thus subjugate his body to his divine soul, then good would triumph over the world, the sparks would be freed, and evil would cease to exist."[52] Each act of goodness brings the world closer to redemption, as each act of evil endangers it. "Every individual Jew now has the personal task of sharing in the task of restoring cosmic harmony by avoiding evil and doing good . . . A burden of active responsibility thus falls on the individual."[53] If Din is to be read as a "space Jew," his mission in helping Grogu is much more complex than merely a change of heart. It is an ethical and spiritual imperative. In this sense, the concept of applying midrashim to non-biblical texts allows us to explore not only what makes a particular text Jewish, but also what Jewishness does to the text, and what the text has to say about Jewishness.

NO BELIEF, ONLY DEEDS

One important Jewish parallel in *The Mandalorian* is the presence of a religion that does not focus on a central belief and does not proselytize. The Mandalorian people show no interest in expanding their tribe through conversion. People like Din Djarin are adopted into the tribe as foundlings in need of care in much the same way as an adopted gentile child may be raised into Jewishness and become Jewish, but no Mandalorians approach outsiders and attempt to convince them that their "Way" is correct and should be followed by all. This is in contrast to the Jedi interest in the Force, which, although not universal, takes on a democratizing element in films such as *The Last Jedi*[54] and *Rogue One*,[55] in which "ordinary people" who are not Jedi are encouraged to engage with the mystical Force, or in *The Phantom Menace*,[56] when Anakin is recruited to become a Jedi because of his potential. Throughout the original trilogy, characters even try to convince Han Solo to care about the Force, about which he is initially skeptical, before he eventually "converts" to understanding and respecting it. Mandalorians, by contrast, do not appear to worship anything mystical or a God at all. Their religion is apparently untied to divinity or abstract belief. They have a series of rules to follow, and certain cultural practices and physical items are significant, such as when Din says, "weapons are a part of my religion,"[57] but no God or gods seem to dominate. Arguably, this diverges from most of Jewish practice, which maintains a monolithic understanding of God. However, this understanding is complicated by many religious texts and beliefs among Jewish people. Many kabbalists do not see God as embodied or even a being at all, and Reconstructionist Jews reject "a divinely revealed legislation," while keeping observance and community. "In abandoning the belief in a personal, supernatural god, it moves closer to the secularist position."[58] In contrast, as revealed in a significant *Clone Wars* arc, the Force is directly tied to a pantheon of religious deities known as The Father, the Son, and the Daughter, a clear parallel to the Christian trinity.[59]

Most importantly, although the Mandalorian religion maintains several beliefs, it prioritizes deeds and actions over them; there is no apparent *central* belief that a single figurehead is the key to redemption and salvation. Belief is not tied to identity for Mandalorians, nor for many Jews. Although Din initially believes Bo-Katan is not a "real" Mandalorian because she takes off her mask, anybody who has seen *Clone Wars* or *Rebels* knows this to be false. Whereas Christianity and being a Jedi are a matter of choice alone (Ahsoka leaves the Jedi Order, as does Anakin when he pledges himself to the Dark Side), the Mandalorian people are ethnoreligious. Although conversion appears to be possible and people like Din born outside the tribe can be adopted into it, somebody like Bo-Katan, born a Mandalorian on the planet Mandalore, cannot choose to no longer be a Mandalorian. It is a part of her identity that is untethered from belief or choice. Similarly, Orthodox Jews do not believe anybody born Jewish ever loses their Jewishness, regardless of the choices they make. Although other sects of Judaism disagree on this front, it is important to note that *The Mandalorian* depicts multiple sects of Mandalorians with a multitude of disagreements on key religious issues, as will be discussed in the final section.

HALAKHA, TIERED *MITZVOT, PIKUACH NEFESH*

If being a Mandalorian is more about shared values and culture than belief in an entity or faith, what values do Mandalorians share? In Jewish tradition, core values are called *mitzvot,* and *The Mandalorian* has much to say about such *mitzvot*, the Hebrew word for "precepts" or "commandments."

In *Jewish Values in a Changing World*, Rabbi Yehuda Amital argues that "one of the fundamental principles of *halakha* is the distinction between different levels with regard to various realms."[60] He provides an example from *Yoma* in the *Talmud*: if someone is extremely hungry and only impure/improperly slaughtered animals are available to eat, the hungry person should be given the impure food.[61] "The underlying assumption in all these and similar lists," he writes, "is that in the world of Halakha it is important to distinguish between levels."[62] One of the reasons this is important is that sometimes *mitzvot* may directly contradict one another in a given scenario, so one must choose the more important *mitzvah* to follow. Here, Amital draws on *Sotah* in the *Talmud*: "Who is a 'pious fool?' One who sees a child struggling in a river, and says: 'After I remove my *tefillin*, I will save him.' But by the time he removes his *tefillin*, the child is already dead."[63] In Judaism, preserving life stands above basically all the other commandments, and to save someone, one is obligated to break taboos. The term *Pikuach nefesh*, meaning "watching over a soul," describes the law that the preservation of human life supersedes all other *mitzvot*.[64] Valuing Grogu over rules about helmets is not a matter of breaking religious codes, but a matter of embracing them. This example of differentiating between levels of *mitzvot* is similar to Din Djarin's decisions regarding breaking rules of the code of Mandalore.

In the season two episode, "The Believer," Din must make several decisions that bend or break the rules of the Mandalorian "Way."[65] First, he trades his Mandalorian helmet for an Imperial helmet in order to sneak into an Imperial refinery. Then, when things get really desperate, he bares his face to a scanner. He does so because this is his only option in order to obtain information to save Grogu from Moff Gideon. His partner in crime, Mayfield, initially ridicules him about his religious values, saying, "Seems to me like your rules start to change when you get desperate. I mean, look at ya. You said you couldn't take your helmet off, and now you got a Stormtrooper one on, so what's the rule? Is it that you can't take off your Mando helmet, or you can't show your face? 'Cause there's a difference."[66] Later in the episode, however, after Din must face Mayfield and several Imperials helmetless in an unambiguous breaking of the code, in order to maintain their cover, Mayfield is more understanding. "You did what you had to do," he tells Din; "I never saw your face."[67] The episode frames this as a horrifyingly vulnerable ordeal, but one Din willingly undergoes to save his adopted child. Without an understanding of Jewish religious beliefs, which both include strict moral codes and also allow those codes to be broken for more important ends, Din's actions read as a violation of his beliefs. But if the Mandalorian people are read as Jewish, no such conflict arises.

In Kevin Melrose's "The Mandalorian Just Violated His Most Sacred Vow," for *Comic Book Resources*, Melrose writes, "Din is willing to sacrifice his own life for the sake of The Way, but he isn't willing to sacrifice the Kid's. That shouldn't come as a surprise, considering the lengths he's gone to protect the foundling, another principle of the Way of the Mandalore. And it appears that rule outweighs the other."[68] In contrast, Hannah Shaw-Williams looks for loopholes that could allow Din's actions in "The Mandalorian: Every Code Loophole That Lets Din Djarin Remove His Helmet" for *Screen Rant*.[69] Although Shaw-Williams points out several such loopholes, Din really does not need any to justify his actions. Rabbi Amital's argument about *mitzvot* as tiered explains the Mandalorian's actions.

To analyze Din's prioritizing of one *mitzvah* over another, the rules of The Code of Mandalore must be understood. The Mandalorian must never let his face be seen, as established in "Sanctuary." But another, more important rule appears to be taking care of other members of one's Mandalorian clan, which, for Din, includes Grogu. The creed by which Grogu is under Din's care and the Armorer's charge to reunite the child with "its own kind"[70] thus appear to take precedence over rules about wearing helmets.

In the final episode of season two, Din once again removes his helmet to bid farewell to Grogu as the child departs with Luke Skywalker.[71] This moment, while dramatic and satisfying for viewership as it emphasizes the depth of Din's love for Grogu, is more difficult to parse. It could be read as Din beginning to care less about his Mandalorian identity and "The Way," or it could be read as him once again making an exception on the basis of another *mitzvah*/code. Finally, it could be read as Din's shifting understanding of what it means to be a Mandalorian and what parts of Mandalorian identity are most important to him.

WHO IS JEWISH/A MANDALORIAN?
AN ARGUMENT FOR PLURALISM

There are three distinct kinds of Mandalorians in *The Mandalorian*: first, we have the Children of the Watch, the group to which Din belongs; second, we have the Night Owls, the group of Mandalorians led by Bo-Katan; lastly, we have the lone Boba Fett. Din, Bo-Katan, and Boba Fett all have vastly different views about what being a Mandalorian means. The four major sects of Judaism similarly disagree on who is a Jew.[72] On this issue, once again, many Jews follow *halakha* for guidance, whereas others do not see *halakha* as binding. While Orthodox and Conservative Jews recognize Jews only if they fit *halakhic* definitions, many Reform and Reconstructionist Jews have a broader definition of Jewishness.[73] *Halakhically*, only children born to Jewish mothers or those who have undergone conversion are Jewish.[74] Reform and Reconstructionist traditions typically allow for patrilineal descent and also offer conversion processes that Orthodox Jews may not be willing to accept.[75] And these distinctions do not even account for Karaite Jews, who follow the Torah alone and believe Jewishness is passed only patrilineally, or other minority cultures like Ethiopian Jews.[76] Furthermore, as stated previously, Orthodox Jews believe that those born Jewish who have converted to another religion or entirely left the practices related to Judaism behind are still Jewish, whereas Reform groups would consider such people no longer Jewish. In *The Mandalorian*, the legitimacy of one's *Mandalorian-ness* is a frequent concern for our protagonists, and the Mandalorians with different backgrounds have differing views about who "counts" as Mandalorian and what the "true" Mandalorian way entails.

The most striking scene related to this disagreement over Mandalorian authenticity occurs in the season two episode, "The Heiress," in which Din Djarin meets Bo-Katan Kryze.[77] After Bo-Katan and her crew of Night Owls save Din and Grogu from an attack at the hands of some quarren, Din tells her, "Thank you. I've been searching for more of our kind," but he's stunned when the Night Owls remove their helmets. Instantly, he decides they're not Mandalorians as he accuses them, demanding, "Where did you get that armor?" Bo-Katan's pitying look and lack of confusion suggest she's familiar with his sect. She politely but firmly proves herself by explaining that the armor has been in her family for three generations, but this explanation is not enough for Din. "You do not cover your face. You are not Mandalorian," he argues.[78] The argument that ensues will feel familiar for any Jewish person who has had a religious disagreement with another Jewish person of a different sect or tradition. Bo-Katan and Din Djarin both have deep-seated prejudices against the "wrong" kind of Mandalorian. "He's one of *them*,"

Bo-Katan realizes. She then explains how the broader universe works outside his people's narrow teachings and tells him he is a member of "The Watch," which she calls "a cult of religious zealots that broke away from Mandalorian society" with the goal of "re-establish[ing] the ancient way."[79] Her language here is telling. The words *cult* and *zealots* imply not just fanaticism and intolerance, but also illegitimacy. Indeed, cartoon fans had been watching Din with confusion, as *Star Wars: Rebels* protagonist Sabine Wren and other Mandalorian characters are seen removing their helmets often. Further, the cartoon casts Bo-Katan as the ruling duchess's younger sister, arguably heir to the throne, and absolutely an insider trained in their culture and history.

Although these kinds of disagreements may feel familiar to anyone religious, such as Catholics who frequently find themselves at odds with Protestants, *The Mandalorian* makes several rhetorical moves to characterize this conflict as distinctly Jewish. First, we have the helmets, which closely mirror *kippot*. Orthodox Jewsish men always cover their heads with *kippot*, whereas most Reform Jewsish men only wear their *kippot* within Temple or within the context of religious events. The *kippah* and traditional clothing become a constant marker of Jewishness for Orthodox Jews that is absent from other Jewish groups, who often don't project Jewishness publicly outside of religious scenarios.

Another major marker of Jewishness in *The Mandalorian*'s religious conflict is oppression. Aside from the obvious examples (i.e., genocide and resorting to a profession considered undesirable and/or taboo by the larger public), we also have the use of the word "Mando" as shorthand for "Mandalorian." Throughout the show, every character refers to the titular Mandalorian as *Mando*, and it appears to be his nickname, but, when used by certain characters, it almost sounds like a slur. Characters who clearly hate the Mandalorian for his culture sneer the word. Historically, the shortening of the name of a people group can become a slur, as with *Japanese*. The internet seems divided on the nature of "Mando" and whether or not it constitutes a racial epithet within the world of *Star Wars*.[80] This argument seems to mirror the use of the word *Jew*, which is not a slur in and of itself, but it is often used in place of "Jewish person" by anti-Semites as if it were.[81] The word *Jew* has at various times been the preferred word for a Jewish person and a pejorative, and, even today, its usage maintains this mixed messaging. Some consider the word to have been reappropriated,[82] whereas others find it the best word to use. According to the *American Heritage Guide to Contemporary Usage and Style*, the use of "Jew" as an attributive is almost always pejorative (i.e., "Jew lawyer").[83] However, when used as a noun, it comes down to intent. This can be seen in the opening scene of the first episode, "The Mandalorian," in which the first lines spoken to the protagonist are by a character in a bar looking to start a fight: "You spilled my drink. . . . Hey, *Mando*! I said, 'You spilled my drink . . . '"[84] Whether or not the label is a pejorative, it's certainly not being used pleasantly here. This opening scene, in which the Mandalorian quickly dispatches his opponent, serves the dual function of establishing the protagonist's power and skill and showing the way the world views Mandalorians.

With these religious and ethnic parallels clearly drawn as the backdrop for the religious conflict, the question becomes, "What is *The Mandalorian* saying about multiple kinds of Jews/Mandalorians and how they should interact? Is the show making a moral or practical argument of some kind?" By the end of the second season, the show makes a clear argument for Jewish and Mandalorian pluralism.

As Roberta Rosenthal Kwall writes in her 2020 article for the *Jerusalem Post,* "Disagreement can be the basis of Jewish unity—even during a pandemic." "We would all do well to remember that strong disagreement regarding Jewish practice has always been part of the fabric of Jewish law and life."[85] Kwall writes that, despite disagreements about religious practice and political and social issues, "there is still a shared past, present and hopefully future."[86] In a statement that parallels the thesis of *The Mandalorian*, Kwall writes that, "although there seems to be little consensus on what the essence of Judaism is—or on what it should be—this lack of agreement may actually foster unity because it allows many types of Jews to feel an attachment to their heritage."[87] In a time when it is particularly dangerous to be Jewish, she argues, "a sense of unity among the Jewish people matters more than ever," and "when all streams of Judaism accept the inevitability of differences and appreciate the good faith function of each space on the Jewish religious spectrum, the Jewish people are at their strongest."[88] This argument for this sort of pluralism is present in two separate instances in *The Mandalorian*'s second season. In *The Heiress*, shortly after Din and Bo-Katan's argument, in which he calls her a fake Mandalorian and she calls him a zealot, Bo-Katan saves Din from an angry quarren and then buys him a drink. In an extremely telling line, she says, "Our enemies wanna separate us. But Mandalorians are stronger together."[89] Accordingly, Din agrees to help Bo-Katan with her mission to take down an Imperial freighter. After they succeed in their mission, she tells him, "Your bravery will not be forgotten. This is the way." Din echoes the reply: "This is the way."[90] In this moment, the two characters show that they have learned to accept one another as legitimate Mandalorians. They have also proven that "unity among the [Mandalorian] people" is a powerful force against their enemies, especially the remnants of the Nazi-coded Empire.

This unity becomes relevant once again in the final episode of season two, in which Bo-Katan, Boba Fett, and Din all team up to save Grogu and reclaim the Darksaber.[91] The parallels become complicated here, because the language related to reclaiming Mandalore mirrors discussion related to Zionism by real-world Jews. "We will help you. In exchange, we will keep that ship to retake Mandalore . . . Mandalorians have been in exile from our home world for far too long," Bo-Katan explains.[92] She wants to recruit Din to join her, but he is largely uninterested in Mandalore the planet. His identity as a Mandalorian does not have ties to a particular piece of land in the way that Bo-Katan's does. Although the disagreement about whether reclaiming their destroyed homeland is a worthy cause and the narrative of exile are familiar for Jews, the parallel does not extend beyond this comparison because there is no analogue for Palestinians, and the Mandalorians are less than a generation removed from their home planet; furthermore, the show has yet to explore what the population of Mandalore looks like post-Imperial razing. The comparison to Zionism here, then, serves only to show further disagreement among Mandalorians about a large issue and to highlight themes of exile and diaspora, rather than staking a clear stance related to Zionism, Israel, and Palestine.

The Fetts' contribution to the Mandalorian–Jew metaphor is more ambiguous than Din's or Bo-Katan's. Jango Fett, the bounty hunter who became the template for the clone army in the *Star Wars* prequels, also had one "unaltered" clone whom he considered his son, Boba Fett. The status of these two Fetts as Mandalorians is disputed by *Star Wars* creators and fans alike. Much of this is a result of Disney's replacement of the old canon, leaving a large gap in Jango Fett's history and altering Boba's. In the Legends (pre-Disney) canon, Jango Fett was a Mandalorian who was a prominent figure in the Mandalorian Civil War and eventually became the leader of the True Mandalorians.[93] However, in the "Creating Mandalore" featurette on *The Clone* Wars: Season Two DVD set, Dave Filoni claims that George Lucas said the Fetts were not legitimate Mandalorians.[94] After the new Disney canon was established, Lucasfilm Story Group member Pablo Hidalgo stated that the Fetts are not Mandalorians, but they might claim to be Mandalorians.[95] Within the new canon, bits and pieces of the old canon remain, either as small references for fans ("easter eggs") or direct re-creations of aspects of the old canon, leaving Jango's relationship to Mandalorian history and culture in flux. For instance, in episode fourteen of *The Mandalorian*, the chain code of Boba's armor (formerly Jango's) mentions Jango's mentor, whose name is partially revealed in the episode as "Jaste . . . " likely a reference to the Legends character Jaster Mereel. Furthermore, when Din Djarin tells Boba, "Your father was a foundling," Boba responds, "Yes. He even fought in the Mandalorian Civil Wars."[96] Jango may no longer have canon ties to the title of "Mandalore" but he *is* canonically a Mandalorian, at least if *The Mandalorian* is privileged as canon above the earlier statements of Hidalgo. However, Boba's status as a Mandalorian is frequently disputed and called into question by other characters.

In the aforementioned season two finale, "The Rescue," Bo-Katan tells Boba Fett, "You are not a Mandalorian," and Boba replies, "Never said I was."[97] The parallel to Jewishness here could go in multiple directions. *The Mandalorian* does not show how Mandalorian identity is passed other than through conversion/adoption into the tribe. It is heavily implied that the children of Mandalorians are automatically considered Mandalorians as well, but there is no mention of rules about patrilineal or matrilineal descent. Just as a person who does not consider themselves Jewish may say that they have Jewish heritage because they have a Jewish father or other Jewish ancestor, Boba mentions that "The armor was given to my father, Jango, by your forebears."[98] In other words, Mandalorians accepted Jango as a member of the tribe, but Boba makes no claims about his own membership. Boba does not have a Mandalorian mother, marking a possible parallel to the children of Jewish fathers and goyim mothers. Of course, Boba has no mother at all and is merely a clone of Jango, complicating this comparison further. There is also the possibility that Bo-Katan considers Mandalorian identity to be tied to a specific set of ideas or practices (The Way), and because Boba has no interest in The Way, he does not qualify as Mandalorian. This could serve as a parallel for atheist, agnostic, or other nonreligious/nonobservant Jews, who may feel ostracized from their community.

There are big questions left unanswered by the first two seasons of *The Mandalorian* regarding Jewishness and pluralism. *The Mandalorian* makes an argument for disparate Jews working together toward a common goal against their oppressors, but beyond that, what does this pluralism entail? Once Din and Bo-Katan have finished fighting the Empire, what comes next? Will they respect one another's differences in the long term and forge a long-lasting alliance? What place does Boba Fett have in this fight, and will he ever be seen as a Mandalorian himself? As with real-world Nazis, unfortunately, the Empire doesn't seem to be going anywhere. Between the events of *The Mandalorian* and *The Force Awakens*, the defunct Empire has regrouped into a new identity, The First Order, which is written to parallel Neo-Nazis in many ways.[99] And although the Empire's hatred of Mandalorians is always framed as political and unrelated to underlying prejudice, and, furthermore, the Empire is just as interested in exterminating Jedi as they are in killing Mandalorians, the reality of the Mandalorians forever facing oppression at the hands of one entity or another feels inevitable. Perhaps the goal of pluralism and solidarity need not extend beyond recognizing one another's legitimacy and fighting a shared oppressor.

Certainly, future seasons of the wildly popular *Mandalorian* will pose more questions and offer or deflect further answers. The parallels to Jewishness may become further tangled or full of contradictions, especially as the show seems to be building up toward reclaiming Mandalore, which may or may not have further parallels with Zionism. However, this uncertain future does little to nullify the Jewishness of the show; the first two seasons are steeped in this Jewishness, and the show makes moral arguments based on this parallel. It is not enough to say that Mandalorians parallel Jews; it is more important to say that *The Mandalorian* makes a compelling argument for a particular Jewish reality: one in which texts both reify and reinterpret parent texts, intertextuality defines storytelling, *mitzvot* are seen as tiered, *pikuach nefesh* is given its due, and Jewish pluralism and solidarity are important tools for fighting for a better world.

NOTES

1. *The Mandalorian*, season 2, episode 8, "Chapter 16: The Rescue," directed by Peyton Reed, written by Jon Favreau, featuring Pedro Pascal, aired December 18, 2020, on Disney+.

2. Charlotte Gartenberg, "Is There a Jew Under the Mandalorian's Mask?" *Tablet,* November 14, 2019. www.tabletmag.com/sections/news/articles/is-there-a-jew-under -the-mandalorians-mask.

3. Gartenberg.

4. Gartenberg.

5. *Star Wars: Episode V—The Empire Strikes Back*, directed by Irvin Kershner, featuring Mark Hamill and Harrison Ford, written by Leigh Brackett and Lawrence Kasdan (1980; San Francisco, CA: Lucasfilm Ltd, Buena Vista Home Entertainment, 2019), DVD.

6. David West Reynolds, Don Bies, and Nelson Hall, *Star Wars: The Visual Dictionary* (New York: DK Publishing, 1998), 52.

7. Gartenberg.

8. Evgeny Finkel and Volha Charnysh. "Property Stolen during the Holocaust Made Some Communities Richer, even 70 Years Later." *The Washington Post,* August 8, 2017. www.washingtonpost.com/news/monkey-cage/wp/2017/08/07/holocaust -plunder-left-some-combig%20munities-richer-even-70-years-later-what-does-that -mean-for-mosul.

9. *The Mandalorian*, season 2, episode 3, "Chapter 11: The Heiress," directed by Bryce Dallas Howard, written by Jon Favreau, featuring Pedro Pascal, aired November 13, 2020, on Disney+.

10. *The Mandalorian*, season 1, episode 8, "Chapter 8: Redemption," directed by Taika Waititi, written by Jon Favreau, featuring Pedro Pascal, aired October 30, 2020, on Disney+.

11. "Way of the Mandalore," *Wookiepedia*, April 10, 2021. starwars.fandom.com/ wiki/Way_of_the_Mandalore.

12. "The Heiress."

13. Lucasfilm Ltd, "The Legendary Star Wars Expanded Universe Turns a New Page." *Star Wars*, April 25, 2014. www.starwars.com/news/the-legendary-star-wars -expanded-universe-turns-a-new-page.

14. Daniel Wallace, Ryder Windham, and Jason Fry, *The Bounty Hunter Code* (San Francisco: Chronicle Books, 2013), 131.

15. Valerie Estelle Frankel, *Hunting for Meaning in the Mandalorian: An Unau- thorized Guide to Homages, Symbols and Backstory* (USA: LitCrit Press, 2020), 63.

16. *Mandalorian*, "Chapter 8: Redemption."

17. Karen Traviss, *Imperial Commando: 501st* (New York: Del Rey, 2009), 158.

18. Curt Schleier, "Q&A: Jon Favreau on Spielberg, 'Iron Man,' and Being a Model Actor," *Forward,* August 1, 2011. forward.com/ schmooze/140685/q-and-a-jon-favreau-on-spielberg-iron-man-and-bei.

19. Schleier.

20. Matthew Belloni, "Jon Favreau Unveils 'Star Wars' Series 'The Man- dalorian,' Marvel Plans and a New Venture," *The Hollywood Reporter*, August 21, 2019. www.hollywoodreporter.com/news/jon-favreau-unveils-star-wars-series -mandalorian-marvel-plans-a-new-venture-1233239.

21. Belloni.

22. Times of Israel Staff, "Jojo Rabbit Director Says Critics Wouldn't Be as Harsh if They Knew He's Jewish," *The Times of Israel,* February 12, 2020, www.timesofisrael .com/jojo-rabbit-director-says-critics-wouldnt-be-as-harsh-if-they-knew-hes-jewish.

23. John C. Lyden, "Whose Film Is It, Anyway? Canonicity and Authority in 'Star Wars' Fandom," *Journal of the American Academy of Religion* 80, no. 3 (2012): 775.

24. Lyden, 775.

25. Lyden, 775.

26. Lyden, 783.

27. Lyden, 783.

28. Lyden, 783.

29. Noah Dominguez, "The Mandalorian Enlisted the Help of Stormtrooper Group the 501st Legion," *Comic Book Resources*, December 29, 2019, www.cbr.com/the -mandalorian-501st-legion-stormtrooper-extras.

30. *Disney Gallery: The Mandalorian*, season 1 episode 1, "Directing," directed by Bradford Baruh, aired May 4, 2020, on Disney+.

31. Lyden, 777.

32. Geoffrey Wigoder, ed., "Midrash," *The Encyclopedia of Judaism* (New York: Macmillan, 1989).

33. Alexander Freer, "Faith in Reading: Revisiting the Midrash-Theory Connec- tion," *Paragraph* 39, no. 3 (2016): 336.

34. Freer, 336.

35. Daniel Boyarin, *Intertextuality and the Reading of Midrash* (Bloomington and Indianapolis: Indiana University Press, 1994), 19.

36. Susan A. Handelman, *The Slayers of Moses: The Emergence of Rabbinic Inter- pretation in Modern Literary Theory* (Albany: State University of New York Press, 1982), 47.

37. Marsha Kinder, *Playing with Power in Movies, Television, and Video Games: From Muppet Babies to Teenage Mutant Ninja Turtles* (Berkeley. University of California Press, 1991): 4. ark.cdlib.org/ark:/13030/ft4h4nb22p.

38. Lincoln Geraghty, "Transmedia Character Building Textual Crossover in the Star Wars Universe." In *Star Wars and the History of Transmedia Storytelling*, ed. Sean Guynes and Dan Hassler-Forest (Amsterdam: Amsterdam University Press, 2018), 117.

39. Geraghty, 118.

40. Geraghty, 188.

41. Geraghty, 121.

42. Geraghty, 122.

43. *The Mandalorian*, season 2, episode 1, "Chapter 9: The Marshal," directed by Jon Favreau, written by Jon Favreau, featuring Pedro Pascal, aired October 30, 2020, on Disney+.

44. Wendy Zierler, *Movies and Midrash: Popular Film and Jewish Religious Conversation* (Albany: State University of New York Press, 2017), 14.

45. Zierler, 5.

46. *The Mandalorian*, season 1, episode 3, "Chapter 3: The Sin," directed by Deborah Chow, written by Jon Favreau, featuring Pedro Pascal, aired November 22, 2019, on Disney+.

47. *Mandalorian*, "Chapter 8: Redemption."

48. *The Mandalorian*, season 2, episode 7, "Chapter 15: The Believer," directed by Rick Famuyiwa, written by Rick Famuyiwa, featuring Pedro Pascal, aired December 11, 2020, on Disney+.

49. *Mandalorian,* "Chapter 8: Redemption."

50. *Mandalorian*, "Chapter 8: Redemption."

51. *Mandalorian,* "Chapter 8: Redemption."

52. Geoffrey Wigoder, ed., "Luria, Isaac," *The Encyclopedia of Judaism* (New York: Macmillan, 1989).

53. Nicholas De Lance, *An Introduction to Judaism* (Cambridge: Cambridge University Press, 2000), 206.

54. *Star Wars Episode VIII: The Last Jedi*, directed by Rian Johnson (2017; Burbank, CA: Buena Vista Home Entertainment, 2018), DVD.

55. *Rogue One: A Star Wars Story*, directed by Gareth Edwards (2016; Burbank, CA: Buena Vista Home Entertainment, 2017), DVD.

56. *Star Wars Episode I: The Phantom Menace*, directed by George Lucas (1999; Beverly Hills, CA: 20th Century Fox Home Entertainment, 2001), DVD.

57. *The Mandalorian*, season 1, episode 2, "Chapter 2: The Child," directed by Rick Famuyiwa, written by Jon Favreau, featuring Pedro Pascal, aired November 15, 2019, on Disney+.

58. Nicholas De Lance, *An Introduction to Judaism* (Cambridge: Cambridge University Press, 2000), 82.

59. *The Clone Wars*, season 3, episode 16, "Altar of Mortis," directed by Brian Kalin O'Connell, written by Christian Taylor, aired February 4, 2011, on Cartoon Network.

60. Yehuda Amital, *Jewish Values in a Changing World*, ed. Amnon Bazak, trans. David Strauss, trans. and ed. Reuven Ziegler (Jersey City: KTAV Publishing House, 2005), 55.

61. Amital, 55.

62. Amital, 56.

63. Amital, 58.

64. Geoffrey Wigoder, ed. "Pikku'ah Nefesh," *The Encyclopedia of Judaism.* (New York: Macmillan, 1989).

65. *Mandalorian*, "Chapter 15: The Believer."

66. *Mandalorian*, "Chapter 15: The Believer."

67. *Mandalorian*, "Chapter 15: The Believer."

68. Kevin Melrose, "The Mandalorian Just Violated His Most Sacred Vow," *Comic Book Resources*, December 11, 2020, www.cbr.com/mandalorian-spoilers-chapter-15 -shows-face.

69. Hannah Shaw-Williams, "The Mandalorian: Every Code Loophole That Lets Din Djarin Remove His Helmet," *Screen Rant,* December 12, 2020, screenrant.com/ mandalorian-din-djarin-remove-helmet-code-rules-break.

70. *Mandalorian*, "Chapter 8: Redemption."

71. *Mandalorian*, "Chapter 16: The Rescue."

72. Geoffrey Wigoder, ed., "Patrilineal Descent Controversy," *The Encyclopedia of Judaism* (New York: Macmillan, 1989).

73. Wigoder, "Patrilineal."

74. Wigoder, "Patrilineal."

75. Wigoder, "Patrilineal."

76. Geoffrey Wigoder, ed., "Karaism," *The Encyclopedia of Judaism* (New York: Macmillan, 1989).

77. *Mandalorian*, "Chapter 11: The Heiress."

78. *Mandalorian*, "Chapter 11: The Heiress."

79. *Mandalorian*, "Chapter 11: The Heiress."

80. Leah Marilla Thomas, "The Newbie's Guide to the Star Wars Lingo in *The Mandalorian*," *Refinery29*, November 15, 2019, www.refinery29.com/en-us/2019/11 /8819115/mandalorian-star-wars-terms-vocabulary-disney-plus.

81. Susan Sommercamp, "'Jew.' Why Does the Word for a Person of My Religion Sound Like a Slur?" *The Washington Post,* May 3, 2016, www.washingtonpost .com/news/acts-of-faith/wp/2016/05/03/jew-why-does-the-word-for-a-person-of-my -religion-sound-like-a-slur.

82. Sommercamp.

83. "Jew." In *The American Heritage Guide to Contemporary Usage and Style*, ed. Steven Kleinedler and Susan Spitz (New York: Houghton Mifflin Company, 2005), 269.

84. *The Mandalorian*, season 1, episode 1, "Chapter 1: The Mandalorian," directed by Dave Filoni, written by Jon Favreau, starring Pedro Pascal, aired November 12, 2019, on Disney+.

85. Roberta Rosenthal Kwall, "Disagreement Can Be the Basis of Jewish Identity—Even During a Pandemic," *The Jerusalem Post,* April 22, 2020, www.jpost.com

/opinion/disagreement-can-be-the-basis-of-jewish-unity-even-during-a-pandemic
-625528.

86. Kwall.

87. Kwall.

88. Kwall.

89. *Mandalorian*, "Chapter 11: The Heiress."

90. *Mandalorian*, "Chapter 11: The Heiress."

91. *Mandalorian*, "Chapter 16: The Rescue."

92. *Mandalorian*, "Chapter 16: The Rescue."

93. Haden Blackman and Ramon F. Bachs. *Jango Fett: Open Seasons* (Wilwaukie, OR: Dark Horse, 2002).

94. "Creating Mandalore." In *Star Wars: The Clone Wars the Complete Season Two*, DVD, created by George Lucas (Burbank, CA: Warner Home Video, 2010).

95. Pablo Hidalgo, @pablohidalgo, "The Fetts Aren't Mandalorian, though I Suppose Jango Claimed to Be from Concord Dawn at Some Point," Twitter post, January 29, 2016, 11:30 p.m. twitter.com/pablohidalgo/status/693214698003644417.

96. *The Mandalorian*, season 2, episode 6, "Chapter 14: The Tragedy," directed by Robert Rodriguez, written by Jon Favreau, starring Pedro Pascal, aired December 4, 2020, on Disney+.

97. *Mandalorian*, "Chapter 16: The Rescue."

98. *Mandalorian,* "Chapter 14: The Tragedy."

99. Eliana Dockterman, "J. J. Abrams Says Nazis Inspired the New Star Wars Villains." *Time*, August 25, 2015. time.com/4010014/j-j-abrams-star-wars-force-awakens-villain-nazi.

WORKS CITED

Amital, Yehuda. *Jewish Values in a Changing World*. Edited by Amnon Bazak. Translated by David Strauss. Edited by Reuven Ziegler. Jersey City: KTAV Publishing House, 2005.

Baruh, Bradford, director. *Disney Gallery: The Mandalorian*. Season 1, episode 1, "Directing." Aired May 4, 2020, on Disney+. www.disneyplus.com/video/4b9bc917-870c-4f72-b60b-a5f0d0b3313d.

Belloni, Matthew. "Jon Favreau Unveils 'Star Wars' Series *The Mandalorian,* Marvel Plans and a New Venture." *The Hollywood Reporter*, August 21, 2019. www.hollywoodreporter.com/news/jon-favreau-unveils-star-wars-series-mandalorian-marvel-plans-a-new-venture-1233239.

Blackman, Haden, and Ramon F. Bachs. *Jango Fett: Open Seasons.* Wilwaukie, OR: Dark Horse, 2002.

Boyarin, Daniel. *Intertextuality and the Reading of Midrash*. Bloomington and Indianapolis: Indiana University Press, 1994.

Christian Taylor, writer. *The Clone Wars*. Season 3, episode 16, "Altar of Mortis." Directed by Brian Kalin O'Connell. Aired February 4, 2011, on Cartoon

Network. Disney+, 2021. www.disneyplus.com/video/75e60bba-9b85-4531-aec2 -7f3b9ed18e4c.

"Creating Mandalore." In *Star Wars: The Clone Wars The Complete Season Two.* Created by George Lucas. Burbank, CA: Warner Home Video, 2010. DVD.

De Lance, Nicholas. *An Introduction to Judaism.* Cambridge: Cambridge University Press, 2000.

Dockterman, Eliana. "J. J. Abrams Says Nazis Inspired the New Star Wars Villains." *Time*, August 25, 2015. time. com/4010014/j-j-abrams-star-wars-force-awakens-villain-nazi.

Dominguez, Noah. "The Mandalorian Enlisted the Help of Stormtrooper Group the 501st Legion." *Comic Book Resources,* December 29, 2019. www.cbr.com/the -mandalorian-501st-legion-stormtrooper-extras.

Edwards, Gareth, director. *Rogue One: A Story Wars Story.* 2016; Burbank, CA: Buena Vista Home Entertainment, 2017. DVD.

Famuyiwa, Rick, writer. *The Mandalorian.* Season 2, episode 7, "Chapter 15: The Believer." Directed by Rick Famuyiwa, featuring Pedro Pascal. Aired December 11, 2020, on Disney+. www.disneyplus.com/video/9cda1e7b-d890-4bc9-a765 -eb8d691cf91d.

Favreau, Jon, writer. *The Mandalorian.* Season 1, episode 1, "Chapter 1: The Mandalorian." Directed by Dave Filoni, featuring Pedro Pascal. Aired November 12, 2019, on Disney+. www.disneyplus.com/video/30ea8a44-797d-4da8-b776 -2e3636a2bf5a.

Favreau, Jon, writer. *The Mandalorian.* Season 1, episode 2, "Chapter 2: The Child." Directed by Rick Famuyiwa, featuring Pedro Pascal. Aired November 15, 2019, on Disney+. www.disneyplus.com/video/0e2b152d-6736-4635-8b0d-4c15f7bb5253.

Favreau, Jon, writer. *The Mandalorian.* Season 1, episode 3, "Chapter 3: The Sin." Directed by Deborah Chow, featuring Pedro Pascal. Aired November 22, 2019, on Disney+. www.disneyplus.com/video/8d1a536a-6815-4afe-ae71-cab7b3004a36.

Favreau, Jon, writer. *The Mandalorian.* Season 1, episode 8, "Chapter 8: Redemption." Directed by Taika Waititi, featuring Pedro Pascal. Aired December 27, 2019, on Disney+. www.disneyplus.com/video/2bb20bd2-cdcd-4f4c-b6bd-62339fb14087.

Favreau, Jon, writer. *The Mandalorian.* Season 2, episode 1, "Chapter 9: The Marshal." Directed by Jon Favreau, featuring Pedro Pascal. Aired October 30, 2020, on Disney+. www.disneyplus.com/video/ed92dc4e-7b61-4ade-aeab -6a9d0eff808b.

Favreau, Jon, writer. *The Mandalorian.* Season 2, episode 3, "Chapter 11: The Heiress." Directed by Bryce Dallas Howard, featuring Pedro Pascal. Aired November 13, 2020, on Disney+. www.disneyplus.com/video/6af69e26-d6f3-4914 -b417-0ceaedec6668.

Favreau, Jon, writer. *The Mandalorian.* Season 2, episode 8, "Chapter 16: The Rescue." Directed by Peyton Reed, featuring Pedro Pascal. Aired December 18, 2020, on Disney+. www.disneyplus.com/video/2b916945-c54e-4dc1-a250 -811aa302e07f.

Favreau, Jon, writer. *The Mandalorian.* Season 2, episode 6, "Chapter 14: The Tragedy." Directed by Robert Rodriguez, featuring Pedro Pascal. Aired December

4, 2020, on Disney+. www.disneyplus.com/video/f0b3a47d-d833-4725-b46f
-a2cf974271f6.

Finkel, Evgeny. and Charnysh, Volha. "Property Stolen during the Holocaust Made
Some Communities Richer, even 70 Years Later." *The Washington Post,* August
8, 2017. www.washingtonpost.com/news/monkey-cage/wp/2017/08/07/holocaust
-plunder-left-some-combig%20munities-richer-even-70-years-later-what-does-that
-mean-for-mosul.

Frankel, Valerie Estelle. *Hunting for Meaning in The Mandalorian: An Unauthorized
Guide to Homages, Symbols and Backstory.* USA: LitCrit Press, 2020.

Freer, Alexander. "Faith in Reading: Revisiting the Midrash-Theory Connection."
Paragraph 39, no. 3 (2016): 335–357. DOI: 10.3366/para.2016.0205.

Gartenberg, Charlotte. "Is There a Jew Under the Mandalorian's Mask?" *Tablet,*
November 14, 2019. www.tabletmag.com/sections/news/articles/is-there-a-jew
-under-the-mandalorians-mask.

Geraghty, Lincoln. "Transmedia Character Building Textual Crossovers in the Star
Wars Universe." In *Star Wars and the History of Transmedia Storytelling*, edited by
Sean Guynes and Dan Hassler-Forest. Amsterdam: Amsterdam University Press,
2018, 117–128. www.jstor.org/stable/j.ctt207g5dd.12.

Handelman, Susan A. *The Slayers of Moses: The Emergence of Rabbinic Interpretation
in Modern Literary Theory.* Albany: State University of New York Press, 1982.

Hidalgo, Pablo. @pablohidalgo, "The Fetts Aren't Mandalorian, though I Suppose
Jango Claimed To Be from Concord Dawn at Some Point," Twitter post, January
29, 2016, 11:30 p.m. twitter.com/pablohidalgo/status/693214698003644417.

"Jew." In *The American Heritage Guide to Contemporary Usage and Style.* Edited by
Steven Kleinedler and Susan Spitz. New York: Houghton Mifflin Company, 2005.

Johnson, Rian, director. *Star Wars Episode VIII: The Last Jedi.* 2017; Burbank, CA:
Buena Vista Home Entertainment, 2018. DVD.

Kershner, Irvin, director. *Star Wars Episode V: The Empire Strikes Back.* featuring
Mark Hamill and Harrison Ford, written by Leigh Brackett and Lawrence Kasdan.
1980; San Francisco, CA: Lucasfilm Ltd, Buena Vista Home Entertainment, 2019.
DVD.

Kinder, Marsha. *Playing with Power in Movies, Television, and Video Games:
From Muppet Babies to Teenage Mutant Ninja Turtles.* Berkeley: University of
California Press, 1991. ark.cdlib.org/ark:/13030/ft4h4nb22p.

Kwall, Roberta Rosenthal. "Disagreement Can Be the Basis of Jewish Unity—even
During a Pandemic." *The Jerusalem Post,* April 22, 2020. www.jpost.com/opinion
/disagreement-can-be-the-basis-of-jewish-unity-even-during-a-pandemic-625528.

Lucas, George, director. *Star Wars: Episode I: The Phantom Menace.* 1999; Beverly
Hills: 20th Century Fox Home Entertainment, 2001. DVD.

Lucasfilm Ltd. "The Legendary Star Wars Expanded Universe Turns a New Page."
Star Wars, April 25, 2014. www.starwars.com/news/the-legendary-star-wars
-expanded-universe-turns-a-new-page.

Lyden, John C. "Whose Film Is It, Anyway? Canonicity and Authority in 'Star Wars'
Fandom. *Journal of the American Academy of Religion* 80, no. 3 (2012): 775–786.
www.jstor.org/stable/23250724.

Melrose, Kevin. "The Mandalorian Just Violated His Most Sacred Vow." *Comic Book Resources*, December 11, 2020. www.cbr.com/mandalorian-spoilers-chapter-15 -shows-face.

Reynolds, David West. *Star Wars: The Visual Dictionary.* New York: DK Publishing, 1998.

Schleier, Curt. "Q&A: Jon Favreau on Spielberg, 'Iron Man,' and Being a Model Actor." *Forward,* August 1, 2011. forward.com/ schmooze/140685/q-and-a-jon-favreau-on-spielberg-iron-man-and-bei.

Shaw-Williams, Hannah. "The Mandalorian: Every Code Loophole That Lets Din Djarin Remove His Helmet." *Screen Rant*, December 12, 2020. screenrant.com/ mandalorian-din-djarin-remove-helmet-code-rules-break.

Sommercamp, Susan. "'Jew.' Why Does the Word for a Person of my Religion Sound Like a Slur?" *The Washington Post*, May 3, 2016. www.washingtonpost.com/news /acts-of-faith/wp/2016/05/03/jew-why-does-the-word-for-a-person-of-my-religion -sound-like-a-slur.

Thomas, Leah Marilla. "The Newbie's Guide to the Star Wars Lingo in *The Mandalorian*." *Refinery29*, November 15, 2019. www.refinery29.com/en-us/2019 /11/8819115/mandalorian-star-wars-terms-vocabulary-disney-plus.

Times of Israel Staff. "Jojo Rabbit Director Says Critics Wouldn't Be as Harsh if They Knew He's Jewish." *Times of Israel*, February 12, 2020. www.timesofisrael.com/ jojo-rabbit-director-says-critics-wouldnt-be-as-harsh-if-they-knew-hes-jewish.

Traviss, Karen. *Imperial Commando: 501st.* New York: Del Rey, 2009.

Wallace, Daniel, Ryder Windham, and Jason Fry. *The Bounty Hunter Code.* Chronicle Books, 2013.

Wigoder, Geoffrey, ed. *The Encyclopedia of Judaism.* New York: Macmillan, 1989.

Wookiepedia. "Mandalorian." *Wookiepedia,* April 10, 2021. starwars.fandom.com/ wiki/Mandalorian.

Zierler, Wendy I. *Movies and Midrash: Popular Film and Jewish Religious Conversation.* Albany, NY: State University of New York Press, 2017.

Chapter Eleven

Zombies and Educating Jewish Brains

Rabbi Matthew Nover and Heather Nover

The 2010s were a peak time for zombies in pop culture. The TV show *The Walking Dead* had recently premiered, the book *Pride & Prejudice & Zombies* was a huge hit, and there were frequent conversations around our Shabbat table about a zombie apocalypse. How would *halakhah* (often translated as Jewish law) deal with such an end of the world scenario? One day, after Shabbat, we (Heather and Matt) started thinking about how we could bring the topic into the supplementary school at which we both taught. We love any opportunity to engage learners by applying popular culture to Jewish ideas. By the end of the week, we created a full curriculum spanning topics from "what are zombies" to "can you loot during a zombie apocalypse," including a potential Nerf obstacle course with fake zombies. We launched it in the spring semester, with each of us teaching it to different age groups. By the end of that semester, Matt had used a passing period between teaching our zombie classes to propose to Heather. But you aren't here for our love story; let's talk about zombies and *halakhah*.

Halakhah, as mentioned previously, is often translated as Jewish Law; however, that law applies to all aspects of life. As Tevye the Milkman from Sholom Aleichem's *Fiddler on the Roof* says, it applies to "how to eat, how to sleep, how to wear clothes."[1] It is not only a system of law, but of ethics and theology. Some even hold that the attempt to interpret and apply halakhah is an attempt to understand and make real the will of the divine.[2]

The basis of the system relies on the idea that there were two Torahs given to Moses at Mount Sinai during revelation. The first, the written Torah (*Torah SheBikhtav*), is the written Torah we are used to seeing today. The second is the oral Torah (*Torah SheBaal Peh*), which was transmitted down through the generations via an oral tradition. It was compiled into the Mishnah and edited by Rabbi Yehudah HaNasi around 200 CE. That tradition is then debated, interpreted, and expounded on by the rabbis in the Talmud (both Babylonian and Jerusalem). The Babylonian Talmud was edited and compiled by the end of the sixth century CE. Imagine if you took the U.S. Constitution, all the laws passed by the U.S. Congress, all U.S. federal, district, appeal, and Supreme Court rulings, and transcripts since the inception of the United States and put them together into one work. Then imagine that the lawyers and judges went out to a bar and shared stories, and that those stories and conversations were incorporated as well. There's a reason it takes seven and half years to study the whole thing at the pace of a page per day. It's also worth noting that the Talmud is not written as a law code. It is very rare for the Talmud to say, "This is the law." To determine that, you need experts.

After the Talmud was compiled, halakhah entered into a new era, where people would send questions to famous and knowledgeable rabbis, who would then research the answer and respond. The responses were *teshuvot,* or responsa. While we have numerous codes of *halakhah* that have attempted to assemble, clarify, and summarize halakhah, the process of *she'elot uteshuvot* (asking questions and receiving responsa) remains the same even today. People will approach their own rabbi or knowledgeable Jew to ask for an opinion on what they should do in a particular situation. That could be anything from "I was stirring my coffee and some of the milk got knocked into the slow cooker filled with stew. Is it kosher?" to "My parent is very ill. What does Judaism say about dealing with those approaching death?" The best *teshuvot* are ones that give clear, concise answers, but also reveal their sources and citations. By doing so, the author allows the reader to examine the strength of the argument and not simply have to rely on the author's authority.

Whether it is termed Jewish law or Jewish values, *halakhah* is a major part of Jewish life. In North America, both the Conservative and Reform movements publish collections of denominational responsa, as do many individual Orthodox communities. We rely on *halakhah* to help us understand the world, and how to act in it as ethical, caring, Jewish people. And we must care about ethics even in the worst of situations, such as a zombie apocalypse.

Before you say that there is no way this would be helpful, and the rabbis of old would reject this outright, we want to remind you that the Talmud does not analyze cases like those of modern courts. Modern courts look at the common case, what is most likely to happen. The Talmud loves to examine the liminal cases, the boundary cases, the "but what if" cases. This spirit is what prompted the course we taught, and so many others like it.

In fact, the idea of *halakhah* being relevant even in unique or troubling circumstances is deeply rooted in Jewish history. When Ilan Ramon z"l went to space in 2003, he consulted rabbis to find out how to observe Shabbat while rapidly orbiting the Earth. In the Pithiviers, Bergen-Belsen, and Vaihingen concentration camps, among others, Jews commemorated *Pesach* (Passover) despite conditions of near-starvation. The role of *halakhah* in Jewish life has a vast variation. Some may consider it strictly binding as it is written. Others consider it to be a system that is still very active and creative. Some consider it to be something to be studied to preserve those parts that are meaningful while removing other parts that are incongruous with modern life. Still others, like Reconstructing Judaism (formerly the Reconstructionist Movement), understand it as "Past understandings of *halakhah* have a vote but not a veto in our formulations of contemporary halakhah."[3] No major North American Jewish denomination says that *halakhah* is irrelevant. It is simply a range of adaptation and adoption.

That, in and of itself, is the point of this course. *Halakhah* is deeply relevant to modern Judaism but is something not often spoken about in many liberal synagogues and schools. How can we expect anyone to care about halakhah if all we say is "It's Jewish law"? That is the same as telling teenagers, "You will never use this in your life." Rather, the goal of this course was to show how Judaism exists and is relevant outside of the synagogue. How it can impact daily life. Incorporating popular culture allowed us to explore the values inherent in the *halakhic* system, to show its relevance to modern life, and have a bit of fun with it as well.

We taught this course to eighth–twelfth grade Jewish students in a once-a-week supplementary Jewish high school program for an hour each week. By the end of the course, we wanted students to be able to discuss the relevance of halakhah to contemporary life, having explored the concepts by applying them to scenarios involving zombies.

Most of the class itself was discussion based and used source sheets. We adapted some of the sources and used them in this chapter, which is written in the style of a *teshuva* or responsum. It is formatted to match those written and published by the Committee on Jewish Law and Standards, which is a Jewish legal authority and advisory committee associated with the denomination of Conservative Judaism. Certain abbreviations are common and can be found in a table of abbreviations at the end of this section. All Hebrew texts and translations are taken from Sefaria, unless otherwise noted. While it pretends to be serious, it of course is parody. Zombies do not exist, and there is no cause for worry about a zombie apocalypse anytime soon. But if they did . . .

HM 425.2022[4]

Killing the "Living Dead"

She'elah (Question): Is it permitted to kill a zombie?

Teshuvah (Response): In times of danger and destruction, Judaism always encourages us to be moral actors in the world. In some cases, that may require a diminishment of the self, of putting others first. But that principle is not absolute. In cases of danger to life, the halakhic system relies on the concept of Pikuach Nefesh, or the primacy of saving a life. This principle overrides every other principle and law in Judaism, save only the prohibition on idol worship, the prohibition on certain, specific intimate relations, and the murder of another human being.[5]

During a zombie apocalypse, however, how do we balance morals and safety? Faced with what seem to be supernatural humans who desire only to kill and eat us, how do we protect ourselves and our humanity?

But before diving into the ethical issues surrounding the destruction of the living dead, we have to define our terms. After all, the understanding of ethics changes based on the frame of reference. Destroying a plant is different than destroying an animal is different than destroying a machine is different than destroying a person. So before anything else we must answer: "What is a zombie?"

There have been many different models, from the sci-fi romance of *iZombie* and the Disney Channel Original Movie *Z-O-M-B-I-E-S* to the mutated horrors of the *Resident Evil* franchise. Rather than take on each variation in turn, this *teshuvah* will explore two major models that seem to match this situation: zombie as an infected human, and zombie as an animated corpse.

ZOMBIE AS INFECTED HUMAN

The model of zombie as infected human is best described and analyzed by Max Brooks, bestselling author of *World War Z* and also the son of comedy icon Mel Brooks. He describes in his work *The Zombie Survival Guide* that zombies form after being infected with the virus "Solanum." He explains:

Solanum works by traveling through the bloodstream, from the initial entry point to the brain. Through means not yet fully understood, the virus uses the cells of the frontal lobe for relocation, destroying them in the process. During this period, all bodily functions cease. By stopping the heart, the infected subject is rendered "dead." The brain, however, remains alive but dormant while the virus mutates its cells into a completely new organ.[6]

This virus is only transmitted through direct fluid contact, but is always transmitted upon exposure, and always leads to transformation into a zombie.[7]

It is also important to note, that, once transformed, a zombie is only interested in killing and eating living beings, and that the only reliable and safe
method of stopping a zombie is through the destruction of the brain.[8]

These facts provide us with a clear description: the zombie is human, but
presents a clear, present, and immediate danger to humans in its vicinity. It
will, given the opportunity, pursue and kill any human within its path. What
should we do? It turns out that halakhah has long considered similar scenarios.

Rodef

Rabbinic literature has a category for a human being who is on their way to
do harm to another: a *rodef,* or pursuer. We learn from the Mishnah quoted
in b. Sanhedrin 73a

"ואלו הן שמצילין אותן בנפשן הרודף אחר חבירו להרגו"

"And these are the ones who are saved at the cost of their lives; (A *rodef,* meaning) One who pursues another to kill him"[9]

The Mishnah explicitly states that it is permitted to kill someone who is on
their way to kill another. We see later in the halakhic codes

הרודף אחר חבירו להרגו והזהירוהו והרי הוא רודף אחריו אפי' היה הרודף קטן הרי כל ישראל
מצוויים להצילו באבר מאברי הרודף ואם אינם יכולים לכוין ולא להצילו אלא א"כ יהרגו לרודף
הרי אלו הורגים אותו אע"פ שעדיין לא הרג

One who pursues his fellow in order to kill him, and was warned, and continued
in his pursuit: Even if the pursuer was a minor, every Jew is commanded to save
the pursued, even at the cost of one maiming one of the pursuer's limbs. If it
is impossible to save the pursued without killing the pursuer outright, then the
pursuer should indeed be killed, even though he has not yet performed the act.[10]

One is not required to wait until the zombie has begun to hunt and kill.
Rather, the moment that a zombie appears, it is required to stop the zombie.
And as we learn from Max Brooks, only lethal force can truly stop a zombie.
Given the evidence, a zombie is considered a *rodef* and must be stopped, even
at the cost of its own existence. The principle of *pikuach nefesh* (saving a life)
applies only to the potential victims, and not to the zombie itself.

ZOMBIE AS ANIMATED CORPSE

One of the beauties of halakhic argument is that it can hold two different sides at the same time. If one were to think that a zombie could not possibly be considered a living human, then the main alternate model would be to consider it an animated corpse. Ignoring the theological issues that arise from that model, we then need to consider: is it permissible to destroy a corpse?

In his responsa on alternative burial practices, Rabbi Jeremy Kalmonofsky examines the laws surrounding the treatment of a dead body and highlights what he sees as the essential value of these commandments:

> An alternative view has some support, too. For instance, others hold that the essential mitzvah is the prohibition against המת הלנת, leaving a body unattended. Ancient Jews regarded an unburied corpse with horror. Abandoning a person's remains to putrefy in public or be eaten by scavenger animals was considered a disgrace worse than death. The core reason for mortuary norms, the Talmud [b. Sanhedrin 47a] proposes, is to avoid בזיון, abjection. This anxiety was so serious that it inspired the laws of met mitzvah, the command that even high priests or Nazirites must violate the purity of their special status to tend to abandoned corpses [b. Berakhot 19b–20, m. Nazir 7.1=47a].[11]

Just based on this exploration of values, one could argue that the transformation of a corpse into a zombie is an insult to the honor of the dead, and actions should be taken to cease its animation (meaning: kill or destroy it). While this provides a certain degree of freedom, different methods of destruction could be just as injurious to the honor of the dead. However, a discussion elsewhere in Jewish sources provides an even stronger case.

We see a discussion in Tractate Ketubot 17a about the case of a bridal procession that encounters a funeral procession. Who should take precedence? The conclusion is that the bridal procession should proceed first. The values are not explicitly stated there, but the case appears on page 11 of Tractate Semachot, where it is made more explicit:

המת והכלה שהיו מקלסין ובאין זה כנגד זה מעבירין את המת מלפני הכלה מפני שכבוד החי
קודם את המתים.

> When a dead person and a bride are being honored and [the two processions] approach one another, we cause the funeral procession to make way for the bridal procession, because the honor of the living takes precedence over the honor of the dead.[12]

"The honor of the living takes precedence over the honor of the dead" permits one to value the honor of a living human over that of a dead one.

This would certainly apply in the case of an animated corpse attacking a living human. It would be permitted to desecrate or destroy the animated corpse to preserve one's own honor, a standard far lower than necessary to invoke the principle of *pikuach nefesh*, which overrides almost all other halakhic considerations.

DESTRUCTION BEFORE TRANSFORMATION

While the idea of a supernaturally animated corpse provokes additional horror, the halakhic discussion of these cases is supremely simple. Applying the principles of "The Honor of the Living overrides the Honor of the Dead" and *pikuach nefesh* leads to the conclusion that almost any action can be permitted to stop or destroy a zombie. And while Jewish law places a value on honoring the body of the dead, it can be said that having the corpse as a rotting, animated horror that seeks to kill is more of a desecration than destroying that body by whatever means necessary.

Rather, the complication comes when viewing a zombie as an infected human. In that model, we must consider the case of a human who has been infected, but not yet transformed. While not completely parallel, the halakhot regarding terminal illness provide some guidance. Just as before, one of the guiding values is the preservation of life. But to what point? The Tosafot, a commentary on the Talmud written and compiled between 1100 CE–1350 CE, describes that even the tiniest fragment of life (Chayei Sha'ah) is important. Their commentary to the Babylonian Talmud tractate Avodah Zarah explains:

לחיי שעה לא חיישינן—והא דאמרינן ביומא (דף פה.) מפקחין עליו את הגל בשבת לחוש לחיי שעה אלמא אלמא חיישינן דאיכא למימר דהכא והתם עבדינן לטובתו דהתם אם לא תחוש ימות והכא אם תחוש ולא יתרפא מן העובד כוכבים ודאי ימות וכאן וכאן שבקינן ודאי הודאי למיעבד הספק:

There are grounds to say that in both sources we should act for his benefit, for there [in Yoma] if you do not care [about "the life of the hour"], he will die, and here, if you do care [about "the life of the hour" and therefore prohibit the Gentile physician from treating him], he will not be healed by the Gentile and will certainly die. So here and there we abandon the certain [course of action] to do that which is doubt [fully appropriate][13]

It is appropriate to take action to preserve life wherever feasible. But some cases cannot be solved by medical treatment, and zombification is one of them.

The Shulchan Aruch gives some guidance for someone who is actively dying. Crossroads Hospice explains that this stage is when patients are very close to death but have not yet passed.[14] This stage has long been recognized in Jewish law and has a technical term: The Goses.

הגוסס הרי הוא כחי לכל דבריו. אין קושרין לחייו ואין סכין אותו ואין מדיחין אותו ואין פוקקין את נקביו ואין שומטין הכר מתחתיו ואין נותנין אותו על גבי חול ולא על גבי חרסית ולא על גבי אדמה. ואין נותנין על כריסו -- לא קערה ולא מגריפה ולא צלוחית של מים ולא גרגיר של מלח. ואין משמיעין עליו עיירות ואין שוכרין חלילין ומקוננות ואין מעמצין עיניו עד שתצא נפשו. וכל המעמץ עם יציאת הנפש ה"ז שופך דמים. ואין קורעין ולא חולצין ולא מספידין עליו ולא מכניסין עמו ארון לבית עד שימות ואין פותחין עליו בצדוק הדין עד שתצא נפשו: הגה: וי"א דאין חוצבין לו קבר אע"פ שאינו עמו בבית עד אחר שימות (ריב"ש סי' קי"ד). ואסור לחצוב שום קבר להיות פתוח עד למחר שלא יקברו בו המת באותו היום ויש סכנה בדבר (רבינו ירוחם בשם ר"י החסיד ז"ל). וכן אסור לגרום למת שימות מהרה כגון מי שהוא גוסס זמן ארוך ולא יוכל להפרד -- אסור להשמט הכר והכסת מתחתיו מכח שאומרים שיש נוצות מקצת עופות שגורמים זה. וכן לא יזיזנו ממקומו. וכן אסור לשום מפתחות ב"ה תחת ראשו כדי שיפרד. אבל אם יש שם דבר שגורם עכוב יציאת הנפש-- כגון שיש סמוך לאותו בית קול דופק כגון חוטב עצים או שיש מלח על לשונו ואלו מעכבים יציאת הנפש -- מותר להסירו משם דאין בזה מעשה כלל אלא שמסיר המונע (הכל בהגהת אלפסי פ' אלו מגלחין)

One in a dying condition is considered a living being in all respects. We may not tie up his jaws, nor may we anoint him with oil, nor wash him, nor stop off his organs of the extremities, nor may we remove the pillow from under him, nor may we place him on sand, clay-ground or earth, nor may we place on his stomach a dish, a shovel, a flask of water or a globule of salt, nor may we summon the towns on his behalf, nor may we hire pipers and lamenting women, nor may we close his eyes before his soul departs. And whosoever closes [the dying person's] eyes before death is regarded as one who sheds blood. One may not rend garments, nor bare the shoulder in mourning, nor make a lamentation for him, nor bring a coffin into the house in his presence before he dies, nor may we begin the recital of *Ẓidduk Haddin* before his soul departs. *Gloss: Some say that we may not dig out a grave for him. although it is not [done] in his presence, [i.e.,] in the house—before he dies. It is [likewise] forbidden to dig out any grave to be [left] open until the next day, in which the corpse will not be buried the same day, and there is danger in this. It is likewise forbidden to cause [aught] to hasten the death of one who is in a dying condition, e.g., one who has been in a dying condition for a long time, and could not depart—[the law is that] we may not remove the pillow or the mattress from under him [just] because some say that there are feathers from some fowl which cause this [prolongation of death]. He may likewise not be moved from his place. It is also forbidden to place the Synagogue keys under his head in order that he may depart. However, if there is aught which causes a hindrance to the departure of the soul, e.g., [if] near that house there is a knocking sound, viz., a wood-cutter, or there is salt on his tongue, and these hinder the departure of the soul, it is permitted to remove it therefrom, for there is no [direct] act [involved] in this, since he merely removes the hindrance.[15]*

This passage can seem somewhat confusing until one makes the differentiation between active and passive steps. One cannot take an active step to hasten death. But one can remove impediments to death. What does this mean? With modern medicine, one can keep the heart beating and the lungs moving forever. In some cases, where healing is possible or a person can continue to live and act in the world, then these are devices that preserve life. However, there may be times where a person is unable to act in the world and is unable to survive without these machines. In these cases, it may be appropriate to remove these devices that are simply preventing death from occurring, and not prolonging life.

What does this mean for us? Simply put, one cannot destroy an infected human before they have turned. For all the person knows, a cure has just been discovered, or what is being assumed to be a zombie bite and infection is actually another, treatable illness.[16] While steps can be taken afterwards to destroy a zombie to preserve the lives of others, it is not permitted to destroy an infected human before they have turned, as the value of preservation of life applies even for Chayei Sha'ah, a moment of life.

IMMEDIATE DANGER OR POTENTIAL DANGER

Most of the discussion so far has dealt with the zombie as immediate threat to self or others. But what about zombies that are wandering in places where there are no people, or where people cannot even exist. All the previous rulings were based on situations of immediate danger to human life. Can these zombies, which represent no immediate threat, be destroyed? What does Jewish law say about potential dangers?

There are a variety of potential comparisons, though none of them deal directly with zombies in the text. B. Shabbat 42a examines whether one may move a thorn (likely to cause injury) in the public domain on Shabbat. Generally, moving anything in the public domain on Shabbat is prohibited, and even moving it in small amounts is prohibited. Here, though, it is permitted because it causes a threat to the masses. A threat of injury to the public permits one to override some of the laws of Shabbat.

Looking into the halakhic codes, the discussion of potential danger becomes more explicit. The Shulchan Aruch explains:

צריך ליזהר מליתן מעות בפיו שמא יש עליהן רוק יבש של מוכי שחין ולא יתן פס ידו תחת שחיו
שמא נגע ידו במצורע או בסם רע ולא יתן ככר לחם תחת השחי מפני הזיעה ולא יתן תבשיל
ולא משקים תחת המטה מפני שרוח רעה שורה עליהם ולא ינעוץ סכין בתוך אתרוג או בתוך
צנון שמא יפול אדם על חודה וימות: הגה וכן יזהר מכל דברים המביאים לידי סכנה כי סכנתא
חמירא מאיסורא ויש לחוש יותר לספק סכנה מלספק איסור (ב"י בשם הש"ס) ולכן אסרו לילך

בכל מקום סכנה כמו תחת קיר נטוי או יחידי בלילה (שם) וכן אסרו לשתות מים מן הנהרות
בלילה או להניח פיו על קלוח המים לשתות כי דברים אלו יש בהן חשש סכנה (רמב"ם) ומנהג
פשוט שלא לשתות מים בשעת התקופה וכן כתבו הקדמונים ואין לשנות (אבודרהם ומרדכי ס"פ
כל שעה רוקח סימן ער"ה ומהרי"ל ומנהגים) עוד כתבו שיש לברוח מן העיר כשדבר בעיר ויש
לצאת מן העיר בתחילת הדבר ולא בסופו (תשובת מהרי"ל סי' ל"ה) וכל אלו הדברים הם משום
סכנה ושומר נפשו ירחק מהם ואסור לסמוך אנס או לסכן נפשו בכל כיוצא בזה ועיין בחושן
משפט סימן תכ"ז:

One must refrain from putting coins in one's mouth, lest it's covered with dried
saliva of those afflicted with boils. He should not put the palm of his hand in
his armpit, lest his hand touched a metzorah [generally translated as a leper;
refers to someone who is impure due to the affliction of the biblical disease of
Tzara'at] or a harmful poison. He should not put a loaf of bread under his armpit, because of the sweat. He should not put a cooked item or drinks under the
bed, since an evil spirit rests on them. He should not stick a knife in an etrog or
a radish, lest one fall on its edge and die. *Gloss: Similarly, he should be careful
of all things that cause danger, because danger is stricter than transgressions,
and one should be more careful with an uncertain danger than with an uncertain
issur (prohibition). They also prohibited going into a dangerous place, such as
under a leaning wall, or alone at night. They also prohibited drinking water
from rivers at night or putting one's mouth on a stream of water and drinking,
because these matters have a concern of danger. It is the widespread custom
not to drink water during the equinox, and the early ones wrote this and it is
not to be changed. They also wrote to flee from the city when a plague is in the
city, and one should leave at the beginning of the plague and not at the end.
And all of these things are because of the danger, and a person who guards his
soul will distance himself from them and it is prohibited to rely on a miracle in
all of these matters.*[17]

While the explicit prohibitions seem strange to modern eyes, the principle
seems to be quite clear: one should avoid carelessness that would put oneself
in a dangerous situation. In fact, Rabbi Moshe Isserles, who wrote the gloss,
explains that possibly violating a prohibition is less important than potentially
putting oneself into a dangerous situation.

Both of these sources would seem to argue that it is clear that one should
avoid a dangerous situation, even by potentially violating explicit commandments in the Torah. Yet, both of these sources are arguing when that potentially dangerous situation is an immediate consequence. The situation these
sources explore is more akin to sounding loud noises to try to attract zombies
or walking into a dark basement in a zombie-infested area.

The situation of zombies in the desert is more akin to a potentially dangerous situation that is significantly disconnected from any actual person.
Strangely enough, sources exist about these situations explicitly in teshuvot
regarding medical research, a few centuries ago.

The Noda BiYehudah, a two-volume collection of responsa written by Rabbi Yechezkel Landau in Prague during the 1700s, explores the necessity of medical research through autopsy. Specifically, he explores the balance between the potential desecration of a corpse (a value explored earlier) and the potential knowledge gained that might lead to the saving of a life. In a common responsum format, Rabbi Landau includes the question:

ע"ד קונטריסו אשר שלח אלי אשר העריך מערכה בנדון השאלה שבאה אליו מק"ק לונדון במעשה שאירע שם באחד שחלה בחולי האבן בכיסו והרופאים חתכו כדרכם בעסק רפואה במכה כזו ולא עלתה לו תרופה ומת ונשאלו שם חכמי העיר אם מותר לחתוך בגוף המת במקום הזה כדי לראות במופת שורש המכה הזאת כדי להתלמד מזה בהנהגת הרופאים מכאן ולהבא אם יקרה מקרה כזה שידעו איך יתנהגו בענין החיתוך הצריך לרפואה ושלא להרבות בחיתוך כדי למעט בסכנת החיתוך אם יש בזה איסור משום דאית ביה ניוול ובזיון להמת הזה או אם מותר משום דאתי מיניה הצלת נפשות להבא להיות מיזהר זהיר במלאכה זו על תכליתה.

Regarding your treatise, which you sent to me, and which offers a presentation of the issue that you were asked about by the holy community of London: It happened that someone was ill with a gallstone. The physicians performed surgery, as usual for such an affliction, but it did not cure him, and he died. The sages of that city were asked if it is permissible to dissect the cadaver in that place to see evidence of the root of the affliction, and to learn from it for the future practice of medicine, so that if such a case occurs again, they know how to perform the surgery necessary for a cure without incising him too much, thus minimizing the risks of the surgery. Is this prohibited because it constitutes desecration and disgrace of this corpse, or is it permitted because it leads to the future saving of lives, so that they may take the utmost caution in their craft?[18]

The question, then, is whether an autopsy may be performed to add to medical knowledge and acknowledging the competing values of honoring the dead and saving a life. Rabbi Landau explores different reasons for embalming the body, or even for autopsies, including that an autopsy of a murder victim could possibly save the murderer from capital punishment. However, he goes on to say the following:

את כל אלה כתבתי לפי דבריכם שאתם קורים זה פיקוח והצלת נפש. אבל אני תמה הלא אם זה יקרא אפילו ספק הצלת נפשות א"כ למה לכם כל הפלפול והלא זה הוא דין ערוך ומפורש שאפילו ספק דוחה שבת החמורה ומשנה מפורשת ביומא דף פ"ג וכל ספק נפשות דוחה שבת ושם דף פ"ד ע"ב ולא ספק שבת זו אלא אפילו ספק שבת אחרת ע"ש. ואמנם כ"ז ביש ספק סכנת נפשות לפנינו כגון חולה או נפילת גל, וכן במס' חולין שם גבי רוצח הפיקוח נפש לפנינו וכן אפילו לענין ממון שם במס' ב"ב ההיזק לפנינו אבל בנדון דידן אין כאן שום חולה הצריך לזה רק שרוצים ללמוד חכמה זו אולי יזדמן חולה שיהיה צריך לזה ודאי דלא דחינן משום חששא קלה זו שום איסור תורה או אפילו איסור דרבנן שאם אתה קורא לחששא זו ספק נפשות א"כ יהיה כל מלאכת הרפואות שחיקת ובישול סמנים והכנת כלי איזמל להקזה מותר בשבת שמא יזדמן היום או בלילה חולה שיהיה צורך לזה ולחלק בין חששא לזמן קרוב לחששא לזמן

רחוק קשה לחלק. וחלילה להתיר דבר זה ואפילו רופאי האומות אינן עושים נסיון בחכמת
הניתוח ע"י שום מת כי אם בהרוגים ע"פ משפט או במי שהסכים בעצמו בחייו לכך ואם אנו ח"ו
מקילים בדבר זה א"כ ינתחו כל המתים כדי ללמוד סידור אברים הפנימים ומהותן כדי שידעו
לעשות רפואות להחיים. ולכן האריכות בזה הוא ללא צורך ואין בזה שום צד להתיר. ולדעתי
שגגה יצאה מלפני כבוד מעלתו שמיהר להשיב להקל.

I have written all of this in accordance with your words, for you call this saving lives. But I am puzzled. If this is considered even a questionable case of saving lives, why must you engage in all of these mental gymnastics? It is clear and explicit that even an uncertainty supersedes the severity of Shabbat, and there is an explicit mishna on Yoma 83 that the possibility of saving a life supersedes Shabbat. And there on 84b it states that not only an uncertainty concerning the present Shabbat, but even an uncertainty concerning a different Shabbat [supersedes]. However, this all applies when there is a present case of uncertainty concerning a risk to life—such as a sick person or collapsed building. Similarly, in the case in Hullin regarding a murderer, the risk to life is present. So too in the monetary case in Bava Batra, the potential damage is present. But in our case, there is no ill person who needs this. Rather, they want to study this discipline in case they encounter a sick person who requires it. We certainly do not supersede any Torah prohibition or even a rabbinic prohibition due to such a slight concern. For if you call this concern "an uncertainty pertaining to a life," then any task related to healing—grinding and cooking medicine or preparing a scalpel for bloodletting—will be permitted on Shabbat, perhaps they will encounter a sick person who requires it that night or the next day. It is also difficult to distinguish between concern for the need arising in the near future and concern for the need arising in the distant future. Heaven forfend that such a thing should be permitted. Even gentile physicians do not gain surgical experience with just any corpse, but only with those put to death by the law or with those who themselves consented to it while living. If we, God forbid, are lax in this matter, they will operate on every corpse to learn anatomy and physiology, so that they may know how to cure the living. Therefore, this is all unnecessarily lengthy, and there is no lenient approach whatsoever. In my opinion, your Excellency was mistaken in rushing to respond leniently.[19]

Rabbi Landau specifically identifies that there is no immediate danger to life here and views the potential to save a life as "slight." In this case, he argues, the principle of *pikuach nefesh* does not apply, and therefore all other laws and legal principles remain in effect.

While all other sources focus solely on the idea that *pikuach nefesh* overrides almost every law, Rabbi Landau identifies that there is a limit to *pikuach nefesh*, namely that it must present an immediate danger to life, and the action being taken must have real chance to preserve that life.

Therefore, a zombie that does not present a reasonable, or reasonably immediate, danger to life cannot be destroyed, whether due to the principle of honoring the dead, or that it no longer qualifies as a *rodef*.

P'SAK DIN (CONCLUSION)

1. A zombie is considered a *rodef*, and if near humans, may be destroyed immediately.
2. Even for one who regards a zombie as an animated corpse, it is permitted to destroy a zombie, as the honor of the living takes precedence over the honor of the dead.
3. The principle of *pikuach nefesh* does not apply to a zombie, as its existence is a danger to any human in its immediate vicinity. Any steps can be taken to destroy it.
4. One cannot destroy a human before they have turned into a zombie, even if they have symptoms.
5. One cannot destroy a zombie if they do not present a reasonable, or reasonably immediate, danger.

TABLE OF ABBREVIATIONS

BT—Babylonian Talmud—The Talmud is the textual record of generations of rabbinic debate about law, philosophy, and biblical interpretation, compiled between the third and eighth centuries and structured as commentary on the Mishnah with stories interwoven. The Talmud exists in two versions: the more commonly studied Babylonian Talmud was compiled in present-day Iraq, while the Jerusalem Talmud was compiled in Israel.[20]

CE—Common Era—A way of distinguishing years that is parallel to BC and AD, but remains secular.

HM—Hoshen Mishpat—A section of the Shulchan Aruch dealing with civil law, including jurisprudence, testimony, harming others, and health.

SA—Shulchan Aruch—The Shulchan Arukh ("Set Table") is the most widely accepted code of Jewish law ever written. Compiled in the sixteenth century by Rabbi Joseph Karo, it is a condensed and simplified version of the Beit Yosef, a commentary that Karo wrote on the Tur. Karo's rulings are in accordance with Sephardic traditions; the text of the Shulchan Arukh also includes the glosses of Rabbi Moshe Isserles, which cite Ashkenazic traditions.[21]

YD—Yoreh Deah—A section of the Shulchan Aruch dealing with ritual slaughter, kashrut, conversion, mourning, niddah, tzedakah, usury, and laws applicable in Israel.[22]

Z"L—Zichrono / Zichrona/ Zichronam Livracha—May their Memory be a blessing—used after the name of someone who has died.

NOTES

1. *Fiddler on the Roof,* directed by Norman Jewison (USA: United Artists, 1971).

2. "Halakhah: Structure of Halakhah," *Encyclopedia.com,* January 25, 2022, www.encyclopedia.com/environment/encyclopedias-almanacs-transcripts-and -maps/Halakhah-structure-Halakhah

3. Daniel Cedarbaum, "Reconstructing Halakhah," *Reconstructing Judaism,* May 6, 2016, www.reconstructingjudaism.org/article/reconstructing-Halakhah.

4. "Halakhah, Shulchan Arukh—Sefaria," *Shulchan Arukh (Sefaria),* accessed February 1, 2022, www.sefaria.org/texts/Halakhah/Shulchan%20Arukh.

5. SA YD 157:1

6. Max Brooks, *The Zombie Survival Guide: Complete Protection from the Living Dead* (Baltimore, MD: Cemetery Dance Publications, 2014), 2.

7. Brooks, 3.

8. Brooks, 18–19.

9. BT Sanhedrin 73a

10. SA HM 425:1

11. Jeremy Kalmanofsky, "Alternative Kevura Methods," *Rabbinical Assembly,* 2017, www.rabbinicalassembly.org/sites/default/files/public/Halakhah/teshuvot/2011 -2020/alternative-burial.pdf, 9.

12. BT Semachot 11:6.

13. Tosafot to BT Avodah Zarah 27b. Translation Courtesy Rabbi Eliot Dorff.

14. "What Is Active Dying?" *Crossroads Hospice,* accessed January 25, 2022, www .crossroadshospice.com/hospice-resources/end-of-life-signs/what-is-active-dying/.

15. SA YD 339:1

16. Case study illustrated in *Zombieland: Double Tap,* directed by Ruben Fleischer (Culver City, CA: Sony Pictures, 2019), DVD.

17. SA YD 116:5

18. Noda BiYehudah II, Yoreh Deah 210.

19. Noda BiYehudah II, Yoreh Deah 210.

20. Talmud, Sefaria.

21. Halakhah, Shulchan Arukh.

22. Sefaria.

WORKS CITED

Brooks, Max. *The Zombie Survival Guide: Complete Protection from the Living Dead*. Baltimore, MD: Cemetery Dance Publications, 2014.

Cedarbaum, Daniel. "Reconstructing Halakhah." *Reconstructing Judaism,* May 6, 2016. www.reconstructingjudaism.org/article/reconstructing-Halakhah.

Fleischer, Ruben, dir. *Zombieland: Double Tap*. Culver City, CA: Sony Pictures, 2019, DVD.

"Halakhah, Shulchan Arukh—Sefaria." *Shulchan Arukh. Sefaria.* Accessed February 1, 2022. www.sefaria.org/texts/Halakhah/Shulchan%20Arukh.

"Halakhah: Structure of Halakhah." *Encyclopedia of Religion. Encyclopedia.com.* January 25, 2022. www.encyclopedia.com/environment/encyclopedias-almanacs -transcripts-and-maps/Halakhah-structure-Halakhah.

Jewison, Norman, dir. *Fiddler on the Roof.* United States: United Artists, 1971, DVD.

Kalmanofsky, Jeremy. "Alternative Kevura Methods," *Rabbinical Assembly,* 2017. www.rabbinicalassembly.org/sites/default/files/public/Halakhah/teshuvot/2011 -2020/alternative-burial.pdf.

"What Is Active Dying?" *Crossroads Hospice*. Accessed February 1, 2022. www .crossroadshospice.com/hospice-resources/end-of-life-signs/what-is-active-dying.

Williams, Brian A. *Preparedness 101: Zombie Pandemic*. United States: United States Department of Health and Human Services, Centers for Disease Control and Prevention, 2012.

Chapter Twelve

The Quest for the Kosher Dragon

Who's the Mensch in Middle-earth?

Arthur S. Harrow

As a Jewish reader of fantasy literature, it can sometimes be a little frustrating when allegory and religious references pop up and they are either from Christian literature or are Christian interpretations of Jewish literature. We sometimes play the game, when watching a TV show or movie, of asking "Who's the Jew?" and it seemed like it was time to take a look at the works of J. R. R. Tolkien in this light. So let's put aside our many well-worn copies of *A Canticle for Leibowitz* (a gift received frequently because "Well, we know you like science-fiction and this is the Jewish science-fiction book"), and embark upon the strangest quest ever imagined: to find something in the works of Tolkien that a Jewish reader could identify with, and to find this as much as possible within the text of the published works (*The Silmarillion, The Hobbit,* and *The Lord of the Rings*). In the course of this search, we will look at possible Jewish references that are really a stretch; possible Jewish references that would be horrifyingly offensive; possible Jewish references that are more positive but are definitely from the non-Jewish perspective; and finally something that is both positive, Jewish, and most importantly, consistent with the Jewish point of view . . . which was unexpected, counterintuitive, and very gratifying. One might even say eucatastrophic.

A recent article asked the question, "Are dragons kosher?"[1] Now putting aside the question of whether dragons chew their cud (and whether it counts that given a chance they will chew *your* cud) and whether St. George needed to have a *shochet*, a ritual slaughterer, at hand to make sure the dragon was killed in a kosher fashion, the bigger question arises, as it has on a frequent basis: where is the Jewish reference in the fantastic literature that we all love?

It's not always easy being on the outskirts of the big crowd. It is true that Tolkien, C. S. Lewis, and lots of other authors draw subtly and not so subtly on their Christian background. That's okay; one writes from one's experience. Still, it sometimes makes enjoying the stories a little harder for those who are not Christians. For example, when someone says, "This is obviously a reference to this incident in Timothy." One loses track of the times that someone in a discussion says, "This makes me think of what Luke said" and having to keep from answering, "Use the Force." For those who are not Christian, the reference is obscure. Moreover, sometimes the references are to Eden or Noah's Ark but are interpreted through a Christian viewpoint, so they can be jarringly different from the way we may be thinking of that reference. Someone talks about the snake being Satan and the impulse to say "No, the snake was only a snake; *ha-satan* translates as 'the opponent' and doesn't connote an anti-God" must be suppressed. There have been moments in various discussion groups at which one just longs to find something that is recognizable from the Jewish perspective. Worse yet, sometimes the references are so horrifyingly offensive that the book cannot be read.

The search for something that a Jewish reader can identify with in C. S. Lewis must be abandoned; Aslan is not a subtle lion. But Tolkien is much less overtly Christian than Lewis, and one has high hopes. Here, the task at hand is to find a religious reference or allegory that speaks to the Jewish reader, something in the works of Tolkien with which a Jewish reader and lover of fantastic fiction can identify.

THE MYTH OF GOLLUM THE GOLEM

There are numerous webposts insisting that Tolkien got the name Gollum from the Golem.

The first reaction to this is "Yeah, right, just because the names sound the same Tolkien would have used it for this pivotal character." When one researches the etymology, there is evidence that Tolkien was inspired by the Old Norse for gold or ring, as scholar Woody Wendling notes:

> The hypothesis of Douglas Anderson, who annotated *The Annotated Hobbit*, is that Tolkien got the name "Gollum" from Old Norse "Gold." The Old Norse word *gull* means "gold." In the oldest manuscripts it is spelled *goll*. One inflected form would be *gollum*, "gold, treasure, something precious." It can also mean "ring," as is found in the compound word fingr-gull, "finger-ring." These are points that may have occurred to Tolkien.[2]

Still, a little more reading is warranted to show why the Golem is not a likely candidate.

Continuing with etymology, the word *golem* is translated as "an embryo" according to Brown-Driver-Briggs's Hebrew and English Lexicon; it occurs once in the Bible, in Psalm 139:16 where the possessive word *galmi*, or *my golem*, is used in a sentence in Hebrew "*galmi ra'u eytzmi*" that translates as "Your eyes saw my imperfect substance."[3] The *Mishnah* (collection of Jewish laws) uses the term for an uncultivated person.

In Jewish folklore, the Golem is a creature of clay or mud that is brought to life by inscribing certain words (frequently *Emet*, or Truth) on its forehead. Traditionally, a Golem is created to protect the Jewish community. The Golem is characteristically mute, and when (inevitably) it starts acting out of control, erasing the first letter of the activating word causes it to return to an inanimate lump of clay. Interestingly, if one erases the first letter of *Emet* (truth), it changes to *Met* (which in Hebrew means death)[4]; that may be an interesting discussion for another time.

Speaking of an interesting talk for another time, it is notable that the most famous Golem in all of Jewish folktales is the golem of Prague, often described as created by the very real historical character rabbi Judah Lowe (when you travel to Prague, visit the Rabbi's grave and then dine at the local kosher eatery, the Restaurant U Golema). Who else lived in Prague?

Karel Capek, author of a little play you might have heard of about artificial creatures working in a factory. The name of that play, which may well have been inspired by the local legend of the artificial creature, is *R.U.R., Rossum's Universal Robots*. So it doesn't take a reread of all of the works of Asimov to see the Jewish roots of robots. (Having said that, you absolutely should reread all the works of Asimov. Again, a discussion for another time.)

So, one might think that Tolkien took the name of an incomplete creature to be the name of Gollum, who is certainly in many ways a primitive, poorly formed hobbit.

This does not stand up to scrutiny because despite there being similarity in the names, Gollum is clearly not a golem. The characteristic of a golem is that it is an unliving creature that is brought to life essentially by magic and can be ended the same way. Gollum, on the other hand, is a creature with sentience and a soul who makes moral choices, and he speaks, albeit in a most interesting way, yes, my precious. It is, in fact, key to his significance in the story that he can make decisions, act on his own, and is not the puppet of some other being. He is definitely not someone who, when death smites the swollen brooding thing that inhabits its crawling hill and holds it all in sway, will wander witless and purposeless and then feebly die.[5] That's a troll.

THE MYTH OF DWARVES BEING JEWS

Next, let's talk about the Oliphaunt in the room: Jews and Dwarves. Of course, this mostly relates to the Dwarves that we meet in *The Hobbit.* First of all, the Dwarvish language takes its roots from Hebrew. As Zak Cramer observes in his essay "Jewish Influences in Middle-earth":

> Khuzdul, the language of the Dwarves, mimics Hebrew, with its guttural con- sonants, triliteral roots, and typical constructions. To give but one example,[8] Gimli's battle cry at the siege of the Hornberg is *Baruk Khazad!* (Axes of the Dwarves!). *Baruch* means bless in Hebrew and Gimli's war cry recapitulates the traditional form of a Jewish blessing—orthodox Jews can be heard saying *baruch HaShem* many, if not hundreds, of times a day. It means something like bless (or thank) God.[6]

This deliberate association of Dwarves with Judaism has been discussed a lot, and not in small part because Tolkien sometimes used phrasing that perhaps could have been more elegant. In 1955 he wrote in Letter 176, "I do think of the 'Dwarves' like Jews: at once native and alien in their habita- tions, speaking the languages of the country, but with an accent due to their own private tongue."[7] And in an interview on the BBC in 1971, he said of the Dwarves, "of course are quite obviously—wouldn't you say that in many ways they remind you of the Jews? . . . Their words are Semitic, obviously, constructed to be Semitic."[8]

Now we understand this to be a linguistic reference. But not long after that interview, people started saying that Tolkien said the Dwarves are Jews.

Why is that a problem?

Well, consider this: The Dwarves are short guys with dark beards. They drive a hard bargain; they know the value of a treasure down to the last gold coin. Finally, in *The Hobbit*, at least, their quest is to gain their long- forgotten gold.

This plays into some unfortunate (to use an understatement) stereotypes of Jews. Further, when someone says, "It's been a long time since Shakespeare wrote about Shylock," one can point to nasty cartoons in the press in the early twentieth century (and not just in Germany) playing into the stereotype of the swarthy-bearded money-counter, or to current comments among the conspiracy-minded about George Soros and his "internationalist millionaire friends," or the "Rothschild Orbital Space Laser." To make it more personal, those of us who grew up in the Deep South may recall the "Jew test" when people would drop a coin on the ground because "If you bend down to pick up the coin it means you're a Jew."

There are other discussions of this where people say, "Well, everyone in *The Hobbit* is greedy; it's not just the Dwarves." However, the question is not whether characters are greedy; it's whether a particular group as a whole is portrayed as intrinsically greedy. Regrettably, there is a passage in Chapter XII of *The Hobbit* that points in this direction: "There it is: dwarves are not heroes but calculating folk with a great idea of the value of money; some are tricky and treacherous and pretty bad lots; some are not but are decent enough people like Thorin and company, if you don't expect too much."[9] Rebecca Brackmann in her essay "'Dwarves Are Not Heroes': Antisemitism and the Dwarves in J. R. R. Tolkien's Writing" observes about the Dwarves' visit to Elrond, with the wise Elf's concern about their quest, "The Dwarves' avarice in this universe is, apparently, so legendary that it even shapes how other races interact with them."[10] Their behavior once they've recovered the treasure is the most deplorable—they instigate a war by refusing to share—though some is the Lakemen's original property and the Lakemen are in dire need. Instead, Thorin retreats to his treasure room, as "The lust was heavy on him" as a species trait.[11] Meanwhile, the Dwarves hole up in their mountain "caressing and fingering" their treasure in an odious celebration of greed.[12]

One can see how that might be disturbing.

Now, this is not what Tolkien meant. Why should we think this (other than a belief that the professor was a good guy)?

First of all, we know that the Dwarves were driven out of their homeland by a monster. True, the Dragon was attracted by their great wealth, but it wasn't something the Dwarves did that specifically caused them to lose their home (unlike their earlier exile from Moria, when the Balrog was released from its imprisonment because "the Dwarves dug too greedily, and too deeply, and disturbed that from which they fled, Durin's Bane."[13] The Jews, in our own tradition, lost our home, our Temple, and our traditional way of life due to our behavior. As the Bible tells it, the kings of Israel practiced idolatry, and ignored a long stream of prophets sent by God to persuade them to change their ways. As a warning, God split the kingdom into Israel in the north and Judah in the south (containing the capital of Jerusalem and the holy Temple therein). Five centuries before the common era, the Assyrians conquered Israel, carrying off many of its people who, known as the Ten Lost Tribes, remain a historical mystery. In the neighboring Kingdom of Judah, Jeremiah prophesized about the Babylonian threat and warned the Jews of terrible devastation unless they stopped worshipping idols and being cruel. At last, the Babylonians conquered Judah, destroyed the Temple, and carried the Jews off to captivity in God's punishment for their not keeping the covenant.[14] Does that sound like the Dwarves?

Secondly, Tolkien tells us that the Dwarves keep their language secret, a secret they did not willingly unlock, even to their friends.[15] As a philologist, that has to have great significance to him. Also, as a philologist, he would know that Hebrew, while not a living language until its revival by Eliezar Ben-Yehuda in 1882, was taught in universities from the Middle Ages to the present. Yes, while not a spoken language it was kept alive as a language of lore and scholarship. Does that sound like the Dwarves?

It doesn't sound like the Dwarves. That's why when Tolkien says, "Don't they remind you of the Jews," he was speaking as a philologist; he meant their language reminds people of the Jews' language.

Now, hold on just a fringe-twirling minute! Hebrew was a language not used except as a tongue of scholarship? And the Jews were exiled because of their hubris and sins? If we are going to play "Who's the Jews," something does come to mind here: don't the Elves fit the description?

ELVES AS JEWS

As we learn in *The Silmarillion*, the source of all things Elvish, the Elves came first. They are the people of the stars; their greatest leader had as the symbol of his house a multi-pointed star. They established civilization before Men came along, and they were the first to have "true knowledge." As seen in the main series, they are very familiar with the theology of Middle-earth and frequently sing praises to the Valar, especially Elbereth, and they do this while wandering across the Shire, after dinner in Rivendell, and at various times in Lorien; there is no sense of any fixed religious rituals.

Tolkien's Elvish language is recognizably derived from Hebrew roots. His names like Galadriel, Tinúviel, and Gilthoniel share the *-el* suffix seen in Jewish angel names (as well as his middle name Reuel), there meaning "God." Other Elvish names like Amroth, Iarwain Ben-Adar, Melkor, and Elessar also share Hebrew derivation.[16] Cramer adds:

> The name *Rohirrim* clearly has Hebraic inspiration. While the language of Rohan, at least as presented in the "translated" text of *The Lord of the Rings*, is clearly inspired by Anglo-Saxon, the name *Rohirrim* is not native to that language—it is the Sindarin word for that people. In Hebrew, nouns and verbs are largely built up out of a system of three letter, or triliteral, roots. When *im* is added to a root of this kind, it is the standard way to make a plural or collective noun. *Rohirrim*, *Galadhrim*, and *Haradrim* are all typical of this very normal Hebrew construction.[17]

The Elves were exiled from their homeland, their sacred promised land, because of their sins: the pride of Fëanor, his desire to possess the Silmarils and the light of the Trees for himself, his urge to be the leader of his people and have all go according to his will. The Silmarils, as Tolkien's works explain, were three gems that Fëanor crafted in the First Age, which captured the light of the Two Trees of Valinor—a creation source that shares symbolism with Eden or the primordial light of heaven (created in Jewish tradition on the first day, before the light of the sun). When evil destroyed the trees, Fëanor refused to undo his own craftsmanship to return light to the world. Out of fear he would lose his position (provoked by the evil Morgoth's whispers), he began rabble-rousing, until he left with his followers from their paradise of Valinor, where their creators dwelled. This legend in many ways references Eden. Further, Fëanor's possessiveness over his jewels became Gollem-like, a sin that added to the world's imbalance. He and his seven sons vowed eternal violence against any who might take the Silmarils. He returned to take kingship of his people, the Ñoldor, but they rejected him. Enmity followed, with a sundering of their peoples and eternal exile that echoes the story of the Ten Lost Tribes. There is even a prophecy, offered by the divine Mandos, that following Morgoth's final return and defeat, Fëanor will be released from the Halls of Mandos and break open the Silmarils, restoring the heavenly light the people have been denied. Bliss will fill the world in a messianic age recognizable to all Bible readers.[18]

The sin for which the Jews were driven into exile is held by our scholars to be *sinat chinam*, baseless hatred.[19] Jeremiah preached repeatedly about the hungry and poor whom the rich neglected to care for. Fëanor's sins—greed and pride—were likewise combined with unkindness to outsiders. Further, after the Jews returned from exile, they once again neglected the commandments, so the Second Temple was destroyed by the Romans in 70 CE, the people carried off once again. Further, during the Roman Rebellion, which led to the 1,800-year exile, there was infighting between different factions that splintered the resistance against the common enemy. Sound like the leaders of the Ñoldorin rebellion much? They sing by the river of Beleriand something along the lines of "If I forget thee, oh Valinor."

On the other hand . . .

The theology of Middle-earth complicates matters. The Elves are destined to fade before the after-comers (the humans), with whom there is a certain animosity because this is known in advance. The after-comers are promised to escape from the world and go to dwell with the Divine after death, and to have a place in the Second Music after the end of the world. The Elves are stuck here, and their fate after the End is unknown,[20] rather like the vision of Dante where the Jews and the Righteous Pagans get to stay in the more upscale suburbs of hell; not damned per se but not getting out either. The Elves' time is past, and they are replaced by Men, who will enter a paradise the Elves never will achieve.

This sounds a lot like Supersessionism, the belief that Christianity replaces Judaism. Brackmann similarly notes this concept in *The Silmarillion*'s creation story of the Dwarves, who are more clumsily formed than the "Children who were to come."[21] Each race, Dwarves then Elves, is allowed by the gods to live as they wish and prosper, but they are rough templates for the paragons who will follow. As Brackmann concludes, in Tolkien's vision, "They are not the chosen people."[22]

One is also reminded of the medieval art form called *Ecclesia et Synagoga,*[23] where many churches, especially in France, England, and Germany, had decorations showing two graceful female figures, usually on the outside of the building. The Church is shown erect and triumphant, bearing a cross; the Synagogue is usually blindfolded and dejected, bearing a broken staff and sometimes decorated with the Tablets of the Ten Commandments.

The relationship between Elves and Men seems to echo this; the Jews had their time in the sun and now they fade away as the After-comers inherit the world from them.

Obviously, Jews do not view theology in this way: we believe we accepted God's covenant and continue to uphold it correctly by obeying the commandments in the Torah and commentaries. As far as the afterlife, Jews believe all humans have a soul (*neshama,* or God's breath). The soul learns through the body that does good deeds on earth, and after death, it flies up to heaven.[24] This afterlife includes all people, not just Jews, as Isaiah 60:21 says, "Your people are all righteous. They will inherit the land forever. They are the shoot of My planting, the work of My hands, in which I glory."

However, life's goal is not to do good deeds to earn passage to *Olam Ha-ba* (the World to Come) but to create paradise on earth through the eventual coming of the Moshiach (the Anointed One), a great human leader. At this time, the dead will revive and return to earth to make a paradise here. Repeated through the Bible is the promise of eternal life (Psalms 37:29) upon a precious land, "as the days of heaven upon the earth" (Deut.11:21). More on this later.

So far, the Elves may be Christian progenitors, but their nature imagery and magic make them a better parallel for Druids or other pagans than for Jews, even a Christian view of Jews. It is also notable that while in *The Silmarillion* it is made clear that the Elves dwelt with the Valar, the representatives of God, there does not seem to be much evidence of anything that resembles worship other than songs to Elbereth sung in the woods, or after dinner at Elrond's house. Jewish worship services are distinct, whether in ancient times (sacrifices and offerings in the Temple) or in modern times (prayers and readings from sacred writings at specified times and dates). Indeed, Tolkien writes in Letter 156:

The High Elves were exiles from the Blessed Realm of the Gods (after their own particular Elvish fall) and they had no "religion" (or religious practices, rather) for those had been in the hands of the gods, praising and adoring Eru "the One," Ilúvatar the Father of All on the Mt. of Aman.[25]

All the peoples lack formal religion—they cry out to the Valar like Elbereth but don't worship in temples.

The concept of the Elves being Jews is unsatisfying. This is certainly not the place we perceive for ourselves in the world (and the world to come); and the "religious" behavior of the Elves has no similarity to Judaism. It is interesting that this dynamic of the Elves being replaced by Men is most prominent in *The Silmarillion*; in *The Lord of the Rings*, it's more that the Elves are fading and leaving and there is not such a firm suggestion of this. This leads to the next section, where evidence suggests a better answer.

THE BEST REFERENCE

Let's look at *The Lord of the Rings* and read about another group. Men at the end of the First Age were granted a land that was protected, the Land of Gift called Númenor. Their language, Adunaic, also uses the Semitic language roots. Cramer explains:

> even the very name Adunaic is Hebraic. In Hebrew *adon* means lord and is used both as a divine title as well as a human honorific. . . . The resonance with Hebrew *adon* and the sense of Númenor as the land of lords cannot be overlooked. The Númenóreans were the lords of Middle-earth in the second age. And their descendants were lords in at least the beginning of the third age and, through the line of Elessar (or Aragorn), in the fourth age as well.[26]

In that land, they grew wise and prosperous as long as they remembered their relation with the Divine powers. "In the midst of the land was a mountain tall and steep, and it was named the Meneltarma, the Pillar of Heaven, and upon it was a high place that was hallowed to Eru Ilúvatar . . . and no other temple or fane was there in the land of the Númenóreans."[27] We are also told that the Númenóreans, led by their King, would ascend to the Hallow three times a year to bring offerings to Eru Iluvatar and there none might speak any word, save the King only.[28] This is reminiscent of the three Pilgrimage Festivals, where the people would come to the Temple Mount to bring offerings, and the ritual of Yom Kippur, where the High Priest would enter the Holy of Holies and he only would speak the Name of God. Unlike the Elves, who sang songs of praise to the Valar and don't appear to mention Ilúvatar, the Men were worshiping Eru the One. Further, they were worshiping Him in a way that is very reminiscent of the practice in the times of the Temple in Jerusalem when there were three Pilgrimage Festivals that involved the people coming to the Temple to bring offerings to the Lord. Tolkien himself, in a letter in 1954, commented on this: "The Númenóreans thus began a great new good, and as monotheists; but like the Jews (only more so) with only one physical centre of 'worship': the summit of the mountain Meneltarma."[29]

During the decay of Númenor, we are told that "the offering of the first fruits to Eru was neglected, and men went seldom any more to the Hallow."[30] In the Bible, such lines are common, always before a great warning or a great disaster. Elijah warns Ahab of forthcoming consequences saying, "The children of Israel have forsaken Thy covenant, thrown down Thine altars, and slain Thy prophets with the sword" (Kings I 19:10). Further, critic Jane Chance Nitzsche notes that with Morgoth's corruption "the desire for power and godlike being is the same desire for knowledge of good and evil witnessed in the Garden of Eden."[31]

Later, when the evil servant Sauron came to Númenor, he seduced the King and his followers, telling them that Eru was a phantom invented by the Valar and convincing them to worship his lord Morgoth and to make human sacrifices. To sum up, those that previously made pilgrimages three times a year to bring offerings to the One were at this point worshiping a false god. Because of this, their kingdom was destroyed, and the survivors escaped into exile. They were led by Elendil, leader of the "Faithful," who maintained a strong friendship with the Elves and preserved the old ways of Valinor. Elendil, his sons, and their supporters fled the downfall of Númenor at the end of the Second Age, escaping to Middle-earth in nine ships. In Middle-earth, Elendil founded the realms of Arnor and Gondor. He eventually led a war there against Sauron, one that his descendent Aragorn completed in *The Lord of the Rings*. So the Faithful of Númenor were exiled from their Promised Land due to their sins after a history that recalls the rise and fall of the ancient Jewish nation. But then the metaphor repeats itself.

The exiles who crossed the sea established a kingdom, which shortly after its founding was divided into the North and South (and the North kingdom of Arnor disappeared, while the South kingdom of Gondor long endured). Even when the (North) kingdom disappeared, the line of kings continued in exile, as it was prophesied that this line would endure. The Men, like the Elves, clearly have some things in their backstory that are resonant with the Jewish experience. Notably, the House of Elendil and his forefather Eärendil are both associated with a star.

In terms of "modern" Men at the time of the War of the Ring, it is notable that there are still among the "High Men" practices that suggest not only worship of Eru, but also hints of Jewish ritual practices. When Frodo and Sam are dinner guests of Faramir, we see that it is a Gondorian (and therefore

Númenorean) custom to pause before eating and taking a moment to "look to Númenor that was, to Elvenhome that is, and to that which is beyond Elvenhome and which shall ever be."[32] They pause before eating to consider their past before exile, as well as to that which is eternal. This should be reminiscent of the Kiddush which precedes meals in Jewish custom, which reminds us of being brought out of slavery and praising God. Jews in the diaspora also pray toward Jerusalem, the lost land where they hope to return.

Let's also add, as we must in the world of Tolkien, a bit of philology. The Hebrew word *Moshiach*, from the three-letter root *met-shin-chet*, means "the anointed one," or, to speak plainly, the king. This word is frequently pronounced *Messiah*, especially outside the world of traditional Judaism; but its theological meaning is very different depending on who is using it.

Christian View of the Messiah

The Christian Messiah is a Divine being who is here to save humanity from their sins; who has returned from death; who on his return will establish an eternal kingdom and banish death. If we look for this Messiah in the *Lord of the Rings*, we would think of Gandalf. He indeed is more angel than mortal, and when he dies fighting an ancient evil, the Balrog, the Divine powers restore him to life. However, he does not establish rule; he does not vanquish death (except on a personal level); he defeats the Enemy and then returns from whence he came.

Jewish View of the Messiah

In Judaism, *Moshiach*, the anointed one, is a mortal man who will restore the kingdom and initiate an era of peace. The great Jewish philosopher Rambam described *Moshiach* as a human paragon, descended from the ancient line of kings, a scholar of the ancient lore, keeper of the commandments, a gifted orator, and a warrior for God.[33]

His coming will be announced by the prophet Elijah, who has returned from heaven. If we look for *Moshiach* in *The Lord of the Rings*, we would find Aragorn, with Gandalf playing the role of Elijah. Aragorn is indeed a mighty warrior, but also a scholar who uses forgotten herb lore to save Frodo and Éowyn even as it proves his royal lineage. He is careful to honor his oaths and obey the moral laws of Middle-earth, even to refusing the temping Ring. He is the last hope of the free peoples of Middle-earth, and finally restores the lost kingdom in which they're all united in peace. With his ascension, the people live without fear and the ancient tree blooms once more. Gandalf, who performs miracles with divine power, is his herald, uniting the people before him and riding to Gondor to announce his coming. Aragorn, unlike

Gandalf, dies permanently when he's grown old, and passes the throne to his heir, in a natural, human fashion. The tradition of the human savior is very easy to see in the story Tolkien gives us. Moreover, that is a story that is both positive rather than pejorative and consistent with the Judaism that we know. It is even more intriguing that an author characterized by his Catholicism would present a story that could be read more like Jewish *Moshiach* than the Christian Messiah.

TO SUM UP

I. Gollum is *not* a Golem.
II. The Dwarves are *not* Jews.
III. The Elves are a little like Jews, although there are some significant differences. But if they are Jews, they are Jews as others see us, not as we see ourselves and our own history.
IV. The Númenórean Men might be Jews: their history of worship of the One God, their fall into the worship of false gods that leads to exile, their continued practices that suggest Jewish ritual, and the story that reads more like *Moshiach* than the Christian Messiah makes their story very much like the Jewish story the way we see it.

And so ends the quest. We can look at the works of Tolkien and say, "We can find a people in this whose history reminds us of the Jews, whose practices appear to be similar to the Jews, and who, most importantly, look the way Jews appear to ourselves and not the way others might see us."

CONCLUSION

Now, to return to the Kosher Dragon. (Or at least the Kosher Dragon Roll. Anyone who can send me a picture of a Chinese restaurant named the Kosher Dragon will have my eternal gratitude.)

It is not enough for the Dragon to be potentially kosher (hooves, cud-chewing, etc.). It must be killed and prepared in a kosher fashion if you want to find it on your plate (and no judgment will be made if that is in fact your choice; each to his own, as they say).

There is another Hebrew word to be aware of: *mashgiach.*

When it comes time to serve up that Kosher Dragon, you are going to need the *mashgiach*, because the *mashgiach* is the food supervisor; his or her job is to make sure that the laws of kashrut, of keeping kosher, are observed during food preparation.

So . . .

When *Moshiach* comes, we will live in peace and harmony.

But when *mashgiach* comes, we shall live in peas and hominy.

NOTES

1. M. Roth, "Are Dragons Kosher?" *My Jewish Learning,* April 7, 2015, www .myjewishlearning.com/2010/02/23/are-dragons-kosher.

2. Woody Wendling, "The Riddle of Gollum: Was Tolkien Inspired by Old Norse Gold, the Jewish Golem, and the Christian Gospel?" *Inklings Forever* 6, Taylor University, 2008. library.taylor.edu/dotAsset/62ebac33-e9d1-4788-8a6d-08f27aef48cd. pdf.

3. Alden Oreck, "Modern Jewish History: The Golem," *Jewish Virtual Library,* www .jewishvirtuallibrary.org/the-golem

4. Oreck.

5. J. R. R. Tolkien, *The Return of the King* (New York: Houghton Mifflin, 1996), 227.

6. Zak Cramer, "Jewish Influences in Middle-earth," *Mallorn* 44 (August 2006): 10.

7. J. R. R. Tolkien, "Letter 176," December 8, 1955 in *The Letters of J. R. R. Tolkien*, selected and edited by Humphrey Carpenter (Boston, MA: Houghton Mifflin, 1981), 229.

8. J. R. R. Tolkien, interview by Denys Geroult, "Now Read On," BBC, 1971, *Tolkien Library.* www.tolkienlibrary.com/press/804-Tolkien-1971-BBC-Interview.php.

9. J. R. R. Tolkien, *The Hobbit, or There and Back Again* (Boston: Houghton Mifflin, 1996), 225.

10. Rebecca Brackmann, "'Dwarves Are Not Heroes': Antisemitism and the Dwarves in J. R. R. Tolkien's Writing," *Mythlore* 28, no. 3/4 (109/110) (2010): 91, *JSTOR,* www.jstor.org/stable/26814913.

11. Tolkien, *Hobbit,* 237.

12. Tolkien, *Hobbit,* 237.

13. J. R. R. Tolkien, *The Two Towers: Being the Second Part of The Lord of the Rings* (Boston: Houghton Mifflin, 1996), 331.

14. Lawrence H. Schiffman, "Jerusalem: Twice Destroyed, Twice Rebuilt," *The Classical World* 97, no. 1 (2003): 32. doi:10.2307/4352823.

15. J. R. R. Tolkien. *The Return of the King: Being the Third Part of The Lord of the Rings* (Boston: Houghton Mifflin, 1996), 410.

16. Cramer, 13.

17. Cramer, 13.

18. J. R. R. Tolkien, *The Shaping of Middle Earth* (New York: Houghton Mifflin, 1986), 115.

19. Elliot B. Gertel, "Because of our Sins?" *Tradition: A Journal of Orthodox Jewish Thought* 15, no. 4 (1976): 68. www.jstor.org/stable/23258405.

20. J. R. R. Tolkien, *The Silmarillion: The Epic History of the Elves in The Lord of the Rings* (Boston: Houghton Mifflin, 1977), 42.

21. Tolkien, *Silmarillion,* 19.

22. Brackmann, 87.

23. Johannes Heil, "Ecclesia et Synagoga." In *Encyclopedia of Jewish History and Culture Online,* 2017, dx.doi.org/10.1163/2468-8894_ejhc_COM_0190

24. Leila Leah Bronner, *Journey to Heaven: Exploring Jewish Views of the Afterlife* (USA: Urim Publications, 2015), 34–35.

25. J. R. R. Tolkien, "Letter 156." November 1954, in *The Letters of J. R. R. Tolkien*, selected and edited by Humphrey Carpenter (Boston, MA: Houghton Mifflin, 1981), 204.

26. Cramer, 11.

27. Tolkien, *Silmarillion,* 261.

28. J. R. R. Tolkien, *Unfinished Tales* (Boston: Houghton Mifflin, 1980), 166.

29. J. R. R. Tolkien, "Letter 156." November 1954, in *The Letters of J. R. R. Tolkien*, selected and edited by Humphrey Carpenter (Boston, MA: Houghton Mifflin, 1981), 204.

30. Tolkien, *Silmarillion*, 266.

31. Jane Chance Nitzsche, *Tolkien's Art* (New York: St. Martin's Press, 1979), 192.

32. Tolkien, *Two Towers,* 320.

33. Bronner, 82.

WORKS CITED

Brackmann, Rebecca. "'Dwarves Are Not Heroes': Antisemitism and the Dwarves in J. R. R. Tolkien's Writing." *Mythlore* 28, no. 3/4 (109/110) (2010): 85–106. *JSTOR,* www.jstor.org/stable/26814913.

Bronner, Leila Leah. *Journey to Heaven: Exploring Jewish Views of the Afterlife.* USA: Urim Publications, 2015.

Cramer, Zak. "Jewish Influences in Middle-earth." *Mallorn* 44 (August 2006): 9–16.

Gertel, Elliot B. "Because of Our Sins?" *Tradition: A Journal of Orthodox Jewish Thought* 15, no. 4 (1976): 68–82. *JSTOR,* www.jstor.org/stable/23258405.

Heil, Johannes. *"Ecclesia et Synagoga."* In *Encyclopedia of Jewish History and Culture Online,* 2017. dx.doi.org/10.1163/2468-8894_ejhc_COM_0190.

Nitzsche, Jane Chance. *Tolkien's Art*. New York: St. Martin's Press, 1979.

Oreck, Alden. "Modern Jewish History: The Golem." *Jewish Virtual Library*, www .jewishvirtuallibrary.org/the-golem.

Roth, M. "Are Dragons Kosher?" *My Jewish Learning,* February 23, 2010. www .myjewishlearning.com/2010/02/23/are-dragons-kosher/

Schiffman, Lawrence H. "Jerusalem: Twice Destroyed, Twice Rebuilt." *The Classical World* 97, no. 1 (2003): 31–40. doi:10.2307/4352823.

Tolkien, J. R. R. *The Hobbit, or There and Back Again*. Boston: Houghton Mifflin Co, 1996.

Tolkien, J. R. R. *The Letters of J. R. R. Tolkien*, selected and edited by Humphrey Carpenter, Boston, MA: Houghton Mifflin, 1981.

Tolkien, J. R. R. "Now Read On." By Denys Geroult. BBC, 1971. *Tolkien Library.* www.tolkienlibrary.com/press/804-Tolkien-1971-BBC-Interview.php.

Tolkien, J. R. R. *The Return of the King: Being the Third Part of The Lord of the Rings*. Boston: Houghton Mifflin Co, 1996.

Tolkien, J. R. R. *The Shaping of Middle Earth.* New York: Houghton Mifflin, 1986.

Tolkien, J. R. R. *The Silmarillion: The Epic History of the Elves in The Lord of the Rings.* Boston: Houghton-Mifflin Co, 1977.

Tolkien, J. R. R. *The Two Towers: Being the Second Part of The Lord of the Rings.* Boston, Houghton Mifflin, 1996.

Tolkien, J. R. R. *Unfinished Tales*. Boston: Houghton Mifflin, 1980.

Wendling, Woody. "The Riddle of Gollum: Was Tolkien Inspired by Old Norse Gold, the Jewish Golem, and the Christian Gospel?" *Inklings Forever* 6. Taylor University, 2008. library.taylor.edu/dotAsset/62ebac33-e9d1-4788-8a6d-08f27ae-f48cd.pdf

Chapter Thirteen

Avatar: The Last Airbender and Judaism

Several Curious Connections

Ellen Levitt

Avatar: The Last Airbender and its follow-up series *The Legend of Korra* are two of the most popular animated series of the early twenty-first century. The moving storylines, the depth of the characters (major and minor), the timeless themes and struggles, the intriguing plotlines, the exciting action and fight scenes: all of these have contributed to an enduring series. When they were made available again on Netflix in 2020, after their initial broadcasting in the early 2000s on Nickelodeon, they drew a great deal of attention once again. Although *Avatar* was primarily geared toward children, and *Korra* geared especially toward teenagers, many adults (particularly the parents of said children) eagerly watched as well.

The ethnic groups most closely associated with the *Avatar* series are Asian, Inuit, and Indian subcontinent peoples. Various forms of martial arts and the flow of energy or Chi (Qi) as well as meditation, yoga, chakras, and such are all explored during the series. Although some stereotyping takes place, to a great extent these two series show positive, negative, and gray areas reflecting Asian culture as it is understood today. In addition, girls and women are shown to be strong and intelligent, as well as crafty and malevolent; both genders have their share of good characters and bad.

Yet one can also make a case for *Avatar: The Last Airbender* and *Korra* as having intriguing similarities to Jewish practices, beliefs, rituals, and culture. Granted, they compare well to many societies and other fictional series (such as the *Harry Potter* books and films). But there are some striking Jewish comparisons worth exploring.

Certainly, there are themes that are considered universal in *Avatar:* fighting for justice, getting an earnest and thorough education, learning to excel, discovering teamwork, and so on. And while there is much about *Avatar* that reflects aspects of Asian societies and belief systems, there are many links to other religions, such as Judaism. Of course, some might look upon Aang, the main protagonist, as a Christ-like figure. But he is actually more akin to personalities within Judaism—Moses, or Jonah, or others.

After viewing both series twice, and reading online comic strip versions of *Avatar,* I noticed certain things in *Avatar* that seemed to be Jewish or "Jewish-adjacent" in content; the four nations and four main types of benders reflect the prevalence of four in Judaism, particularly in Passover rituals.

As with particular key personalities in the Torah and Jewish scriptures, there is thoughtful character development and maturation evident in several characters of *Avatar* and *Korra*. "It presents the audience with an unexpected level of character development, revealing a psychoanalytic process of unconscious conflict, repetition, and emotional resolution through relationship."[1] We see this happening with Judah and a bit with Esau, as well as Joseph and King David, in the Jewish texts, based upon their successes and errors. Likewise in *Avatar* we see this particularly with Zuko, who goes from being a young proto-villain to a heroic figure, as well as with *Korra* as she stumbles through the pressures of being a teenaged Avatar.

Another general feature of both the *Avatar* and *Korra* series is respect for animals. Many of the main and secondary characters in both series have pets and animal species that they cherish (Aang's Appa and Momo pets, Sokka's pet Hawky, Toph's reverence for the badgermoles, etc.). There are Jewish laws that govern preventing the suffering of living creatures, "tsa'ar ba'alei hayim." (For example, in Proverbs 12, "the righteous person regards the life of his beast."[2]) There are also talking/communicating animals in *Avatar*, and they might remind some of Balaam's donkey. (The talking owl Wan Shi Tong is a prime example.)

Aang and Korra, who are both young Avatars, frequently go into meditative states in order to seek advice and healing from past Avatars. Both also rely upon living mentors for advice and encouragement, echoing Jews who consult with rabbis and scholars. Uncle Iroh offers incisive, powerful advice to Prince Zuko, Tenzin guides Korra, Guru Pathik teaches Aang, and other characters fill similar roles.

We could draw comparisons between certain biblical figures and the *Avatar* characters, as well as other Jewish personalities over time.

BRIEF SYNOPSIS OF *AVATAR: THE LAST AIRBENDER* AND *KORRA*

There are three seasons of *Avatar* and four seasons of *Korra*. In *Avatar*, Aang, the last surviving Airbender, and his first two friends, siblings Sokka and Katara, and later Toph, accompany Aang as he travels far and wide, and learns how to bend water, earth, and lastly fire. Aang is sought after by the Fire Nation, particularly Prince Zuko, who wants to restore his honor by capturing Aang. Other people around the world are anxious to see Aang succeed and bring about peace and harmony in the world, after a hundred years' war waged by the Fire Nation against everyone else, in their ferocious quest for power.

In *Korra,* the teenage girl Avatar works hard to learn all her bending, while battling various enemies, some of whom are members of her extended family, as well as less malevolent critics who still cause her trouble. She has a close set of friends, including the brothers Mako and Bolin, Asami, as well as Aang's son Airbender Tenzin and his family. Near the end of season two, Korra loses her connection to all the previous Avatars, and at the end of season three, she suffers a particularly brutal assault from a small group of enemies, whom she and her allies manage to subdue. The end of season four is upbeat and has a provocative element. It is also important to mention that Korra is one of the rare female starring protagonists of color in an animated series.[3] This diversity is notable and has been applauded by viewers and educators.

If there is a storyline in the Torah that has a somewhat similar trajectory, it would be that of Joseph. He is coddled when very young (as was Aang, to an extent); he then suffers greatly and embarks upon a unique journey that involves self-discovery, and leads to salvation for much of the world, as with Aang. Both Joseph and Aang have engaging personalities, as well. Aang will have closer friends than Joseph, who does gain allies but does not seem to have a close friend who can also critique him when necessary.

Korra could be compared to Moses, who endures a series of struggles, both when he is young and old; to Jonah, who like Korra, dodges certain responsibilities in his role of prophet; and a bit to Yael, who killed Sisera, the enemy general, in a wily manner.

CENTRAL THEMES OF *AVATAR* AND *KORRA*: JEWISH INSPIRATIONS?

The *Avatar–Korra* series focuses on a few timeless themes that have driven so much literature and art throughout time. Among these are good versus evil; the individual versus the group, including the importance of family and friends; the struggle for and maintenance of power; maturation and how/why it manifests in certain individuals.

Jewish scripture delves into these themes in a variety of ways. Good versus evil, including piety versus sinfulness, is a key factor in the Noah flood saga, in the book of the prophet Jonah, in the story of Esther, and elsewhere. But there are times when key Bible figures make mistakes (Jonah running away from his calling to Nineveh, Noah getting drunk, etc.), which show us that humans, no matter how good, are not perfect. In *Avatar,* the most righteous of characters do things that are sometimes incorrect, including Aang (such as when he takes on a false identity at a school), and Katara and Sokka (when the siblings bicker). Korra certainly makes some curious judgment calls as well, as when opting to follow her evil uncle as a mentor, or when she assumes a different identity for several months and does not inform her parents and Tenzin of her whereabouts. We see that these cartoon characters are multilayered and do need to mature. Even Tenzin, depicted largely as a wise man, has episodes of imperfection and impatience (with Korra, with the new Airbenders after the Harmonic Convergence, with Lin the police chief, etc.). Fortunately, Tenzin does admit to his wrongdoings, and thus is a strong role model.

A major tenet of Judaism is the importance of the group, the people of Israel. Even with crucial patriarchs and matriarchs, Moses, and the other prophets, all are seen as human and part of a continuum. This is quite different from Christianity, for example, which places Jesus as the key figure and the son of God. *Avatar* has similarities to the Jewish faith, in that the Avatar (Aang in the first series, Korra in the second) is part of a continuum of Avatars, or Prophets, as one may describe them. Both of these youthful Avatars need the assistance of their close friends in order to achieve their central goals. Aang relies greatly upon Sokka, Katara, and Toph, and later Zuko (as well as certain teachers and the guru) and Korra relies greatly upon Mako, Bolin, and Asami, as well as Tenzin as her primary role model, and to a lesser extent other adults such as Lin, Suyin, Varrick the entrepreneur, and others.

In fact, we can see that neither Aang, or Korra can be at peak performance without the support and skill sets of their friends and allies. And the Jewish people cannot be at their peak performance without the correct actions of and care for other Jews. "All Jews are responsible for each other" (Kol Yisrael Arevim Zeh La Zeh) is a tenet of Jewish communality.

One of the more emotional quotes from *Avatar,* about friendship and how it can resonate throughout generations, is when the past Avatar Roku says to Aang, "Some friendships are so strong they can even transcend lifetimes."[4] This piece of advice to Aang helps the young Avatar to bolster his confidence and sense of mission.

The struggle for and maintenance of power in *Avatar* is shown to be the overriding objective of the Fire Nation, and in *Korra* there are four different examples of people and groups that try to have power or at least be the leaders. Perhaps the most curious (and ambiguous) season is three, with Zaheer and his followers who believe in a form of anarchy, the overthrowing of title and power, and who wreak havoc and hurt Korra greatly. Their philosophy is at great odds not only with that of Korra but would also be at great odds with Jewish history. Zaheer and his crew, the Red Lotus, would be against the kings of Jewish history, against the leadership of Moses as well. Would Zaheer relish living in the lawless times of Noah, prior to the Flood? Or in the Tower of Babel, when languages were drastically changed, leading to confusion?

Korra offers critiques on different forms of government and leadership: there are wise leaders such as Tenzin and buffoons such as Prince Wu; there is the totalitarian leadership of Kuvira, who promises safety to those who pledge loyalty, which fools some people to an extent (such as the well-intentioned Bolin). Is Tenzin modeled, even slightly, upon a wise Jewish king such as Solomon? Tenzin has his moments of frustration and melancholy as did Solomon, who wrote about it in the book of Kohelet (at least, it is assumed that he was the author of this work). Tenzin is consumed with nurturing the small community of Airbenders so that it does not die out, and this has been a great weight upon him for most of his life.

As for maturation, we see throughout the two series how Aang and Korra develop and gain insight, as well as the storyline of Zuko, who goes from being consumed by anger and revenge, to being a friend and teacher for Aang. At one point, Aang announces, "The past can be a great teacher," a pithy adolescent assessment that has depth.[5] Zuko's is even a story of transformation, with his realization that he should be an ally to Aang and not an enemy. In certain ways, Judah was transformed from a petty man to a true leader, even though he was not the eldest of Jacob's sons. His interactions with Joseph and the other brothers, and with Tamar, particularly changed him.

An unusual aspect of the *Avatar* series in particular is that the classic dichotomy of righteous people versus evil people is at times upended. We see that in the Old Testament as well: Abraham, Jacob, Moses, Miriam and others have occasionally lapses. They are not perfect. In *Avatar*, "Moral ambiguity abounds, and people from all nations see the conflict as, variously, an opportunity or a tragedy; there are Earth Kingdom citizens who have become cynical or apathetic after generations of fighting, and those from the Fire Nation who are fully capable of doing good."[6] People in *Avatar* and in *Korra*, as well as in the Torah, are multidimensional.

DID JEWISH SUFFERING INSPIRE THE
SUFFERING OF THE AIR NOMADS?

One of the most horrific details and plot catalysts in the *Avatar* series is the Air Nomad Genocide, perpetrated by the Fire Nation. In its quest for world domination, the Fire Nation sought the newest Avatar at the time and targeted the Air Nomads because they knew that in the Avatar birth cycle, the Air Nomads were next in the series. The Air Nomads were slaughtered en masse by the Fire Nation—except for Aang and his flying buffalo Appa, who escaped, and then managed to be frozen in a submerged iceberg.

He was discovered by two Southern Water tribe teens, sister Katara and brother Sokka, freed from his icy state, and the story progresses on from this. We soon learn that Aang feels deep regret for running away from his people, realizes that he could have helped them or even saved them, and experiences survivor guilt.

The holiday of Tisha B'Av commemorates the destruction of the First and Second Temples of the Jews; other disasters in Jewish history are also reflected upon during this saddest day in the Jewish calendar. And on Yom Kippur day, there is a section of the mussaf service called Martyrology. A feature of this is the accounts of the Ten Martyrs, rabbis who were slaughtered in horribly graphic manners. In addition, there are days such as Yom HaShoah that mark mourning over the Holocaust's impact on Jews.

The Jewish people have suffered through, yet survived, the horrors of the Crusades, the Inquisition, pogroms in Europe and in the Middle East such as the Farhud, the Holocaust, and more. Slavery, ghetto life restrictions, expulsions, blood libel accusations, pogroms small and large, and the systematic killings and dehumanization programs of the Nazi regime and cooperating nations: all these decimated the Jewish population, caused untold grief and pain, and echo throughout history. Yet every time a group tried to erase the Jews from the world, they failed.

Returning to the fate of the Air Nomads, in terms of sheer numbers, their genocide at the hands of the Fire Nation is perhaps worse than that of the Jews during the Holocaust. To have just one survivor of an ethnic group is unspeakable, and that has never happened to the Jews as a whole. Nor has it happened to the Native Americans, nor the Cambodians, nor many other groups that were targeted for extinction.

And Aang does experience an adolescent version of survivor guilt and regret over his running away, even though at the time he fled, he did not realize how severe would be the genocide of his people. Holocaust survivor guilt and the guilt that their children and grandchildren have grappled with have been studied at length. The grieving process that Aang is shown to go through is a version of this, made tolerable for a youthful audience. An example of advice given to Aang when he is at his saddest (when his beloved pet Appa is taken away) is offered by Katara, who comforts Aang by telling him, "I know sometimes it hurts more to hope and it hurts more to care. But you have to promise me that you won't stop caring."[7] This is heavy but realistic, and mature, insight offered from one teen to another in *Avatar*.

UNCLE IROH: A TEACHER WITH A PAINFUL PAST

Uncle Iroh is undoubtedly wise and a brilliant fighter and strategist. He acts as a mentor to Zuko in his toughest days. Can we consider him a rabbi for his nephew Zuko? He does teach Zuko quite a bit, much of it in a spiritual and psychological fashion, sometimes indirectly and with curious lessons. In the *Korra* series he imparts wisdom in the Spirit World to Korra. As a key figure in the Order of the White Lotus, a group that included brilliant and powerful people from all the nations of the world, he sought and revered balance and harmony (and tea, copious amounts of soothing tea). He is learned and often easygoing, although extremely tough under pressure.

Would that qualify him as a rabbi? Not quite, but he is an extremely helpful mentor and teacher for Zuko and Korra, and to a lesser degree, other characters in the series. Perhaps he has more than a bit of King Solomon in his personality.

But Iroh also suffered a great deal over his years: he was shunned by his family and considered a traitor; his own son was killed; he is imprisoned in the third season of *Avatar* and treated poorly there. He overcomes many obstacles, and his devotion to Zuko becomes his primary goal. He is the Rabbi Akiva of the *Avatar* realm.

Many fans of *Avatar* have plumbed the sayings and actions of Iroh and have acclaimed his complexities. One oft-quoted Iroh statement is when he tells his nephew Zuko that "You must never give in to despair. Allow yourself to slip down that road, and you surrender to your lowest instincts. In the darkest times, hope is something that you give yourself. That is the meaning of inner strength."[8] Not only is that meant to steer Zuko on the right path, but it is also Iroh speaking to himself, or to a younger version of himself when his own son died in combat. Iroh encapsulates in this statement something that would resonate with Jewish prisoners in Nazi death camps. It can be seen as a parallel to the twelfth statement of the Ani Ma'amin, part of the Thirteen Principles of Moses Maimonides, and the source of a haunting song of faith in the coming of the Messiah "although he may tarry."[9]

KORRA

An interesting comparison can be made between Korra and the prophet Jonah. At times Korra feels invincible, while at others she is rather reluctant to have the weight of the world's woes on her shoulders.

She knows she has a role to fulfill, as far as keeping the world's energy balanced. And her role is difficult, rare, and provokes skepticism amongst many people, just as it had been with the ancient prophets. Not everyone flocks to a prophet; not everyone wants to hear the admonishments of a prophet if the wise words are in conflict with one's agenda!

Among the strong females in the Old Testament are Sarah and Rebecca, the prophetess Deborah, Yael (who impales Sisera), and others. Perhaps a comparison could even be drawn between Korra and Hagar, who flees from her mistress Sarah but does heed the word of the angel of God.

Another interesting comparison could be drawn between Korra and Queen Esther. Both are young women thrust into difficult, at times awkward situations in which the well-being of communities is at stake. Korra has to meet and even confront people (especially adults) who make her uneasy and who even threaten her; Esther risks her life by approaching King Ahashverosh, unbidden. And she also has to deal with the odious Haman, the villain of the Book of Esther.

SIBLING RIVALRY

Sibling rivalry is one of the oldest sources of conflict and drama in history, and it has provided the plot strife for many writers and playwrights over the years. *King Lear* is rife with it; *Joseph and the Amazing Technicolor Dreamcoat*, with its biblically derived story, is as well. *Little Women, The Godfather, East of Eden, The Brothers Karamazov* and so many other novels, plays, musicals, TV shows, and films explore siblings fighting.

There are major "plotlines" in the Torah that are driven by sibling rivalries: Cain and Abel; Noah's three sons; twins Jacob and Esau; sisters Leah and Rachel; Joseph versus Jacob's other sons; even squabbles amongst Moses, Aaron, and Miriam. Pivotal sections of the Old Testament show that siblings do not always live in familial harmony and sometimes their fights can wreak havoc. At times the arguments seem quaint while others are deeply divisive.

In *Avatar*, Aang is an only child, so he is spared this friction, but there are times when sister Katara and brother Sokka of the Water Tribe argue, often due to their different abilities and personality quirks. The much harsher sibling feud is between Prince Zuko and Princess Azula of the Fire Nation.

The spats between Sokka and Katara are realistic, and at times comic. Teasing and one-upmanship are on display. But for the most part they both get along because they are fighting for the same cause. And their parents are rendered as loving and nurturing, so they support each other.

In contrast, Zuko and Azula were raised in a tense family situation, and coupled with their own pressures, these two have one of the nastiest showdown battles of the animated series. Their duel over who will be the Fire Lord is far beyond the typical sibling squabble. From a physical and psychological standpoint, they are enemies. And at the end, do we pity Azula or rejoice in her defeat?

We could certainly compare and contrast the animosity and power struggle between two of King David's sons, Adonijah and Solomon. Adonijah attempted to usurp the throne that was meant for Solomon, and Adonijah was eventually executed for this. Probably because the battle between Zuko and Azula was viewed by children, Azula is not killed, but she is imprisoned and shown to be suffering from mental illness.

The majority of sibling rivalries in the Old Testament are within single-gender groupings. One of the few mixed-gender sibling disagreements is when Miriam lodges complaints against Moses; this incident has its consequences but is not a life or death situation. Compared to the Zuko–Azula running feud, especially their big battle, the Miriam–Moses incident seems tamer. But in both cases, there is a definite power play.

Later in *Korra* we see sibling rivalry incidents hashed out between the three grown children of Aang and Katara, and Toph's two daughters Lin and Suyin. Aang and Katara had three children together: Bumi, Kya, and Tenzin. While all three have great affection for each other, there are resentments underneath the veneer because Tenzin is the only Airbender, and thus Bumi (a non-bender until much later in life) and Kya (a Waterbender like her mother) feel that their father showered much more attention upon Tenzin. They realize that it was done with great purpose, but there are hurt feelings that do flare up on occasion. In season two of *Korra* the trio have a painful discussion and work through their familial jealousies.

The resentment between Toph's two daughters Lin and Suyin is an easy compare–contrast with that of Leah and Rachel in Bereshit. Lin and Suyin had quite different personalities, had a mother who gave them abundant freedom but also seemed ambivalent about her role as a mother, and neither girl knew her father (and on top of that, they each had a different father). Due to Su's rebellious hijinks as a teenager, Lin broke with her, and they did not speak to each other for many years.

Their reconciliation is drawn out and painful, especially for Lin; but once they do, their relationship blossoms, and Lin's personality changes dramatically. There are definite parallels here to Leah and Rachel; Leah and Lin, both the older daughters, carry around much more resentment toward their younger sister. In a switch with the Torah comparison, Lin, the older sister, has no children while the younger, Su, has five children (while Leah had six sons and one daughter and Rachel had two). And while the reconciliation between Lin and Suyin is a moving and emotional event, there really isn't a reconciliation between Leah and Rachel, especially because Rachel dies much younger.

Another parallel could be drawn between Jacob and Esau, who had great animosity toward each other, especially due to their father, Isaac's, different treatment, and then the sold birthright and deathbed blessing incidents. Years later they do reconcile, and while Lin and Suyin never reach the point where one desires to kill the other, the reconciliation episodes have emotional similarities.

In contrast, there is a set of mixed-gender twins in *Korra,* introduced in season two, that is harmonious and rather quirky. Brother Desna and sister Eska are a peculiar team. Although often portrayed as stonily humorous, they are both powerful characters, and their transformation from supporting their father and being icy toward their cousin Korra to being allies of Korra (once they realize how selfish and horrible their father has been) is significant and shown to be a sign of their maturity.

There are three other sets of brothers in the *Korra* series, two of which are acrimonious, and one caring and supportive. When we first meet Mako and Bolin, these two orphans are literally teammates on a pro-bending team. Throughout the four seasons of *Korra* we see them as comrades who sometimes argue, and have different personalities (as well as different bending abilities), but they usually have the same main goals. We could compare them in a way to Moses and Aaron, although Moses was considerably more important than Aaron, and both Mako and Bolin have equal importance for the *Korra* series.

In season one, viewers do not even realize that Amon and Tarrlok are brothers. Amon is the leader of a non-bending movement, whereas Tarrlok is an important politician in Republic City. Later in the series they realize that they are long-lost brothers. We also see flashbacks to their childhood, which was happy at first but later turned violent and manipulative, due to their father's cruelties and exploitation. At the end, Amon goes by his birth name, Noatak, and in a shocking denouement, Tarrlok kills them both.

Another brother spat over power occurs in season two, between Tonraq (Korra's father) and his younger brother Unalaq. These two brothers of the Water Tribe are presented as strong individuals, but the younger is crafty and manipulative, and creates a situation in which he is the more powerful leader. He also has a wild goal to bridge the spirit world with the human world.

Later he becomes so power hungry that he has Korra's father imprisoned, and he attempts to become a Dark Avatar, not only surpassing his older brother but also his niece, the rightful Avatar. In the end, Korra defeats (and kills) Unalaq, but her link to the past Avatars has been severed in the process. This is a shattering situation for Korra, dispiriting her in many ways.

What could this be compared to in Jewish scripture? Perhaps this has echoes of Adonijah and Solomon. It also could be compared with Cain and Abel, and the psychological pain that runs through this storyline. Jealousies that end in fratricide are shocking, and the Torah had the first version of this.

These frightening plotlines are fleshed out in *Korra,* which expected a more mature audience that could grapple with power struggles, interfamily fighting, and other hostile and even quite violent episodes.

After all this, the childish and sweet arguments between Tenzin's three older children (daughters Jinora and Ikki, and son Meelo) are a relief, a way to contrast the painful clashes that flare between the other sets of siblings in the series. Tenzin is shown as a flawed but ultimately caring father, while Amon and Tarlok's father, Yakone, is a criminal and a horrid dad. We can see in *Korra* that bad parenting often leads to troubled children. An exception to that is how Desna and Eska turn out to be good (if strange) despite the efforts of their devious father, Unalaq.

In the Torah, Isaac's major flaw is how he favors one son over another; his own childhood includes the bewildering and frightful Akeidah (near sacrifice). Jacob then ends up favoring Joseph over the other sons, and the jealousies cause great disruption. However, there is also the positive Master Plan theme within this, and even Joseph forgives his brothers because he realizes that their cruelties toward him as an adolescent have ultimately saved them from starvation because he is in Egypt and has such great, extensive power there.

Thus, the imperfections and power plays of families are integral to Jewish scripture and to the *Avatar–Korra* franchise.

UNUSUAL MENAGERIES—RESPECT FOR ANIMALS

A beloved aspect of the *Avatar* and *Korra* series is the unusual hybrid animals—at least, they are hybrid to us. Some of those featured include Appa, a flat-tailed flying bison; Naga, the polar bear dog; the rabaroo species that is a combination of rabbit and kangaroo. There are many scenes in both animated series where we see the human characters interacting affectionately with their pets.

Jewish scripture mentions many of the animals with which we are familiar today, but there are others that are somewhat fantastic, mythic, and at the very least curious: the Behemoth mentioned in the Book of Job, which may have been an elephant or hippo . . . or may have been something else. The Leviathan, also mentioned in Job, was a rather weird and large sea creature. The fourth chapter of Lamentations (Eikha) mentions a few rather odd animal creatures. The cockatrice, mentioned in the King James edition of Isaiah, is a kind of hybrid. A Cherub, as described in Ezekiel, had the faces of a human, ox, eagle, and lion, as well as bull hooves.

Obviously, *Avatar* is not the only fictional series that has strange beasts and creatures, as exemplified through the *Harry Potter* canon (especially the *Fantastic Beasts* spinoff) and the novel *The Island of Doctor Moreau*, by H. G. Wells. But this is yet another way in which *Avatar* and Judaism do share some iconic beings. In *Avatar,* the use of these creatures (as in *Harry Potter* and other series geared toward children and adolescents) serves to entertain but also spur the imagination. It's as if we are challenging youth to imagine living beings that are hybrids in a positive (although also occasionally ghoulish) light. In Jewish scripture, these unusual creatures serve religious purposes, such as to frighten and instill awe in followers of the faith.

We can see frankly that in *Avatar* and in Jewish religious texts, there are typical animals such as dogs, horses, deer, and fish; and there are also occasional appearances by very strange animals. And the very first Avatar, Wan, dealt with spirits and hybrid creatures who spoke directly to him; these are reminiscent of Balaam's ass, who spoke directly and frankly with him. However, in the Torah this was an extremely rare incident, whereas in *Avatar* and *Korra,* spirits and animals communicate frequently with some of the featured characters.

FOUR: A PIVOTAL NUMBER

In Judaism, the number Four is quite significant. And in the *Avatar–Korra* series, Four is also important. Coincidence? Probably not.

Four in Judaism: Passover in particular has sets of four. The Four Questions; the Four Sons; The Four Promises; the Four Cups of Wine. Sukkot has the Four Species: the palm branch (lulav), hadas (myrtle), arava (willow), and etrog (citron). They represent the four types of Jews in service to G-d. Four is also prominent in the Torah: four Matriarchs (Sarah, Rebecca, Leah, and Rachel); four women who give birth to Jacob's children (Leah, Rachel, Bilhah, and Zilpah).

A more gruesome quartet in Jewish liturgy is "the sins for which we deserve the four kinds of death inflicted by the Court of Law: stoning, burning, beheading and strangling," mentioned in the Evening Service of Yom Kippur.[10] And there are "four sins so great that God blocks the sinner's way toward repentance," as described in the ArtScroll Mesorah Series volume on Yom Kippur.[11]

Four is also essential to the *Avatar–Korra* canon. The most obvious Four are the four main Nations, and bending abilities: water, earth, fire, and air. It is important for them to be balanced, and with the Fire Nation as conquerors, this imbalance threatens much of the world.

And Four is important because the Avatar must be a master of all four styles.

The link between the Four Nations of *Avatar–Korra*, and the Foursomes of Passover and Sukkot have clear connections. All four are necessary and part of a larger scheme. We learn a great deal about human psychology and capabilities within the scheme of four.

CONCLUSION

There are many connections between Jewish scripture, practice, and thought, and the realm of the animated *Avatar* and *Korra* series. We can easily draw parallels between these two "worlds."

This seems too much of a coincidence and is certainly intriguing, and worthy of discussion and research. Even though the *Avatar* and *Korra* series star Asian people and feature variations of martial arts, there is quite a bit of Judaica and Jewish history echoed throughout the two TV shows.

Avatar and *Korra* are among a select group of animated series, seen on TV and in the theaters, that can be enjoyed on superficial levels, but also in deeper dimensions.

NOTES

1. Dr. Carol Panetta, "Avatar: The Last Airbender: A Psychoanalytic Review or How a Kids' Show Can Teach Analysis," *Boston Graduate School of Psychoanalysis,* April 12, 2016, bgsp.edu/avatar-the-last-airbender.

2. David L. Lieber, Jules Harlow, and The Rabbinical Assembly, *Etz Hayim: Torah and Commentary* (New York: The United Synagogue of Conservative Judaism, 2004).

3. Jenna Jones, "Avatar vs. Legend of Korra: The Feminist Debate," *The Journal, the New Source for Webster University,* September 10, 2020.

4. *Avatar: The Last Airbender,* season 3, episode 6, "The Avatar and the Fire Lord," directed by Ethan Spaulding, written by Elizabeth Welch, aired October 26, 2007, in broadcast syndication, Paramount, 2015, DVD.

5. *Avatar: The Last Airbender,* season 3, episode 13, "The Firebending Masters," directed by Giancarlo Volpe, written by John O'Bryan, aired July 15, 2008, in broadcast syndication, Paramount, 2015, DVD.

6. Alex Barasch, "The Stunning Second Life of 'Avatar: The Last Airbender,'" *The New Yorker,* July 5, 2020, www.newyorker.com/culture/culture-desk/the-stunning -second-life-of-avatar-the-last-airbender.

7. *Avatar: The Last Airbender,* season 2, episode 12, "The Serpent's Pass," directed by Ethan Spaulding, written by Michael Dante DiMartino and Joshua Hamilton, aired September 15, 2006, in broadcast syndication, Paramount, 2015, DVD.

8. *Avatar: The Last Airbender,* season 2, episode 5, "Avatar Day," directed by Lauren MacMullan, written by John O'Bryan, aired April 28, 2006, in broadcast syndication, Paramount, 2015, DVD.

9. *HaSiddur HaShalem*, Daily Prayer Book, trans. and annotated by Philip Birnbaum (New York: Hebrew Publishing Company, 1977).

10. *ArtScroll Mesorah Series: Yom Kippur,* 6th ed., trans. Benjamin Yudin (New York: Mesorah Publications, 1999).

11. ArtScroll Mesorah Series: Yom Kippur.

WORKS CITED

ArtScroll Mesorah Series: Yom Kippur, 6th ed. Translated by Benjamin Yudin. New York: Mesorah Publications, 1999.

Barasch, Alex. "The Stunning Second Life of *Avatar: The Last Airbender*." *The New Yorker,* July 5, 2020. www.newyorker.com/culture/culture-desk/the-stunning-second-life-of-avatar-the-last-airbender

DiMartino, Michael Dante, and Joshua Hamilton, writers. *Avatar: The Last Airbender.* Season 2, episode 12, "The Serpent's Pass." Directed by Ethan Spaulding. Aired September 15, 2006, in broadcast syndication. Paramount, 2015, DVD.

HaSiddur HaShalem, Daily Prayer Book. Translated and annotated by Philip Birnbaum. 1949. New York: Hebrew Publishing Company, 1977.

Jones, Jenna. "Avatar vs. Legend of Korra: The Feminist Debate." *The Journal, the New Source for Webster University,* September 10, 2020.

Lieber, David L., Jules Harlow, and The Rabbinical Assembly. *Etz Hayim: Torah and Commentary.* New York: The United Synagogue of Conservative Judaism, 2004.

Machor Abodat Israel, translated by S. Singer, N. Adler, and A. Th. Philips. New York: Ziegelheim, 1946.

O'Bryan, John, writer. *Avatar: The Last Airbender.* Season 2, episode 5, "Avatar Day." Directed by Lauren MacMullan. Aired April 28, 2006, in broadcast syndication. Paramount, 2015, DVD.

O'Bryan, John, writer. *Avatar: The Last Airbender.* Season 3, episode 13, "The Firebending Masters." Directed by Giancarlo Volpe. Aired July 15, 2008, in broadcast syndication. Paramount, 2015, DVD.

Panetta, Dr. Carol. "Avatar: The Last Airbender: A Psychoanalytic Review or How a Kids' Show Can Teach Analysis." *Boston Graduate School of Psychoanalysis,* April 12, 2016. bgsp.edu/avatar-the-last-airbender.

Tanach: The Stone Edition, The Torah/Prophets/Writings. Translated by Rabbi Nosson Scherman. 1957. Brooklyn, NY: Mesorah Publications, Ltd., 1996.

Welch, Elizabeth, writer. *Avatar: The Last Airbender.* Season 3, episode 6, "The Avatar and the Fire Lord." Directed by Ethan Spaulding. Aired October 26, 2007, in broadcast syndication. Paramount, 2015, DVD.

Chapter Fourteen

The Twilight Zone as Jewish Science Fiction

Judy Klass

There is a 1995 documentary about the life of Rod Serling that was pre-sented as part of the *American Masters* series on PBS. The film is called *Rod Serling: Submitted for Your Approval.*[1] It contains a lot of good information and context; many well-chosen clips; and interesting interviews with actors, peers, and collaborators and with Serling's widow, daughters, and brother. It also contains a few cheesy touches. It opens with a black and white sequence depicting doctors operating in a hospital, with *Twilight Zone*-ish music play-ing, that presents the death of Serling at age fifty in 1975 as if it is a sequence from that remarkable show he created—while Lee Grant narrates. The film features a Rod Serling imitator reading aloud Serling's written thoughts. Of course, one can understand, with the sparse amount of audio interview mate-rial available, and the distinctiveness of Serling's way of speaking, why that choice was made. (And the authors of books like *Last Stop, The Twilight Zone: The Biography of Rod Serling,* by Joel Engel, and *Serling,* by Gordon F. Sander, also feel a need to play around with *Twilight Zone* tropes and scriptwriting formats as their books open.)

The film mentions that Rod Serling was born in 1924 on Christmas Day: "a suitable start to a charmed childhood." It does not mention that Serling was Jewish. Serling did grow up with Christmas trees in his house, and books about him, like his daughter Anne's memoir *As I Knew Him: My Dad, Rod Serling*, mention that he liked Christmas for a sense of wonder and magic associated with it, not for religious reasons. Serling's mother, Esther, was from an Orthodox household. His father, Sam, was a Reform Jew who did not prioritize keeping kosher or having his sons bar-mitzvahed (neither was), and he told them: "I am not a good Jew, but I think I'm a good person. If you want to be very religious, that's up to you. My own philosophy is, I take people for what they are, not where they go to pray."[2] These words made a big impression on his younger son, Rod. He grew up attending synagogue on the High Holy Days in Binghamton, New York, and was involved with the Jewish Community Center there. He later married a Gentile woman and joined her Unitarian church (though he was not one to attend services), finding Unitarianism's liberal, non-sectarian values congenial—but he identified as a Jew ethnically and culturally throughout his life. He lit Yahrzeit candles for his parents and remained "Jewish" in other ways.

The documentary talks about Serling soaking up "the New Deal aspirations of his parents" and includes a clip from the film *Seven Days in May* for which Serling wrote the screenplay, referencing dangerous demagogues like Senator Joe McCarthy—but it does not give a sense of what FDR and the New Deal meant to many Jewish Americans, or how the American Jewish community, in general, reacted to the House Un-American Activities Committee (HUAC) and the McCarthyism that so often targeted Jews. Books about Rod Serling communicate that his father was more conservative than his mother but loved FDR and taught his sons that the United States was a beacon of hope for immigrants as much for its Bill of Rights and democracy as for the financial opportunities it provided.

The documentary presents Serling as part of a group of interesting young writers who got their start during the Golden Age of Television, but does not look at how many of those writers who chafed at the banality of television in the late 1950s (Paddy Chayefsky, Reginald Rose) were Jewish, and how Jewishness may have informed the sociopolitical concerns they wanted to explore—along with directors who were involved with *Playhouse 90* at CBS at the same time as Serling, such as Sidney Lumet, Arthur Penn, and half-Jewish John Frankenheimer. (*Playhouse 90* ran from 1956 to 1960, presenting ninety-minute dramas, live, and it is remembered as representative of television's "Golden Age," and as a training ground for many talented people.)

The *American Masters* documentary is worth watching—but it is also worthwhile to take a look at Rod Serling as a practitioner of Jewish science fiction and fantasy, and to provide more context for how his Jewishness may have affected Serling's writing, especially on *The Twilight Zone* (1959–1964), for which he is most remembered.

Engel, Sander, and Nicholas Parisi in his book *Rod Serling* write about Binghamton as a kind of idyllic small town: a source of lifelong nostalgia for Serling, and the inspiration for *Twilight Zone* episodes like "Walking Distance" and "A Stop at Willoughby" where harried, weary protagonists look to visions of small-town innocence for salvation.

Everybody has to have a hometown," Serling wrote. "Binghamton's mine. In the strangely brittle, terribly sensitive make-up of a human being, there is a need for a place to hang a hat or a kind of geographical womb to crawl back into, or maybe just a place that's familiar because that's where you grew up. When I dig back through memory cells, I get one particularly distinctive feeling—and that's one of warmth, comfort, and well-being.[3]

But Engel and Sander both stress that there was an undercurrent of anti-Semitism in Binghamton. Serling was blackballed from a Jewish high school fraternity for dating Gentile girls, and from another high school fraternity for being Jewish. "'It was the first time in my life I became aware of religious differences,' he said, still stung by the incident, thirty years later."[4] The father of a girl he dated at a Jewish camp felt he was not sufficiently religiously Jewish.

Growing up during Hitler's rise to power also shaped Serling, as he would hear his father angrily talk about what was going on in Germany. Anxious to prove himself, though he was considered too short, he talked his way into the paratroopers right after high school: a dangerous group to join. His time in New Guinea training for jungle combat was grueling. His experience fighting to retake the island of Leyte in the Philippines from the Japanese scarred him. Memories of shooting a Japanese soldier on a baseball field, staring down the barrel of a gun, sure he was about to die, only to have a G.I. behind him kill the Japanese soldier about to shoot him, and seeing a friend, another funny Jewish kid named Mel Levy, killed by falling supplies during an air drop, all left marks on Serling, leading to lifelong struggles with nightmares and insomnia, and a need to write—to work through what he was feeling. His time in Japan after Japan's surrender made him optimistic about people's ability to get past prejudices and work through problems. Many sources of information about Serling quote what he told the *Los Angeles Times* in 1967: "I happen to think that the singular evil of our time is prejudice. It is from this evil that all other evils grow and multiply. In almost everything I've written, there is a thread of this: man's seemingly palpable need to dislike someone other than himself."

Serling first established himself on television (in those early days of live drama) in 1955 with a script called "Patterns" about the ruthlessness of corporate America, and he had another major success with "Requiem for a Heavyweight" about a boxer—Serling himself had done some boxing. (Both of those television dramas, like Chayefsky's "Marty" and Rose's "Twelve Angry Men," would later be reborn as feature films.) But he ran into troubles with networks and sponsors when he tried to write about this issue of prejudice that was so important to him. In 1955, a fourteen-year-old African American boy from Chicago named Emmett Till was visiting Mississippi, and allegedly he whistled at a white woman running a small store. Her husband and other men kidnapped, beat, and killed the child, and were exonerated in court by other white Southerners, though they later admitted in a magazine that they were the murderers—and the incident helped to galvanize the Civil Rights Movement of the 1950s and 1960s. Serling wrote several scripts inspired by the murder of Emmett Till. Each time, he was thwarted by the timorousness of those above him in the television hierarchy. Told he could not write about Blacks and whites, he wrote "Noon on Doomsday" about an attack on an elderly Jewish pawnbroker. But when white citizens councils in the South heard that the script was, at least allegorically, about what happened to Emmett Till, they were outraged:

> The murdered Jew was changed to suggest an unnamed foreigner, the locale moved from the south to New England . . . and ultimately it became a lukewarm, vitiated, emasculated kind of show. By the time they finished taking Coca-Cola bottles off of the set because the sponsor claimed that this had Southern connotation—suggesting to what depth they went to make this a clean, antiseptically rigidly acceptable show, why it bore no relationship to what we purported to say initially.[5]

The *American Masters* documentary (along with other sources) quotes from what Serling said about the second script:

> By the time *A Town Has Turned to Dust* went before the cameras my script had turned to dust. . . . Emmett Till became a romantic Mexican who loved the storekeeper's wife, but "only with his eyes." My sheriff couldn't commit suicide because one of our sponsors was an insurance firm, and they claimed that suicide often leads to complications in settling policy claims. The lynch victim was called Clemson, but we couldn't use this 'cause South Carolina had an all-white college by that name. The setting was moved to the Southwest in the 1870's . . . the phrase "twenty men in hoods" became "twenty men in homemade masks." They chopped it up like a roomful of butchers at work on a steer.[6]

Another part of the documentary where it might be helpful for viewers to know Serling was Jewish is the discussion of what ended up being the final *Playhouse 90* script to be aired: "In the Presence of Mine Enemies." It was a script about a Jewish family in the Warsaw Ghetto. Serling asked for a guarantee that it would get made before he embarked on months of research. He got the guarantee, only to have the network renege when they found sponsors wary of a drama about a "negative topic" like the Holocaust. Ultimately, "In the Presence of Mine Enemies" was produced during a writers' strike in 1960, when unproduced scripts were scarce, and Serling had already moved on to doing *The Twilight Zone.*

Serling faced a firestorm of criticism for this *Playhouse 90* script, which presented a young Nazi, played by Robert Redford, as being opposed to what Nazis were doing, and depicted discussions of violence and hate on all sides. An older Nazi tells the young man:

"Young Sergeant Lott, I'm going to talk about morality. The morality of hating Jews. Because there is a morality in hatred, Sergeant. It happens to be a clue to survival. Nations can feed on it. They find their strength in it. They're nurtured by it, Lott. But there must be an object of hatred. Suddenly, in front of us, out steps a Jew. An unassimilated foreigner in our midst. And so, we hate him. And in the process, we are unified."[7]

Among those who excoriated *Playhouse 90* for the script was Leon Uris who went on to write a novel about the Warsaw Ghetto, *Mila 18*, and, most famously, the novel *Exodus*. Uris found the "shades of gray" shown among German and Jewish characters reprehensible. Anne Serling quotes a letter her father wrote to "a prominent Jewish leader" about the script:

Neither my Pole nor the German soldier were designed to be representative or symbolic. As a dramatist, I was dealing with individuals—not symbols. As a matter of fact I thought I'd gone to great lengths to make the implication clear that these were exceptions to the rule. The essence of playwriting is conflict and for me to have shown a Jewish point of view in this case would have been simply a restatement of a horror we are already too familiar with. All I was trying to dramatize was that even in a sea of madness, there can be a moment [involving] just a fragment of faith, hope, decency and humanity. Hence, an orthodox rabbi can put his hand on the quaking shoulder of a young German and offer him forgiveness that he cries out for.[8]

To his friend Julie Golden, who liked "In the Presence of Mine Enemies," Serling wrote:

The show has engendered considerable comment both pro and con. I now stand in the middle between two poles of accusation. Either I'm a great and vicious anti-Semite (according to Leon Uris) or I'm a dirty, Jew-loving bastard (from the Steuben Societies of the United States). But I suppose that is what makes ballgames and church attendance.[9]

There are a number of reasons why few writers worked on stories about the Holocaust in the late 1950s. Jewish writers may have been reluctant to draw attention to their own Jewishness, as the United States itself had experienced increased anti-Semitism during the Nazi years. Ralph Medoff in his introduction to *We Spoke Out*, a rare collection of postwar Holocaust fiction, writes: "For American Jews to have spoken loudly about the Holocaust in those days would have run counter to the prevailing national mood. It would have focused on a narrow ethnic concern and emphasized the most somber of topics, at a time when the path to speedy Americanization required embracing a positive, upbeat approach of going along and getting along."[10] Others might shy away from the topic due to the very timidity of the networks and sponsors that Serling encountered, and the kind of furious response he provoked; this was a highly charged, highly sensitive subject in the years right after the war: more than at any other time.

And there are some who still grapple, today, with the question of whether it is possible to create good art about something as unimaginably horrific as the Holocaust—and whether one should even try. What room is there, with such a subject, for "nuance," and for recreating out of chaos and ungraspable horror the order that art demands? An article in *Vice* notes:

> Theodor Adorno famously uttered and then retracted the oft-misinterpreted statement "to write poetry after Auschwitz is barbaric"; over half a century later, when graphic novelist Art Spiegelman was questioned by a reporter about the insensitivity of his Holocaust memoir *Maus*, he retorted, "no, I thought Auschwitz was in bad taste." There is a grain of truth in both dictums. A traumatic event, whether personal or universal, is an illogical outlier and thus it should be near impossible to make any sense of it—to be able to translate that illogic into a poem, book, or painting after an act of barbarism is equally barbaric.[11]

What must have motivated Serling to return, repeatedly, to the topic of the Holocaust, which others avoided for the excellent reasons mentioned above—both pragmatic and philosophical—was the compulsion he felt to explore precisely the unpleasant, difficult topics others evade, and themes like prejudice, scapegoating, and blind hatred. He saw a discussion of those important moral issues as part of his job as a writer.

I teach a Jewish science fiction course at Vanderbilt University. One of the pleasures of the course is turning students on to *The Twilight Zone*. Often, they have never heard of it, and most have never seen it. I tell them: this is a show in black and white, and its creators had almost no budget, they had no CGI, and almost no ability to achieve special effects, as we think of them. They used sound, props, and visuals creatively, but what they mainly relied on, to creep people out and to get them thinking, were assets that more expensive shows that came later did not always have: really strong actors and really strong scripts. Students get caught up in the first episode that we watch: "It's a Good Life," from 1961.[12] Serling wrote the script, but it is based on a 1953 short story by Jerome Bixby, who was Catholic. The Bixby short story explores in great depth what might go through the mind of an omnipotent being with the ability to read thoughts and to casually kill what it has created, as when the child in the story, little Anthony Fremont, makes a bird fly around erratically, and absentmindedly flies it into a rock.

The *Twilight Zone* episode based on the story also plays with the edgy, irreverent idea of an all-powerful God figure as a spoiled child—but it puts more emphasis on the callowness and cowardice of the adults who enable his tyranny and praise him. Little Billy Mumy as Anthony terrorizes his mother and father, played by Cloris Leachman and John Larch, and other adults; the palpable fear the adults feel around the child, as they curry favor with him, is what sells the reality of the story. When Don Keefer as Dan Hollis challenges someone to stand up to Anthony and kill him, Alice Frost as Aunt Amy, whose mind Anthony has scrambled, thinks about it—but no one acts.

When I ask students about whether "It's a Good Life" can be read allegorically, it usually leads to a wide-ranging discussion. It can be seen as an indictment of God, or of any organized religion where one is not allowed to ask too many questions. Some students say they see it as being about communist dictatorships—some compare Anthony to Kim Jong-un. In recent years, unsurprisingly, some have compared Anthony and the adults around him to Donald Trump and his enablers. Some say it's about the dangers of over-indulging children, and a student once suggested that it is a metaphor for how members of the Greatest Generation who had lived through the Great Depression and World War II felt horrified by the smug sense of entitlement of those born after the war: the young Baby Boomers.

I try to let the discussion be student-run, and then I add a few other thoughts: that Serling had also lived through the elevation of fascist strongmen like Hitler, Mussolini, and Franco, and may have had them in mind, as well as, possibly, dictators on the Left. And I talk about the loyalty oaths, self-censorship, and coerced exclamations of patriotism and praise from Americans during the Cold War. I call students' attention to the sequence where Anthony "makes" television, and the adults have to watch Claymation dinosaurs fight each other, and they exclaim that it's "much better than the old television!" This comes from the original Bixby short story, but I say that this part of the episode may also be Serling commenting on the lost potential of the Golden Age of Television in the 1950s that he was part of, and how government bullies, sponsors who did not want to offend anyone, and new TV executives who only wished to please the sponsors, make a buck, and dumb everything down had crushed the potential of the medium.

Serling may have been commenting on what caused him to create *The Twilight Zone* in the first place: a show in which he could explore, allegorically, through science fiction and fantasy, themes that realistic shows avoided.

I am not suggesting that Jewish writers were the only ones to take issue with safe, lowest-common-denominator American television in the late 1950s and early 1960s. Surely, that is one of the objects of satire in Kurt Vonnegut Jr.'s 1961 short story "Harrison Bergeron." Nor am I saying that only Jewish writers like Serling used science fiction and fantasy as a means of discussing, from unusual angles, issues of the day that were generally considered "too hot to handle." No writer—besides Serling—had a style and ethos that permeated *The Twilight Zone* more than did Ray Bradbury, though he only wrote one script for the show: "I Sing the Body Electric," aired in 1962. (Bradbury and other science fiction writers at times accused *The Twilight Zone* of stealing ideas from them, but there are trends and tropes common to speculative fiction in any decade, and motifs in "what if?" stories may repeat themselves.) Bradbury's 1950s science fiction book *The Martian Chronicles*, with a story in which African Americans leave the Jim Crow South to create a colony on Mars, and a later story that stood as a sequel to it, explored in science fiction what other writers were afraid to go near in more "literary" tales.

What I say to my students is that the position of most twentieth-century Jewish Americans as immigrants or the children of immigrants; the fact that many came from Leftist families; the scapegoating of Jews and other minorities in the United States; Jewish history that includes exiles, inquisitions, ghettoization, and pogroms; and revelations about the Holocaust, along with the Jewish tradition of Tikkun Olam—trying to heal the world—made many Jewish science fiction writers (as with Jewish comedians, songwriters, filmmakers and practitioners of other art forms my courses touch on) more likely than most to broach thorny topics, in a time when the gatekeepers preferred the safety of silence.

Another course I teach is on Jews and Hollywood. Neal Gabler in his book *An Empire of Their Own: How the Jews Invented Hollywood* writes about Jewish "moguls"—such as Adolph Zukor, the Warner Brothers, and Louis B. Mayer—and how these self-made immigrants wanted to be seen as patriotic Americans. Gabler documents how the House Committee on Un-American Activities in the late 1930s came to be led by Representative Martin Dies of Texas who appeared wary of Jews, inviting speakers from the Nazi Bund, the Silver Shirts, and the Ku Klux Klan. He was not hostile to Nazis: only communists. He was the first to investigate Hollywood. Representative John Rankin of Mississippi dominated HUAC in the mid-1940s, and he was more openly anti-Semitic. His rhetoric echoed American Nazi attacks on Jews in Hollywood. (Senator Joseph McCarthy, who gave his name to this dark era, came later and was not focused on show business.)

Gabler quotes blacklisted writer Lillian Hellman about how the "moguls" and the men directly under them thought: "'It would not have been possible in Russia or Poland, but it was possible here to offer the Cossacks a bowl of chicken soup.'"[13] Men who had fled persecution as Jews in Europe were terrified by HUAC and McCarthy, and Gabler writes that those men were often politically far more right-wing than the writers who worked for them: writers who wound up getting blacklisted, sometimes with the help of those running the studios. Television shows were often filmed elsewhere in Hollywood (and in New York), but television was a related entity.

The 1976 film *The Front* (written by Walter Bernstein and directed by Martin Ritt, both blacklisted, featuring Zero Mostel and other blacklisted actors) depicts the hunt for "Reds" in television in New York City in the early 1950s, and uses that milieu to comment on what happened throughout the entertainment industry. Many in positions of power in television were not Jewish, but no one making executive decisions at a network wanted to upset a government committee, offend a corporate sponsor, or endanger the bottom line.

After *The Twilight Zone* was canceled, Serling wrote a pilot episode for a new show called *The Challenge*, with Reginald Rose, about a school bus driver who refuses to sign a loyalty oath. Not so surprisingly, it was never filmed, and *The Challenge* never got on the air.

The *Twilight Zone* episodes we watch for my Jewish science fiction class are varied. "Time Enough at Last" is another episode with a script by Rod Serling based on a short story by someone else—in this case Lynn Venable.[14] This was apparently the first time that "the Bomb dropped" on any fictional U.S. television show. The episode aired in 1959, during the first season of *The Twilight Zone*. Of course, this is another iconic episode, and the ending—where Burgess Meredith, the henpecked bookworm, stumbles upon a public library in the ruins of his city, as a solitary survivor of a nuclear attack, only to have an unfortunate accident—has been parodied on *Futurama* and other shows. I see "Time Enough at Last" as a basic text that my students should know. It is also one of the *Twilight Zone* episodes that helps to communicate to them how we all lived during the Cold War: expecting nuclear annihilation at any moment. When I ask students if there is anything particularly "Jewish" about the episode—they sometimes say that the image of the timid man with an overbearing, shrewish wife is a trope of Jewish comedy. They may have something, there.

For me, what defines Henry Bemis's wife as maliciously evil is how she has scrawled on every page of his prized book of poetry, rendering it unreadable. The way Serling scripts that scene evokes Jewish thoughts about how the Torah—but, by extrapolation, other books as well—is to be given respect akin to the respect we show to people . . . and the utter villainy of those who deface and desecrate books.

But the three episodes of *The Twilight Zone* that I show my class that I tie most directly to Jewish science fiction themes of "aliens and alienation" are episodes written entirely by Rod Serling: not based on the work of anyone else. They are "The Shelter," "The Monsters Are Due on Maple Street," and "Eye of the Beholder."

"The Shelter," like "It's a Good Life," aired in 1961 during the third season of the show.[15] The issue of bomb shelters was being debated—should people build them, was there even a point to them—and Serling took that debate from current headlines and fashioned a taut drama. It begins with a musical riff on "Happy Birthday," and a camera pan from a sleepy, smalltown street to one house where a birthday celebration is in progress. Inside the house, Jack Albertson as Jerry gives a joking, affectionate birthday toast to "Doc" Bill Stockton, played by Larry Gates, who has cared for all of his neighbors and their children—and who also comes in for some kidding for the noise he's made building a fallout shelter in the basement. The warm, neighborly atmosphere changes when a radio CONELRAD announcement warns of unidentified flying objects and urges people to get into their fallout shelters, or to take shelter elsewhere.

The guests scatter to their homes, and Stockton and his wife and son head down to their shelter. But soon their friends are back, begging and demanding to be allowed inside. Soon they bring a battering ram into the Stockton basement to knock down the door to the shelter. Everyone is left horrified by their own behavior and the behavior of those around them—including the Stocktons. A notable beat in the episode comes when one of the previously cordial neighbors, Frank Henderson, played by Sandy Kenyon, turns on another, a dark-featured immigrant with a mustache and perhaps a bit of an accent: Marty Weiss, played by Joseph Bernard. Frank tells Marty to shut his mouth: "That's the way it is when the foreigners come over here. Pushy, grabby, semi-American." A few minutes later, he tells Marty: "Nobody cares what you think, you or your kind!" He punches Marty. And yet, Marty soon joins him in the mob intent on breaking down the fallout shelter door.

I used to find "The Shelter" overwrought—an example of Rod Serling being bombastic and over-the-top with his representation of how easily Americans can devolve into a nativistic, violent mob. My thinking has changed in the last few years, and I no longer find the episode so implausible. Sadly, I find that episode, and "The Monsters Are Due on Maple Street," to be quite relevant allegories for the United States that we now live in.

Like "The Shelter," "The Monsters Are Due on Maple Street," from season one in 1960, begins with a kind of celebration of idyllic, sleepy, suburban life in the kind of American small town we associate with the era: from *Leave It to Beaver*, *Father Knows Best*, *The Donna Reed Show*, and all the others.[16] As the *American Masters* documentary makes clear, Serling's connection to smalltown life was genuine. As mentioned, Serling wrote *Twilight Zone* episodes like "Walking Distance" and "A Stop at Willoughby," which communicate a yearning for the lost innocence of childhood and the gentleness and goodness of smalltown life, which he associated with Binghamton, New York, and perhaps with places where he lived later, like Westport, Connecticut.

But there is also a satirical aspect to episodes like "The Shelter" and "The Monsters Are Due on Maple Street," indicating that Serling, as an adult writer, understood the ugliness that a seemingly wholesome, picture-perfect American small town can contain—as Shirley Jackson (who was married to Stanley Edgar Hyman and directly familiar with anti-Semitism as a result) did when she wrote her famous short story "The Lottery." That short story opens with scenes of bucolic picturesqueness, and "The Monsters Are Due on Maple Street" begins in a similarly heartwarming way. An ice cream peddler makes his way down the street in the opening shot, as Serling narrates: "Maple Street, USA. Late summer. A tree-lined little world of front-porch gliders, barbecues, the laughter of children—and the bell of an ice cream vendor. At the sound of the roar and the flash of light, it will be precisely 6:43 p.m. on Maple Street." Boys, one of them carrying a baseball bat, run to buy ice cream as the strange light and sound turn the head of everyone who lives on the block.

Once the power on the block goes out, and a kid relates the plot of a science fiction story or comic book about aliens sending representatives down ahead of them that look like humans, but aren't, the people of Maple Street turn on each other, and every neighbor's personality quirks suddenly seem "suspicious." Again, the escalation of violence and hysteria in this episode once struck me as melodramatic and overdone—but it no longer seems like such a heavy-handed fable. As with "The Shelter," I feel as though we all have been living in it. (I don't get into my changed views with my classes; I simply say that these episodes feel more lifelike and convincing to me than they previously did.) The story the boy tells that sets off the paranoid finger-pointing is meant to be ridiculous, and I tell my classes that Serling and most of his audience would remember when Orson Welles adapted the H. G. Wells novel *The War of the Worlds* into a radio play in 1938, with the story presented as news broadcasts about a Martian invasion that some took to be real, and panic and hysteria ensued.

Neighbors in "The Monsters Are Due on Maple Street" watch each other, hunt each other, question each other . . . and the hostility and fear continue to mount. As in "The Shelter," some neighbors are more foolish, obnoxious, and aggressive than others, but no one is immune to the insanity that turns a community of people living, more or less, in a Norman Rockwell painting into the inhabitants of a hellscape. In "The Monsters Are Due on Maple Street," average Americans are transformed into the very monsters that they, themselves, are pursuing. Unlike "The Shelter," this episode contains no identifiably Jewish characters. (Like other episodes I've discussed, it contains at least one Jewish actor who does not necessarily read as Jewish playing a character who does not read as Jewish.) But "The Monsters Are Due on Maple Street" resonates with McCarthyism and the hunt for "Reds," and with the Holocaust and other moments of when people who have been good neighbors suddenly lose their own humanity and their ability to see the humanity of those who are near them..

There's a twist at the end I won't go into, but Serling sums things up nicely in his outro remarks: "The tools of conquest do not necessarily come with bombs and explosions and fallout. There are weapons that are simply thoughts, attitudes, prejudices—to be found only in the minds of men. For the record, prejudices can kill. And suspicion can destroy. And a thoughtless, frightened search for a scapegoat has a fallout all of its own—for the children, and the children yet unborn. And the pity of it is that these things cannot be confined to the Twilight Zone."

"Eye of the Beholder" is another episode with a twist at the end that I will not spoil.[17] It's an episode that arguably contains feminist themes—because, while "lookism" applies in some ways to everyone, in this episode and in life there is far more discussion of the way that women look. But beyond lookism and questions of what beauty is—the episode broaches the idea of ghettoizing those who are different, as a merciful alternative to killing them or locking them away. The episode features a speech by a societal leader demanding conformity, above all, with the trappings of a speech by a Fascist dictator.

Rod Serling may have handled Holocaust themes better when he broached them in this indirect way. There are episodes where he approaches the topic more directly—such as the third season episode "Deaths-Head Revisited" about a former SS officer who has taken a new name returning to Dachau and being confronted and "tried" by the Jewish prisoners he tortured and killed. Serling later explored similar themes in a novella called "The Escape Route," published in a book called *The Season to Be Wary* in 1967. It was part of the pilot for the 1970s show Serling hosted called *Night Gallery*.[18] "The Escape Route" involves a Nazi who has escaped to South America, but fears he will be brought to trial as Adolf Eichmann was in Israel, and finds his way to project himself into a soothing painting in a museum—until something goes wrong.

Another *Twilight Zone* episode dealing with Nazism directly is the hour-long fourth season episode "He's Alive," with Dennis Hopper as a two-bit neo-Nazi Hitler wannabe, receiving guidance from the spirit of the original.[19] There are powerful moments in it—and yet *The Twilight Zone* may be at its most effective when it is allegorical—when it uses the cloak of science fiction and fantasy the way that some Latin American literature uses magical realism both to evade censure and censorship and to explore themes so large and strange that they would suffer if given a more literal and "on the nose" treatment.

The trauma Serling suffered as a WWII veteran paratrooper manifested in a number of episodes of *The Twilight Zone*—in more ways than just his lingering love of airplanes. He wrote the story, though not the script, for "The Encounter," about a Japanese American young man and a bigoted World War II veteran trading secrets under the influence of a samurai sword.[20] That episode is problematic because the young Japanese American man, played by George Takei, turns out to have had a father who was disloyal to America at Pearl Harbor, and there is no evidence of Japanese American disloyalty of that kind, though that was the kind of baseless charge used to justify people (like George Takei, as a child) being sent to internment camps; for this reason, the episode was removed from U.S. syndication. (Takei has indicated in interviews that the things the two men think about are hallucinations or *Twilight Zone*–type experiences that perhaps should not be taken as factual and literal.)[21]

A source of the fictional veteran's guilt is that he killed the man from whom he took the samurai sword after the man surrendered. And he is still twisted and distorted by the hatred toward the "Japs" that motivated him during the war. As the United States began to bumble its way into Vietnam (which concerned Serling years before most Americans had strong views), the episode could, ultimately, be seen as a reminder to white Americans to see Asians as human beings; it was an attempt, at least, to portray an existential balancing act between two equally flawed men.

Similarly, a third season episode that Serling wrote, "The Quality of Mercy," follows an American GI in World War II eager to hunt down and kill the Japanese . . . who is transformed into a Japanese soldier under an equally bloodthirsty officer out to kill Americans.[22] Even with the mental scars the war visited upon Rod Serling, he retained an ability to see the humanity in people that many Otherized—and a desire to make his viewers see it as well.

Serling wrote several TV scripts with gentle, older Jewish characters later in life. One was "Storm in Summer" starring Peter Ustinov in 1970, about an elderly Jewish man who is the foster father, reluctantly at first, of a Black young boy.[23] The other story aired on *Night Gallery* (a mediocre show where, sadly, Serling did not have creative control as he had had with *The Twilight Zone*) and was a Christmas–Hanukkah fable called "The Messiah on Mott Street."[24] It starred Edward G. Robinson.

The documentary *Submitted for Your Approval* gives the impression that the only feature film project of any significance or merit that Serling was involved with in the years following *The Twilight Zone* was *Seven Days in May*. That film about an attempted military coup in the United States certainly deserves recognition—but Serling should receive more recognition for his work on the *Planet of the Apes* screenplay. The novel by Frenchman Pierre Boulle works as a kind of companion piece to the other great novel by

Boulle, *The Bridge Over the River Kwai*. In that book, the Englishmen in the POW camp and the Japanese soldiers running it see each other as less than human—as apes and monkeys . . . and Boulle's science fiction novel can feel like a logical extension of his more realistic book. Exploring these themes, the 1968 film *Planet of the Apes* is rich in ideas and substance in a way that the recent *Planet of the Apes* films are not.

According to various sources, including a *MeTV* article, Serling wrote a number of drafts of the script, which at times had a large projected budget and at times a small one.[25] Serling believed that the idea of using a certain iconic statue at the end of the film originated with him, though others have claimed credit for it. The consensus view of biographers and critics seems to be that credit should go to him. However, Serling credited Michael Wilson, with whom he shares screen credit for the fun dialogue in the script. (Wilson was long blacklisted, and long uncredited for his work on the film version of Boulle's *Bridge Over the River Kwai*; Glenn Frankel, writing about Carl Foreman, who translated his experience of being abandoned by friends while being blacklisted into his screenplay for *High Noon*, tells of how Wilson and Foreman were cheated out of their Oscars for the screenplay for *Bridge Over the River Kwai*, and how, years later, their widows were invited to a ceremony to pick up the awards.[26])

Serling had a more somber vision than Wilson. But the scope of the ideas in the film and the way it preserves the Swiftian elements of the novel (the wild humans like Nova that the astronauts encounter and that the gorillas hunt are reminiscent of the Yahoos in *Gulliver's Travels*) surely owe a lot to Serling.

There is a 2018 graphic novel written by Dana Gould called *Planet of the Apes: Visionaries* based on Serling's 1964 screenplay for *Planet of the Apes*.[27] The story it presents already shows key elements of what the movie would become, including Dr. Zira emerging as a startlingly strong and dynamic female lead for the 1960s (as she is in the 1963 Boulle novel), the pointless cruelty of the hunt, Dr. Zaius's belief that humans are fundamentally violent and destructive (which seems verified by our penchant for nuclear weapons), the discoveries in the archeological dig site that culminate in the human doll that says "Mama," the destruction of that dig—and the appearance of the iconic statue at the end.

A reader cannot know what has been left out of the graphic novel—which is much less "talky" than a typical Serling script—or what Serling added into his subsequent screenplay drafts. Dr. Zaius in the graphic novel is certainly intent on distorting the scientific record: lobotomizing another intelligent human astronaut and destroying the archeological dig site that provides evidence of an earlier advanced human civilization. But in the graphic novel, no religious motivation gets cited. In Boulle's satirical novel, the orangutans represent the pompous, stuffy academicians in society. In the 1968 American film, they seem more like John Birch Society members, or figures in the tradition of Father Coughlin and Senator John Rankin: mixing religion and reactionary politics, long before the rise of the Moral Majority. Perhaps this was an element added by Left-wing, blacklisted Catholic Michael Wilson, and not Serling. Engel writes that Wilson "made the character of Zaius—in the book just an ignorant and prideful scientist—a type of fifteenth-century grand inquisitor."[28]

In the 1968 film, chimpanzees like Dr. Zira and Dr. Cornelius seem to face quotas and career-destroying discrimination similar to what Jews faced in colleges and medical schools for much of the twentieth century—but, again, I cannot say whether this was a touch added by Wilson or by Serling. But certainly, when we consider the speculative fiction contributions of Rod Serling, *Planet of the Apes* should not be left out of the discussion.

However, in the end, what Serling will be most remembered for is creating *The Twilight Zone,* and scripting so many fine episodes for it. His episodes range from whimsical to heartbreaking, and explore many aspects of fate, ethics, and the human condition. The main purpose of this chapter has been to suggest that one more lens through which to view Serling's episodes is as Jewish science fiction. His preoccupations were similar to those of science fiction writers like Alfred Bester, Isaac Asimov, my uncle Philip Klass/ William Tenn, Henry Kuttner, Harry Harrison, Judith Merril, and others who did much of their work in the same era. For each of these writers, mixed in with the anxieties borne of living in a nuclear age, and having lived through the insanity of World War II and the Holocaust, and the Red Scare, and living with Cold War escalation, was the perspective of a Jewish American even more aware than most of the dangers of perceiving fellow human beings as the Other, and vilifying them.

Like a number of people of his generation, but with more urgency than most, Rod Serling understood the fragility of a decent and democratic way of life where the humanity and the rights of minority ethnic groups and religions, and women as well as men, are respected—and Serling understood far more than most the chaos and darkness that can engulf seemingly warm, kindly, and benign people—when something goes wrong and they reach for a scapegoat, or when persuasive people or troubling events tempt them to live down to their basest impulses. These are hard lessons—which all of us would do well to learn, again and again—from *The Twilight Zone.*

NOTES

1. *Rod Serling: Submitted for Your Approval*, directed by Susan Lacy (1995; USA: Panasonic, 2003), DVD.

2. Anne Serling, *My Dad, Rod Serling: As I Knew Him* (Ohio: Commonweal Book Company, 2021), Kindle edition.

3. Nicholas Parisi, *Rod Serling: His Life, Work and Imagination* (Jackson: University Press of Mississippi, 2018), 9, Kindle edition.

4. Gordon F. Sander, *Serling: The Rise and Twilight of TV's Last Angry Man* (New York: Cornell Paperbacks, 2011).

5. A. Serling.

6. A. Serling.

7. *Playhouse 90*, season 4, episode 16, "In the Presence of Mine Enemies," directed by Fielder Cook, written by Rod Serling, aired May 18th, 1960.

8. A. Serling.

9. A. Serling.

10. Neal Adams, Rafael Medoff, and Craig Yoe. *We Spoke Out: Comic Books and the Holocaust* (San Diego: IDW/Yoe Books, 2018).

11. Ysabelle Cheung, "Art After Auschwitz: The Problem with Depicting the Holocaust," *Vice,* September 15, 2015, www.vice.com/en/article/nz445m/art-after-auschwitz-the-problem-with-depicting-the-holocaust

12. *The Twilight Zone,* season 3, episode 8, "It's a Good Life," directed by James Sheldon, written by Rod Serling, story by Jerome Bixby, aired November 3, 1961, CBS, 2005, DVD.

13. Neal Gabler, *An Empire of Their Own: How the Jews Invented Hollywood* (New York: Anchor Books, 1989), 734.

14. *The Twilight Zone,* season 1, episode 8, "Time Enough at Last," directed by John Brahm, written by Rod Serling, story by Lynn Venable, aired November 20, 1959, CBS, 2004, DVD.

15. *The Twilight Zone,* season 3, episode 3, "The Shelter," directed by Lamont Johnson, written by Rod Serling, aired September 29, 1961, CBS, 2005, DVD.

16. *The Twilight Zone,* season 1, episode 22, "The Monsters Are Due on Maple Street," directed by Ronald Winston, written by Rod Serling, aired March 4, 1960, CBS, 2004, DVD.

17. *The Twilight Zone,* season 2, episode 6, "Eye of the Beholder," directed by Douglas Heyes, written by Rod Serling, aired November 11, 1960, CBS, 2005, DVD.

18. *Night Gallery*, season 1, episode 1, "The Escape Route," directed by Barry Shear, written by Rod Serling, aired November 8, 1969, on NBC, Universal, 2004, DVD.

19. *The Twilight Zone,* season 4, episode 4, "He's Alive," directed by Stuart Rosenberg, written by Rod Serling, aired January 24, 1963, CBS, 2005, DVD.

20. *The Twilight Zone,* season 5, episode 31, "The Encounter," directed by Robert Butler, written by Martin M. Goldsmith, aired May 1, 1964, CBS, 2005, DVD.

21. George Takei, "George Takei Discusses *The Twilight Zone*," *Foundation Interviews,* August 29, 2011. www.youtube.com/watch?v=bA-9iIsAcI0

22. *The Twilight Zone,* season 3, episode 15, "The Quality of Mercy," directed by Buzz Kulik, written by Rod Serling, story by Sam Rolfe, aired December 29, 1961, CBS, 2005, DVD.

23. *Storm in Summer*, directed by Buzz Kulik, written by Rod Serling (1970; USA: Showtime Entertainment, 2001), DVD.

24. *Night Gallery*, season 2, episode 13, "The Messiah on Mott Street," directed by Don Taylor, written by Rod Serling, aired December 15, 1971, on NBC, Universal, 2004, DVD.

25. "Rod Serling Wrote *The Planet of the Apes* Screenplay, but Did He Write the Ending?" *MeTV, February 5, 2018,* www.metv.com/stories/rod-serling-wrote-the -original-planet-of-the-apes-screenplay-but-did-he-write-the-twist-ending.

26. Glenn Frankel, "High Noon's Secret Backstory," *Vanity Fair,* February 22, 2017, www.vanityfair.com/hollywood/2017/02/high-noons-secret-backstory.

27. Rod Serling and Dana Gould (w) and Chad Lewis (a). *Planet of the Apes: Visionaries* (Los Angeles, Boom Studios, 2018).

28. Joel Engel, *Last Stop, the Twilight Zone: The Biography of Rod Serling* (Brooklyn, NY: Antenna Books, 2014), Kindle edition.

WORKS CITED

Adams, Neal, Rafael Medoff, and Craig Yoe. *We Spoke Out: Comic Books and the Holocaust.* San Diego: IDW/Yoe Books, 2018.

Cheung, Ysabelle. "Art After Auschwitz: The Problem with Depicting the Holocaust." *Vice,* September 15, 2015, www.vice.com/en/article/nz445m/art-after-auschwitz -the-problem-with-depicting-the-holocaust

Engel, Joel. *Last Stop, The Twilight Zone: The Biography of Rod Serling.* Brooklyn, New York: Antenna Books, 2014.

Frankel, Glenn. "High Noon's Secret Backstory." *Vanity Fair,* February 22, 2017. www.vanityfair.com/hollywood/2017/02/high-noons-secret-backstory

Gabler, Neal. *An Empire of Their Own: How the Jews Invented Hollywood.* New York: Anchor Books, 1989.

Lacy, Susan, dir. *Rod Serling: Submitted for Your Approval. American Masters*, 1995. USA: Panasonic, 2003. DVD.

Parisi, Nicholas. *Rod Serling: His Life, Work and Imagination.* Jackson, MI: University Press of Mississippi, 2018. Kindle edition.

"Rod Serling Wrote *The Planet of the Apes* Screenplay, but Did He Write the Ending?" *MeTV,* February 5, 2018. www.metv.com/stories/rod-serling-wrote-the -original-planet-of-the-apes-screenplay-but-did-he-write-the-twist-ending.

Sander, Gordon F. *Serling: The Rise and Twilight of TV's Last Angry Man.* New York: Cornell Paperbacks, 2011.

Serling, Anne. *My Dad, Rod Serling: As I Knew Him.* Ohio: Commonweal Book Company, 2021. Kindle.

Serling, Rod, writer. *Night Gallery.* Season 1, episode 1, "The Escape Route." Directed by Barry Shear. Aired November 8, 1969, on NBC. Universal, 2004, DVD.

Serling, Rod, writer. *Night Gallery.* Season 2, episode 13, "The Messiah on Mott Street." Directed by Don Taylor. Aired December 15, 1971, on NBC. Universal, 2004, DVD.

Serling, Rod, writer. *The Twilight Zone.* Season 1, episode 8, "Time Enough at Last." Directed by John Brahm, story by Lynn Venable. Aired November 20, 1959. CBS, 2004, DVD.

Serling, Rod, writer. *The Twilight Zone.* Season 1, episode 22, "The Monsters Are Due on Maple Street." Directed by Ronald Winston. Aired March 4, 1960. CBS, 2004, DVD.

Serling, Rod, writer. *The Twilight Zone.* Season 2, episode 6, "Eye of the Beholder." Directed by Douglas Heyes. Aired November 11, 1960, CBS, 2005, DVD.

Serling, Rod, writer. *The Twilight Zone.* Season 3, episode 15, "The Quality of Mercy." Directed by Buzz Kulik, story by Sam Rolfe. Aired December 29, 1961. CBS, 2005, DVD.

Serling, Rod, writer. *The Twilight Zone.* Season 3, episode 3, "The Shelter." Directed by Lamont Johnson. Aired September 29, 1961. CBS, 2005, DVD.

Serling, Rod, writer. *The Twilight Zone.* Season 3, episode 8, "It's a Good Life." Directed by James Sheldon, story by Jerome Bixby. Aired November 3, 1961. CBS, 2005, DVD.

Serling, Rod, writer. *The Twilight Zone.* Season 4, episode 4, "He's Alive." Directed by Stuart Rosenberg. Aired January 24, 1963. CBS, 2005, DVD.

Serling, Rod, writer. *The Twilight Zone.* Season 5, episode 31, "The Encounter." Directed by Robert Butler. Aired May 1, 1964. CBS, 2005, DVD.

Serling, Rod, and Dana Gould (w) and Chad Lewis (a). *Planet of the Apes: Visionaries.* Los Angeles, Boom Studios, 2018.

Storm in Summer, directed by Buzz Kulik, written by Rod Serling (1970; USA: Showtime Entertainment, 2001), DVD.

Takei, George. "George Takei Discusses *The Twilight Zone.*" *Foundation Interviews,* August 29, 2011. www.youtube.com/watch?v=bA-9iIsAcI0

Conclusion

So how Jewish are all these franchises? Certainly, it varies. *Twilight Zone* truly offered a Jewish creator addressing immediate Jewish issues in a post-Holocaust world, using science fiction as effective cultural criticism. *Superman* was subtler, but his creators were exploring their lives through the immigrant metaphor and did an evocative job, before sending Superman out to fight for the Jewish people. *The Mandalorian, Avatar: The Last Airbender*, and TNG's "Rightful Heir" are admittedly more suggestive and subtle, but they still have cultural criticism to offer about faith and religious adherence.

Some series have crossed the line to the point where they're crying out for sensitivity viewers, as described with *Batman* and *Bombshell* comics, as well as *Arrow* and *Agents of S.H.I.E.L.D.* In all these, skipping over the destruction of the Jewish people in favor of simplified Nazi villains feels like removing Jews from the narrative, something already happening in superhero shows. A suggestion that the Holocaust is the only significant event in Jewish history is also problematic. Likewise, Tolkien's admission about the Dwarves would likely be frowned upon if he said this today, though his messianic concepts fit better.

Golem episodes and novels vary—some authors have come up with brilliant ways to make golems fresh and clever, but the most popular tale with the Talmudic scholar and the hulking destructive killer is highly overused, offering clichéd views of Judaism as well. While the token golem (or rather token Jewish) episode was popular in the multicultural eighties and nineties, this trend is being replaced today with intersectionality—realizing that a person can have more than one identity, even while they should reach across the aisle to support other groups. The recent shows *Penny Dreadful: City of Angels* and *The Man in the High Castle* both stress that Jews and other minorities should make common cause against prejudice.

Moon Knight gives the hero multiple vulnerabilities, as do the Jewish vampire shows *Juda, Split,* and *Shadowhunters* (along with a Jewish werewolf on both versions of *Being Human*). Superheroes too teach banding together and caring for one another's vulnerabilities. In *Marvel's Runaways,* the Jewish character is shunned as a purple-haired activist geek in a group of varyingly marginalized teens. The Jewish characters in *Batwoman, Arrow,* and *Legends of Tomorrow* are damaged superheroes likewise straddling multiple identities. However, as the big franchises introduce representation in diverse races, genders, orientations, and disabilities, they hesitate to tackle religion. And when they do, they're unlikely to bring in Jews. This results in Nazi villains without mention of their victims, superficially written characters failing to practice their religion, and Jewish creators who still hesitate to tell their own stories (with notable exceptions). As representation improves every day, one hopes the Jews won't be left behind.

Index

About the Editor and Contributors

ABOUT THE EDITOR

Valerie Estelle Frankel is the author of over eighty books on pop culture, including *Hunting for Meaning in The Mandalorian*; *The Villain's Journey*; and *Star Wars Meets the Eras of Feminism*. Many of her books focus on women's roles in fiction, from her heroine's journey guides *From Girl to Goddess* and *Buffy and the Heroine's Journey* to books like *Fourth Wave Feminism in Science Fiction and Fantasy*. Her *Chelm for the Holidays* (2019) was a PJ Library book, and now she's the editor of *Jewish Science Fiction and Fantasy* for Lexington Books, publishing an academic series that begins with Jewish science fiction and fantasy through 1945. Once a lecturer at San Jose State University, she now teaches at Mission College and San Jose City College and speaks often at conferences. Come explore her research at www.vefrankel.com.

ABOUT THE CONTRIBUTORS

Mara W. Cohen Ioannides' book chapters are in *Judaism and Gender*, *Search of the Interior Borderlands: Where Does the Midwest End and the Great Plains Begin?*, *Who Is a Jew*, and *Jews and Non-Jews: Memories and Interactions from the Perspective of Cultural Studies*. Her articles span Jewish culture with a number of her articles in: *International Journal of the Study of Music and Musical Performance*, *Elder Mountain: A Journal of Ozarks Studies*, *Women in Judaism: A Multidisciplinary Journal*, and *American Jewish Archives Journal*.

Matthew Diamond is a former educator and a current financial professional at a consulting firm currently residing in San Jose, California. He holds a bachelors in math and economics from UC San Diego and a masters in financial engineering from the Drucker Business School at Claremont Graduate University. He has been reading comic books and sci-fi/fantasy works since he's been in first grade and to this day owns boxes of graphic novels from a multitude of publishers. Matthew has also been a guest speaker and panelist for multiple comic conventions in the Northern California area with topics ranging from "Fourth Wave Feminism" to "The Villain's Journey in Popular Media."

Ari Elias-Bachrach has a BS and MS in computer science from Washington University in St. Louis and The George Washington University, respectively. Now retired from Information Security, he received smicha from Yeshivat Keter Hatorah and was formerly the content director for Sefaria. He resides in Silver Spring, Maryland, with his wife and four children, some of whom he is embarrassed to admit, have gone to the dark side and become *Star Wars* fans. He is an occasional speaker at local synagogues and author for the Lehrhaus. He spends significant time arguing the halachic merits of various sci-fi technologies, and blogs about it at https://www.leolamvaed.com.

Erin Giannini, PhD, is an independent scholar. She has served as an editor and contributor at PopMatters and is the author of *Supernatural; A History of Television's Unearthly Road Trip* (Rowman & Littlefield 2021), and a forthcoming TV Milestones book on *The Good Place*. She is also currently coediting a collection on *Good Omens*.

Arthur S. Harrow received a BA in biochemistry from Rice University in 1979, and an MD from the University of Texas Southwestern Medical School in 1984. He is currently a member of the faculty of internal medicine at Sinai Hospital of Baltimore. He has served as a Jewish lay leader including a term as president of Temple Beth-El in Richmond, Virginia. Dr. Harrow has been reading fantasy and science fiction from an early age. He ranks among his proudest accomplishments being the only person in his medical school class who can legitimately list "comic book villain" on his curriculum vitae.

Caleb Horowitz is a North Carolinian writer and independent scholar. He has taught classes on publishing and fantasy writing at the University of North Carolina Wilmington. His current areas of research include Jewishness in pop culture and trauma studies. When Horowitz is not working on his novel, you can find him writing about Jewishness in *Star Wars*, *Avatar: The Last Airbender*, and *The Lord of the Rings*.

Sarah Katz is an author and graduate of UC Berkeley with a background in cybersecurity. Her other works include the science fiction novel *Apex Five* and short stories published in *365tomorrows, AHF Magazine,* and *Thriller Magazine.* Her nonfiction articles have appeared in *Cyber Defense Magazine, Dark Reading, Infosecurity Magazine, Tech Xplore, Jewish Journal,* and *Middle East Quarterly.*

Judy Klass has had eight full-length plays produced onstage. *Cell* was nominated for an Edgar and is published by Samuel French/Concord. Judy wrote a TOS *Star Trek* novel published by Pocket Books and a YA book published by a small press. Her short fiction has appeared in *Asimov's Magazine, Albedo One, Space & Time, Satire, Wind Magazine, Terra Incognita, Suffusion, Harpur Palate, Outer Darkness, Phoebe, The Courtship of Winds, Bryant Literary Review,* and elsewhere. She wrote about film versions of *Nineteen Eighty-Four* for *Starlog.* She teaches courses, mostly for the departments of English and Jewish studies, at Vanderbilt University.

Ellen Levitt is a veteran teacher and writer. She wrote the trilogy of *The Lost Synagogues of New York City* (www.avotaynu.com) and *Walking Manhattan* (www.wildernesspress.com). She has also written for *The Wisdom Daily, ROUTES, Style & Polity, New York Teacher, The Brooklyn Eagle*, and other publications and websites. She is an alumna of Young Judaea and an active participant in her Conservative, egalitarian congregation in Brooklyn.

Miriam Eve Mora holds her PhD in American immigration and ethnic history from Wayne State University. Her first book, *Carrying a Big Schtick: American Jewish Acculturation and Masculinity in the Twentieth Century*, examines Jewish American identity, focusing on Jewish masculinity in twentieth-century America. In addition, Dr. Mora specializes in anti-Semitism and anti-Semitic rhetoric and has spoken publicly on the subject in several venues. She lives and works in New York City as director of academic and public programs at the Center for Jewish History.

Heather and Matthew Nover are Jewish educators who love looking at Judaism from a variety of viewpoints. Matthew is the assistant rabbi and education director of Beth El Synagogue in East Windsor, New Jersey. Heather is the executive director of the Anshe Emeth Community Development Corporation. They collaboratively wrote a course on zombies and Judaism when they taught together at the Bergen County High School of Jewish Studies. They live in East Windsor with their daughter, Jane, and dog, Jada.

Jonathan Sexton is a lifelong nerd whose passions include Judaism, media analysis, and visual art. As a teenager he placed twice as a runner-up in the Jack L. Chalker Young Writers' Contest held by Baltimore Science Fiction Society. Since then, his artwork has been featured in fanzines. He lives in Maryland, where he spends his free time drawing, writing, arguing about *Batman*, and petting his cat. This is his first nonfiction publication.

Fraser Sherman, born in England, raised in Florida, would still be in the Sunshine State if he hadn't discovered his dream woman lives in North Carolina. He's been a journalist, financial writer, political columnist, and fantasy writer, and most recently published *Undead Sexist Cliches*, a book about bad misogynist beliefs. Fraser's now married to his dream woman, living in Durham, North Carolina, and sharing the house with the world's most perfect dogs. He's been fascinated by golems since his teen years but has no idea why.